About the author
Martin Empson is a longstanding socialist and environmental activist who has written on Marxism, ecology and agriculture. His first book *Land and Labour: Marxism, Ecology and Human History* looked at the changing relations between nature and society through history.

Acknowledgements
Writing this book has incurred a large number of debts. Thanks to the staff of Manchester Central Library and Archive for their help in locating rare publications and to the Working Class Movement Library in Salford for help with material on the Luddites and for finding me an actual truncheon used by the militia against those protesters. A number of individuals read various drafts and made numerous comments and suggestions. If I haven't always followed all their advice I was nevertheless grateful for it. Thanks again to Richard Bradbury, Matt Clements, Graham Mustin and Josh Sutton. At Bookmarks I would like to thank Sally Campbell, Lina Nicolli, Peter Robinson and Carol Williams, for all their work and thanks to Yuri Prasad and Dave Sewell for the cover design. Finally I would like to thank Sarah Ensor for her support and encouragement over many years.

"KILL ALL THE GENTLEMEN"

Class Struggle and Change in the English Countryside

Martin Empson

Bookmarks *Publications*

Kill All the Gentlemen:
Class Struggle and Change in the English Countryside
By Martin Empson

Published 2018
© Bookmarks Publications
c/o 1 Bloomsbury Street, London WC1B 3QE

Quotes from newspapers courtesy of British Newspaper Archive
britishnewspaperarchive.co.uk © The British Library Board

The Fell Types are digitally reproduced by Igino Marini
www.iginomarini.com

Typeset by Peter Robinson
Cover design by Yuri Prasad and Dave Sewell
Printed by Melita Press

ISBN 978-1-910885-69-7 (pbk)
978-1-910885-70-3 (Kindle)
978-1-910885-71-0 (ePub)
978-1-910885-72-7 (PDF)

Contents

Introduction

BRITAIN TODAY is a highly industrialised, urban society. A small percentage of the population live in rural communities and an even smaller part of the working class are employed in agriculture. So why write a book on the historic struggles of the peasants and labourers of England? What relevance do these, often forgotten, movements of the last 700 years have for people today?

In part this book is about celebrating the struggles of ordinary people. When we learn about the history of England, we rarely hear the full story of what happened. Occasionally we hear about Wat Tyler and the Peasants' Revolt and perhaps Jack Cade or Robert Kett's rebellions but if we do, they are explained as isolated incidents that bucked a trend of gradual economic development. The reality, as I have tried to show in this book, is that the history of the English countryside is one of constant class struggle; a fight that, as Karl Marx and Friedrich Engels put it in the *Communist Manifesto*, is "sometimes hidden and sometimes open". This book celebrates the rural class struggle for equality, justice and a better life and through this, hopes to inspire people today.

But this history also has a deeper significance. As a socialist involved in the environmental movement, it is abundantly clear to me that the reason we face a global ecological crisis in the 21st century is because capitalism puts profits before people and the planet. It is a system that systematically degrades the natural world in order to accumulate wealth for the richest. Capitalism arose out of earlier class societies but is marked by a very different set of priorities; under capitalism, everything from land and water to plants and animals is turned into a commodity. Capitalism transformed everything about rural life and agriculture.

There have been extensive debates among Marxists about how to explain and understand the development of capitalism out of feudalism. There are many factors to this debate, including the class struggle between peasant and lord, the interaction between town and country and the growth of trade and manufacturing. In this book I have followed the analysis of Chris Harman who, while engaging with the work of Robert Brenner and others, reasserted the approach of Karl Marx. Harman avoided looking for a single factor that allowed capitalism to begin, but showed how Marx saw capitalism arising from four factors, "the growth of trade...free labour in manufacturing...separation of the peasantry from the land, and...the 'primitive accumulation of capital'." Harman continues by explaining that what was important was the interaction between these individual factors which

> all arose from the way in which the growth of the forces of production within feudalism threw up new relations of production, relations which came into collision with the old society when it entered into crisis.[1]

So capitalism did not immediately replace the old feudal order but saw a prolonged period of transition during which different groups within society fought for their different interests. To give just three examples, we see this in the 16th century in the court of Henry VIII in which ministers had differing ideas of how far the Reformation should go, and why; we see it in Queen Mary's Counter-Reformation; and we see it with those who fought to enclose land or develop market-orientated agriculture in the 17th and 18th centuries. As these groups fought each other for influence and power their conflicts sometimes spilt over into civil wars, rebellions and uprisings. Ordinary people were not passive in the face of these changes and conflicts. As we shall see, they fought to defend their interests and their beliefs, they made up the armies and they struggled to carve out their own futures or protect their historic rights. It is the struggles of these ordinary people in the face of a changing world that make up the narrative of this book.

The rise of capitalism was not an automatic process—its changes were contested at every stage. As Harman points out, Marx showed how the bourgeois revolution that created the conditions for capitalism to develop freely was "centred in the towns but is reinforced by the revolt of the rural classes".[2] But for those at the bottom of rural society, capitalism developed on the back of their historic defeat as they were transformed from peasants into wage labourers; their land taken from them and the countryside carved up in the interests of the rich.

The struggles of the rural population did not begin with the development of capitalism. The history of all class societies is the history of class struggle and the rights and traditions that the English peasantry had were rooted in much earlier battles, so this book begins with the first great mass rebellion of ordinary people against the feudal system: the Peasants' Revolt of 1381.

In order to keep the book to a manageable length, I have focused on England and I have had to ignore events in Wales and Scotland. In part this is about the slightly different histories of these three countries. But it means that I have missed out some fascinating historical episodes which have parallels with the events described here. The Rebecca Riots of 1839-1843 and the Highland Clearances are just two examples which mirror English struggles against tithes and enclosures. I hope to return to these in the future. Because of my focus on rural struggle, I have also neglected some more well known parts of English radical history. Chartism thus forms the backdrop to some events here, but not a separate part of the book. While leading Chartists were concerned with land ownership and through their Land Company hoped to relocate many workers to the countryside, it was primarily an urban struggle and it is told elsewhere.[3]

The title of this book, "Kill all the Gentlemen", comes from an unsuccessful anti-enclosure rising in Oxfordshire in 1596. The Attorney-General claimed that the leader of the rebels, Bartholomew Stere, was motivated "to kill the gentlemen of that countrie and to take the spoile of them, affirming that the commons, long sithens [since] in Spaine did rise and kill all the gentlemen in Spaine and sithens that time have lyved merrily there." The slogan "Kill the Gentlemen" also appears during the Lincolnshire Rising of 1536 and Kett's Rebellion of 1549. It neatly sums up who the lower orders blamed for their problems.[4]

Commons, keep well your harness
Trust you no gentlemen
Rise all at once.

— Bill posted in Leeds, January 1537, following the defeat
of the Lincolnshire Rising and the Pilgrimage of Grace [5]

The Peasants' Revolt of 1381

ON 13 June 1381, 30,000 rebels assembled south-east of London on Blackheath in military formation with banners and flags flying. To the east of London another 20,000 rebels gathered near Mile End. Over the previous few days they had taken control of large areas of England. They had captured castles; numerous villages and small towns had come over to the rebellion; and those who refused to swear an oath of allegiance to "[King] Richard and the True Commons" were killed. The rebels did not destroy indiscriminately but targeted individuals responsible for their exploitation and burnt records that recorded their oppression.

A contemporary chronicler, Thomas Walsingham, a monk at St Albans Abbey, described a famous sermon that the radical priest John Ball was supposed to have delivered at Blackheath. Walsingham was not present and was hostile to the rebellion, so his account should be understood as an attempt to smear both John Ball and the rebels. But Walsingham knew the complaints of the rebels well, so his description of John Ball's sermon gives a glimpse of what inspired the rebels. According to him, Ball began by quoting a couplet that has now become closely associated with him:

When Adam delved and Eve span, who was then the gentleman?

Then John Ball

tried to prove...that from the beginning all men were created equal by nature, and that servitude had been introduced by the unjust and evil oppression of men, against the will of God, who, if it had pleased Him to create serfs, surely in the beginning of the world would have appointed who should be a serf and who a lord. Let them consider, therefore, that He had now appointed the time wherein, laying aside the yoke of long servitude, they might, if they wished, enjoy their liberty so long desired. Wherefore they must be prudent, hastening to act after the manner of a good husbandman, tilling his field, and uprooting the tares that are accustomed to destroy the grain; first killing the great lords of the realm, then slaying the lawyers, justices and jurors and finally rooting out everyone whom they knew to be harmful to the community in future. So at last they would obtain peace and security, if, when the great ones had been removed, they maintained among themselves equality of liberty and nobility, as well as of dignity and power.[6]

In her history of the uprising, Juliet Barker argues that whether or not Ball delivered this speech or was even at Blackheath, Walsingham was putting John Ball "at the spiritual and physical heart of a rebellion which threatened to overthrow the establishment in both Church and state".[7] The monk wanted to forever link Ball's revolutionary ideas with the rebellion that had almost brought his world crashing down.

Over the next few days the rebels were to bring the most powerful figures in England's ruling class to their knees. Several of them, like the hated Archbishop of Canterbury Simon Sudbury and the King's treasurer Sir Robert Hales, were executed. Even as the rebellion was defeated in London, it was still spreading across England and it was only after months of repression, torture and execution that the ruling class regained control.

Tens of thousands of people arrived from many different towns and villages in London. Why did they rebel? Why were they prepared to risk death? What was it about society that made so many people so discontented that they were prepared to leave their homes, their families and their crops and take up arms?

Historian Edmund Fryde suggests the roots of the revolt lay in a "grave deterioration in the quality of government". As the Speaker of the Commons Sir Richard Waldegrave acknowledged, despite the "great treasure continually levied from the commons for the defence of the realm", the government was unable to prevent raids, particularly on Sussex and Kent.[8] Inadequacy in defence certainly contributed to popular anger at the government, but it is not enough to explain the uprising.

There was wider discontent at the way the government was making those at the bottom of society pay more. The taxes that proved to be the prime trigger for the revolt were imposed to raise money for a costly war with France; between 1369 and 1381 at least £1,100,000 was spent on the conflict. Over this same period the government's income, however, "considerably surpassed" that spent on war. The taxes themselves were harsh but they were also changing. Before 1334 there had been a property minimum below which the taxes were not levied. But from 1334 the poorer sections of the population became liable for taxation. Following the reduction in population caused by the Black Death, the fixed taxes hit the smaller populations harder.[9]

After war with France began again in 1369, new taxes based on people not property were introduced hitting areas with larger populations harder. Fryde points out that with the parish tax of 1371, "the assessment of Norfolk was increased by a third and that of Essex by four fifths, whilst the charge of Suffolk was almost doubled. All these shires were in the forefront of revolt in 1381".[10]

Further taxes were needed to raise more and more funds for the war with France. In 1377, the first poll tax had been set at 4d on all persons over the age of 14 and raised £22,000. The second, in 1379, only brought in £19,000 and so in December 1380 the poll tax was increased to 12d per person with the aim of raising £66,666. The rebellion began in the years prior to 1381 with the non-payment of tax. Between 1377 and 1381 a third of those who had paid previously, some 458,356 individuals, disappeared from the records. This non-payment of the tax was "much more universal than the armed risings of May-June 1381" and was most common in the poorest parts of England.[11]

Alongside the imposition of further taxes came government corruption and a popular perception of the king as being the victim of corrupt and traitorous ministers. This is best demonstrated by the watchwords of the rebels themselves who, when challenging each other, would ask "With whom holdes yew?" expecting the answer "Wyth kynge Richarde and wyuth the trew communes."

But the greatest single cause of the revolt was the very nature of feudal society—the exploitation of the peasantry by a ruling class that tried to squeeze as much as possible from those at the bottom of society who created all the wealth.

As we shall see, one of the most "persistent" demands made by the rebels when in negotiations with the king at Mile End and Smithfield was for the abolition of serfdom.

Rodney Hilton, the Marxist historian of medieval peasant revolts, argues that "the earliest elements in peasant protest were the direct consequence of the peasants' attempts to devote as much as possible of the family's labour to the cultivation of the holding, and to keep for the disposal of the family as much as possible of the product of that labour".[12]

This was true of protest through the whole medieval period. But as peasant movements developed, wider questions were raised which often had their roots in changes in medieval society.

The ruling class was very concerned with popular feeling. In France in 1358 there had been a major peasant uprising against the feudal lords and the English lords were concerned that they might face a similar rebellion.

In 1377 they petitioned the parliament of Richard II because "resistance by servile peasants was impoverishing many landowners".[13]

In the 1381 rebellion the demands of the rebels and their actions, particularly the targeting of legal documentation and manorial records, as well as the killing of individuals involved in the legal profession, indicate that they hoped for radical change. Hilton suggests that the "indiscriminate" targeting of lawyers implied the "rebels felt they could wipe out the whole legal system".[14]

The other great pillar of feudal society, the church, was also threatened by rebel demands. Again, Hilton points out that during negotiations at Smithfield, Wat Tyler, one of the leaders of the uprising, proposed:

> No churchmen, whether monastic or secular, were to hold property, but only to be given their reasonable subsistence. The surplus in the parishes, once the parish clergy had received their subsistence, was to be divided among the parishioners. The great property of the possessioners...should be redistributed to the commons. There should only be one bishop at the head of the church.[15]

Another contemporary account by Henry Knighton says:

> The rebels petitioned the king that all preserves of water, parks and woods should be made common to all: so that throughout the kingdom the poor as well as the rich should be free to take game in water, fish ponds, woods and forests as well as to hunt hares in the fields—and to do these and many other things without impediment.[16]

Taken together these demands suggested a radical redrawing of medieval society.

Life in medieval England

At the time of the Peasants' Revolt the vast majority of people in England lived in the countryside in small, scattered and often isolated villages. Almost all the population of the countryside worked the land. They grew their food to eat or to sell in order to provide themselves with other goods. But large amounts of what they produced was not theirs, it went directly to the lord of the manor.

Agriculture was central to the medieval economy, but across the country its organisation varied enormously.[17] The best known type of medieval agriculture was open-field farming, which reached its high point around the time of the Black Death in 1348 in up to a third of England. Though open-field farming was found nearly everywhere across

England, it was concentrated in a band that ran roughly through the centre of the country, from Dorset and Somerset in the south-west, across the Midlands, to Yorkshire and Northumberland in the north-east.[18]

In open-field farming land was divided into large fields. Each of these fields was then divided into separate strips which were divided among the peasant families. Each family had a mixture of strips in various different fields and within the fields, mixed up with the strips of other families. This ensured that there was an even distribution of land around the population—no family would only have infertile land or land most likely to be flooded and the distance someone had to walk to get to their land was similar for everyone. In addition to the open fields, villages also had uncultivated land and woodland which provided pasture for animals. Everyone also had the right to graze their animals on fallow land or land that had been harvested. All this required village-wide organisation.

But however the land was farmed, the key social relationship in medieval society was between the peasantry and the lords who owned the land. This was a society where, in its simplest terms, social relations were between a "landowning military aristocracy on the one hand, and a vast class of peasant-producers, working individual family holdings but also organised in village or hamlet communities, on the other".[19]

The feudal landowners depended on the peasantry. They produced nothing themselves but enjoyed their lavish lifestyles by taking the surplus produced by the peasantry, the extra above what the peasants needed to keep themselves and their families alive.

As Spencer Dimmock has pointed out, it is important to ask why the peasantry felt obliged to pay rent at all to the lords. This he argues was a result of the "imposition of manorial lordship by military force on a potentially free owner-occupying peasantry". This "caging of the peasantry" had taken place after the end of the Roman occupation of England.[20] This period had seen attack and warfare from external forces, such as the Vikings, from which the peasantry wanted protection. Those who could offer or be seen to offer such protection, would demand a part of the peasantry's product in return. Historian Christopher Dyer explains where the lord's power originated:

> Just as they presented themselves as the friends and protectors of their tenants, they also justified their dominance by claiming that peasants had been granted parcels of the lords' land, together with livestock and equipment in exchange for heavy services, making the whole arrangement seem like a reciprocal exchange. But very rarely were lords filling up an empty

piece of countryside. A more common situation was that they took over an inhabited territory, and then to subject it, and above all its population, to their control. In these circumstances they had not given their peasants their holdings, but took away lands they already held, and granted them back on more oppressive terms.[21]

The lords' ability to extract surplus from the peasantry rested on the threat of violence, backed up by a system of laws that restricted peasants' ability to escape their lord or challenge him. Following the Norman Conquest in 1066 the new ruling class instituted a particularly strong feudal system in England. William the Conqueror redistributed the land, keeping some for himself, giving some to the church and a large chunk to a relatively small number of barons who had supported him in his invasion. These nobles swore lifelong allegiance to the king and in turn distributed land to their own followers (knights) who made a similar oath. Thus William created a highly centralised system reaching down to a very local level. Alongside this, a system to police the population was created, a "vast social network" known as frankpledge.[22] This divided England's population into groups of ten who were collectively responsible for the behaviour of each other and had to ensure that a member who was charged with a crime appeared in court. The system had begun to break down by the 13th century, but while it functioned it gave local lords a powerful system of social control.

Lords, including landowners such as monasteries, did not accumulate wealth for the sake of it but for consumption, though they had every interest in trying to increase the wealth they could squeeze from the peasantry to fund buildings, hire soldiers and so on. Lords might also use some of their wealth to build bridges, water mills and improved ploughs. This means, as Harman has argued, that for some of the feudal period, the lords' "concern with increasing the level of exploitation also led some of them to encourage advances in the means of production".[23] We shall return to the importance of this later.

In its simplest form, a lord's manor was essentially in two parts: the land that was directly managed by the lord (known as the demesne) and the land that was held and worked by tenants. The demesne, however, was worked by the tenants of the rest of the land and, on occasion, hired labour. The tenants effectively paid rent for their use of the lord's land through their labour on his fields or strips of land and through the provision of their equipment. In addition to this, some might be obligated to give over a portion of their crops or a sum of money each year. This relationship was known as serfdom.

There was a confusing array of names for the different peasants on a medieval manor, often based on the amount of land held. The historian J L Bolton summarises these.

> Virgaters or half virgaters farmed their own land and the lord's land; cottars, bordars, acremen, with less land of their own probably earned their living by providing the spare labour needed by lord and villein alike. Other men were to be found of course—freemen, specialists, such as the miller or the smith, but the majority of the agricultural population were virgaters, half virgaters or cottars, providing the necessary manpower for labour-intensive arable agriculture.[24]*

The relationship that these tenants had with their lord was extremely one-sided. They could not leave the manor without permission or without paying an annual fee. Their daughters could not marry without permission and the payment of a fee and a peasant could be fined if his daughter got pregnant outside of marriage. When a peasant died his family would have to pay a death tax; he would be obliged to grind his grain at the lord's mill, on payment of a fee; his animals and farming equipment were at the disposal of his lord; and most importantly he would be obliged to engage in work for the lord and possibly other payments of produce or animals. Peasants could not purchase their own land, for this meant they could become free and deprive the lord of his income.

Freemen did not have to perform all the labour that an unfree peasant did, though they might still have to pay "boon work" at periods of intense labour such as the harvest. They also had less "compulsory outgoings" than the unfree peasants. They did, however, still have some restrictions: they had to attend the regular manorial courts and might have to pay on specific occasions (such as the marriage of children).[25]

This feudal relationship had its origins in a society when lords could offer military protection to communities. But by the 14th century the need for such protection was minimal and thus the peasantry was exploited through "coercive sanction". The peasants were mostly unfree, tied to their lords by tradition and legal structures that reached back hundreds of years. Bolton explains that the freemen "were always there, to act as a spur to the unfree".[26]

---

* A virgate (or yardland) was a quarter of a hide, typically between 60 and 120 acres. The physical size varied dependent on the quality of land as it was based on the amount of land that could support a family. Cottars and bordars were peasants who had a right to live in a cottage and to a very small amount of land, perhaps four or five acres.

The precise extent of a lord's ability to exploit the peasants on his land was rooted in tradition and historic legal decisions. Peasants would try to resist changes that would increase their exploitation, and the lord would try to extract as much as he could from their labour.

The records of the manorial courts tell us much about life in medieval times. As the historian Warren Ault points out:

> The records of a manor court are filled with matters pertaining to the lord's estate: whether all those who owed suit of court had come; whether the officers of the manor had been faithful in the discharge of their duties; whether the lord's demesne had been well cultivated, his meadows and woods conserved; whether any had trespassed in his grain or his pasture; whether any had put their sons to clergy or allowed their daughters to marry without leave.[27]

The following examples taken from the Manorial Court Rolls of the village of Great Horwood (now in Buckinghamshire) tell us a little about life in medieval England.

TUESDAY, 11 JULY 1290: "A day is given to the town messor to report the names at the next [court] of all those who were transgressors against the ordinance made recently forbidding lambs to be pastured in the common grain [fields] of the town."

WEDNESDAY, 28 JULY 1305: "It is granted by all the lord's tenants, the free men as well as the villeins, that whoever shall be found guilty of having his mares so tethered that the foals get in the grain of the neighbours shall give the lord 6d as often as he is found guilty before the Gules of August [1 August]."

WEDNESDAY, 26 JUNE 1332: "It is granted and ordained by the whole township of Horwood that no one shall be allowed to glean who can earn his food and a penny a day if there is any one who wishes to hire him... And that no stranger be allowed to glean among them".[28]*

These brief extracts give a sense of the content of the manorial courts' decisions. Year after year, the courts levied fines, decided punishments, elected officials and imposed rules on the population.

Frequently the rolls can be very specific about the duties and obligations a peasant was expected to perform. In May 1320, the Great Horwood manorial court declared that:

---

* Gleaning was the collection of leftover grain that had fallen to the ground after the harvest had been completed.

John Smyth holds of the lord one messuage and one virgate of land ᵼ one butt containing one rood of land, rendering therefore 4s 4d per annum at the aforesaid terms and at the death of the aforesaid John he shall give a heriot namely his best beast and if the said John does not have a beast he shall give the lord as a heriot the produce of the best half acre of land under crop on the said land and for the said heriot the wife of the said John shall remain on the said land for one whole year.*

But the legal documents also list the obligations that John Smyth had to the lord and specify what the lord would give in return:

And he ought also to carry the lord's hay to the court of the lord of the manor for one day with one cart and he with the other customers shall have his food namely a loaf of wheat bread, beer and cheese as food for the said John and his boy, 2d.

And he ought also to reap the lord's grain for one day in autumn with two men without food and this work is worth 4d, and again he ought to reap with the lord with all his family except his wife at the great boon day and the same John shall go to see that his family does their work well and he ought to gather the sheaves together and at noon they shall come for their food to the lord's court at the lord's expense.²⁹

Not everyone in a medieval village was a peasant. Some specialist workers like carpenters, tillers, thatchers and so on might move from place to place. Others, like blacksmiths, might have plots of land in addition to their specialist work. There were also a minority of landless wage labourers who might work the lord's demesne, but also included individuals like ploughmen, carters and shepherds. All of these would have identified with the majority of the population and would have seen themselves as part of "peasant communities".³⁰ Figures with some of these backgrounds played central roles in the 1381 revolt and later struggles.

The church

The church was one of the most powerful forces in medieval society. Its ideologies pervaded all parts of life and its doctrine explained the confusing world which might bring a bumper harvest one year, but famine or plague in the next. Marc Bloch brilliantly describes how religious belief in feudal times was influenced and shaped by earlier ideas:

---

* Messuage means dwelling, a rood is a quarter of an acre and heriot was the belongings, usually an animal, paid to the lord on a tenant's death.

s also nourished on a multitude of beliefs and practices
the legacy of age-old magic or the most recent products of
ll extremely fertile in myths, exerted a constant influence
octrine. In stormy skies people still saw phantom armies
nies of the dead, said the populace; armies of deceitful
red the learned, much less inclined to deny these visions
than to find for them a quasi-orthodox interpretation.[31]

The church also justified the social status quo, a world where the population was divided into three groups: "those who work, those who fight and those that pray". The church rationalised this by arguing that society needed each person to perform their particular role to ensure the correct functioning of the whole. Anyone who tried to change this, or did not perform their role adequately, risked upsetting the whole edifice. In return for performing their role, each person would get recompense that fitted their position.[32] Even the German religious reformer Martin Luther would say in 1525, "An earthly kingdom cannot exist without inequality of persons. Some must be free, others serfs, some rulers, others subjects".[33]

The church's huge network of parish churches, monasteries and cathedrals brought in vast amounts of money in rent, tithes and donations. By the 12th century, the church was the "greatest landlord in Europe",[34] which meant it was one of the largest owners of serfs, who produced vast amounts of wealth from their labour and rent.

In addition, everyone was expected to pay towards the upkeep of the church. Peasants paid tithes to the church amounting to 10 percent of their income either in cash or in the form of grain, animals or other goods.[35]*

But tithes weren't the end of it. When he died, the peasant's family was expected to pay a mortuary fee to the church of their second best beast (the first going to the local lord in lieu of the peasant's inability to render military service any longer). There were payments to the church when getting married, when your child was baptised (essential in a world where it was firmly believed that the unbaptised could not enter heaven) and to bury someone.

It is not surprising that, as A L Morton notes, there was a "general feeling that priests were more interested in their tithes" than helping their congregations. Morton refers to a list of sins written to help the priest when hearing confessions, the "first sin listed is refusal to pay tithes and the next two are neglect to pay promptly and pay in full".[36]

---

* The tithe came from Genesis, when Jacob promises God, "of all that you give me I will give you a tenth" (Genesis 28:22).

In the years before the Peasants' Revolt, anger at the church was everywhere. Discontent was growing at corruption and greed and often fuelled revolts led by figures who contrasted the early Christian church with the wealthy, landowning church of their own time. As Norman Cohn points out,

> there hardly seems to have been a time in medieval Europe when there were no lay preachers wandering through the land in imitation of the Apostles. Such people were known already in sixth-century Gaul; and they continued to appear from time to time until, from about 1100 onwards, they suddenly become both more numerous and more important.[37]

Thus the church played a contradictory role. On the one hand it offered solace and an explanation of the world; on the other it was central to the oppression and exploitation of the mass of the population and its hierarchy grew rich on the proceeds. It is this contradiction that helps to explain two things about the events of 1381 and of other revolts of the period: the importance of itinerant preachers like John Ball and his radical combination of Christianity and democracy and the "conspicuous" involvement of the lower clergy,[38] and the anger and hatred directed at senior religious figures in the church.

Christianity was the key ideology of the Middle Ages in Western Europe. As a result, most peasant movements and uprisings of the period used the language of the Bible. Friedrich Engels wrote that "In the popular risings of the West...the religious disguise is only a flag and a mask for attacks on an economic order which is becoming antiquated".[39] But this, as Graham Mustin has noted, is an over-simplification. A belief that they had god on their side helps explain why rebels were often prepared to challenge the awesome military power of the medieval state. In addition, a vision, often inspired by the Bible, of a promised land where people were equal and food, drink and land were in abundance was a key part of winning potential recruits to a rebel banner.[40]

Resistance

The coercive relationship between lord and peasant meant that those at the bottom of society were constantly attempting to resist the demands of their lords. As one historian points out:

> Most people resisted authority, not by violent disturbances but by quietly ignoring the regulations and conducting their lives in the way that suited them... People learned how to manipulate the system, by exploiting their

influence as officials, concealing acts that infringed the rules, or bending customs and laws in their own favour.[41]

Sometimes the court rolls record attempts to resist or argue against the imposition of new rules by the lord. Take the following example from the manorial records of Great Horwood.

In 1303, two of the village's woodwards demanded that every tenant of the manor should pay them some grain "as of right". Woodwards were officers of the lord whose duty was to ensure that no tree was cut down or had a limb removed without permission. They also ensured that there was no trespass in the woods. The local lord had recently appointed them and demanded his tenants contribute to their upkeep.[42]

In the manorial court the villagers denied that there had ever been a claim on them for grain previously, explaining they had elected the wood-wards historically and were liable for any "default in service" and that they had never contributed to the upkeep of these officials before. The "jury of freemen and others said that the township had never given the woodwards anything unless by the common consent of the whole town."

In the court, the names of six earlier woodwards were given who, the villagers argued, had not been supported by the villagers. Instead they had had use of a piece of meadowland and only had to pay half their rent. Notably, the only time that the village had supported the woodwards was an occasion when one was unable to work and the peasants had donated wheat according to the size of the land they worked.

This story tells us much about life in medieval rural economies. Firstly we see how the lord used the law to try and protect his property, in this case the wood of his forests; he could also appoint officials to enforce this. We see that lords used the manorial courts to enforce and extend their rights and privileges, but they could also be spaces where the peasantry opposed him. Secondly we get a glimpse into the complex social arrangements of medieval society. Interestingly, we also see the collective aspect of village life—once when the villagers organised to support some of their own when they were unable to work, but secondly when they collectively used the courts to protest against their lord's actions. The peasants used the limited legal avenues available to them to plead their case. The peasants' collective memory of village custom and practice was an important part of this struggle as when they "recited" the names of the previous six woodwards.

A study of the Court Books of the Abbey of St Albans found that between 1279 and 1311, 21 courts were held that dealt with "mano-rial labour discipline". These led to 146 convictions for the "deliberate non-performance of labour services". This included refusing to turn up for work on the lord's land or not responding to a summons.[43*]

For J L Bolton the 13th century was the "century of the lord" when "holdings grew smaller, sub-tenancies multiplied and it seems possible that there was, relative to resources, rural overpopulation across a large section of the country." At the same time, a growing economy meant increased demands for agricultural products.[44] The lord wanted more from the peasants, increasing the labour service they owed him, which encouraged resistance from the peasants.

If the manorial courts proved inadequate, a minority could use higher courts. But this was difficult, expensive and only open to those with certain property qualifications. Villeins only had land to farm at the leave of the lord so they had to rely on the local manorial court where the system was stacked against them. Court cases were often dominated by legal arguments about the status of the peasants. These might involve appeals to tradition, oral and written, to prove status and frequently involved complex legal precedents. For instance, some villeins working land that had belonged to the crown during Edward the Confessor's reign (1042-1066) "could claim royal protection against an increase in services" even though the land had been transferred to other lords in the intervening years.[45]

Rodney Hilton quotes an example of a case when the ruling went against the peasants.

> In 1278 the villain tenants of the alien [controlled from outside of England] Priory of Harmondsworth impleaded their lord the Prior that he should not demand from them customs and services in excess of those they owed when the manor was in the king's hands. Domesday Book was searched and it was shown that the manor did not count as ancient demesne. The tenants were therefore declared tallageable at the will of the lord and liable to merchet. The sheriff of Middlesex was ordered to assist the abbot to distrain and to tallage his rebellious tenants.[46**]

Sometimes, if the case went against the peasants, they would take matters into their own hands. After a dispute between the Abbot of Halesowen and his tenants as to whether or not they should be liable for increased service went in favour of the Abbot, the peasants were excommunicated for "laying violent hands on the abbot and his brethren".[47]

---

* Other examples included "grazing beasts on the lord's pasture" and "sheltering strangers at night" see Bolton, 1980, p117.
** Merchet was the fine owed if a villein allowed his daughter to marry without the lord's permission. Tallage was a tax, to distrain was the seizure of property to force payment of taxes.

A changing world

The medieval world was not static. Over the hundreds of years that today we call the Middle Ages there were big social and economic changes. An important example of this was way that the peasants were, in the decades preceding the Peasants' Revolt, increasingly at odds with the existing social order.

Through the 13th century increasing numbers of peasants were working for wages rather than their obligations to a lord as the population grew at a time when the lords were in a relatively strong position over the peasantry. Falling wages, expansion of agricultural land (and hence new rents) and the further division of existing land to meet the demands of a growing peasantry gave more wealth to the lords. Despite a feudal crisis around 1300, the position of the lords looked strong.[48]

But things changed with the Black Death in 1348 which killed around a third of the population. The Black Death and further epidemics throughout the 14th century created a shortage of labour which fundamentally altered social relations by encouraging wage labour in the countryside and prompting peasants to move around looking for better wages.

John Gower, a medieval courtier, landowner, poet and friend of Geoffrey Chaucer complained:

> The shepherd and the cowherd demand more wages now then the master-bailiff was wont to take; and, withersoever we look, whatsoever be the work, labourers are now of such a price that, when we must needs use them, where we were want to spend two shillings we must now spend five or six.[49]

Peasants wanted more and members of the ruling class like Gower hated it.

> Labourers of olden time were not wont to eat wheaten bread; their bread was of corn or of beans, and their drink was of the spring. Then cheese and milk were a feast to them; rarely had they other feast than this. Their garment was of hodden grey: then was the world of such folk well ordered in its estate.[50]

The church's inability to protect people from the plague led some to question it as an institution. As Philip Ziegler writes of the religious reformer and dissident John Wycliff:

> Wycliff was a child of the Black Death in the sense that he belonged to a generation which had suffered terribly and learned through its sufferings to doubt the premises on which its society was based. The church which he

attacked was a victim of the Black Death because of the legion of its most competent and dedicated officers who had perished and, still more, because of the honour and respect which it had forfeited in the minds of men.[51]

This was not helped by the actions of the rich in the aftermath of the epidemic who gave large amounts of money to the church to "beautify their buildings and enhance their standing in the world." At precisely the point when people were questioning the ability of the church to protect them, the rich were donating extra money, recognising its importance in maintaining "social discipline".[52]

John Gower was more perceptive than most and understood that the changing world was leading to conflict. On the eve of the Peasants' Revolt he warned prophetically:

> the lords are sunk in sleep and lethargy, so they take no heed of the madness of the common folk; this thus they suffer this nettle, this is so violent in itself, to grow. He who surveyeth this time of ours may well fear that soon—if God provide no remedy—this impatient nettle will suddenly sting us before men do justice upon us.[53]

In response to demands for increased wages, the ruling class reacted predictably. In 1349 the government introduced the Ordinance of Labourers, legislation to fix wages at the levels they were before the plague. Parliament's words were very clear:

> Because lately a large part of the people, and especially of labourers and servants, has died during the pestilence, and some, perceiving the pressing need of the lords, and the great scarcity of servants, refuse to service unless they receive excessive wages, while others prefer to be in idleness than to get their livelihood by labour…every man or woman in our realm whatever condition, free or bond, being able in body, and below the age of sixty years, not living in merchandise, nor exercising any craft, nor having wherewith to live of his own resources, nor land of his own in whose tillage he may employ himself, and not serving another—if he shall be required to serve in any suitable service, considering his condition, shall be bound to serve him who required him, and shall receive only such wages, allowance, hire or salary, as were accustomed to be offered in the place where he is to serve, in the 120th year of our reign, or in the average five or six years preceding.[54]

Soon after the Ordinance was enacted, further legislation, the Statute of Labourers (1351), was passed which strengthened and reinforced the Ordinance.

Rates of pay were enshrined in law, "one penny a day for weeding or hay making, reapers two pence a day, mowers five pence a day, tillers threepence a day and their boys a penny and a half, same with thatchers, and none with food or drink".[55] The state employed hundreds of commissioners to travel around the country enforcing the new law.

The outbreak of the Revolt

The Peasants' Revolt of 1381 thus had its roots in the exploitation, oppression and poverty inherent in feudal society. Its beginnings lie in the mass evasion of the hated poll tax. The refusal to pay was on an enormous scale. In Kent, the English county whose population was central to the rebellion, the number listed on the tax records in 1377 was 56,557 but by 1381 this had fallen to 43,838. In Somerset over the same period numbers dropped from 54,604 to 30,384. Devon's figures dropped by over a half.[56]

This meant a colossal loss of income for the crown, so in March 1381 the king's council appointed new tax commissioners after sacking those that had overseen the drop in numbers. The new commissioners had greater powers to enforce the payment of taxes and were charged with collecting the missing money.

This meant that resentment exploded into active revolt. A medieval manuscript *The Anonimalle Chronicle* describes what happened when, on the 30 May, Thomas Bampton "steward of a lord, who was regarded as a king or great magnate in that area because of the great estate he kept" arrived in Brentwood, Essex.

> He had summoned before him a hundred of the neighbouring townships and wished to have them form a new subsidy, commanding the people of those townships to inquire diligently and to give their replies and to pay their dues. Amongst these townships all the people of Fobbing gave answer that they would not pay a penny more... On this, Thomas menaced them strongly, and he had with him two sergeants-at-arms of our lord the king; and for fear of his wrath the people of Fobbing took counsel with the people of Corringham, and the folks of these two townships made levies and assemblies and sent messages to the men of Stanford-le-Hope to urge them to rise too, for their common profit. And then the men of the three townships came together to the number of a hundred or more and with one assent went to Thomas Bampton and roundly gave him answer that they would have nothing to do with him nor give him one penny. On this Thomas ordered the sergeants-at-arms to arrest these folks and put

them into prison; and the commons rose against him and would not be arrested, but tried to kill Thomas and the two sergeants.[57]

The Peasants' Revolt had begun. The men of Fobbing, Corringham and Stanford "took to the woods" to avoid reprisals and sent messages out through Essex. Messages reached the capital too, as two London butchers, Adam Attewell and Roger Hang, rode across Essex telling the population that the people of Kent and London were ready to join them.[58]

On Sunday 2 June, Sir Robert Belknapp arrived with soldiers at Brentwood with "indictments against various persons". He was met with a full-blown uprising from across the region. *The Anonimalle Chronicle* tells us what took place.

> The commons rose against him and came before him and told him that he was a traitor to the king and the realm, and that it was of pure wickedness and malice that he wished to put them in default by means of the false inquests made before him. And because of this evil they caused him to swear on the Bible that he would never again hold such a session nor act as a justice in such inquiries. And they made him tell them the names of all the jurors, and they took all that they could catch and cut off their heads and cast their houses to the ground and Sir Robert took his way home with all possible speed.[59]

The Chronicle is an account of the rebellion written by its victorious enemies so its authors had every reason to portray the rebels as blood-thirsty. However, while we have to be careful of its accounts, we also get a sense of the first few days of the rebellion:

> the high master of the hospital of St John of Clerkenwell in London had a very beautiful and delectable manor-house in Essex, where he had ordered victuals and other necessities to hold his chapter general, and it was well furnished with wines and suitably appointed, as befits such a lord and his brethren. And at this time the commons came to the manor and ate the victuals and drank three tuns of good wine and rased the manor-house to the ground and set it alight.[60]

The same day that Sir Robert was driven out of Brentwood by the rebels (he was tied backward on his horse), Kent began its rebellion when the abbot of Lesness monastery was forced by a band of armed men to swear allegiance "to them". In their history of the revolt, Philip Lindsey and Reg Groves note that this was likely to be the first use of the oath of the rebels, to "King Richard and the True Commons".[61]

It might seem strange that rebels who had suddenly turned on their lords and masters would swear allegiance to the king. But, as is common in revolts by the peasantry, the rebels believed that the king was not at fault for the high taxes and their misfortunes. Instead, they blamed traitors and corrupt ministers around Richard II, who they imagined were exploiting his youth for their own gain (Richard II was only 14 when the revolt broke out). Most of the peasants moving into rebellion did not see the system as something that had to be changed; instead they wanted to remove the worst offending ministers and make changes such as fairer taxes. An example of this is when some Kentish rebels gathered and agreed that:

> no one who dwelt near the sea in any place for the space of 12 leagues should come with them, but keep the coasts of the sea from the enemies, saying amongst themselves that there were more kings than one and they would not suffer or have any king except King Richard.[62]

One of the complaints of the population of Kent was that the state was failing to provide coastal protection from raiders during the wars with France. So important was protecting the coast that the rebels left people behind to prevent an invasion to overthrow King Richard rather than enrolling them into their army. But the misplaced trust in the king as a neutral figure above his ministers would be one reason for the defeat of the revolt.

Further actions by senior figures in the king's government helped to enrage the peasantry. On 3 June, Sir Simon Burley, vice-chamberlain of the king's household, arrived in Gravesend with two sergeants-at-arms. He was there to find Robert Belling, who he claimed was one of his serfs who had run away. Sir Burley appears not to have noticed the seething discontent among the population of Kent who came to bargain with him for Belling. Even *The Chronicle* notes Sir Burley's arrogance:

> the good folks of the town came to make a bargain for the man in civil fashion, because of their respect for the king; but Sir Simon would not take less than £300... The good folks prayed him to lessen the sum, but they could not come to terms... But Sir Simon was very angry and irritable, and greatly despised these good folk, and for haughtiness of heart he bade his sergeants bind the said man and take him to Rochester Castle...after his departure the commons began to rise, gathering to them the men of many townships of Kent.[63]

On 5 June, a commission arrived in Canterbury to enforce the collection of taxes. One of those in this group was John Legge, who was thought to have been involved in the arrest of Belling. They were driven off after a short fight, though the rebels "let them return unharmed to emphasise their respect for the king's authority which these men represented".[64] For Legge this was a short reprieve as he was executed by the rebels in London nine days later.

By now, the rebels were making links between risings in different areas. Juliet Barker notes how the Kent rebels crossed the Thames twice to bring rebels from Essex to inspire rebellion in Dartford.[65] Rebellion there had begun a few days earlier when John Tyler (unrelated to the more famous leader of the Revolt) killed a tax collector, hitting him so hard with his staff that "the brains flew out of his head".[66] The rebellion in Dartford targeted the home of Nicholas Heryng (or Herring), a "former escheator of Kent... justice of the peace and steward of the king's lands in the county...[and] a member of the reassessment commission".[67]* Later the rebels were to target other properties of his around the county. This targeting of individual officials who were seen to have a role in the poll tax or a history of particular oppression of the peasantry was a feature of the Revolt.

The rebels at Dartford, under the leadership of a baker, Robert Cave, set off with those from Gravesend towards Rochester. Rochester Castle remains an imposing solid stone keep overlooking the River Medway. In 1381 it was a powerful reminder of the feudal order; the tallest castle in England "its dungeons were filled with those who had stolen from hunger or who had escaped bondage or who had simply and inadvertently fallen foul of the law".[68] Individuals like Robert Belling were held here and these were the people the rebels wanted to release.

The rebels laid siege to the castle and

> the constable defended himself vigorously for half a day, but at last, for fear that he had of such a multitude of men deaf to reason from Essex and Kent, he delivered up the castle to them. And the commons entered and took their companion and all other prisoners out of prison.[69]

Rochester Castle had never fallen to a foreign enemy; in 1216 it had fallen only after a two-month siege by King John which cost 60,000 marks.[70] For the castle to surrender to a peasant army after half a day's siege must have given enormous confidence to the rebels and helped further stimulate the rebellion, as Mark O'Brien explains:

> The fall of Rochester Castle became a clarion call to the peasants throughout England to rise and it is from this moment that the rebellion

---

* An escheator was someone responsible for collected the property of those who died without heirs for the Crown.

became a threat to the ruling class, not just on a local but also on a national scale.[71]*

The Gravesend rebels returned home in victory. But the rest of the growing army headed south towards Maidstone where the "hedge priest" John Ball was imprisoned.

John Ball, Jack Straw and Wat Tyler[72]

We know very little about the majority of those who took part in the Peasants' Revolt. We know some of their names from indictments and trials that took place in the repression that followed. Some accounts give more details of the leaders, though these are often contradictory.

The anonymous author of *The Anonimalle Chronicle* makes it clear what they thought of John Ball, a "chaplain of evil character" who was "esteemed amongst the commons as a prophet, and labored with them day by day to strengthen them in their malice".[73]

The contemporary accounts usually emphasise that the rebels in 1381 were peasants, calling them "rustics", "common men" or, more generally, "commons" or "plebs".[74] As we shall see, the rebellion was in no way just restricted to peasants, it pulled in individuals from rural communities, especially those who had close links to the peasantry, such as village artisans. In particular the "lower clergy", vicars and parish priests often played a leading role with nearly 20 individuals being recorded. Some of these clerics joined the rebellion because their meagre livelihoods and low wages had little to do with the great wealth of the church. As Hilton explains:

> They, like other wage-earners, were subject to the provisions of the Statute of Labourers. The rectors and vicars had their own grievances, such as the frequent clerical taxes...fees payable to the diocesan officials and very frequently a rather poor income. The vicars were particular sufferers, since in their parish the tithes and other income to which rectors would normally be entitled were largely appropriated by the monasteries.[75]

But it was not just the poorest of clergy who rebelled, some well-to-do members also took part and their involvement cannot simply have been economic. The clergy were "more literate and more likely to be familiar with general concepts about the rights of men and the duties of governments than the custom-dominated laity".[76] As Karl Marx pointed out, religion is simultaneously the "opium of the people" but it is also the

---

* Juliet Barker notes that the rebels had captured the family of the castle's constable and used them to make him open the castle. Barker, 2014, pp175-176.

"cry of the oppressed" and the Bible is full of material that could be used to question the status quo. John Ball seems to have been adept at using biblical imagery to expose the hypocrisy of the rich and the official church and inspire rebellion against them.

There have been attempts to link John Ball to wider radical movements within the church. An account written some 40 years after he was executed, supposedly based on John Ball's confession, accused him of being linked to John Wyclif and the Lollard movement. Wycliff, who was based in Oxford, was a radical critic of the church whose teachings included ideas that criticised the wealth of the church and later,

> stood against compulsory penance and absolution, against papal indulgences—bought by sinners to wipe out their sin—and masses for the dead, for he rejected the theory of purgatory where souls went through a kind of probation while their living relatives and friends purchased masses until they had purchased the soul's right of entry into heaven.[77]

Such teachings worried the church, but it is unlikely that John Ball had learnt from Wycliff. Ball had been preaching his own ideas for decades before Wycliff spoke out. Indeed Ball had been first imprisoned in the 1360s. It is possible that Ball had heard Wycliff, or at least his supporters, speak but attempts to link Ball to Wycliff were really about discrediting the Lollard movement in the years after the uprising.

In the aftermath of the Black Death, Ball's "preaching would seem to have been directed against the widespread immorality" but he quickly began to develop wider social criticisms. He argued against the tithes that impoverished the poor and the conditions that ordinary people had to live and work under. Unsurprisingly, the church did not like this and in 1366 Ball was "summoned" to a meeting with the Archbishop of Canterbury. Ball was not the only critical preacher and the archbishop was keen to clamp down on those stirring up trouble. He declared that people should not listen to Ball's preaching and threatened those who did with excommunication. Ball continued to preach however and was eventually excommunicated and imprisoned. After his release, no longer able to preach in church, he began to preach to congregations in churchyards at the end of services and in other public spaces.[78]

The medieval chronicler, Jean Froissart, described a sermon by John Ball:

> things cannot go right in England and never will, until goods are held in common and there are no more villeins and gentlefolk, but we are all one and the same. In what way are those whom we call lords greater masters

than ourselves? How have they deserved it? Why do they hold us in bondage? If we all spring from a single father and mother, Adam and Eve, how can they claim or prove that they are lords more than us, except by making us produce and grow the wealth which they spend? They are clad in velvet and camlet lined with squirrel and ermine, while we go dressed in coarse cloth. They have the wines, the spices and the good bread: we have the rye, the husks and the straw, and we drink water. They have shelter and ease in their fine manors, and we have hardship and toil, the wind and the rain in the fields. And from us must come, from our labour, the things which keep them in luxury.

Froissart adds that many ordinary people agreed with him and would spread his message onward:

> Some, who were up to no good, said 'He's right!' and out in the fields, or walking together from one village to another, or in their homes, they whispered and repeated among themselves: 'That's what John Ball says, and he's right'.[79]

Another famous leader of the Revolt was Jack Straw. Straw's name has been closely associated with the rising in popular myth and contemporary accounts. He is mentioned by Chaucer in *The Canterbury Tales* and various contemporary accounts list him as being Wat Tyler's second in command. Two pubs in Hampstead in the north-west of London were named Jack Straw's Castle after the legend that he addressed crowds while standing on a hay cart (the castle) on nearby Hampstead Heath. But we don't have much hard evidence for Straw at all. Some accounts even conflate him together with Tyler and *The Anonimalle Chronicle* doesn't even mention Straw.

Historian Alastair Dunn says that: "Although Straw's identity as a real individual should be accepted, the evidence is far less convincing than that for Wat Tyler and John Ball, and historical constructions of his place in the Rising rest heavily on his popular 'canonisation' in the chap-books and pamphlet of literature of later centuries".[80]

Legal inquisitions held after the rising describe Straw as one of the rebellion's leaders and a John Rakestraw along with Watte Tegheler is recorded as having made a proclamation in the church of St John in Thanet, Kent, to raise two hundred local men to attack the home of William de Medmenham and destroy the rolls.[81] But there are few other references to Straw. A detailed confession supposedly made by Straw prior to his execution is almost certainly a fabrication by Thomas Walsingham.

Following the death of the rebel leaders their reputations grew stature as later generations turned them into folk heroes, figures in stage plays and poems. This was true of no one more so than Wat Tyler.

We also know little about Wat Tyler. *The Anonimalle Chronicle* says he was from Maidstone and his name suggests he worked tiling roofs, there is some speculation he was a soldier, though, as Barker points out, there is no evidence for this in the muster rolls of the time.[82] Dismissed as the "leader of the ruffians and rustics from Kent"[83] by Thomas Walsingham, Tyler certainly commanded the respect of the rebels. During the uprising in St Albans, rebels there sent a delegation to London to find Wat Tyler and get his support for their actions. According to Walsingham, they wanted to "receive power from Wat Tyler...for they believed that there would in future be no more important man than Tyler within the kingdom and that the laws of the land would be henceforward invalid".[84] Tyler's death while negotiating with King Richard ensured his name has gone down in history. Whether or not he was the central leader of the Revolt is open to question, though he certainly played a key mobilising role in Kent.

Some historians of the Peasants' Revolt have seized on references to a "great society" and interpreted this as referring to a co-ordinating body for the rebellion, perhaps imagining a conspiratorial organisation or revolutionary party. For instance, Phillip Lindsey and Reg Groves assert that: "The Great Society had, beyond doubt, been busy, drawing men from here, from there, and choosing the leaders, although in certain places, such as Cambridge itself, they were elected by the vote of the people".[85]

This is conjecture. When revolutionary movements explode onto the historical scene, ruling classes are so shocked they often believe that they must be engineered by some hidden organisation. The ruling class in 1381 could not believe that the mass of the peasantry were capable of widespread rebellion without the involvement of outside agitators. In fact, as we shall see, the history of rural rebellion often sees the authorities focus on perceived agitators or political organisation even where none were present. This is the origin of the "Great Society" and in her detailed account of 1381, Juliet Barker notes that "the phrase was in common parlance and meant no more than a large crowd or gathering".[86]

But arguing for the absence of an organisation such as the Great Society is not to suggest that there was no organisation in 1381 at all. We have already noted that there was co-ordination between groups of rebels such as those on opposite sides of the Thames in Kent and Essex and we know of individuals who rode from town to town spreading the message of rebellion. We also know of John Ball's letters, sent out to urge people to rise and we know that people from different villages and towns gathered together to organise. Ball in particular must have made many friends and contacts as he travelled from village to village speaking in squares and churchyards. As each village rose, messengers and delegations were sent out to urge their neighbours to join them. The rebels would have used existing relationships to strengthen their rising and individuals like Ball, Tyler and Straw were able to put themselves at the heart of these networks.

The peasant armies converged on Maidstone where John Ball had been imprisoned by the Archbishop of Canterbury, Simon Sudbury. Ball had correctly predicted he would be freed by 20,000 men. At Maidstone the rebels met and discussed their aims. Already the rebels had, as they converged on the town, burnt and destroyed symbols of their serfdom, in particular legal and manorial documents which listed the rights and obligations of tenants and serfs. Now they made Wat Tyler "their chief",[87] electing him as their leader. John Ball sent out letters around the country announcing the uprising and urging people to rise and organise. These letters are remarkable documents. Despite their coded language, they are a call to arms and show that Ball had the respect of communities around the country. The letters were copied and passed on, and give a programme about what to do: the time has come, get together trusted people, elect a leader and follow our example. At his trial, John Ball took credit for the letters, which had been found on numerous captured rebels.[88] Here are three examples.

> John Ball greeteth you all,
> And doth to understand he hath rung your bell,
> Now with might and right, will and skill,
> God speed every dell.

> John Shepe, sometime St Mary priest of York, and now in Colchester, greeteth well John Nameless and John Miller and John Carter, and biddeth them that they beware of guile in borough and standeth together in God's name and biddeth Piers Plowman to go to his work and chastise well Hob the Robber, and take with him John Trueman and all his fellows and no more, and look that ye shape to one head and no more.*

> John Ball greeteth you well all, and doth you to understand that he hath rungen the bell.[89]

---

* John Shepe (Shepherd) in the second letter is a pseudonym for John Ball himself.

From Maidstone the rebels headed towards Canterbury. On the way they recruited those that they met (including those making a pilgrimage to Canterbury) to the rebellion and "in every village, the chief upholders of oppressive laws and corrupt government were hunted out, their houses ransacked and documents burnt".[90] They were "cheered by everyone", according to Froissart, and

> 4,000 of them entered into the minster church of St Thomas and, kneeling down, they cried with one voice on the monks to elect a monk to be Archbishop of Canterbury, 'for he who is now archbishop is a traitor, and will be beheaded for his iniquity'.[91]

The archbishop was Simon Sudbury and he was indeed beheaded later in London. Canterbury Castle was destroyed by the rebels, the prison broken open and Sudbury's home was destroyed. Again, the rebels targeted individuals such as the county sheriff, burning his records. The rebels asked if there were any "traitors" in the town and "the townsfolk said that there were three and named them. These three the commons dragged out of their houses and cut off their heads".[92]

The Anonimalle Chronicle tells us that 500 Canterbury men joined the rebel army, the remainder were left to "guard the town". From Canterbury, the rebels marched towards London. Froissart gives us a sense of how their march pulled in more support:

> They drew in all the people from the villages they went near, and they passed by like a tornado, levelling and gutting the houses of lawyers and judges of the King's and Archbishop's courts, and showing them no mercy.[93]

In Essex, similar events were taking place. The rebels controlled towns and villages including Colchester, which had fallen without a struggle.

> Everywhere, unjust officers of the government were attacked: John Ewell, escheator of the county, for example, was beheaded at Langdon Hills; the manor of the sheriff John Sewell, at Coggeshall, was looted, as was that of John Ginsborough, one of the county justices. The rich house of Hob the Robber—Sir Robert Hales—at Cressing Temple was destroyed on the 10th, and the home of Admiral Edmund de la Mare was ransacked, many of his official papers being carried on pitchforks by some of the rebels on their march to London.[94]

As in Kent, official documents were destroyed and with the county under rebel control, the Essex peasant army marched on London. On the evening of 12 June, the Kentish rebel army was camped on Blackheath, perhaps 30,000 of them. A similar number from Essex gathered at Mile End east of London. Inside London, up to 50,000 citizens were awaiting them. The speed with which the rebels had subdued Kent and Essex and then marched on London was "an impressive tribute to Tyler's capacity for organising".[95]

London

When the uprising broke out the king was at Windsor Castle. He returned to the capital, sending messages to the rebels asking "why they were raising a rebellion in his land." The rebels reply, according to *The Anonimalle Chronicle* was that "they were rising to deliver him and to destroy the traitors to him and to his kingdom". *The Chronicle* then suggests an exchange of messages between the rebels and the king, who tried to stop the rebels advancing closer to London. *The Chronicle* describes a large council meeting at the Tower of London with up to 600 people. While this figure seems large, the meeting involved the most important and powerful men in the country, including the Archbishop of Canterbury, the Bishop of London, the Treasurer of England and the earls of Buckingham, Kent, Arundel, Warwick, Suffolk, Oxford and Salisbury.[96]

The king agreed to go to meet the rebels on the morning of Thursday 13 June. He travelled by barge to Greenwich, accompanied by his retinue in four other barges. What they found at Greenwich shocked them. Instead of the disordered peasant rabble they expected, gathered on the banks of the Thames was a large army displaying "two banners of St George and forty pennons".[97]*

Froissart described what happened next.

> When the King and his nobles saw the frenzied crowds on the bank, the boldest of them were frightened and his barons advised the King not to land. They began to turn the barge away and upstream again. The King called: 'Sirs, what have you to say to me? Tell me. I came here to talk to you.' Those who could hear him shouted with one voice: 'Come on land, you! It'll be easier that way to tell you what we want.' The Earl of Salisbury, speaking for the King, replied: 'Sirs, you are not in a fit condition for the King to talk to you now'.[98]

Froissart's account describes the rebels as being set "aflame with fury" by this dismissal and the army took up the cry "To London! Straight to

---

* A pennon was a long, swallow tailed flag, often attached to the end of a lance.

London". They stormed towards the city, destroying everything in their way, but particularly the Marshalsea prison in Southwark:

> they broke and threw down to the ground all the buildings of the Marshalsea, and took out of prison all the prisoners who were held captive there for debt or felony.

They also destroyed the homes of the officials who ran the prison. At the same time the Essex rebels

> reached Lambeth, near to London, a manor of the Archbishop of Canterbury, and entered the buildings there, and destroyed many goods of the archbishop, and burnt all the books of the register and rolls of remembrance of the chancery which they found there.[99]

Once in London the rebels targeted buildings associated with leading figures of the government. According to another contemporary account by a "monk of Westminster", in Clerkenwell the rebels "killed all those who opposed them and burnt all the houses there as well as the manor of Highbury, which Robert Hales...had recently built". Hales was "Hob the Robber", Treasurer of England and central to the poll tax. Hales and the Archbishop of Canterbury "hid themselves in the Tower of London with the king".[100]

The scale of the destruction in London would have been impossible without the active involvement of the population of the city itself. The mass of London sympathised with the grievances of the thousands who had marched on the capital. Rodney Hilton points out that the contemporary chroniclers all agree that the entry of the rebels into London was because the London population forced the keepers of the gates to open them. Froissart has the "common people of London" gathering together and saying "Why not let these good people come into the town? They are our own people and they are doing all this to help us". This is clearly a fanciful description, but captures the widespread support for the rebellion within London.[101]

The Anonimalle Chronicle describes how the rebels

> surged on to the [London] bridge to pass into the city, but the mayor was just before them and had the chain drawn up and the drawbridge lifted to stop their passage. And the commons of Southwark rose with them and cried to the keepers of the bridge to lower the drawbridge and let them in, or otherwise they would be undone. And for fear of their lives the keepers let them enter, though it was against their will.[102]

Froissart embellishes this, saying the people of London welcomed the rebels with food and drink:

> So the gates had to be opened and all those famished men entered the town and rushed into the houses which had stocks of provisions. Nothing was refused them and everyone made haste to welcome them in and set out food and drink to appease them.

Never one to miss an opportunity to slander the rebels, Froissart then describes the rebels proceeding to

> kill a wealthy man called Richard Lyon, whose servant Wat Tyler had once been during the wars in France. On one occasion Richard Lyon had beaten his servant and Wat Tyler remembered it. He led his men to him, had his head cut off in front of him and then had it stuck on a lance and carried through the streets. So those wicked men went raging about in wild frenzy, committing many excesses on that Thursday throughout London.[103]

There is no doubt that brutality and violence took place during the capture of London. But the reality is that rather than behaving in a "wild frenzy", the rebels were incredibly disciplined and avoided wanton destruction and murder. Damage tended to be aimed at buildings, individuals and institutions that were hated for their exploitation and oppression of ordinary people.

Along Fleet Street, one of the most important places in London for legal and administrative buildings, the rebels targeted a number of buildings and liberated the prisoners in the Fleet prison. The rebels again showed their desire to end serfdom by attacking the Temple, a key location for English law, systematically destroying the "books and rolls and remembrances". Even the roof tiles were removed to leave them open to the elements.[104]

From Fleet Street, the rebels marched on the Savoy Palace. This was one of the most sumptuous buildings in London. It was owned by the Duke of Lancaster, better known as John of Gaunt, who had spent a fortune on maintaining it. Thomas Walsingham wrote that it was "unrivalled in splendour and nobility within England".[105]

John of Gaunt

Gaunt was probably the most powerful individual in England; he owned enormous estates all over the country, and was extremely wealthy. His influence extended onto the continent—he claimed the title of "King of Castile" through his marriage, and his wealth had enabled him to lead military expeditions into France. Being the son of the previous king, Edward III, and the uncle of Richard II gave him a powerful position in England's ruling class. At times Gaunt had effectively run the country when Edward III was ill, but when Richard II was crowned king at the age of ten, Gaunt was pushed out of direct involvement in the ruling councils.

Gaunt's power and influence were resented by others in the ruling class and when parliament met in April 1376, towards the end of Edward III's reign, it challenged corruption at court. The regional representatives "were critical of what they regarded as the abuse of royal powers", earning it the title of the Good Parliament.[106]

> This parliament was reflecting the interests of a new and ever-growing mix of smaller merchants and lower gentry who wished to check the power of the court over their social and business affairs. When Peter de la Mere, speaker for the Good Parliament, laid out the chief grievances to John of Gaunt and said that the 'king has with him certain councillors and servants who are not loyal or profitable to him or the kingdom', he considered himself to be speaking for the 'Commons of England'.[107]

The Good Parliament refused to agree further taxes until the royal administration was reformed and decided to impeach some of Gaunt's allies. Gaunt himself managed to escape being targeted and once parliament ended he manoeuvred to undermine its work, starting by having Peter de la Mere imprisoned in Nottingham Castle.

A new parliament met in early 1377. It was much friendlier to John of Gaunt and his interests (possibly because he packed it with loyalists), reversing some of the decisions of the previous parliament, and passing the first poll tax. But 1377 also saw the death of the elderly Edward III and Richard II's coming to the throne.

Gaunt was associated with corruption, extreme wealth and the poll tax, but another reason that he was disliked by Londoners arose from his dispute with the church. The church opposed the inclusion of clergy in the poll tax of 1377. John of Gaunt had also become the patron of John Wycliffe whose radical views about the church and its wealth challenged the ecclesiastical establishment. Wycliff was summoned to London to be questioned by William Courtney, Bishop of London, and at this meeting was accompanied by Gaunt who proceeded to treat the Bishop with disdain. So rude and threatening was Gaunt towards the Bishop and the church in general that the crowds who had gathered rioted in protest. Despite popular support for Wycliff, the hatred of Gaunt came to the fore and he was lucky to escape with his life. The next day Gaunt's Savoy Palace was attacked for the first time and possibly would have been destroyed had not Courtney dispersed the mob. Such was popular dislike for Gaunt that his coats of arms were attacked and his servants would not wear his uniform in public.[108]

But four years later, in 1381, John of Gaunt's Savoy Palace was burnt to the ground.

> They broke open the gates and entered the place and came to the wardrobe, and they took all the torches they could find and set fire to all the sheets and coverlets and beds and head boards of great worth, for their whole value amounted, it was said, to 1,000 marks. And all the napery and other things which they could find they carried into the hall and set it on fire.[109]

The palace was packed to the rafters with objects of art and value. Alastair Dunn quotes Walsingham's account describing the rebels systematically destroying Gaunt's wealth. They

> tore the golden cloths and silk hangings to pieces and crushed them underfoot; they ground up jewels and other rings inlaid with precious stones in small mortars, so that they could never be used again.

Dunn then quotes *The Westminster Chronicle*:

> With priceless objects in full view and under their hands as they assembled them, the yokel band did not dare to purloin any of the valuables since anybody caught in any act of theft was hauled away, without trial or judgement, to death by beheading.

Similarly, Dunn highlights Henry Knighton's account that tells us that one looter was killed by his own side, while the rebels shouted that they were "zealots for truth and justice, not thieves and robbers". As Dunn rightly points out, this was not unrestrained looting, rather this was an attempt to "deconstruct [Gaunt's] possessions" perhaps even an attempt to "purify the city".[110]

That's not to say that no-one looted, at least two Kentish men were indicted for stealing and another, probably exaggerated account, says that 32 men were burnt alive after they had drunk so much of Gaunt's wine that they were unable to escape.[111] But the destruction of the Savoy, along with legal records and the opening of prisons was a statement by the rebels that they were fighting for fundamental change. They must have been disappointed that John of Gaunt was away from London.

The Anonimalle Chronicle concludes that: "the commons of Kent received the blame for this arson, but some said that the Londoners were really guilty of the deed, because of their hatred for the said duke".[112]

The rebels then marched towards Westminster, burning a number of properties and destroying Westminster and Newgate prisons. From the earliest days of the rising, prisons were targeted and the inmates freed. Alistair Dunn suggests that this implies "collusion" between the rebels and a "criminal underclass".[113] But this ignores the fact that the rising was a class revolt of the oppressed against the oppressors. The breaking open of prisons is a common feature of rebellions and revolutions, as exemplified by the storming of the Bastille in July 1789 during the French Revolution. As the masses rise, they can both identify with other oppressed groups and free those who have been the victims of the system. The London prisons, like Rochester Castle, would have been filled with those who had turned to crime from poverty, as well as those victimised by the feudal system.

However, this identification with the oppressed did not extend everywhere. One tragic example of this is the way that during the rebellion the rebels targeted foreigners in the city. Pogroms against Jews were not uncommon in medieval Europe and in 1290 Edward I had expelled the Jews from England. But during the 1381 Revolt there was another group who received the wrath of the rebels. Froissart describes rebels going "from street to street, killing all the Flemings they found in churches, chapels and houses. None was spared".[114] According to *The Anonimalle Chronicle*, Flemings sheltering in the church of St Martin's in the Vintry near the Thames were killed a few days later during the slaughter of between 140 and 160 people on Friday, 14 June.[115] These attacks took place outside London as well, with attacks on Flemings in "at least five East Anglian towns" according to the historian Erik Spindler. *The Anonimalle Chronicle* says that the rebels "reserved special hatred for the Flemings" announcing that anyone who captured Flemings should behead them. Other "aliens" such as the Lombards were targeted for robbery but not murder.[116]

Geoffrey Chaucer refers to this episode in *The Canterbury Tales*, suggesting that the rebels "enthusiastically pursued" Flemings as a high point of the revolt.[117]

> Certainly old Jack Straw and his army
> Never raised shouting half so loud and shrill
> When they were chasing Flemings for to kill

Why were Flemings targeted like this? One suggestion is that they were clearly outsiders. This is put forward by Erik Spindler who points out the way that language was considered a key part of the test of who was a Fleming.

And many fflemynges loste here heedes at that tyme, and namely they that koude nat say 'breede and chese', but 'case en brode'.[118]

Language tests like this occurred in other medieval riots and Spindler suggests that they originate in a test mentioned in the Bible (Judges 12:6) when 42,000 Ephraimites were killed for not being able to pronounce the Hebrew word "shibboleth" (ear of wheat).[119]

We know little about who the Flemings were. Those killed in Southwark ran or worked in brothels, and we can speculate that those massacred at St Martin's in the Vintry worked in the weaving community which had existed there for some years.[120] Spindler speculates that numbers of Flemings may have come to England from 1360 onwards to escape plague, floods and political crisis. The proximity of Flanders meant that London and the east coast may well have been the place where many of these refugees made their home.

Spindler suggests that the rebels attacked Flemings "to become more English". By targeting the Flemings they were able to unite themselves into a community. While all the contemporary chroniclers refer to this massacre, the evidence remains scant. Spindler's conclusion is based on an analysis of the text and the language used in the accounts: "They killed [the Flemings] because the only relevant characteristic the rebels shared was to be English, and to kill a Fleming in June 1381 was to become a little more English".[121]

I find this conclusion troublesome. While it is very likely xenophobia and prejudice existed against Flemings and other foreigners in England, it seems to me there was far more that united the rebels than simply the notion of Englishness even if this actually meant much to the mass of the population in 1381. Certainly the rebels were united in their hatred of the rich, the powerful and the higher ranks of the church. It is more likely that the murder of the Flemings was a horrible part of the uprising orchestrated by a part of the rebellion, rather than reflecting the sentiments of all those involved. Uprisings are never pure as those involved carry the prejudices and ideas of the past with them and the accounts we have of the uprising are usually from authors who hated the rebellion. Chaucer's words sound particularly heinous in this regard smearing all of Jack Straw's followers with the hatred of foreigners and likening them to people hunting a fox.

On the night of 13 June the rebels gathered outside the Tower of London. Inside, King Richard and many of the most senior members of the English nobility gathered and argued about what to do.

Richard II and his council

The Tower of London was one of England's most formidable strongholds. Fully manned it would have been able to withstand a major assault, but there was no standing army in medieval times. One of the roles of lords under feudalism was to summon armies when they were needed for war, so the number of troops in London was minimal when the rebels stormed the city. Nonetheless, medieval castles were designed to withstand sieges and by retreating to the Tower, the king and his entourage were probably in the safest place they knew.

As the commons camped outside the Tower of London on the evening of Thursday, 13 June 1381, the king, together with his closest advisers discussed what to do. Froissart describes the scene:

> You can well imagine what a frightening situation it was for the King and those with him, with those evil men all shouting and yelling outside like devils.[122]

The speed and scale of the rebellion had taken England's finest completely by surprise so it is no wonder that initially the king's lords "did not know how to advise him and all were wondrously abashed". Their first plan involved attacking with their small groups of men "at midnight, fully armed, down four different streets, and fall on those evil men, the whole sixty thousand of them". According to Froissart, the king's advisers thought that the rebels would all be drunk by then and that the loyal and wealthy men left in London would be able to assemble enough forces and the rebels would be "killed like flies".[123]

Others spoke against this plan, fearing "the rest of the common people in London" and, according to Froissart, the Earl of Salisbury recommended that the king

> appease them by fair words, that would be the better course. Promise them everything they were asking. If we begin something that we are unable to finish, there will be no stopping things before we and our heirs are destroyed and all England is laid in ruins.[124]

This plan was agreed, and the scene was set for one of the most extraordinary concessions by a ruling class to a mass, revolutionary movement.

Mile End

On Friday 14 June 1381, the king and an entourage went to meet the rebels. They met at 7am at Mile End, then "a fine open space...situated in the middle of a pleasant meadow". *The Anonimalle Chronicle* contains a detailed list of those who went with the king, though it must be treated with caution. It is unlikely for instance that his mother came along, particularly given that violence was expected. *The Chronicle* also records that the Archbishop of Canterbury and other targets of the rebels did not come and attempted to escape through the "Little Water Gate" by boat on the Thames, but were thwarted by a woman who raised the alarm.

We cannot know how many rebels assembled at Mile End to hear the king. *The Anonimalle Chronicle* suggests a gathering of 100,000 and Froissart says over 60,000. The rebels also left a guard at the Tower of perhaps 400.[125]

The Chronicle describes the king arriving and "the commons all knelt down to him, saying; 'Welcome, our lord, King Richard, if it pleases you, and we will have no other king but you."

Wat Tyler then petitioned the king in the name of the commons "that he would suffer them to take and hold all the traitors who were against him and the law; and the king granted that they should take at their wish those who were traitors and could be proved traitors by the law."

He continued:

They required that no man should be a serf, nor do homage or any manner of service to any lord, but should give fourpence rent for an acre of land, and that no one should serve any man but at his own will, and on terms of regular covenant.[126]

Froissart suggests that the language was much simpler:

We want you to make us free for ever and ever, we and our heirs and our lands, so that we shall never again be called serfs or bondmen.[127]

The king agrees to these demands:

he would confirm and grant them their freedom and all their wishes generally, and that they should go through the realm of England and catch all traitors and bring them to him in safety and that he would deal with them as the law required.[128]

Froissart's account differs again in description, if not tone.

That I grant you. Now go back home in your village companies as you came here, but leave two or three men behind to represent each village. I will have letters written at once and sealed with my Great Seal for them to take back with them, granting you all that you ask freely, faithfully and absolutely. And in order to reassure you still more, I will order my banners to be sent to you in each bailiwick, castlewick and borough. You will find no hitch in any of this, for I will never go back on my word.[129]

The king offers to send his personal banners to each region to show his sincerity: "I pardon you everything you have done until now, provided that you follow my banners and go back to your own places in the way I told you."

The rebels took the king at his word. But their interpretation was not what the king intended; they thought that they had been given leave to find the traitors. A crowd of rebels stormed the Tower of London and there they captured and killed some of the nobles that they most associated with their oppression.

It is likely that these victims were expecting their fate. *The Chronicle* says that Archbishop Sudbury spent his last hours in prayer. Alongside the Archbishop of Canterbury, Sir Robert Hales the Treasurer of England; William Appleton, a physician to the Duke of Lancaster; and John Legge, the King's sergeant-at-arms were beheaded on Tower Hill. Their heads were put on poles and displayed on Tower Bridge.[130]*

The storming of the Tower was a complete inversion of the established order. Guards were powerless, or unwilling, to do anything, not even to stop the rebels intimidating the king's mother. Thomas Walsingham's account is full of salacious details.

> Few who would ever have believed that such rustics, and most inferior ones at that, would dare...to enter the chamber of the King and of his mother with their filthy sticks; and, undeterred by any of the soldiers, to stroke and lay their uncouth and sordid hands on the beards of several most noble knights. Moreover, they conversed familiarly with the soldiers, asking them to be faithful to the ribalds and friendly in the future... After the rebels had done all these things...they arrogantly lay and sat on the King's bed while joking, and several asked the King's mother to kiss them.[131]

But the most powerful examples of how weak the ruling class's position was were the charters granted by the king following the meetings at Mile End. He may have had no intention of allowing these to ever be enforced, but the wording he used shows how strong the rebels were.

---

* Interestingly John of Gaunt's son was in the Tower but escaped. He went on to become Henry IV after usurping Richard II's throne.

Here is the text of a charter sent to Hertfordshire showing how far the king went to appease the rebels.

> Richard, by the grace of God, King of England and France and Lord of Ireland, greets all of his bailiffs and faithful subjects whom these letters reach. Know that, by our special grace, we manumit all of our lieges and individual subjects, and all others, of the county of Hertfordshire, and all of theirs whomsoever they may be, from all bondage, which we make quit by these present letters; and also that we pardon those same lieges and subjects, of all felonies, crimes, transgressions and extortions, committed by them, or by any of them, whatever they have done or perpetrated, and also of outlawry or judgements, which have been passed on them, or any of one of them, and which have or will be promulgated on this occasion; and we grant to all and any of them our entire peace. In witness whereof we have made these letters patent. Witnessed by myself at London, on the fifteenth day of June of our fourth year.[132]

Clerks set about writing out similar charters for different parts of the country. As each one was finished and marked with the Great Seal of England, it was carried triumphantly back to the home town or village, but tens of thousands of rebels still remained in London.

These were extraordinary charters which effectively abolished serfdom and transformed social relations. As Juliet Barker has pointed out, Richard also decreed that "all his subjects were to be free to buy and sell within every city, borough, market-town or other place in the realm of England". This concession effectively removed all the "closely guarded monopolies and privileges" limiting the ability of the rich to extract money through tolls, taxes or monopolies on facilities like mills. This was a significant undermining of the economic organisation of medieval society.[133]

But England's feudal aristocracy had no intention of allowing these charters to become law. At the first meeting of parliament following the rebellion, the country's new treasurer Sir Hugh Segrave, declared "when the trouble had partly ceased, our same lord the king, by the advice of his council then about him, had the said grants revoked and repealed for they had been made and granted under compulsion, contrary to reason, law, and good faith, to the disinheritance of the prelates and lords of his aforesaid realm".[134]

In her book on the Revolt, historian Juliet Barker suggests that Richard II was in "sympathy" with the rebels. Indeed, at the same parliamentary meeting the king raised again the question of ending villeinage:

the king wishes to know the will of you, my lords, prelates, lords and commons here present, and whether it seems to you that he acted well in that repeal and pleased you, or not. For he says that if you wish to enfranchise and make free the said villeins by your common agreement, as he has been informed some of you wish to do, he will assent to your request.[135]

Barker interprets this as Richard II's support for the ending of serfdom and his regret at the repeal of the letters sent out from Mile End. We can never know exactly what Richard was thinking as he met the rebels in Mile End, with his capital burning around him. Much might be made of Richard's youth—he was only 14—but it is difficult to imagine that any king would willingly decree the end of the social structures that provided him and his class with their wealth. It may well be true that Richard was sympathetic to some of the demands of the rebels though it is noteworthy that nothing was said about abolishing the Statute of Labourers.[136]

It is likely that Froissart's account is more accurate. The night before Richard went to Mile End, his advisers suggested making the concessions in the hope that this would disperse some or all of the rebels from the capital. They had no intention of enforcing them and knew that they could be abolished as soon as they had served their purpose. As the history of revolutionary movements has shown many times since 1381, embattled ruling classes are often willing to grant concessions in order to gain a breathing space in the midst of revolution. Richard II and those around him were no different and any sympathy Richard had with the rebels evaporated as he helped lead the repression in the aftermath of the Revolt.

The strategy was partly successful as many rebels left London with the charters. But this also had the effect of spreading the revolt as the rebels could legitimately claim a significant victory. It is notable that some of the biggest acts of the rebellion took place after the meeting at Mile End.

Smithfield

The next day was a Saturday and the rebels continued their work in London. Famously they went to Westminster Abbey and John Imworth, marshal of the Marshalsea prison—"a tormentor without pity"—was found at the shrine to St Edward. Despite churches traditionally being seen as sanctuaries, the rebels pulled him out and executed him. The king issued a statement asking all to return home "without doing any more evil" but, as the *Chronicle* points out, the "commons paid no heed".[137]

Later in the day Richard himself visited Westminster to pray at the tomb of Edward the Confessor, his patron saint. Afterwards he arranged to meet the remaining rebels at Smithfield. What took place there was another incredible encounter between an embattled king and his revolutionary subjects and has been the source of much discussion ever since.

According to the detailed account in *The Anonimalle Chronicle*, the two sides arranged themselves opposite each other; the commons "in battle formation, in great numbers". The king asked the Lord Mayor of London, William Walworth, to bring Wat Tyler to meet him. Tyler

came to the king in a haughty fashion, mounted on a little horse so that he could be seen by the commons. And he dismounted, carrying in his little hand a dagger which he had taken from another man, and when he had dismounted he half bent his knee, and took the king by the hand, and shook his arm forcibly and roughly, saying to him, 'Brother, be of good comfort and joyful, for you shall have within the next fortnight 40,000 more of the commons than you have now and we shall be good companions.' And the king said to Wat; 'Why will you not go back to your own country?' And the other replied with a great oath that neither he nor his fellows would depart until they had their charter.

Tyler then outlined his demands:

there should be no law except the law of Winchester, and that there should be henceforth no outlawry in any process of law, and that no lord should have any lordship, except only to be respected according to their rank among all folks, and that the only lordship should be that of the king; and that the goods of Holy church should not remain in the hands of the religious, nor of the parsons and vicars, and other church-men; but those who were in possession should have their sustenance from the endowments and the remained of their goods should be divided amongst the parishioners; and no bishop should remain in England save one...and that all the lands and tenements now held by them should be confiscated and shared amongst the commons... And he demanded that there should be no more bondmen in England, no serfdom nor villeinage.[138]

The king, at least according to *The Anonimalle Chronicle*, agreed to this and commanded Tyler to return home immediately.

As Alistair Dunn points out, we have no other source for these demands. *The Westminster Chronicle* states only that the rebels demanded a "revised charter of liberty". But there is agreement that the cause of the violence that then erupts was Wat Tyler's behaviour.[139]

Wat Tyghler...called for a flagon of water to rinse his mouth because he was in such a heat, and when it was brought he rinsed his mouth in a very rude and disgusting fashion before the king.[140]

Tyler's behaviour outraged the king's followers and one yeoman insulted Tyler, who would have killed him had William Walworth not intervened. Tyler is supposed to have stabbed Walworth, who was uninjured because of his armour, but struck Tyler in turn on the neck and head. Following this one of the king's yeoman, Ralph Standissh, stabbed Tyler two or three times with a sword, mortally wounding him.[141]

Tyler's alleged rudeness is mentioned elsewhere—an account written in the late 14th century, comments that Tyler "failed to uncover his head".[142] Walsingham describes the mounted Tyler angry at a knight, Sir John Newton, who himself refused to dismount. In a temper, Tyler attempted to attack Newton, leading to his arrest by Walworth and then the attack.[143]

All the accounts of Tyler's death come from hostile authors. This explains the portrayal of Tyler as rude and so having no right to speak to the king. Whatever the exact reasons, Tyler fell to the ground badly wounded. Sometimes history turns on moments like these. As Tyler fell to the ground, his army of rebels began to "bend their bows" to fire. Had they unleashed their arrows, there would have been a massacre of a significant section of England's ruling class.

Perhaps with this possibility in mind, Richard II spurred his horse towards the rebels shouting, as their king and their leader, to leave the field. At the same time Walworth rode back to London to raise a force to protect the king. The rebels were completely disorientated. *The Anonimalle Chronicle* explains that the wounded Wat Tyler had been taken to a nearby hospital, from where Walworth, upon his return, dragged him and beheaded him at Smithfield.

> the mayor caused his head to be set upon a pole and carried before him to the king...when the king saw the head he had it brought near him to abash the commons and thanked the mayor warmly...when the commons saw that their leader, Wat Tyghler was dead in such a manner, they fell to the ground among the wheat like men discomforted, crying to the king for mercy and many of them took to flight.[144]

Thomas Walsingham describes the commons being surrounded by armed men who had rallied behind Walworth:

> They immediately surrounded the entire band of rustics with armed men, just as sheep are enclosed within a fold until it pleases the labourer

to choose which he wants to send out to pasture and which he wants to kill.[145]

Walsingham says that the knights wanted to avenge their shame by killing one or two hundred of the rebels, but were prevented by the king. In the repression that was to follow the Revolt, he wouldn't be as reticent. In the immediate aftermath of Tyler's murder, the king rewarded those who had saved the situation. William Walworth was made a knight, as were four others including Ralph Standissh. Standissh had served Richard's father for many years, but was without wealth. A few months later, Richard rewarded Standissh even further making him constable of Scarborough Castle and ensuring he received an income worthy of his new rank.[146]

The death of Tyler and the dispersal of the rebels from London was not the end of the revolt. As we have seen, the letters written by Richard at Mile End were used to help spread the rebellion. The story of what took place outside of London demonstrates how deep the Revolt went.

Rebellion outside London

Wat Tyler's death had little immediate impact on the rebellion outside the city. Even as the fires in London were dying down, the Revolt was spreading across the country. The rebellion that began in Essex and Kent led to thousands marching on the capital. But thousands more rebellious peasants remained in their villages and others spread the Revolt outwards. Frequently the regional uprisings were fuelled by historic disputes and grievances. One example of this is the story of that in St Albans.

The people had been in dispute with their overlord, the Abbot of St Albans, for well over a century. The abbot claimed that he had the right to control the freedoms of the people in the area, which included rights over grazing, hunting and so on. A focus of contention between the abbot and the people was the right to use hand mills. The abbot insisted that the abbey was the only place that people could use mills. For the people, the "hand-mills...had become a potent emblem of their struggle against the abbot's assertion that they were his villeins".[147]

In 1274 popular rebellion had tried to break the hold of the abbot over them, and again in 1326-1327. In 1327, following a march to London by the townsfolk,[148] the king recognised St Albans as a borough, which meant that the townspeople were not considered villeins of the abbot. But in 1331 this was revoked by the new king, Edward III. In order to emphasise his complete victory, the abbot had the people's handmills seized and used as paving stones in the abbey's parlour.[149] The symbolism of the monks walking over the stones was not lost on the inhabitants of St Albans. For 50 years disputes raged with the abbey and in 1381 the situation was ripe for rebellion.

We have already encountered Thomas Walsingham's account of the rebellion. Walsingham was a monk at St Albans and his reports are the basis for much of what we know about what happened in the town. Walsingham tells us that St Albans villeins went to London and "began to discuss their subservience to the monastery and the methods by which they could achieve the aims they had long secretly desired: namely, to have newly defined boundaries around their town within which they might pasture their animals freely; to enjoy fishing rights in various places without dispute; to possess hunting and fowling rights in certain places; and to be able to erect hand-mills where they pleased".[150]

Crucially they also demanded that their town should be outside the jurisdiction of the abbey's bailiff. As we have already seen Walsingham tells us that the rebels wanted "power from Walter Tyler...for they believed that there would in future be no more important man than Tyler within the kingdom and that the laws of the land would be henceforward invalid". It is possible that this was an attempt by Walsingham to smear the St Albans delegation by association with Tyler and the wider rebellion because, rather contradictorily, he also says that some of the St Albans rebels also wanted authority from the king, directing the abbot to restore their rights.

Walsingham claims that the "chief agent" in all this was William Grindcobbe, who had been "educated, nourished and maintained" at the monastery and that it was because of this that Grindcobbe was able to extract letters from the king after kneeling six times.

Walsingham's description of these events is filled with contempt and loathing of ordinary people. While much of this is directed at Grindcobbe who he sees as betraying the abbey, there is a snobbish class anger directed at the lower orders. But reading between Walsingham's account of "fools", "mobs" and "butchers", an amazing account of a medieval agrarian revolt shines through as he describes how the population took control of their town and reorganised it in their interests, as well as extracting revenge on those who they saw as being linked to the oppressors.

The first thing the rebels did after the deputation returned to St Albans was to destroy woodland enclosures that the abbot had built. Walsingham says that the "fools" spent the whole night breaking folds and gates and a building belonging to the person responsible for collecting payments for those who used the abbey's mills.[151]

But Walsingham's "fools" were getting organised; now calling themselves "citizens", as he contemptuously notes, they met together the next day and called on everyone to arm themselves. A large crowd gathered and discussed what to do next. Firstly, they agreed to destroy any remaining gates and fences, then they returned to town and met with "rustics and commons" from neighbouring towns. Walsingham suggests the crowd was now 2,000 people but seemingly cannot believe that so many people would assemble in hatred at the abbey as he assumes that they have been forced to do so on under threat of violence. The crowd joined their right hands in an oath of loyalty to one another and, as a symbol of their new control over the local commons, a rabbit was caught and fixed to the town pillory.[152]

The crowd then marched to the monastery and ordered the opening of the prison, freeing all the prisoners with the exception of one who was executed on the spot. We don't know why this individual was punished like this: perhaps the crowd thought he was guilty of a crime against them all. Walsingham uses the event to depict the crowd as "judges and butchers" and describes their "devilish shouting", apparently learnt in London at the killing of Archbishop Sudbury. It seems unlikely that the St Albans rebels had been present there, so again Walsingham is trying to smear the rebels. Indeed, as Juliet Barker notes, the reality was that the uprising in St Albans was relatively non-violent and "by men who knew their rights and were determined to get them legally acknowledged and preserved in written evidence so that they could not be overturned again".[153]

According to Walsingham, at around 9am Richard of Wallingford arrived in St Albans. He had ridden from London with a letter from the king and a banner of St George. Planting this in the ground outside the abbey, he called the rebels to meet around it and following a brief discussion, he took the king's letter into the abbot. The text of the letter was preserved by Walsingham.

At the petition of our beloved lieges of the town of St Albans, we will and command that (as law and rights demands) you cause to be delivered to the said burgesses and good men of the town certain charters in your custody which were made by our ancestor, King Henry...concerning common, pasture, fishing rights and several other commodities mentioned in the said charters; so that they have no reason to complain hereafter to us for this reason.[154]

Despite clear instruction from the king, the abbot prevaricated, claiming that he couldn't find a particular charter demanded by the rebels. Other records were found and burnt, including financial bonds paid to guarantee good behaviour. The millstones were also dug up. The prevarication meant that an order arrived from Richard II cancelling his earlier letters. But despite this, the abbot conceded much to the rebels. He confirmed the king's general freeing of serfs and agreed to remove the rights of his bailiff to hold court in the town. From all around St Albans, tenants of the abbey arrived to demand their own freedoms. Many of these were very specific and concerned particular grievances, but all fitted in with the general demands raised by St Albans. The manors of Watford and Cashio, for example, no longer had to pay tolls connected with the abbot's bridge and park, no longer had to pay to use the abbot's windmill and could use their own hand mills. Walsingham seethed with anger at the abbey's changing fortunes, "according to their foolish minds there would be no lords thereafter but only king and commons".[155]

But on 29 June, Sir Walter Lee arrived with many soldiers and Grindecobbe was arrested. The villagers were not willing to give up their leader easily; they raised a £300 bail and employed a lawyer and Lee found he couldn't get a jury to indict the rebels. Nevertheless the balance of forces was on the side of Lee and Grindecobbe was returned to jail. The townspeople had to pay £200 in compensation, the abbot's house was to be rebuilt and the mill stones were once again returned to the abbey. Though they had to return their new charters, the townspeople carefully copied them, perhaps hoping to preserve evidence of their victory for future battles. Despite the lack of violence in the St Albans revolt, Grindecobbe and other rebel leaders were harshly punished. No less a figure than the king's Chief Justice Tresilian was set to try the rebels. Tresilian initially persuaded some jurors to name names, promising them their own pardons. But they eventually withdrew these and Tresilian fell back on the threat of violence, suggesting that if the jurors did not indict, they would suffer the same penalty as the rebel leaders. Fifteen rebels were eventually hanged in July 1381, 80 others were jailed.[156]

When released on bail from Hertford prison, Grindecobbe had spoken about what the revolt meant, and urged his fellow citizens to continue their struggle. His speech serves as an epithet for all those who were hanged by Tresilian in St Albans the next month. Their punishment, wildly in excess of any actual crimes, was revenge for having challenged the existing order:

Fellow citizens, for whom a little liberty has now relived the long years of oppression, stand firm while you can and do not be afraid because of my persecution. For if it should happen that I die in the cause of seeking to acquire liberty, I will count myself happy to end my life as such a martyr. Act therefore now as you would have acted if I had been beheaded at Hertford yesterday. For nothing could have saved my life if the abbot had not called back his esquires in time. They had accused me of many things and had a judge partial to themselves and eager to shed my blood.[157]

Despite orders that the rebels' bodies should remain hanging as a warning to others, they were cut down secretly and buried. The king himself ordered the bodies found and to be hung again, this time in chains. The vindictiveness of the punishments caused even further discontent with tenants leaving in such numbers that the harvest was threatened. They were rounded up and brought back to their manors.[158]

The closeness of Thomas Walsingham to the St Albans revolt has left us with a detailed account of what must have happened in myriad different towns and villages throughout rural England during the Peasants' Revolt. While the people of St Albans had a long history of struggle with their lords, this was no less true of many other places throughout the country. The tenacity, solidarity and bravery of the people of St Albans terrified Walsingham and the ruling class. That is why men like William Grindecobbe lost their lives and why their punishments were so vicious.

Bury St Edmunds and the Revolt in Suffolk

As in St Albans, there was a long history of dispute between the abbey of Bury St Edmunds and the wider population.[159] Bury was a sizeable town with a large cloth industry and trading networks to Cambridgeshire and East Anglia. The town was wealthy and the abbey was getting rich on tolls and rents and controlling services ranging from a mint to the rights to collect manure.

In 1327 the abbey had been the focus of riots that had led to the burning of buildings and manor houses. But in 1381 this anger had an additional focus. Two years previously, a new abbot had been elected by the monks. But almost simultaneously another abbot had been appointed by the pope. The townspeople favoured the pope's nominee, Edmund Brounfeld, a Bury monk who had been in Rome. Given the history of dispute between town and abbey, they didn't want an abbot selected by the monks. Brounfeld, however, was rejected by the abbot and the king had him imprisoned. So while the dispute was temporarily abated, it was simmering in the background as the uprising started.

In June 1381, John Wrawe, a former priest from near Sudbury in Suffolk, led a band of Essex rebels into Suffolk. Wrawe had been at a larger gathering of rebels from across the areas north-east of London and he led rebels to Richard Lyon's manor of Overhall. The next day the rebels moved on to the village of Cavendish, where the king's justice, John de Cavendish, had hidden his valuables in the church. Wrawe then led the rebels to Bury St Edmunds, where a proclamation was made urging the people of the town to join them or face beheading. The home of the prior of the abbey was attacked and bands of men were sent to nearby towns to extract money. The first building in Bury to be targeted was that of the prior, followed by the home of John de Cavendish. Both men had already fled the town as the rebels approached.

Juliet Barker describes Cavendish as "one of the most hated men in Suffolk". He had sat on all sorts of royal bodies, including ones "enforcing the Statute of Labourers", but had also worked closely with the abbey and had been involved in the repression after the riots of 1371. This helps to explain why when Cavendish made it to Lakenheath he was recognised. Before he could escape in a boat across the river to Norfolk, a woman called Katherine Gamen pushed the boat into the river trapping Cavendish on the bank where the rebels captured and executed him.[160]*

After a long trek avoiding angry locals, and eventual betrayal by his own guide, the prior too was captured and beheaded. Walsingham tells us that the prior "was a worthy and artistic man" who "took care to protect the rights of his monastery". Condemned to death by "his own serfs and villeins". The prior's body was left in a field for five days as no one was prepared to bury him.[161] But his head, like that of Cavendish, was carried back to Bury and both men's heads were displayed on the ends of poles.

These killings and the desecration of corpses may sound barbarous. But the rebels were not randomly killing. In Bury St Edmunds, and elsewhere, the rebels were both taking revenge on those who had oppressed them and demanding that named monks be handed over to them from the monastery. Following the pattern elsewhere, prisoners were released and the rebels also demanded and received papers and deeds, as well as the abbey's treasure. After the revolt the townspeople had to pay the king and the abbey 2,000 marks for damage and injuries.[162]

* The killing of Cavendish at Lakenheath is notable for being one of the few incidents in the records of 1381 when women are mentioned. In addition to Katherine Gamen, a Margaret Wrighte was also named for her involvement in Cavendish's death. See Dyer, 1994, p239.

The revolt in Suffolk wasn't limited to Bury. Bands of rebels attacked and targeted property and individuals across the county. According to one document, the rebels in Suffolk looted gold, silver, spoons, belts and rings as well as beer, corn and animals.[163] On 19 June a large rebel band attacked Mettingham Castle where the local well-to-do had sought to protect their treasure. We shouldn't be surprised that people took the opportunity of rebellion to seek to improve their lot, but we should also note that as in many other places the rebels destroyed court rolls and legal documents and targeted individuals who were associated with their oppression.

The key figure in the Suffolk revolt was John Wrawe. Wrawe was captured after the collapse of the revolt in western Suffolk. He was taken to London were he confessed, giving evidence against his fellow rebels. This didn't save him and he was hanged, drawn and quartered in London.

Norfolk

The revolt in Norfolk began with the spread of revolt from Suffolk, led by rebels influenced by John Wrawe. Rebels entered the county from Cambridgeshire and Suffolk, often targeting places with links to those areas, such as estates belonging to Bury St Edmunds Abbey or sites with wider political links. Homes and estates in Norfolk linked to people involved in raising poll taxes were also attacked. In one case, a royal commissioner, Edmund Gurney (who was also the steward of Gaunt's Norfolk estates), and John Holkham, a justice of the peace, fled to the coast and boarded a boat. The two eventually escaped rebels who commandeered another boat and chased them for miles along the coast.

A major gathering of rebels took place on 17 June 1381 in Rougham, targeting the property of John Rede, a "professional tax-gatherer". Rede was hated for many reasons, not least his implementation of the poll tax. Rede had made many enemies, which explains why his home was "thoroughly looted and demolished: goods worth one hundred shillings were taken, including grain, horses...his pigs and even his mill-stone". It is notable that the rebels at Rougham included "people from all ranks in society" who came from Suffolk, Cambridgeshire and west Norfolk. Forty Rougham rebels (including five women) were later charged with "violent breaking, entering and assault".[164]

Separate, but linked to these events, was the rebellion in the north-east of the county. For days rebels had been riding around villages calling on people to assemble at Mousehold Heath, just outside Norwich. The Heath would become famous for its association with Kett's Rebellion in

1549, but in 1381 it was the site for a gathering of rebels who used it to launch an attack on Norwich, then the fifth largest town in England. The rebels here seem to have been under the leadership of Geoffrey Lister, a dyer from Felmingham.

The Norfolk rising attracted at least one of the local gentry Sir Roger Bacon. It is not clear why Bacon joined the rebellion, but it may have been due to his frustrations at the way that war with France had been run.[165] But Bacon was unusual, as Juliet Barker points out. A large proportion of Norfolk's workforce were "craftsmen and tradesmen or working for wages as servants and labourers...exactly the sort of people... who felt most trapped and exploited by the manorial system and government legislation".[166]

As with London and other towns, the occupation of Norfolk did not lead to mass destruction and looting. The rebels did target individuals, executing Reginald de Eccles, a justice of the peace, whose property, along with that belonging to others, was confiscated. But Eccles was only one of two executed in Norwich. Based in Norwich, Lister spread the rebellion, sending out groups to target particular sites and solve issues. For instance, Roger Bacon led a group to Great Yarmouth to challenge a royal charter that gave the town a monopoly on coastal trade and the right to levy large tolls on fishermen from other towns, long a source of anger for local people. The charter was torn in two, one piece being sent to John Wrawe in Suffolk and the other kept for Lister. Again the homes of individuals were targeted for destruction and looting. In Yarmouth's case, this included two people who "had been impeached for corruption in the Good Parliament".[167]* As part of this rebellion a "mass invasion of the religious houses of north-east Norfolk" took place, with manorial records being destroyed at 56 places, and we know of "incidents connected to the revolt at ninety-five further places".[168]

Lister saw an opportunity to solve outstanding questions of oppression, but also to instigate a new type of social order. He became known as the "king of the commons" and ran a "court" which gave judgment on issues brought to it by ordinary people, as well as touring local villages to proclaim "the programme of the 'True Commons'". Lister and the rebels had captured the whole of Norfolk in a week. But now they must have heard of the killing of Wat Tyler and events in Smithfield. Receiving news that an armed force led by Henry Despenser, Bishop of Norwich, was

---

* While in Yarmouth, Roger Bacon used the opportunity to solve a personal issue. He abducted a William Clere, the heir of a local lawyer who had obtained one of Bacon's properties. Clere was imprisoned until he surrendered over the manor to Bacon, who then sold it back to him three days later. See Barker, 2014, p343.

heading to Norfolk, Lister organised a delegation to the king in London "for a pardon" and a charter for Norfolk. Three of Lister's most trusted comrades headed to London with two prisoners. Unfortunately, the band ran into Despenser in Suffolk. Despenser was on the way back from Cambridge, where he had executed leaders of the rebellion and put down a major uprising in the town. He was in no mood for justice and executed Lister's delegates, freeing the two gentlemen.[169]

We get a sense of Bishop Despenser's justice from Henry Knighton's account of his actions at Peterborough:

> He prevented the malefactors from carrying out their aims and scattered the mob, paying them back as they deserved. Sparing no one, he sent some to death and others to prison. Several of the rebels fled to the church for protection but fell into the pit of perdition they had dug themselves: for those who had not feared to destroy the ramparts of the church did not deserve its immunity. Some were struck down with swords and spears near the altar and others at the church walls, both inside and outside the building. Just as they had spared no one from their own furious vengeance, so the bishop's eye now spared none of them... For the bishop gladly stretched his avenging hand over them and did not scruple to give them final absolution for their sins with his sword.[170]

The bishop went wherever he heard of rebels, according to Knighton, to "meet and disperse them, crushing their arrogance at its root".

Having beheaded Lister's delegates and "fixed up the heads of these traitors at Newmarket",[171] Despenser then marched with his troops to put down the rebellion in Norfolk.

Geoffrey Lister and the rebels retreated from Norwich and sent out messages calling on supporters to join them. According to Thomas Walsingham, the rebels built a camp at North Walsham, digging a ditch and using furniture, shutters, gates and stakes to protect themselves. Sounding trumpets, the bishop charged in "like a whirlwind" and the "warlike priest" spared no-one. Those that ran away were hunted down and Geoffrey Lister was captured and sentenced to "drawing, hanging and execution". Bishop Despenser was, however, a man of god, and heard Lister's confession, absolved him and went with him to his execution.

Cynically he "held up the rebel's head to prevent it knocking on the ground while he was being dragged".[172]*

The end of the Revolt

Despenser brought the revolt in Norfolk to an end. His summary execution of rebels, and military action against their holdouts, together with the defeat of the rebels in London meant the rebellion had passed its high point. His actions, however, were unusual. Elsewhere local nobility seldom challenged the rebels and indeed it was not until 18 June that the king ordered action against the rebellion:

> Because we understand that various of our subjects have risen in various counties of England, against our peace and to the disturbance of the people, and have formed various gatherings and assemblies in order to commit many injuries against our faithful subjects, and because they affirm and inform our people that they have made the said assemblies and risings by our will and with our authority we hereby notify you that these risings, assemblies and injuries did not and ought not to derive from our will or authority, but that they displease us immensely as a source of shame to us, of prejudice to the crown and of damage and commotion to our entire kingdom… Wherefore we command and order you to have this publicly proclaimed, in the places where it seems to you this can be best and most quickly done to preserve the peace and resist the said insurgents against our peace; you are to do this to the limit of your ability and with force, if necessary…you must command all and each of our liegemen and subjects to desist completely from such assemblies, risings and injuries and return to their homes to live there in peace, under penalty of losing life and limb and all their goods.[173]

Given the events of the Revolt, this seems a defensive response from the king, who probably recognised that he did not need mass repression. Richard also did not use the two armies that he already had mobilised for war with Castile, both well placed to intervene against the rebels. Together these armies had around 5,000 men. Given the speed with which the rebels had captured London it would have been difficult for Richard to get them to the capital in time. But it is notable that in

---

* Juliet Barker points out that contemporary records suggest Lister was beheaded not hanged and an account written several years after 1381 says that Despenser persuaded the rebels to surrender without a battle. Her conclusion is that while there is no proof a battle was fought between Despenser and the Norfolk rebels, "it is likely that at least some rebels were cornered and put up a fight". See Barker, 2014, p351.

the repression that followed Richard did not feel the need to employ a full-scale military operation.[174]

The Anonimalle Chronicle gives us one version of how the revolt ended:

> the king sent out his messengers into various districts to take the evil doers and put them to death; and many were taken and hanged in London and other cities and towns in the south country. And finally, as God willed, the king saw that too many of his lieges would be undone and too much blood spilt, so he took pity in his heart...it was ordained with their assent that the commons ought to have grace and pardon for the misdeed, on condition that they should never rise again, on pain of loss of life and members.[175]

But the king was far from merciful. As the Westminster chronicler noted:

> the royal judges were now everywhere to be seen in session, inquiring into the activities of the conspirators and giving the guilty short shrift. Gibbets rose where none had been before, since existing ones were too few for the bodies of the condemned.[176]

The king authorised commissions to enforce peace and bring the rebels to justice. We have already encountered the head of one such commission, Sir Robert Tresilian, who ended the rebellion in St Albans. On 17 June a commission was sent out to Kent, with the king's elder half-brother Thomas Holand, Earl of Kent, Sir Thomas Trivet and 12 horsemen and 25 archers. On 20 June the Earl of Suffolk led 500 soldiers to Suffolk and travelled on into Norfolk, hearing testimony along the way.[177] But these were not impartial commissions designed to find out the reasons for revolt and solve injustice. Instead, these commissions acted as judge and executioner. The commission to Essex, headed by a large local landowner and working with other local gentry, was not likely to take the side of the peasants. Indeed, many local rebels decided to resist but, despite building barricades and digging ditches to defend themselves against Buckingham's troops at a place called Billericay, they were massacred. Buckingham then travelled all the way to Gloucester, where, by coincidence, his wife also owned large estates, and put down the rising there.[178]

Tresilian went to St Albans, executing rebels along the way, to preside over John Ball's trial. Ball had been captured in Coventry and was brought to St Albans to be tried in the presence of the king. Thomas Walsingham tells us that Ball was sentenced to "drawing, hanging, beheading, disembowelling and...quartering" and was executed on 15 July.[179]

Jack Straw was captured and executed in London, his head probably being exhibited at London Bridge. Walsingham tells us he was executed together with other "leaders of the commons" including "John Starlying of Essex who boasted that he had executed the archbishop".[180]

The suppression of the rebels was violent but arbitrary. As Juliet Barker points out, in St Albans Tresilian sentenced 15 to death and 80 to prison, though no killing had taken place there. In contrast at Bury St Edmunds, where there had been extensive killing and destruction, the king fined the town 2,000 marks and "the townsmen escaped with their lives and liberty".[181]

The young king put himself at the heart of the repression. He was present at the trial and execution of John Ball and according to several chronicles led an armed force to Essex to put down the rebels (though we should take with a pinch of salt Walsingham's suggestion that the king had 40,000 troops for this task).

There is a telling story in Thomas Walsingham's account of the rising, in which rebels in Essex send a message to the king to find out whether they were to be granted the liberty they desired. The king responds to their representatives:

> you wretched men, detestable on land and sea, you who seek equality with lords are not worthy to live... So give this message to your colleagues from the king. Rustics you were and rustics you are still; you will remain in bondage, not as before but incomparably harsher. For as long as we live and, by God's grace, rule over the realm, we will strive with mind, strength and goods to suppress you so that the rigour of your servitude will be an example to posterity. Both now and in the future people like yourselves will always have your misery as an example before their eyes; they will find you a subject for curses and will fear to do the sort of things you have done...you may keep your lives if you decide to return to us and remain faithful and loyal.[182]

We have to be careful reading this as the actual words of the king. However it gives a sense of how the rebels were viewed by Walsingham (and presumably those around him) in the aftermath of the rising. Whether or not the speech took place, the king and his government certainly had no intention of letting another rising occur.

In November 1381 parliament met in the aftermath of the rebellion. Proceedings were dominated by discussion of what to do. The king wanted to pass rules to return his country to peace and said he wished to provide against another rising...of the same sort and to seek and discover the ways by which the malefactors may be punished...to investigate and search for the causes and principal reasons for the said risings, so that when these have been discovered and known, and completely removed, people will have confidence in the remedy.[183]

The king raised the question of the charters he had approved at the height of the rebellion, which effectively freed the serfs and gave in to their demands, and were then repealed. He asked whether parliament endorses his actions or whether it actually wanted to free the peasants.

But now the king would like to know the wishes of you, my lords prelates, lords and commons here present, and if it seems to you that he did well by this repeal and to your pleasure or not. For he says that if you desire to enfranchise and make free the said villeins with your common assent—as it has been reported to him that some of you wish—the king will assent to your request.[184]

Richard and his government were now securely back in power and in a position to look like they were concerned about the state of the kingdom and the commons, while doing little to change the status quo. It is highly unlikely Richard really thought parliament might want to abolish serfdom and when Sir Richard Waldegrave responded in his capacity as Speaker, he laid the blame for the revolt not on serfdom but on corrupt individuals:

And there are grievous oppressions throughout the country because of the outrageous multitude of embracers of quarrels and maintainers, who act like kings in the country, so that justice and law are scarcely administered to anybody. And the poor commons are from time to time despoiled and destroyed in these ways, both by the purveyors of the said royal household and others who pay nothing to the commons for the victuals and carriage taken from them, and by the subsidies and tallages levied upon them.[185]

This corruption together with "outrages" by raiding from the country's enemies were given as the root cause of the rebellion. But nothing was said about the issues that the rebels repeatedly raised as demands "from abolition of all forms of villeinage and freedom from tolls and customs to the revocation of the Statue of Labourers".[186] Parliament did pardon people and towns, including those members of the nobility who had killed rebels, as well as those rebels who had committed treason. This sounds magnanimous, but as Juliet Barker points out, a rebel who wanted a pardon had to first admit their involvement in the rebellion and then pay for it. A year later parliament got the king to make a second pardon which removed the need to pay for all except several hundred named rebels.[187]

Parliament granted commissioners powers to arrest those who took part in meetings or actions aimed at encouraging future uprisings and the right to use violence to suppress them through the raising of military forces.[188] Parliament was keen to make sure that in future there should be no confusion or doubt about whether or not individuals like Bishop Despenser had the right to murder those who were rebelling against injustice.

The legacy of 1381

Beyond the immediate gains that may have resulted from the killing of a particular abhorrent lord or abbot, the plundering of their goods and wealth or the destruction of manorial records, the Peasants' Revolt had little lasting impact for those at the bottom of society. But while the rebels may have been defeated and many killed, their legacy was significant.

Firstly, the defeat was not total. Even in the immediate aftermath of the suppression, some were unwilling to give up. In September 1381 in Kent, Thomas Harding called together a meeting and planned to kill three of the local gentry. The plotters hoped to send agitators to Essex and force the king to grant the Mile End charters again. They were betrayed. Tresilian presided over their trial and nine plotters were executed.[189]

In September 1382, another more serious attempt to instigate rebellion took place that was clearly linked to the previous year's Revolt.[190] Thomas Walsingham tells us that:

> certain people in Norfolk...made a conspiracy and assembled in iniquity with the firm intention, if fortune favoured them, of capturing and killing the Bishop of Norwich and all the great men of the country unexpectedly. In order to increase their power, they determined to go secretly to Saint Faith's fair and force all the people gathered there either to swear to support them or to suffer immediate slaughter.[191]

The plans, which have been described as a "well-devised scheme", included the occupation of the Abbey of St Benet as a stronghold against reprisals.[192] The Bishop of Norwich was none other than Despenser; clearly the 1382 rebels hoped to get revenge for his suppression of the Revolt. The authorities were worried enough to execute ten people when the conspiracy was betrayed.

In 1393 a chronicler of a rising in Cheshire, noted that: "men all over England were sure another general insurrection was at hand".[193]

But the greatest legacy of the Great Revolt of 1381 was in the way it has inspired, and continues to inspire, those fighting against oppression. The names of Jack Straw, Wat Tyler and John Ball in particular came to represent the struggle for justice and were often referred to by rebels that followed in their footsteps. The ruling class never forgot the few weeks when the peasant masses managed to capture some of their most important towns and cities and killed many senior figures. In the run up to the English Civil War in 1642, for instance, King Charles 1 warned that if his parliamentary opponents didn't stop making radical demands, then:

> this splendid and excellently distinguished form of government, [would] end in a dark equal chaos of confusion, and the long line of our many noble Ancestors in a Jack Cade, or a Wat Tyler.[194]

The Revolt of 1381 was part of a long tradition of resistance to feudalism by those at the bottom of society. The Revolt was national, but it was shaped in localities by the experience of feudalism. Those who rebelled were not just the poorest but, in the words of Rodney Hilton, a "cross section" of medieval rural society. On occasion even members of the gentry, such as Sir Roger Bacon, joined in.

Serfdom survived 1381, but the Revolt began the process which culminated in its end. The historian V H Galbraith concluded that as villenage became increasingly economically unprofitable, it was not abolished "it just faded away".[195] After 1381, things were never quite the same, but they were not completely different either, which is why it was barely 70 years before the peasantry exploded in revolt again.

2

Jack Cade's revolt

CADE: Be brave, then; for your captain is brave, and vows reformation. There shall be in England seven halfpenny loaves sold for a penny: the three-hooped pot; shall have ten hoops and I will make it felony to drink small beer: all the realm shall be in common; and in Cheapside shall my palfrey go to grass: and when I am king, as king I will be—

ALL: God save your majesty!

CADE: I thank you, good people: there shall be no money; all shall eat and drink on my score; and I will apparel them all in one livery, that they may agree like brothers and worship me their lord.

DICK: The first thing we do, let's kill all the lawyers.

CADE: Nay, that I mean to do.

— Shakespeare, *Henry VI, Part II*, Act IV, Scene II

"By this toun, by this toun, for this array the kyng shall lose his Croune"

— John Frammesley, or Ramsey, a London wine merchant, was executed for singing this chant through London in the run up to the Revolt[196]

THE NEXT rebellion to shake the English state to its very foundations is known by the name of its leader, Jack Cade.* It took place in a very different set of circumstances to the 1381 uprising. Its roots lay in the political, military and financial crisis that arose as England's Hundred Years' War with France approached its end. We know a great deal about the demands of the rebels, as this was "the first popular rebellion in English history to produce a coherent programme of grievances, requests, and remedies in the form of written, publicised manifestos".[197]

Henry V had carved out an enormous area of France to be part of his Kingdom and the Treaty of Troyes with France ensured his heir would

---

* Unlike the 1381 Revolt, there are far fewer accounts of Jack Cade's rebellion. The most well known, that depicted in Shakespeare's *Henry VI, Part II*, is almost entirely inaccurate. The best summary is Harvey, 1991, upon which I have drawn heavily here. An accessible recent account of the English occupation of France and its defeat is Barker, 2006. A comprehensive account of the rule of Henry VI can be found in Griffiths, 1981, which has an excellent chapter on the events of 1450. Studying the Cade revolt today, it is easy to sympathise with the historian Robert Furley who wrote in 1874 that it has been "often recorded, though, until of late, not very accurately." Furley, 1874, p385.

be the first joint king of the two countries. But Henry v's early death meant his heir, Henry VI, was only nine months old. Initially England and its French territories were governed by a council overseen by two of his uncles, the Duke of Bedford and the Duke of Gloucester. Henry VI took over at the age of 16 in the year 1437. He was a weak and ineffective leader: militarily inept, he preferred lavishing wealth on his friends and family and was enormously in debt.

According to historian I M W Harvey, Henry was at best "regarded as a hapless idiot, and at worst as a predatory menace to his country's domestic finances and its foreign affairs." Popular criticisms of the king noted in the 1440s included: "He was a fool, a simpleton", "he had murdered his uncle, the duke of Gloucester", "losing all the wealth of the crown", "no soldier" and "Henry were better dead".[198]

An indictment in 1450 inquired whether John and William Merfeld of Brightling in Sussex had said

> That the king was a natural fool and would often hold a staff in his hands
> with a bird on the end, playing therewith as a fool, and that another king
> must be ordained to rule the land, saying that the king was no person able
> to rule the land.

Such jocular criticisms of the king had far more serious conclusions. This indictment continues by noting that John Merfeld had also claimed that, "He and his fellowship would rise again and when they were up they would leave no gentleman alive but such as they pleased to have".[199]

Henry VI's inability, or unwillingness, to lead the country meant that a number of other figures came to be influential within royal circles. This "court party" included William de la Pole, the Duke of Suffolk. Many of Suffolk's men were to play key roles in the events that were to follow, particularly as several, including Suffolk himself, were linked with the defeats in France. Others, such as the lords Thomas Daniel, John Trevilian and John Say, were not of such high rank, but were nonetheless hated for their greed, holding positions which had gained them wealth and favour from the king.[200]

Many of them held numerous positions, controlled large areas of land and were significant political figures. Thomas Daniel, for instance, was sheriff of Norfolk and Suffolk from 1446-1447, a justice of the peace for Norfolk and constable of Castle Rising, MP for Cornwall (1445-1446) and Buckinghamshire (1447 and 1449) and held a number of offices for the king. Such were the individuals around Suffolk, whose "adherents were most prominent in Norfolk, Suffolk, Kent, Surrey and Sussex. They took over these areas both socially and politically, impinging upon some of the older established gentry. The courtiers went about the buying up of estates and the securing of property in a rapacious and often violent manner...made rich pickings for such opportunists".[201]

The areas under Suffolk's influence were run like his personal kingdom, a rule marked by violence and corruption. Judicial hearings from the end of 1450 document the "persistent bullying, extortion, and harmful interference in county life and government" protected by senior figures in the government.[202] In 1438, for instance, Thomas Tuddenham, John Heydon and Thomas Brigge threatened the population of Norwich that they would inform the Duke of Suffolk that their city was planning to rise against the king unless a bribe was paid. Tuddenham and Heydon were both justices of the peace and didn't neglect opportunities to extort money from individuals under threat of having goods seized or being imprisoned under false charges. This was the "complete breakdown of effective law and order although the processes and functions of the law continued as a charade played out by its misusers".[203]

One of Suffolk's key allies was James Fiennes. Fiennes, known as Lord Saye and Sele, eventually became lord treasurer in September 1449 and was on the king's council. During the 1440s he had extensive official positions throughout Kent, including being warden of the important Cinque Ports. He was "chamberlain of Henry's household, constable of Dover castle, [and] warden of the Cinque Ports". Like Suffolk's other friends, Fiennes was happy to use his power to grab more wealth and land and to use his position to control those who wanted access to the king. Fiennes and others stopped clergy from preaching before the king unless their sermons had been checked beforehand and prevented them speaking on particular subjects such as "the king's own conduct, or the conduct of his privy council".[204]

In 1450, the rebels of Kent named "four great extortioners", William Crowmer, Stephen Slegge, William Isle and Robert Est, all of whom were involved in corruption, violence, injustice and the abuse of their positions for personal gain.[205]

As I M W Harvey explains,

> Est and his kind were able to carry on as they did unchecked because they were never brought to court during the 1440s... The presence of such fellow criminals as Saye and William Isle on the commissions of the peace must have been of assistance... If the allegations made by the commons of Kent in 1450 concerning the activities of the king's bench are accurate, then the royal courts of law were used as vehicles of exploitation in the country.[206]

War and peace

But while there was plenty to complain about regarding corruption and lawlessness, the growing crisis over English possessions in Normandy during the 1440s was stirring popular discontent. The 1440s saw a number of attempts to make peace with France. In 1444 the Treaty of Tours was signed agreeing a 21-month truce and Henry VI married Charles VII's 15-year-old niece by marriage, Margaret of Anjou. This was a somewhat one-sided arrangement. Margaret brought little in the way of dowry to the English coffers and was a fairly minor royal figure. The Duke of Suffolk was central to these agreements, which fuelled speculation that he was in the pay of France.[207]

In his desperation to end the war, Henry made a number of strategic mistakes. In 1440 he gave up one of his most valuable and important hostages, the Duke of Orleans, whom he hoped would return to France and agitate for peace. Opposed to this measure was the popular Humphrey, Duke of Gloucester, one of the leading figures in the campaign to keep England's French possessions and its claim to the French throne. In 1445 Henry further undermined his position by giving Maine back to the French. Suffolk's enemies argued that he had engineered this, making rash promises as part of the peace negotiations or acting "without the assent, advice or knowledge of your other ambassadors".[208] As a result, popular songs and poems of the day alleged that "Suffolk normandy hath swold".[209]

Despite England's new queen and the return of Maine, the crisis continued. Rival forces at the royal court continued to jockey for position, and in February 1447 parliament was summoned. On the day of his arrival the Duke of Gloucester was arrested and died a few days later of an apparent stroke. As he lay sick, some 40 of his entourage were also arrested. Gloucester had been a longstanding opponent of Suffolk's faction and an important political figure for half a century and was very popular with the people. Whether he was murdered or not, it was a popular belief that Suffolk had had him killed, which in turn implicated the king.

Crisis

This was the backdrop to the wider crisis that led to the revolt of Jack Cade. As Harvey explains:

> These years saw...the outcome of years of cumulative mismanagement so disastrous that the people of whole regions of England were finally provoked into a demonstration of protest and hostility.[210]

The king's revenue from taxes was dropping and the costs of war were rising. Henry's favouritism led him to grant money, exemptions from taxes and land to his friends at court, while lavishly spending money on the building of his college foundations at Eton and Cambridge. By December 1446 the country's treasurer was unable to provide any money for the defence of Normandy if war broke out again. The parliament that met in February 1449 was unwilling to grant further cash and so "the provisioning of Normandy at this crucial time suffered because the Commons could not trust those who were in favour around the king to make proper use of the taxation of the people of the realm". Income from taxes on imports and exports had also dropped dramatically. In particular exports of woollen cloth to Holland and Flanders had massively declined as a result of the war. Imports of goods from these countries were banned which further heightened the financial crisis. This helps to explain the involvement of labourers in the cloth and wool industries in the revolt that followed.[211]

By the time the next parliament met in June 1449, there was growing concern about popular discontent, so much so that in a debate over the supply of the Normandy garrisons concern focused initially on "measures for dealing with disorder at home".[212]

By the next parliament, which ran from November 1449 to June 1450, discontent was already breaking out into open rebellion. In parliament, noted for its "financial inaction", MPs sat while "Normandy was slipping out of English hands" and splits grew at the top of society. In November there was an attempt to assassinate Lord Cromwell, one of the king's critics. The would-be assassin, William Tailboys, was linked to Suffolk and those who wanted to arrest Suffolk now had even more grounds.[213]

The crisis on the other side of the Channel grew as the French scored victory after victory in their attempt to retake Normandy. By the end of 1449 the threat of invasion seemed very real as the last of England's territory in France was captured. Bureaucratic inefficiency and lack of money meant that troops gathered for the defence of the country were left to get restless in Portsmouth. In early January, when Bishop Moleyns finally arrived in the city with cash for some of their back pay, 300 soldiers and sailors "dragged him out of his lodgings to a field and killed him". The bishop may have kept some of the money for himself, but it is likely the most important reason for his murder was that he was a close associate of Suffolk.[214]

In January 1450 a small uprising broke out in Kent, led by Thomas Cheyne. He gathered rebels from villages on the east coast of Kent, between Sandwich and Dover, and hoped to gain support from much wider afield. They listed those they wanted to see beheaded, including Suffolk and Lord Saye, and organised themselves militarily, hiding their identities with aliases such as "King of the Fairies", "Queen of the Fairies" and "Robin Hood". Cheyne took the name "the hermit Blewbeard". At its peak the rising may have involved thousands.[215]

The rebellion was stopped at Canterbury. Cheyne was captured, tried and hanged, drawn and quartered. His head was sent to be displayed at London Bridge and the rest of the body parts were sent to "London, Norwich and two of Clinque Ports". It is a mark of the level of discontent that it was difficult to find people to transport Cheyne's remains.

Nicholas Jakes was executed for trying to encourage rebellion in Westminster, again plotting to execute leading government figures, though he was caught before anything actually happened. Near Winchester at the start of February, rebellion began as an ex-soldier gathered an army, including troops who had been involved in the killing of Bishop Moleyns, and flew "a red flag of defiance and threatening war against the king".

In February and March 1450, parliament formally accused Suffolk of a series of crimes. Suffolk escaped the charges related to affairs with France and on the remainder the king had his friend banished for five years from the beginning of May. The duke barely made it back to his home in Suffolk as a London crowd attempted to capture him. Discontent was now at fever pitch. Posters appeared across London bemoaning the state of the realm, at home and in France. Anger was so great that the king got the "sheriffs of London and Middlesex, Kent, Surrey, and Sussex to make proclamation against the carrying of arms".[216]

This popular discontent was matched by anger in parliament about the king's finances (he was enormously in debt) and the wider political situation. When rebellion finally exploded, the trigger was Suffolk's fate.

Rebellion

As the Duke of Suffolk was being taken across the Channel into exile, a second ship came alongside and the duke was taken aboard, given an arbitrary trial by the crew, and executed. No one knows who was responsible but what was important was that many people in Kent believed the rumour, perhaps arising from a threat made by Lord Saye, that Kent would be "made a wilde forest" in revenge for the extrajudicial killing.[217] In fact this appears to have been the spark that ignited the whole region in open rebellion.

Kent had suffered more than most from the trials and tribulations of the previous years. Suffolk's men and others linked to the king's household had used the land and people to line their own pockets and the war had hit the area hard too. French raids on coastal villages and towns hit ordinary people and ports suffered from the reduced economic activity, particularly the export of wool and cloth. Thousands of soldiers who passed through Kent on their way to war, or the refugees who fled the towns captured back from the English, needed to be fed and looked after. Support for the king's troops was supposed to be compensated by the state, but reimbursement was often slow if it ever arrived at all. News and rumours of defeats in France, fuelled by refugees, further unsettled the people: after all, the French army was now only the other side of the Channel.[218]

By end of May, Kent was in open rebellion. According to I W A Harvey, this coincided with the major Rochester fair which brought in people from across the region, an opportunity to plan, gather information and spread rebellion.[219]

The rebellion of May 1450 was different to the uprising in 1381. While both of them involved a cross section of rural society,

> The rebel complaints of 1450 reflect the frustrations and resentments of practically all sections of Kentish society, including the substantial and well-to-do, the townsmen and the traders as well as the peasantry and yeomen.[220]

But while those listed as pardoned after the rebellion included many gentlemen and former and future MPs, the majority were agricultural workers, yeoman or labourers, with many more not identified. Helen Lyle lists the trades of many of those pardoned after the revolt, a cross section of these include; tinkers, carters, farriers, servants, brewers, innholders, people from many different cloth trades, masons, thatchers, joiners, butchers, bakers and "men connected with sea or river traffic". Yeoman and labourer "are terms applied to many", so while the rebels were a cross section of society, the mass of those who marched on London were from the lower classes and the majority were from "agricultural" trades.[221]

By the time of the rebellion, few in Kent worked as unfree peasants. Most were small peasant producers, who had a "reputation for litigiousness" in defence of their rights.[222] The rare example of landowners still demanding "residual labour dues", such as the estates of the Archbishop of Canterbury or those of Battle abbey, were clearly an issue for resentment and during the rebellion tenants refused to pay these customary dues.[223]

By June rebels were meeting across Kent and had elected a leader, Jack Cade, "the Capitayne of the oste" or "captain of Kent". We know little about who Cade was, though at the time there were many rumours and theories. He was often known as John Mortimer, a name possibly chosen to associate Cade with the ancestors of the Duke of York, which had great political implications at the time. York was associated with critical opposition to the king and had a claim on the throne, but he was given no prominence in later rebel proclamations. The king believed Cade to have come from Ireland, where the Duke of York was posted and where he had lands. As far as can be concluded with any certainty, Jack Cade had some link with south-eastern England before the rebellion, and possibly was a yeoman from Hurstpierpoint in Sussex. Accounts of the rebellion describe him as "ribaud", "knave" or a "sympylle man".[224]*

Cade did not receive quite the levels of support that his predecessors in 1381 had. In early June 1450, his army of 4,000 arrived at Canterbury and waited three hours without receiving any support, after which they headed toward London. While some towns remained careful about committing to Cade, who was sending out appeals for support, other groups of rebels were converging on the capital or joining Cade's army. The hesitancy from some is shown by the town of Lydd which made a gift of a porpoise to Cade, "to have his friendship" instead of joining the rebellion. This gift may seem strange, but at the time porpoises were considered royal fish, belonging to the crown. Lydd may not have joined the rebellion, but its community leaders were making a statement about how they saw Cade, or hoping that he would leave them alone if they flattered him enough.[225]

News of the rebellion led parliament, which was meeting in Leicester, to be adjourned on 6 June and the king ordered a force to "go against the traitors and rebels in Kent and to punish and arrest the same". But this response was not quick enough to prevent the rebels reaching London. By 11 June Cade and his army were camped on Blackheath in a camp protected with stakes and ditches. The rebels must have been confident that they would be supported by Londoners as Cade sent orders to merchants in the city for arms and money or risk losing their heads.[226]

Over the course of the uprising, the rebels produced a number of manifestos of demands. The first of these, possibly produced as early as May, is dominated by concerns relevant to the population of Kent, which might reflect its use as a mobilising tool in preparing the rebellion, "a manifesto to launch a campaign".[227]

The "complaints and causes of the assembly on Blackheath" begins:

---

* The Duke of York had a claim to the English throne because he was descended, through his mother, from Edward III's second surviving son.

Fyrst hit is opynly noysyd that Kent shuld be dystroyd with a ryall power & made a wylde fforest for the dethe of the duke of Suffolk of wyche the commones there was nevyr dede doer.[228]

The extensive document continues, listing a host of complaints and demands. Beginning with the fear that Kent would be turned into a forest for the murder of Suffolk, a crime which the people denied any involvement with, it continues by highlighting corruption, and requesting the king does something to rein in those who were oppressing the population. As Harvey summarises:

> They wanted something done about the inconvenience and nuisance caused to the tax collectors in Kent by the requirement that they sue out writs of exemption for the barons of the Cinque Ports... Another issue was the way in which the officials of the court of Dover outstepped their jurisdiction; others, the rigging of the elections of the knights of the shire in Kent and the need for the holding of the sessions of the peace in two separate ends of the county... Alongside these county issues they were complaining that the king should restore to himself the Crown revenues he had granted away, that his natural counsellors among the aristocracy should be restored to their proper ascendancy in the king's council, and that inquiry should be made throughout the land to find out who the traitors were who caused the French possessions to be lost...remaining complaints concerned the extortions and grave abuses of office of royal household men and their colleagues.[229]

This was no revolutionary document. It was a series of radical demands by a cross section of the population that wanted an end to the abuses and corruption of Henry VI's reign. This, in part, explains the involvement of a cross section of the population rather than just those at the bottom. But it was enough of a challenge to demand a military response from the king. Estimates for the size of Cade's force on Blackheath vary dramatically, suffering from the exaggeration of medieval chroniclers, but it was undoubtedly thousands strong.

The demands placed at Blackheath differed from the earlier emphasis on Kent. This is not surprising as the rebels had arrived at the capital, and were now talking to the king and to the wider population who they were hoping to win to their cause. As Griffiths writes:

> This second document is in no sense a peculiarly Kentish document; rather does it express universally felt grievances in a mood more of sorrow than of anger: 'These ben the poyntes, mischeves, and causes of the gederynge and

assemblynge of us, youre trew lege menne of Kent, the weche we triste to God for to remedye, with helpe of hym oure Kynge, our Soveraigne lorde, and all the comyns of Inglond, and to dye therefore'. Its main purport is a detailed indictment of 'the false traytours abowte his hyghnesse' for their greed, deceit, and maliciousness, and for their mismanagement of the king's affairs. This was no narrow, sectionalist complaint, but a skilful plea for the restoration of sound and equitable government.[230]

Even before the king arrived back in London the city's leadership had begun to make preparations to defend the city. Armed guards patrolled 24 hours a day, siege engines were stationed to fire at attackers, armourers were forbidden from selling outside of the city and so on. Some of these defences were limited, so for instance the four hand-guns provided to guard London Bridge were clearly not enough "when one considers the speed and accuracy of contemporary firearms" and the thousands of rebels assembled outside the capital.[231]

The king initially wanted to lead a force to drive off the rebels, but was convinced to adopt a different tactic. Instead, on 16 June, a delegation of those who "stood highest in the social and political hierarchy of the realm" was sent to meet the rebels, including Archbishop Stafford (Kent's biggest landowner), the bishop of Winchester, the former bishop of Rochester and the Duke of Buckingham. Most of the group had extensive interests in Kent and were hoping to persuade the rebels to leave. They returned with a petition of demands, "the desires of the trewe comyns of your soueraign lord the King".[232]

The petition demanded the king punish Suffolk's men as traitors, as well as those who had killed the Duke of Gloucester and others. Once again the question of the loss of France was raised as a key point and "mention of their particular grievance of the abuse by county officials of the writs sealed under the green wax of the exchequer"—in other words the abuses of position and authority by officials to line their own pockets. The document also highlighted three issues of particular importance to the Kentish rebels, purveyance (the right of the king to purchase goods at lower rates), the Statute of Labourers and Kent's extortioners—"Slegge, Crowmer, Isle and Est". The rebels declared their loyalty to the king and Cade "issued a proclamation forbidding any destruction of property or other lawless behaviour".[233]*

---

* The original reads "all the extorcions may be leif down, that is to sey, the grete extorcion of grene wex, that is falsly vsed to the perpetuall distruccion of the Kynges liege men and the Comons of Kente". For the full document see Harvey, 1991, p191.

This was unacceptable to Henry and he decided to send in his military forces, but when, on 18 June, they arrived at Blackheath they discovered that the rebel army had left during the night, perhaps having heard of the king's plans. Henry sent a small force under Sir Humphrey and William Stafford which encountered the rebels near Sevenoaks but, in the ensuing battle, the king's force was destroyed—both Staffords and 40 men were killed. This defeat was a significant turning point in the rebellion. Not only did it give confidence to the rebels, and possibly prevent them dispersing, but it also made it clear that the king was prepared to use force. At the same time as this battle, several of the king's men were leading 2,000 troops in a campaign of robbery and intimidation around Kent.[234]

The defeat of the Staffords also led to further divisions in the king's camp. At Blackheath some of the king's retainers began to side with Cade and threatened to join the rebels unless those regarded as traitors (including the Lords Saye and Dudley, John Trevilian, John Say and Thomas Daniel) were arrested. Probably in an attempt to undermine this new threat, Henry VI had Lord Saye arrested and imprisoned in the Tower of London. Just how calculated this was is unknown because the king panicked and "publically encouraged the seizure of others who were popularly regarded as traitors". Back in London on 20 June he attempted to meet with Saye and offer him protection but remarkably the constable of the Tower, the Duke of Exeter, refused to let the prisoner go. The king then fled London to Kenilworth Castle in the Midlands on 25 June, leaving the defence of London to the mayor and town council. This incredible reversal of fortunes led Jack Cade to return to Blackheath on 29 June.[235]

The rebels return[236]

Harvey quotes a contemporary account of the rebel army at its second arrival at Blackheath as "a force marshalled and disciplined in military manner, but edgy and aggressive".[237] While the force may have been numerically smaller than earlier in the month, it was more confident and at the beginning of July, Cade's force occupied Southwark on the south bank of the Thames. Cade himself made the White Hart Inn his headquarters.

Cade had not been idle. A rising in Colchester, Essex, was the result of him sending a John Gibbes to argue for rebellion, which eventually took place on 1 July. Other Essex rebels arrived at Mile End to be joined by the Colchester rebels. This growing force was hard to control—Cade had to execute one of his captains to maintain discipline—and there was looting and robbery in Southwark. At the beginning of July it was looking remarkably like a repeat of the 1381 uprising with rebels armies camped at Mile End and south of the river.

On 3 July, the king's commission to examine "treasons, felonies and insurrections" in London and around began. In the tense atmosphere, a fight broke out and the ropes on the drawbridge on London Bridge were cut, preventing the guards from blocking access to Cade's army. As Cade's men entered the city, he made proclamations declaring that anyone looting would be executed. But this was not as disciplined a force as in 1381 and the rebels immediately began stealing goods. One hostile contemporary account describes what happened when Cade and the rebels entered London:

> when he had entered the city at once he and his men fell to robbery, and robbed certain worthy men of the city and put some of them into prison till they had paid notable sums of money to save their lives.

Jack Cade is described as riding around like a victorious lord:

> The said captain rode about the city bearing a naked sword in his hand, armed in a pair of brigadines, wearing a pair of gilt spurs, and a gilt salat [helmet] and a gown of blue velvet, as if he had been a lord or a knight, and yet he was but a knave, and had his sword borne before him.[238]

The presence of Cade and the rebels in the city forced the hand of those judges sitting on the king's commission who had dared to remain. A number of well-known figures, including John Say, John Trevilian and Thomas Daniel, were indicted for treason and other crimes. While these figures had not remained in London, Lord Saye was still in the Tower and he was taken to the Guildhall and charged with treason, including involvement in the death of the Duke of Gloucester. He was found guilty and quickly beheaded. His son-in-law, William Crowmer, another figure hated by the rebels, was also killed.

Several others targeted by the rebels were also executed over the following days. These killings were accompanied by systematic looting and robbery, though the homes of those targeted were often those who were against the rebels or who had been identified beforehand as enemies. One group even went away from London to Surrey, where in Beddinton, north of Croydon, they robbed the house of Nicholas Carew a Surrey justice of the peace linked to the Fiennes family who, as we have seen, were long associated with the extortion in the south-east.

The authorities could not allow this to continue and so they planned to attack Cade's encampment. But the rebels heard of the plan and, after releasing prisoners from the Marshalsea prison to increase their numbers, Cade led an attack. They were met on London Bridge by troops under Lord Scales from the Tower of London and the battle raged from "9 o'clock in the evening to 10 o'clock on the morrow; and many men were slain on both sides".[239]

Cade's men were under-equipped when compared to the regular troops who had immense resources from the Tower and were led by experienced soldiers, including Matthew Gough, a veteran of the war with France. Nonetheless, Cade's army burnt the drawbridge after seeing the gates shut in their faces. By morning there were several hundred dead.

The damage to the bridge and the sealing of the gates meant that the rebel army had been forced out of the city. But Cade's men did not give up. Rebellion was growing outside the city and on the same day Cade's supporters in Essex were raising more men to join his army. Negotiations were "held in St Margaret's church, Southwark, between Cade and the archbishops of Canterbury and York and the Bishop of Westminster"[240] and as a result, a general pardon was issued to the rebels. As with the 1381 rebellion, it is worth reflecting that a peasant army had again forced the English state to its knees and the rebel leaders were able to negotiate terms directly with some of the most powerful figures in the land. On 6 and 7 July, hundreds of names were added to the pardon, including that of Cade's alias, John Mortimer.[241] The king issued a

> Pardon to John Mortymer of all murders, insurrections, treasons, felonies, misprisions, offences, impeachments, confederacies, conspiracies, interlocutions, ignorances, negligences, plundering, spoliations, robberies, contempts, forswearings and misdeeds and of all penalties, punishments and forfeitures incurred thereby.[242]

The sheer breadth and general nature of this pardon helped lead to many hundreds of people who did not take part in the rebellion, or indeed were active in opposing it, including their names.* A more detailed pardon for Cade reads

> General pardon to John Mortymer, at the request of the queen, though he and others in great number in divers places of the realm and specially in Kent and the places adjacent of their own presumption gathered together against the statutes of the realm to the contempt of the king's estate; and

---

* Harvey notes that the list of names of those pardoned can be broken into three rough groups. A minority who did not rise, a group representing their communities which might have been implicated simply by being on the route of a rebel march, and the rebels themselves. See Harvey, 1991, p192.

if he or any other wish for letters of pardon, the chancellor shall issue the same severally.[243]

Cade left London, with some of his men, sending (according to the *English Chronicle*) his "pillage" by barge to Rochester. Despite the pardons, when Cade left London he tried to capture Queenborough Castle in the north of Kent, perhaps knowing how former rebels had been treated in 1381 despite the concessions granted to them. But the castle resisted their attack and Cade lost some of his men. Discontent still existed in the south-east, with Cade's supporters "agitating" in his support in various towns and villages. On 10 July a writ was issued declaring Cade a traitor.[244]

Cade could be charged with treason again because it was discovered that Mortimer was not his real name, invalidating the earlier pardon. A reward of 1,000 marks was announced for the person who killed Cade, 500 marks for his lieutenants and five marks for Cade's followers. The rebel leader was chased across Kent and on 12 July he was captured and killed. Cade's naked body was taken back to London and identified as the rebel leader by the wife of the White Hart's innkeeper. It was then beheaded and quartered.[245]

After Cade

Jack Cade's death did not mean the end of popular discontent. While the revolt of 1450 was not on the same scale as that of 1381, it certainly had resonances outside of its key areas in the south-east of England. In July 1450 there were disturbances in Suffolk, Gloucestershire, Wiltshire, Hampshire, Dorset and Somerset, in addition to those already described.[246] Suffolk was in a "state of widespread unrest and lawlessness"[247] and Wiltshire saw large scale protests and violence. Wiltshire was a key textile producing region and was suffering from the economic downturn in the industry. But it was not immune from the wider social anger that had inspired Cade's followers.

The property of the Bishop of Salisbury, who was linked with the Duke of Suffolk and was Henry VI's confessor, was repeatedly targeted by mobs. They stole animals, valuables and other belongings from him, in particular targeting the bishop's baggage train as he travelled across the region away from London. One report states that among the gold and silver valuables taken was the huge amount of £3,000. The bishop was eventually captured as he celebrated mass at a monastery. A crowd of at least a hundred, and possibly many more, dragged him from the church altar, denounced him as a traitor to the king and beat him to death.

In Salisbury there appears to have been an uprising dominated by anti-clerical sentiments. Salisbury had been a town which had seen a Lollard rising in 1431 and in the political chaos of 1450, hundreds rose, "alleged to have wanted to destroy all ecclesiastical houses in the county, and to have exacted sums of money from canons of the cathedral".[248] The crowds also rode out of the city and attacked a manor belonging to the bishop, taking the lead from the roof, swans from his pond and 300 sheep. The killing of the Bishop of Salisbury seems to have unleashed pent up anger at the local church, with a number of attacks on houses belonging to religious figures, as well as the bishop's palace in Salisbury. Court rolls and other legal documents were also destroyed.

Elsewhere in England there were risings and sporadic protests. In Hampshire there was an "anti-clerical rising" in Crawley. The protesters marched on the abbey of Hyde, near Winchester, and "threatened the abbot with mutilation". He survived but the rebels got £100 from him. On the Isle of Wight, a counsellor of the Bishop of Chichester was beheaded by a mob.[249]

Near Southampton rebellion took an unusual turn as the targets of the anger there were the Italian merchants based in the town. These merchants traded with Europe through the port and contracted out textile work to the local population. The centre of this work was the village of Romsey and some of those workers marched on Southampton to "robbyd the lumbardes". This was not like the murder of Flemings during 1381, rather this seems to have been an attempt to "wreak revenge on their Italian masters". But the people of Southampton protected the traders and the leaders of this local uprising were imprisoned.[250]

The killing of the Duke of Suffolk and the murder of his followers gave confidence to Suffolk's enemies. Suffolk still had many adherents, though, and while in some places local risings took care of them, elsewhere their own aristocratic rivals took the opportunity to settle scores and strengthen their position. As two historians put it, "Where there was a powerful group of Suffolk's opponents among the county notables, they took charge of proceeding against his underlings using the established legal machinery, and they restrained the rest of the population from revolting".[251]

After the main rebellion ended and Jack Cade was killed, discontent continued for three years, particularly in Kent, the heart of the uprising. I M W Harvey's book gives a real sense of the extent of these local riots, risings and rebellions. On several occasions, local figures declared themselves to be Captain's of Kent, such as William Parmynter, who led a Kent-based rising from August to September 1450. The Parmynter rising, like others that took place in the region over the months and years following Cade's rebellion, probably involved only a few hundred people. But that there were repeated such events indicates that England was still seething with discontent.

In part this is likely because the main demands of the rebels were ignored by the king. Despite the pardon issued in July, and a conciliatory commission sent to Kent to hear grievances which indicted a number of people, little seems to have changed. At the end of January 1451, the king set out on a "judicial progress" through Kent with a thousand men. This commission was to look at events since the pardon of July 1450 in the area, though it "did not make too nice a distinction between those who had risen after 8 July and those, supposedly now immune, who had risen before". Some 30 villagers were hanged for treason and the carts carrying the bodies back to the capital to be displayed led to the king's trip being described as a "harvest of heads".[252]

Some reacted to this show of force by trying to rise again. The day after executions took place in Canterbury, agitation was taking place in and around Maidstone to organise to go to Canterbury and demand a pardon from the king, threatening him with 5,000 armed men. But such ambitions were not matched by reality. Others were cowed by the punishments. When the king returned to London at the end of February, some 3,000 former rebels are said to have gathered on Blackheath, "prostrating themselves before him naked to the waist and with cords tied around their necks" to beg forgiveness.[253]

During Cade's rebellion the rebels were keen to make it clear that they did not see Henry VI as the problem, but now he was seen as an enemy. The Court Patent Rolls for April 1451 include a pardon given by a king keen to show himself to his subjects as "he desires God to be to him" to Thomas Michelle, a baker, who, inspired by Cade,

> levied war against the king in Kent and elsewhere in the realm, proposed to annul the laws and customs of the realm, to destroy the king and realm, to spoil the lords spiritual and temporal and the king's lieges of their goods and enrich themselves affirming that they would hold all things in common, and on 26 September, 29 Henry VI, [1450], at Sevenok and elsewhere in Kent imagined the king's death and assembled to the number of twenty and more to make war and levied such war against the king until 27 January.[254]

In April 1451 rebels gathered in two parts of Kent "planning to do away with the king and the lords spiritual and temporal of the realm" and planned "to set up a dozen peers from among themselves to rule the country".[255] The discontent spread widely, including into Sussex, where at Rotherfield a gathering declared "they wanted the heads of certain Sussex gentlemen, especially of those who were against Jack Cade". The main leader of the April events was Henry Hasilden who paid with his life.[256]

Discontent in the aftermath of the Cade rebellion continued in Essex too, where there was a "similar, but not entirely parallel, pattern of plotting, uprisings, and lawlessness" to that in Kent.[257]

In September 1450, for instance, in Colchester, after declaring that Cade was still alive, rebels rioted and Richard Taillour, a brick maker, was imprisoned. This provoked a group of heavily armed men, including John Shaket, a fuller, to break into the jail and release Taillour. Shaket was indicted, but pardoned in February 1451, for saying that

> John Cade *alias* John Mortimer, captain of Kent, was living, and that they would stand with him and die in his treasons.[258]

In May 1452 there was a significant outburst of rebellion again in Kent, known as Wilkyns' Rising.[259] John Wilkyns was a pedlar from Stratford-upon-Avon who had lost everything because of his debts. This probably fuelled his anger that the demands of 1450 had not been met. Many of those who rallied to his side did so from villages that had risen with Hasilden the previous year. Again, hundreds took part, demonstrating that discontent had not died. As Harvey summarises, this uprising had links back to the Cade rebellion but was taking things much further:

> The insurgents' alleged demands were for an assortment of political and religious reforms. They wanted the petitions sought in the last parliament by them and all Kent put into effect 'even in the unwilling teeth of the king'; they wanted to do away with the power of the bishops; they desired that priests should possess nothing more than a chair and a candlestick for reading; and they, like certain men of Essex late in 1450, asserted that Cade was 'alive and their chief captain in carrying out their decisions'. It was suggested that York's son, the earl of March, was going to arrive in Kent with a great posse of Welshmen to help them obtain these petitions.[260]

Wilkyns was caught and hanged with 28 others. A few were fined and most pardoned, some for the second time. In August 1452 some of those who had supported Wilkyns were involved in a rising east of Maidstone. This rebellion also wanted to see Cade's petitions granted and proposed that secret letters be sent to the Duke of York or the Earl of Devon. They also made lists of those public figures they wanted to punish, including "officers of the king in Kent labouring against the county". Interestingly, as Harvey explains, there is an echo of the Peasant's Revolt as the rebels were alleged to have planned to kill these men and "place bills on their corpses explaining that they had been so killed because this was how it was done in the time of Jack Straw".[261]

The Duke of York

Following the events of 1450, the Duke of York, returned from Ireland, was increasingly seen as an alternative to Henry VI, particularly in Kent where he had strong links. As Harvey explains:

> York...had not been involved during the years immediately preceding 1450 in the diplomatic and military failures in France, and who was clearly not an associate of Suffolk, was one of the few magnates to command the respect of the common people.[262]

Later chroniclers worked hard to allege links to the rebels of 1450 and after with York. While it seems unlikely that York was involved with Cade's rebellion, he did attempt to use Kent for his own campaign to take the throne.

In September 1450, York wrote two letters of complaint to the king. One of these was to declare his innocence; the other was a list of demands for change in parliament. York was portraying himself as a "champion of reform".[263] This may have had some effect, for in November a small rising in Navestock, Essex, took place declaring that they expected a new king soon.[264]

In November 1450 parliament met in London. It elected York's chamberlain, Sir William Oldhall, as speaker, a good omen for the duke. Parliament then discussed a bill calling for the permanent dismissal of 29 individuals who were around the king, including key figures linked to the former Duke of Suffolk. Henry was not prepared to go this far, but his position was weak enough that he suggested an alternative which banished the 29 for a year "from his presence", except lords and "certain persones which shall be right fewe in nombre the which have be accustumed contynuelly to waite upon his persone". It was a terrible attempt at compromise and was received badly by ordinary people, leading to parliament being stormed with shouts for "Justice".[265]

The discontent that had provoked the uprising was not going to die down easily. Protests continued, particularly targeting the Duke of

Somerset, who was associated with the French defeats. Properties of his in Suffolk and Dorset were attacked and the duke himself had to be rescued from a mob and taken to the Tower of London for safety. York could not afford to associate with behaviour like this and in December he helped the king punish one looter who was executed. York also joined a "great show of strength" by riding with the king and other lords and their retinues through London.[266]

But York did not give up his ambitions and in early 1452 the duke sent letters out in an apparent attempt to get the southern part of the country to rise in rebellion. Having gathered his own forces, he marched on London, but found the city gates sealed. York then went to Dartford where he had property and apparently expected that the population of Kent would rise for him. They did not. The king marched on Dartford with an army and forced York to capitulate.[267]

While the lack of support for York's ambitions demonstrates that the region had been cowed to a certain extent by the royal repression, the continued protests of 1452 show that many had not given up on their aims of winning reforms. Indeed these struggles were only temporarily brought to a halt when the Duke of York was eventually made Protector and Defender of England while the king was laid low through mental illness.[268]

The last uprising of this period took place in April 1456 after York had resigned from his second period as Protector. This five-day rising was led by a tailor, John Percy, who also called himself John Mortimer. The rebels came from a small number of villages in the Kentish Weald, a "strongly localised disturbance". Unusually, it seems that many of those who followed Percy only did so out of compulsion.[269] This, however, seems to have been the end of any significant disturbances. It is notable, though, that during the Wars of the Roses the region was a strong supporter of the Yorkist rebellion against Henry VI when the Earl of Warwick landed at Sandwich with his supporters in June 1460 before marching on London. Those who flocked to Warwick's rebel flag came, in Harvey's words, mostly "from the counties which had produced the petitioners-turned-rebels of 1450".[270]

Few of the demands of Jack Cade and the subsequent rebels were realised. Indeed, many of the most hated figures that were the main targets of the rebel anger continued to prosper under Henry VI.

What did come out of this period of political turmoil, as the country entered into a period of civil war, was the emergence of the commons of Kent as a "remarkably independent political force", as Harvey puts it. Their support for the Yorkist cause in 1460 was less out of support for that side than because the "Yorkist lords wanted reform". So, in March 1461 men from Kent and Essex travelled to London to see Edward IV, the first Yorkist king, crowned. But the people of Kent were prepared to support whoever "appeared to be the best guarantor of good government", something that was sorely lacking in the years following Jack Cade's rebellion.[271]

Cade's rebellion has gone down in history as a rising against the inadequacies of Henry VI's rule and the greed of those around him. However, the involvement of a cross section of medieval society in the rebellion has sometimes been used to downplay the radical nature the rebellion. Harvey notes that the events show the growth of a "social group below that of the aristocracy and the gentry...who did not own villages, but carried weight in their communities as village notables." She points out that this group would go on to play an important role as "instigators of revolt" in the following century.[272]

But this social group could not and would not have stormed London and forced the king to flee without the involvement of thousands of men and women who had their own fears and dreams. When the main rebellion had been defeated and Cade's rebels returned to their homes, it was these ordinary people who continued to rise and resist the king. On occasion, such as with the Sevenoaks rebels who plotted to "hold all things in common", we get a glimpse of these dreams. It is why many believed Jack Cade was not dead and would return and it is why today we should continue to celebrate the rebellion of 1450.

3

Episodes of Tudor rebellion

THE WARS of the Roses (1455-1487) engulfed England in civil war. The origins of the conflict lay in the different claims to the English throne of the powerful Houses of York and Lancaster. The economic and social crises that followed the weak rule of Henry VI and the end of England's Hundred Years' War with France fuelled the fires. The Wars of the Roses involved a complex series of alliances, with key figures frequently changing their allegiances.[273] The crown changed hands on several occasions and each king would decry the "revolts" or "rebellions" of his opponents. These rebellions need not concern us here for these were top-down mobilisations of military forces by feudal lords intent on expanding their wealth, power and influence and have little in common with the rebellions we have discussed so far; though on occasion, as we have seen with Kent in the summer of 1460, people who had hoped for change rallied to the banners of the side they thought might bring this about.

The Wars of the Roses ended when Henry Tudor defeated Richard III at the Battle of Bosworth in 1485, becoming Henry VII. With his coronation, Henry VII brought in the Tudor era, his descendants ruling until 1603 when Elizabeth I died childless.

The Tudor period was marked by numerous revolts. Some of them involved attempts to usurp the crown, such as that by Perkin Warbeck. Others were economic and social rebellions, several of which threatened the throne from below. In this chapter we will look at two key events in brief, before discussing the rebellious year of 1549.[274]

The Tudor world

Tudor England was a tremendously unequal society. The two most important classes were the gentry and the commons, the mass of the population. The majority of those at the bottom of society were tied workers who owed obligations to a local lord, though "serfdom" by this point meant little. For the majority of the population, life was extremely difficult. As one historian of the Tudor "poor", A L Beier, puts it "England began the Tudor and ended the Stuart age with a great army of needy persons, possibly the majority of the country's inhabitants". Beier quotes taxation records that suggest that between a third and a half of the English population lived "in or near poverty" in the 1520s. The number of the poor, or those needing relief, rose and fell, frequently dependent on the success of the harvest. But the years 1500-1650 were "hard times", with the poor getting poorer in part because of the rise of the population, which grew from 2.3 million in 1520 to 4.8 million in 1630. Labour was increasingly plentiful and "real wages for agricultural and industrial labour actually fell by up to 50 percent in the period".[275]

Life in the countryside was changing and the changes were having a significant impact upon people's lives and wealth. Part of this was as a result of enclosure—this was the parcelling up of common land with hedges and fences. In Tudor times it frequently meant a switch from arable to sheep farming. These changes were made by the landowners and were hated by the peasantry who lost their common rights and sometimes their whole livelihoods. As we shall see, one common aspect of rural rebellion in Tudor times (and later) was the uprooting of hedges and the destruction of fences. Enclosure was particularly resented because it led to the loss of common land that was usually used for grazing animals. But it also meant "a change to individual farming from a communal system in open-fields".[276]

There was a second process that is sometimes lumped in with enclosures but was not the same. This is engrossing—the merging of smaller farms to make larger ones. This was usually done by wealthier farmers who wanted larger areas to graze sheep for their wool. It could have an enormous impact, as Beier explains: "Engrossers wiped out a large share of the 2,000 villages deserted between 1086 and 1700". With the smaller population of the 15th century, the merging of farms mattered less as land might well be vacant. But as the population grew the farms were not broken up again and this increased demand for land, driving up rents, as well as increasing the numbers of landless poor.[277]

The growth of sheep farming was blamed for this rural poverty and despair. As one contemporary complaint had it:

> Who will maintain husbandry which is the nurse of every county as long as sheep bring so great gain? Who will be at the cost to keep a dozen in his house to milk kine [cows], make cheese, carry it to the market, when one poor soul may by keeping sheep get him a greater profit? Who will not be contented for to pull down houses of husbandry so that he may stuff his bags full of money?[278]

Sheep had always been kept—primarily for the manure they produced. But farming sheep on a scale large enough for the textile industry required capital, something that only larger and wealthier farmers had. The question of enclosure was not simply of concern to those losing land or unable to get land; the ruling class was also worried. There were parliamentary commissions in 1517 and 1548 to examine the issue. In 1517, the Commission of Inquiry into Enclosures noted what everyone knew, that many people,

> not having before their eyes either God or the benefit and advantage of our realm or the defence of the same, have enclosed with hedges and dykes and other enclosures certain towns, hamlets and other places...where many of our subjects dwelt and there yearly and assiduously occupied and exercised tillage and husbandry, and have expelled and ejected the same our subjects dwelling therein...and have reduced the country round the houses, towns and hamlets aforesaid, and the fields and lands within the same, to pasture and for flocks of sheep and other animals to graze there for the sake of their private gain and profit.[279]

In 1533-1534, Henry VIII even passed an act limiting the number of sheep that one farmer could own to 2,000.[280]

The growing population, the demand for land, high rents and low wages meant that rural England in the 16th century was increasingly in crisis. Julian Cornwall notes in his history of the 1549 peasants' revolts that the "agricultural community existed in a state of acute tension arising from the profound changes that were taking place in farming methods".[281] Peasants and small farmers had to fight to maintain their lands and their rights. In the first instance this would mean an appeal to local custom through manorial courts. Cornwall notes that some of these farmers, often small landlords, became experts in defending their rights which they knew inside out: "popular lore had it that the Norfolk farmer carried his copy of Lyttleton on Tenures with him when he went a-ploughing".[282]*

The Cornish rebellion of 1497

The first major rebellion of the Tudor era began in Cornwall. The Cornish had supported Henry Tudor's claim to the throne. Despite his Welsh birth, Henry VII claimed direct descent from the mythical King Arthur, a figure with strong cultural importance in the region. Henry deliberately encouraged this, naming his first-born son, the Duke of Cornwall, Arthur. Cornwall was one of the poorest parts of England, distant from the capital. Fishing and trading links to the continent especially Brittany

---

* Lyttleton on Tenures is one of the first books written on English property law.

and a language that was similar to Breton and Welsh helped make the Cornish feel autonomous from the rest of the country. Many people did not speak English at all.[283]

But despite the hopes of the Cornish that Henry VII's coronation would introduce a golden age for the region, his rule benefited the rich rather than the majority. Mark Stoyle emphasises the way that this encouraged a further separation between the Cornish gentry and the majority of the population. This gentry became increasingly tied to the English court, which

> encouraged them to abandon their native traditions, thus widening the cultural divide which was already growing up between the greater gentry of Cornwall (few, if any, of whom were Cornish-speakers) and the common people.[284]

In 1495-1496 new rules were introduced to regulate the tin mining industry, one of the region's most important and historically independent industries. When the population refused to accept this, the king suspended the stannaries, the unique local legal institutions which conferred extensive rights and privileges on Cornish tin miners and towns dependent on the industry. This betrayal of Cornwall's hopes in Henry VII, combined with the ongoing decline of Cornish culture under the encroachment of English (Cornish stopped being a majority language at the end of the 15th century) helps explain the May 1497 uprising.[285] The tin industry was also a source of ongoing discontent for the people of Cornwall. The miners made little from their hard, dangerous work. But the Worshipful Company of Pewterers in London, who controlled the trade, made enormous profits.[286]

The imposition of taxes to fund Henry VII's war against Scotland was the final straw. The rebellion began in the village of St Keverne in the far west under the leadership of Michael Joseph An Gof (a blacksmith). The rebels moved eastwards to Bodmin and there the protest was given a new direction by a local lawyer, Thomas Flamank, who put the legal case against Henry's war taxes.

A contemporary account, written by Polydore Vergil, describes how

> Thomas Flammock, a lawyer, and Michael Joseph, a blacksmith, two bold rascals, put themselves at the head of the rising... When they saw that the mob was aroused they kept shouting that it was scandalous crime that the king, in order to make a small expedition against the Scots, should burden the wretched men of Cornwall who either cultivated a barren soil, or with difficulty sought a living by digging tin.[287]

In his history of the reign of Henry VII, first published in 1622, Francis Bacon described Flamank's speech:

> He told the people, that subsidies were not to be granted or levied in this case; that is, for wars in Scotland...and war was made but a pretence to poll and pill the people. And therefore it was good, they should not stand now like sheep before the shearers, but put on harness, and take weapons in their hands. Yet to do no creature hurt; but go and deliver the king a strong petition, for the laying down of those grievous payments, and for the punishment of those that had given him that counsel; to make others beware how they did the like in time to come: and said, for his part, he did not see how they could do the duty of true English-men, and good liege-men, except they did deliver the king from such wicked Ones that would destroy him and the country.[288]

The rebels began their march on London gathering support and numbers as they proceeded. The march was orderly, gathering supporters as they travelled eastwards, including some discontented individuals from the clergy and gentry, losing its "exclusively Cornish nature". Up to 15,000 rebels arrived at the capital and, after a brief engagement with 500 of the king's troops, they marched around the south of London. The rebels hoped to gain support from Kent. According to Bacon, Flamank had told them that "Kent was never conquered and that they were the freest people of England".[289]*

Nonetheless, for a rebel army of this size to have reached London was an enormous problem for Henry VII. Luckily for him, the army Henry was preparing to attack Scotland could be turned on his own people. Camped, as previous rebel armies had, on Blackheath overlooking the capital, the failure to gather additional support from Kent and the preparations for battle led to many fleeing. But some 10,000 remained to face the king's better equipped army of 25,000.[290]

> The rebels maintained the fight for a small time, and for their persons shewed no want of courage; but being ill armed and ill led, and without horse or artillery, they were with no great difficulty cut in pieces, and put to flight. And for their three leaders, the lord Audley, the blacksmith, and Flammock, as commonly the captains of commotions are but half-couraged men suffered themselves to be taken alive. The number slain on the rebels' part were some two thousand men... On the King's part there died about three hundred, most of them shot with arrows, which were

---

* Stoyle says between 3,000 and 6,000 Cornishmen crossed into England.

reported to be of the length of a tailor's yard; so strong and mighty a bow the Cornishmen were said to draw.[291]

Thomas Flamank and Michael Joseph were both captured and then hanged, drawn and quartered. Joseph is said to have declared at this execution that he "should have a name perpetual, and a fame permanent and immortal".[292]* According to Bacon, Lord Audley "was led from Newgate to Tower Hill, in a paper coat painted with his own arms; the arms reversed, the coat torn". Being gentry, Audley was spared being hanged, drawn and quartered; instead he was beheaded at Tower Hill. Understanding that Cornwall was "unquiet and boiling",[293] the king avoided a great deal of further bloodshed, though he imposed heavy fines on the regions that had supported the rebellion.

In September 1497, the pretender to the crown, Perkin Warbeck, landed in Cornwall and had himself proclaimed King Richard IV at Bodmin. His choice of Cornwall as the site to launch his campaign for the throne was based on a hope that Cornish discontent would bring large numbers flocking to join his rebellion. While the numbers were smaller than he must have hoped, Warbeck was still able to raise an army of 6,000 to try and capture the key town of Exeter. After this failed, Warbeck was captured and taken to London.[294]

While the Cornish rebellion of 1497 failed to achieve its aims, it was the first in a long tradition of Cornish risings closely linked with resistance to the undermining of Cornwall's historic semi-independence. According to Mark Stoyle:

> Although the unprecedented series of risings and near-risings which gripped the West Country between 1537 and 1549 had a multiplicity of causes...the disturbances cannot be fully understood unless the deep-seated Cornish hostility towards further assimilation within the British state is also taken into account.

Stoyle notes that it was Cornish speaking west Cornwall that provided the "storm-centre of popular protest".[295] As we shall see later, this would be a powerful threat to future English monarchs who would respond with unprecedented severity.

But while the impact of economic changes would fuel many a rebellion over the course of the period, there was another factor that was

---

* Joseph has in this regard been proved right. His defiant words are inscribed on a memorial to him and Flamank, the "leaders of the Cornish hoist who marched to London and suffered vengeance there June 1497" in Bodmin, erected on the 500th anniversary of the uprising. It is notable that this memorial and others, such as the statue in St Keverne, are part of modern attempts to create a Cornish cultural and national identity.

causing intense discontent. This was the religious changes that were being imposed on the country, beginning with Henry VIII and continuing into the reign of his son, Edward VI.

The English Reformation

In November 1534 parliament passed the Act of Supremacy, which declared that Henry VIII, "the king, our sovereign lord, his heirs and successors kings of the realm shall be taken, accepted and reputed the only supreme head on earth of the church of England".[296]

This break from the Catholic Church and the pope was the culmination of five years of complex interactions between Henry VIII's court and the wider church. However, they reflected wider political interests within England's ruling class. We shall see later how the rise of Protestantism and its challenge to traditional Catholicism was linked to the rise of a new economic class. Because society's ideology in this period was religious, social changes were understood with religious interpretations. How the English Reformation progressed was closely associated with the personal rule of Henry VIII and his economic and political interests. However, there was also growing discontent with the established church. The church was enormously rich, owning vast areas of land, and its leading figures had made themselves wealthy on the back of this. The selling of indulgences, the collection of tithes, church corruption and the wealth of bishops were increasingly seen as being at odds with the teaching of the church itself.* It was this that encouraged figures like the German reformer Martin Luther to challenge established doctrine. A section of society, in particular traders and craftspeople as well as some of the more wealthy merchants, wanted reform of the church. Some of these went on to align themselves with the new Protestant faith.

During Henry VII's reign, the king had married his eldest son, Prince Arthur, to Catherine of Aragon to link England and Catholic Spain in an alliance. Arthur's untimely death threatened this alliance, and Henry VII decided that in order to continue it, his second son, (the future Henry VIII), should marry Catherine. But under church law a papal dispensation was required for this. This was granted by the pope and Henry married Catherine. With the death of his father, Henry became King Henry VIII and now needed a male heir to continue the Tudor line. Unfortunately all of Henry and Catherine's male children died and

---

* Indulgences were a way of reducing punishment for sins after death. They might include reciting a prayer or the completion of a pilgrimage. By the late Middle Ages the granting of indulgences was becoming increasingly commercialised.

Henry looked around for a new wife. Having decided that he wanted to marry Anne Boleyn, Henry now needed a divorce from Catherine, but this time the new pope would not agree.

Anne came from a Protestant family and Henry, though he was a religious traditionalist, was prepared to break with the pope to get his divorce. In search of his divorce, Henry began seeking legal and religious opinion in England and Europe to support his argument that his marriage to Catherine was not really valid. This was led by Thomas Cranmer, an academic at Cambridge University. But Henry also began to attack the Catholic Church, gathering around him ministers and advisers who would facilitate this, most famously Thomas Cromwell. These ministers did not simply reflect Henry's religious interests, but had their own agendas. Cromwell, for instance, was from the newly emerging bourgeoisie, a wealthy merchant keen to strengthen his class's position. He was "instinctively favourable to some kind of Erasmian Protestantism" and helped drive through the break with the pope and the establishment of Henry as head of the Church in England. Cromwell "effected a new political integration of the kingdom...[leaving] a deep mark on much of the machinery of central and local government".[297]

Henry VIII was driven into making reforms in part to strengthen his own position. But he was also motivated by a desire to build alliances at home and abroad. During his marriage to Catherine of Aragon, the daughter of Isabella I of Castile and Ferdinand II of Aragon, he was keen to be seen to maintain the Catholic religion. His desire to marry Anne Boleyn from a Protestant family and the refusal of the pope to permit this helped encourage Henry towards religious reforms. Later, his interest in forming European links with the Lutheran German princes against Catholic Spain strengthened the position of Protestants at court. These twists and turns help in part to explain the rise and fall of various figures, such as Cromwell, in Henry's court.

As Henry VIII's reign progressed the power of the Catholic Church and links with Rome were gradually undermined and eventually broken. Henry replaced the pope as the head of the English Church: ecclesiastical legislation had to be submitted to the crown instead of the pope; bishops were appointed from those nominated by the monarchy; and church taxes were paid to Henry and not Rome. In 1533 the need for a divorce became urgent as Anne Boleyn was pregnant. Henry appointed Thomas Cranmer Archbishop of Canterbury, who then announced that the king's first marriage was invalid and Anne Boleyn, having earlier secretly married Henry, became queen.

Henry's first Act of Succession, passed in March 1534, ensured that the succession would pass only through Henry and Anne's children and declared Princess Mary (the daughter of Henry and Catherine of Aragon) a bastard, removing her from the line of succession. Every Englishman over the age of 14 had to swear an oath accepting this and commissioners were dispatched around the country to enforce it. But they were not always welcome. In June 1534, for instance, the "radical Protestant preacher Hugh Latimer" was dispatched to Exeter to preach on Henry VIII's supremacy. Latimer received "a hostile reception" and when one of his sermons was ended due to a "spectacular nosebleed" it was "gleefully hailed as the judgement of God on his heresies".[298]

As Henry's reign progressed, there was a slow but sure undermining of traditional Catholicism. His own personal adherence to traditional beliefs, however, meant he was not willing to go too far. Henry was, for instance, "committed to the reform of the cult of the saints and of images, but he was ferociously opposed to any deviation from traditional teaching on the Mass".[299] The Reformation process continued under his son, Edward VI, and despite reversals in the counter-reformation during the reign of the Catholic Mary (1516-1558), it was completed by Elizabeth I (1558-1603) who established the Protestant Church. However, at every stage of the Reformation there was resistance—sometimes on a local level and sometimes, as we shall see, on a much larger scale.

In 1535 in Exeter, the Priory of St Nicholas, "noted for its charity to the poor", was dissolved. The women of Exeter rallied outside "some with spikes, some with shovels, some with pikes, and some with such tools as they could get", trapping the workmen who were taking down the roodloft of the church:

> Two of these workmen were Breton carpenters, evidently Huguenots (French Protestants) who had boasted that they would pull down the crucifix 'with all the saints there naming them to be idols'. The women stoned one of the men, who leapt from a tower to escape, breaking a rib in the process.[300]

Armed force was eventually needed to break up the women's protest. Other reforms were as likely to provoke anger. In August 1536, Cromwell abolished many feast days, arguing that these holidays undermined the country's economy. But these feast days were at the heart of many villages' social calendar, occasions for markets and fairs.[301] Further religious changes introduced by Cromwell challenged the ideas and practices that hundreds of thousands of men and women had held dear for their entire lives. This included attacking "the alleged superstitions surrounding the cult of pilgrimage and images, declaring it shall profit more their soul's health, if they do bestow that on the poor and needy, which they would have bestowed upon the said images or relics".[302] Despite this, as historian Andy Wood notes, labouring people in the 16th century often saw the Reformation "in material terms, as yet another plot by the gentry to impoverish the commons and destroy the commonwealth".[303]

It is notable that when Mary's rule temporarily reversed some of the reforms made under Henry and Edward, most ordinary people returned quickly to traditional religious practices. In many places this meant retrieving church goods that had been sold or hidden during the earlier part of the reign. It required the gradual fading away of Catholic practice over many years before these beliefs were extinguished in the minds of most people. But in the short term people were often prepared to fight against religious change.

In many parts of the country these changes helped spark rebellion. In order to respond to this the Tudor authorities further criminalised dissent with the expansion of treason laws. An extra 68 treason statutes were added. Some clarified existing laws, but many were "new categories of secular treason" arising from the need to replace "ecclesiastical jurisdiction over religious dissidence", which had been removed by Henry's break with Rome.[304] Andy Wood explains the importance of these new categories of treason, which were intended

> to prevent religious and political dissidence, regardless of the social place of the dissident. Treason legislation intruded into the political worlds of the court, the parliament, the gentry and the nobility just as much as it did into those of the artisan, farmer and labour.[305]

Henry VIII's 1534 Treason Act and those that followed after his death were specifically designed to stifle criticism of the king, making certain forms of speech, such as calling him a heretic or a tyrant, treasonable. As Wood concludes, the legislation "presumed that the central state ought to exercise control over political speech, writing and publication. The primary target of the sixteenth-century treason and sedition legislation was therefore the public sphere of political speech and action".[306] The responses to the Reformation had scared the ruling class who wanted to make sure that any future rebellion could be prevented or contained.

The new laws were not enough to prevent rebellion, but they did ensure that the king had legal authority to repress uprisings and dissent, as well as punish those who criticised him or led rebellions.

The Lincolnshire rebellion of 1536 [307]

In his classic social history, *A Peoples' History of England*, the Marxist historian A L Morton described the 1536 rebellion known as the Pilgrimage of Grace as "reactionary" in form, a "Catholic movement of the North, led by the still half feudal nobility of that area and aimed against the Reformation and the dissolution of the monasteries". [308]

But this is an inadequate description of a mass rebellion involving tens of thousands of ordinary people who were agitated by the religious changes imposed by Henry VIII, but were also discontented with their social and economic circumstances. At its peak the rebellion threatened the very authority of the crown and Henry VIII's reign might well have come to a premature end. In his history of the reign of Henry VIII, the historian J J Scarisbrick concludes that Henry was saved "not so much by the loyalty of his friends as by the loyalty of the rebels". [309] To understand this, we shall explore the dynamics of the northern revolt.

The year 1536 saw two large-scale connected rebellions. The first, known as the Lincolnshire Rebellion, began in the town of Louth, south of Grimsby. Today St James' church in Louth is one of the most impressive churches in England with its 295-foot high tower, the tallest of any medieval church. In 1536, when the Lincolnshire Rebellion broke out, it was only 20 years old. The local population was intensely proud of their church and over the years it had amassed a wealth of valuables which they considered were under threat.

The Vicar of Louth, Thomas Kendall, was an "extremely orthodox and rigorous Oxford theologian" [310] whose beliefs were being directly challenged by the king's religious reforms. On Sunday 1 October, as Thomas Cromwell's commissioners were travelling across Lincolnshire detailing the wealth of the churches in the area, he preached to the Louth congregation that the "next day they should have a visitation, and advised them to get together and look well upon such things as should be required of them in the said visitation". At the end of the service the yeoman Thomas Foster, referring to the processional crosses the church owned, called out: "Masters step forth and let us follow the crosses this day: God knows whether ever we shall follow them again". [311]

Rumours that church possessions like these would be confiscated were as yet unfounded, but widely believed. Their possible loss through confiscation would have deeply worried church congregations. The wealth of local churches was the result of years of donations by the parish population themselves. In his classic of Tudor history detailing the life of the Devonshire village of Morebath, historian Eamon Duffy details how the church's wealth had been built up. In 1529, for instance, a silver wedding ring had been donated to Morebath's St Sidwell church, which was "melted down to help make a silver shoe, attached to the feet of the statue as a mark of devotion. The commission of this silver shoe coincided with a series of bequests from other parishioners for the painting of the image of Jesus, the gilding of St Sidwell, and the provision of painted cloths for their altar".[312]

Morebath was at the other end of the country to Louth, but there is no doubt that similar bequests had built the wealth of St James over decades. Parishioners who were too poor to donate silver wedding rings would have raised funds for the church in other ways—through the donation of wool or crops or their own labour. The king's threat to the church's wealth was felt as an attack not just on the church but on all those who had donated.

Other wild rumours spread: "there shall be no church within five miles, and that all the rest shall be put down" or that silver chalices would be melted down and replaced with ones made from tin or that there would be taxes on everything from white-bread and animals to weddings and other services.[313]

The next day, before Cromwell's officials arrived, a crowd gathered at the church. They discussed the ringing of the bells as a call to action and then moved to the town hall, where one of the Bishop of Lincoln's staff, John Henneage, was overseeing the election of the town's officers.[314] The bishop was disliked in Lincolnshire because:

> He subscribed to the new religious prescriptions without any sign of remorse and had also played his part in trying to get Henry a divorce from Catherine of Aragon...it was he who was sent to Oxford (where stones were thrown at him) to solicit the university's support. On top of all this he had...informed his dioceses...that saints' days were to be much reduced and that most patronal festivals would henceforth take place every year on 1 October instead of being scattered throughout the calendar.[315]

Anger at the Bishop of Lincoln led to the targeting of his representative, Henneage, who was taken by an armed mob to the church, where Nicholas Melton, a shoemaker known as "Captain Cobbler", made Henneage swear an oath "to be true to the commons, on pain of death".[316]

Following this, a second official, John Frankishe was taken by the mob. Frankishe was the official in charge of the visitation and was made to climb the cross in the market place in a pretend hanging. He was then forced to burn all his papers. On 2 October 1536 some 60 parish priests were in Louth to be examined by the visitation and they were forced to take an oath and promise that when they got home they would ring their church bells to raise their populations in rebellion. From Louth rebels then headed out to the Cistercian nunnery of St Mary in Legbourne a few miles to the east. At the nunnery they seized the commissioners there.[317]

Captain Cobbler called for every man, aged 16 to 60, to gather the following day. More than 3,000 did, including many from nearby villages. They marched on Caistor, a village some 15 miles from Louth, where the commissioners who were touring Lincolnshire for the parliamentary subsidy were based. But before they arrived, the commissioners were surrounded by locals, who, despite attempts to placate the crowd's anger, were forced to flee. Some commissioners were captured and we get an insight into the rebels' motivation from a letter the commissioners were made to write to the king. This letter made it clear that the cause of the assembly was the fear that

> all the jewels and goods of the churches should be taken from them and brought to your grace's Council, and also that your said and faithful subjects should be put off new enhancements and other importunate charges. Which they were not able to bear by reason of extreme poverty and upon the same they did swear us first to be true to your grace and to take their parts in maintaining of the common wealth, and so conveyed us...to the town of Louth...where we as yet remain until they know further of your gracious pleasure, humbly beseeching your grace to be good and gracious both to them and to us to send us your gracious letters of general pardon or else we be in such danger that we be never like to see your grace nor our own houses...further, your said subjects hath desired us to write to your grace that they be yours, bodies, lands and goods at all times.[318]

According to Geoffrey Moorhouse, the rebels also told these commissioners that while the king could have "first-fruits and tenths of every benefice as well as the subsidy", there must be "no more suppressions and no further money taken from the commons". The rebels also wanted Cromwell handed over, with a number of bishops, including the Bishop of Longland, Archbishop Cranmer and the Bishops of Rochester, Ely, Worcester and Dublin. John Porman, who told the commissioners about these demands, was not an ordinary labourer but was described as a "gentleman".[319]

His involvement is our first indication of the complicated part the gentry played in the rising. The gentry did not start the rebellion; indeed, they had to be forced to join it with threats of violence or the destruction of property.[320] But by 4 October, the gentry had taken leading roles in the uprising. They wrote to the king's commander "claiming that their strategy was to divert the commons' energy into petitioning and waiting for an answer at Lincoln rather than marching further south".[321] While most were forced to join the rebellion, many members of the gentry had their own grievances and saw the growing rebellion as an opportunity. This helps explain why they mustered the men in their own wapentakes, or administrative areas.

But the commons certainly expected the gentry would take their side. They did not consider themselves rebels and were "scandalised" when they found captured letters describing them as such.[322] That said, there was certainly distrust of some or all of the gentry. When two members of the gentry, Robert Aske and Thomas Moigne, met, the commons insisted that they did so in their hearing.[323] While the commons wanted the gentry to lead, the gentry never had complete authority.

The role of the gentry in the Lincolnshire uprising and the subsequent Pilgrimage of Grace is contradictory and has often been misunderstood. Some historians have suggested that the uprising was planned and organised by the gentry as a rebellion against Henry VIII, though the evidence is clearly against this interpretation. Instead, the motivation of the richer section of northern society is more contradictory.

The main strategy of the gentry seems to have been to play for time and to try and encourage the king to grant a pardon to the rebels, in order that they might be dispersed. They were frustrated in this latter hope and their actions did not meet with approval from the king. At Louth, on Wednesday 4 October, the gentry divided the commons into wapentakes and, as Thomas Moigne explained,

> everyone of us went to our own wapentakes and persuaded them that they should not go forward but to depart home unto their own houses to such time as they had answer from the king's highness, but that they would not do in no means, but cried to go forward out of hand or else they would destroy and slay us and choose other captains. And then when we did see them in such obstinate and wilful opinions, we determined ourselves for to follow their minds and to stay them when we came to Lincoln by such policies as we could our minds invent, to the intent to weary them and make them spend their money and so by such policy compel them to go home again.[324]

Thomas Moigne was later executed for his role in the uprising and his account should be read as a justification for his actions. But other accounts tend to support the idea that the gentry wanted to be seen to be part of the uprising at the same time as keeping their distance.

The letter sent from Louth to the king explained the concerns of the rebels:

The cause of their assemble was...that the common voice and fame was that all the jewels and goods of the church of the country should be taken from them and brought to your grace's council and also that your said loving and faithful subjects should be put of new to enhancements and other importunate charges which they were not able to bear by reason of extreme poverty.[325]

The letter then continues to ask for a pardon for both the gentry and the commoners and makes clear the continued loyalty of the commons to the king. Crucially, as the historian R W Hoyle notes, the "letter clearly expresses the distance between the commons and its gentry signatories".[326]

At Horncastle, the other centre of the Lincolnshire uprising, a nearly simultaneous insurrection took place. Led by William Leach, it was more violent than the events at Louth, the hated chancellor of the Bishop of Lincoln, Dr John Rayne, being beaten to death and another man hanged. The rebellion may have been led by one man, but "the whole town of Horncastle was congregate with other and no man spake against the rebellion".[327]

From Horncastle the commons went forth to capture local gentry and swear them to their cause. They met them with confidence—Leach is described as meeting the gentry "with his cap on his head". The gentry who surrendered were sworn in. Sir William Sandon, who was more confrontational, who declared the commons "should be hanged in the end for their labours", was sworn in separately after being beaten.[328]

Although the gentry might have had to be forced to join the rebellion through violence or threats of violence, the way they did so determined whether they would have influence with the commons and perhaps be able to halt the rebellion. Hoyle writes that by verbally attacking the rebels, Sandon forfeited "his credit with them and so his ability to influence their action." The commons saw themselves as defenders of the true order of things and loyal subjects of a king surrounded by traitorous advisers. As Hoyle points out, when Sandon denounced the commons as traitors, he was challenging their rebellion by challenging their self-perceived authority to carry it out.[329]

We have an account from Horncastle, made at the trial of Nicholas Leche (or Leach), the priest of Belchford, who helped raise the commons around Horncastle. This describes the central role of the gentry in leading the rising after its initial explosion, but also their distance:

The gentlemen were always together commonly a mile from the commons. What they did he knows not, but at length they brought forth certain articles of their griefs, of which one was that the King should remit the subsidy, and another that he should let the abbeys stand.[330]

But the gentry clearly did not feel that they could impose these demands on the commons. They needed their agreement. The articles were proclaimed and then the gentlemen asked of the rebel crowd,

'Masters ye see that in all the time we have been absent from you we have not been idle. How like you these articles? If they please you say Yea. If not, ye shall have them amended.' The commons then held up their hands and said with a loud voice, 'We like them very well.'

Not all of the demands were ones that the commons raised or possibly understood. Leche explains that:

Amongst other articles there declared, Mr Sheriff and other gentlemen said, 'Masters, there is a statute made whereby all persons be restrained to make their wills upon their lands, for now the eldest son must have all his father's lands, and no person to the payment of his debt, neither to the advancement of his daughters; marriages, can do nothing with their lands, nor cannot give his youngest son any lands.

The report of Leche's trial implies the priest thought the commons did not know what the Act of Uses was and this was a demand that meant more to men of property than to the majority of the commons. Nonetheless they agreed to it. Crucially, Leche also reports that during the Lincolnshire rebellion,

not one of them [the gentlemen] persuaded the people to desist or showed them it was high treason... He thinks the gentlemen might have stayed the people of Horncastle... The gentlemen were first harnessed of all others, and commanded the commons to prepare themselves harness, and he believes the commons expected to have redress of grievances by way of supplications to the King.*

This reliance on the gentry by the rebels helps explain how the Lincolnshire rising ended. Despite a large army—10,000 marched to Lincoln—and the support of the population, the gentry were able to eventually make the rebels return home.

---

* Significant numbers of clergy were involved in the Lincolnshire uprising, including 700-800 priests and monks, some of whom, like Leche, paid with their lives. Moorhouse, 2003, p58.

The rebels converged at Lincoln on 9 October. There the gentry were firmly in control of the commons. A new set of demands was drawn up and a plan was made for a general muster of rebel forces near Grantham. The demands at Lincoln were essentially those that had been raised on a number of occasions since the initial uprising in Louth. Among other demands, the Lincoln articles call for an end to the suppression and dissolution of religious houses, "whereby the service of our God is not wel [maintained] but also the [commons] of yor realme by unrelieved". Secondly, they call for the "acte of use" to be ended because "we think by the sayde act that we your true subjects be clerely restraynyd of ther liberties in the declaration of our wylles concernying our lands". Thirdly, the rebels called on the king to reduce the taxes that his subjects faced on sheep and cattle, "which wold be an importunate charge to theym considering the povertie that they be in all redye and losse which they have sutayned these ii years by past".[331]

The rebels named those persons around the king who were perceived as leading him astray and ruining the kingdom for their own advantage, "the which we suspect to be the lord crumwell and Sir Richard Riche Chanceler of the augmentacion", and the bishops who they saw as being the cause of the problems, especially the Bishop of Lincoln, who was seen as the source of "all the trouble of this relm and the vexation that hath been takyn of yor subjects".*

These demands neatly brought together the interests of the gentry and the commons. Every social movement finds the raising of demands only the beginning of their difficulties. The key question is how to win them. The commons wanted to send the demands to the king immediately, but the gentry urged restraint, preferring to wait until they had a response to their earlier letter.

Henry had decided to mobilise militarily against the rebels. He was aware that the rebels had a significant force, as one report he had received made clear:

> They number 10,000 or 12,000 spears, well harnessed, and 30,000 others, some harnessed and some not... The country rises wholly as they go before them. [The writer] Thinks lord Hosey will be taken tonight or tomorrow by noon, for he dare not stir, and none of his tenants will rise for him. The journeymen will not abide with their masters, and no one is left in the towns who can bear harness.[332]

---

* Richard Riche was the person charged with administering the lands and incomes from dissolved monasteries.

Henry wrote to the rebels via the Duke of Suffolk, who was commanding the royal forces, promising an army of 100,000 would march against them. Reality was different. The royal forces were "badly organised, without the necessary funds to pay what were essentially mercenary troops and did not yet have any ordnance". In contrast the rebel army, while lacking equipment and funds, was made up of men committed to rebellion. Most of the troops in the king's army were only there because their lord had been instructed to raise soldiers. There had to be a real possibility that the rebels would win any pitched battle. It was this fact that forced the hand of the gentry.[333]

The gentry knew that if they lost, they and their families would lose their wealth, titles and land, and likely their lives. If they won, they would still face the problem of being in charge of a rebel army that had even greater confidence and the prospect of England descending into civil war. With the commons increasingly restive, prone to insubordination and ready to march on London, the gentry decided they had had enough.[334]

News from elsewhere was giving confidence to the commons. Two messengers arrived in Lincoln on Sunday 8 October, the first from Beverly and the second from Halifax, both declaring that the commons there had risen and offering assistance. It was with great difficultly that the gentry persuaded the commons to remain in Lincoln. On the Monday the articles were sent to London and once again the commons wanted to march out, but were held back.[335] On Tuesday 10 October, a messenger arrived from the king and was escorted to meet the gentry gathered in the Chapter House, a massive vaulted building which was part of the cathedral.

The gentry wanted to read this privately, but the 300 rebels who had escorted the messenger in insisted that the message be read aloud. This was done, but Thomas Moigne deliberately left out a sentence because it would "stir the commons".[336] When this was exposed by a priest, Geoffrey Moorhouse describes the reaction from the commons:

> There was bedlam in the chamber. Someone shouted that it was time to kill these turncoats and someone else threatened that if any harm befell the commons now, not one gentleman in Lincolnshire would be left alive.[337]

The commons initially decided to see if the gentry would let them march the next morning, then changed their minds and decided to kill them immediately. Knowing that they risked losing control, the gentry gathered those men they trusted most and tried to use them to persuade the remainder not to march. Failing that, they hoped to have a force that could fight.[338] Gathering their trusted men, Moigne says that the gentry:

Opened unto them the danger of our going forward to the displeasure of our prince with the mischief that should ensure thereof. And so moved them to stay until such time as we might hear further of the king's pleasure.[339]

Moigne says the gentry thought "It was better to be slain in our prince's quarrel [than] go forward and be destroyed with our prince's power".[340]

When the commons arrived on Wednesday, they were met by the gentry prepared for battle. The gentry declared that they would not move until they had heard from the king and convinced the commons to await further letters. That evening (11 October), Henry VIII's messenger, Lancaster Herald, arrived and over the course of the next two days the commons were convinced to return home, albeit only after promises that the rebels would be summoned again if there was no pardon from the king.[341]

To what extent can we take Moigne's rather self serving account of the crucial events in Lincoln at face value? Were Moigne and the rest of the gentry genuinely trying to hold back the rebellion, or, in its aftermath, were they trying to cover up their own rebellion? Those gentry who were involved had everything to lose as Henry VIII had executed many "traitors" on far flimsier evidence.

Hoyle argues that there is enough evidence to suggest that Moigne's account is true. In particular, the commons did wait at Lincoln for a response from the king. Letters sent from Lincoln by the gentry "both expressly refer to their use of delaying tactics". For instance, a letter to Sir Edward Maddison says: "we trust, God willing, to find such policy and means to stay them two or three days".[342]

If Moigne and the others really did try and hold back the rebellion, why, despite their initial refusals and reluctance, had they placed themselves in the driving seat? Was it simply to give them time to be able to stop the rebellion when the opportunity arose?

Hoyle argues that this may have been their strategy, but that the gentry also found themselves trapped. They hoped, in Hoyle's words, for a "free and unconditional pardon" because "even association with the rebels jeopardised their own lives", hence the pardon they called for in their letter from Louth. When the king's belligerent letter arrived in Lincoln on Tuesday 10 October, it did not mention a pardon and as the commons disbanded the pardon lost its significance, though it would have helped those like Moigne who were eventually executed for their roles.[343]

What then of the demands sent to the king by the rebels? Recall that some of these specifically related to the Statute of Uses and would have been of particular interest to those with property. Was this simply a cynical manoeuvre by the gentry? Hoyle suggests that the two wings of the rebellion, the one which started in Louth and the other in Horncastle, differed in what they did. He writes:

> The Louth gentry made no attempt to formulate their grievances further after they sent their letter to the king with Sir Edward Maddison. The articles sent to London with George Stanes or Stones of Haltham (south of Horncastle) on Monday, 9 October appear to have originated with the Horncastle arm of the rebellion and were sent to London only after the Louth gentry had insisted on their being toned down.[344]

By the time the Horncastle demands were sent to the king they were "transformed into a set of grievances which the rebels drew to the king's attention, and to which was annexed a request for a pardon". Hoyle points out, for instance, that the demand for the re-establishment of religious houses became a request, then simply a statement which pointed out that the dissolution meant a decline in religious service and hospitality.[345]

But in the aftermath of the rising Henry made it clear that he had no intention of giving in to the rebels. He wrote to the Duke of Suffolk urging him to make sure his proclamation was "read openly".[346] He also responded to the rebel petitions in detail leaving no doubt about his intentions, attacking the very idea that those at the bottom of society should think to change laws or make demands upon the monarch. Henry wrote that he had

> Never heard that princes' counsellors and prelates should be appointed by ignorant common people nor that they were meet persons to choose them. 'How presumptuous then are ye, the rude commons of one shire, and that one of the most brute and beastly of the whole realm and of least experience, to find fault with your prince for the electing of his counsellors and prelates?'

Henry continues rebuking the rebels' demands one by one, repeating the propaganda against the monasteries and justifying his actions as being supported by his own parliament.

> As to the suppression of religious houses we would have you know it is granted to us by Parliament and not set forth by the mere will of any counsellor. It has not diminished the service of God, for none were suppressed but where most abominable living was used... As to the relief of poor people, we wonder you are not ashamed to affirm that they have been a great relief, when many or most have not more than four or five

religious persons in them and divers but one; who spent the goods of their house in nourishing vice.

The letter concluded with an emphatic statement of violence should the rebellion continue:

> We charge you to withdraw to your houses and make no more assemblies, but deliver up the provokers of this mischief to our lieutenant's hands and submit yourselves to condign [appropriate] punishment, else we will not suffer this injury unavenged. We pray God give you grace to do your duties and rather deliver to our lieutenant 100 persons than by your obstinacy endanger yourselves, your wives, children, lands, goods and chattels, besides the indignation of God.[347]

In the aftermath of the Lincolnshire rebellion the people of Louth and Horncastle were ordered to travel to Lincoln and the ringleaders arrested. By November 1536, 140 rebels were imprisoned in Lincoln. While the Duke of Suffolk seemed to accept the arguments put forward by the gentry for their role, the king was not so easily convinced.[348] Forty-six were eventually executed, including members of the gentry like Thomas Moigne as well as Thomas Kendall, the vicar of Louth.[349]

That the executions were delayed until the following year was no surprise. The Lincolnshire rebellion was over, but a further rebellion, on an even larger scale, had broken out and too severe a punishment might have made peace over in Yorkshire much more difficult.

The Pilgrimage of Grace

As the Lincolnshire uprising was coming to an end, a larger and far more widespread rebellion was beginning. Today it is collectively known as the Pilgrimage of Grace, though to be strictly accurate this name should be applied to only part of the uprising. Eventually, much of the north of England would be in rebellion and tens of thousands of people from towns and villages across the region would arm themselves and prepare to battle royal forces. The demands of the rebels during the Pilgrimage varied from place to place and, once again, the gentry played a key but ambiguous role.

The Pilgrimage of Grace cannot be separated from the Lincolnshire uprising. A contemporary letter from Sir Ralph Sadler to Henry VIII's chief minister, Thomas Cromwell, makes this clear,

> As I have passed in these parts, I have communed in divers towns with some of the honest sort...and asked them upon what ground the people

were thus stirred to rebel...they, as men that would excuse themselves, said that they began in Lincolnshire and if they had not risen there, no one man would have risen in the North.[350]

The roughly rectangular area to the north of Lincolnshire, known as the East Riding, was clearly directly influenced by the Lincolnshire rising. The towns and villages would have heard reports of events, likely seen the burning signal beacons and perhaps heard the backwards ringing of church bells. Hull in particular was a key trading town and travellers and refugees brought news of the rising. Panic spread among the gentry who fled to Hull and the castle at Scarborough. Hoyle notes that the gentry fleeing the rebellion tended to attract the commons, as the act of flight was seen as a "hostile act of opposition".[351] Hence both Scarborough and Hull became focuses for rebellion.

The rising began in the market town of Beverley, north-west of Hull, on Sunday 8 October. As in many other places it started with bells being run. At least one account suggests that Robert Aske sent a letter calling on Beverley to rise, though an alternate report has a group meeting and hearing an account of the Lincolnshire rising and deciding to emulate those events. Either way, a call was put out for an assembly and a letter written in support of Lincolnshire. They then agreed to meet again the next day. On Monday the commons approached the local gentry to ask them to lead their rising. Several gentry refused, but within a few days William Stapleton was chosen as a captain. Afterwards Stapleton declared his surprise at being chosen; he was not from Beverley, rather visiting a sick relative in the town. The reason lies in the fact that Beverley had a history of factional internal disagreement and it is likely the commons felt unable to choose one of their own gentry who would command respect from the whole town.[352] As one contemporary account has it:

> William seeing the wild disposition of the said people, the great fear that the honest men were in by reason of the aforesaid dissension amongst themselves and thereby likelihood of great murder, upon all which prem- ises moved to him of the behalf of the said honest men, was much steered thereby to take the governance and rule of the said people and they all continually crying 'Master William Stapleton shall be our captain'.[353]

Stapleton took on the leadership, insisting that the commons forget old arguments and then argued that they disband for the day.

How Stapleton came to be leader of the rebellion at Beverley is important, not because it was exactly the same elsewhere during the

Pilgrimage of Grace, but because it demonstrates that the gentry were often unwillingly pulled into leadership roles, which they felt they could not refuse. Once in a leading role the gentry tried to defuse the rebellion, though frequently this was not enough to save them from the wrath of the king.

We see this process clearly at Beverley. Stapleton constantly attempted to delay, disperse or hold back the rebellion while simultaneously looking like he was giving leadership. As Hoyle puts it, Stapleton "offered the Beverley commons firm leadership, but denied them any *forward* leadership".[354] Pressure from the commons tried to push the movement forward and gradually Stapleton lost his ability, together with other members of the gentry, to prevent the rising spreading, though he remained in a leadership role. Key to this was the arrival of delegates and letters from Lincolnshire in response to Beverley's solidarity letters. Eventually the rebels from Beverley and elsewhere besieged Hull for a week where some of the local gentry had fled.

In this part of Yorkshire the Pilgrimage of Grace was very much a rising of the commons, rather than being initiated by the gentry. Local and national issues created a situation ripe for rebellion. Take events in the area east of Hull, Holderness, which began under the leadership of John Hallam, a farmer from near Watton. Hallam was later tortured and executed for his role and hostile witnesses said he had forced people to rise. Hallam, however, argued that the rebellion involved most of the local population: "no man could keep his servant at plough but that every man that was able to bear a staff went forward toward Hunsley".[355]

Hallam himself had personal reasons to rebel. He had long been in dispute with the Prior of Watton, Robert Holgate, one of the "up and coming men in the church of England, a friend of Thomas Cromwell's and one of the King's chaplains". Holgate had evicted Hallam from his land after insisting "the tenant pay his tithe in cash rather than in kind".[356]

The dispute between the two men came to a head when Holgate, preaching in the church on Sunday 8 October, failed to mention St Wilfrid's holiday on 12 October. This important local holiday marked a local man who had "secured the English church's Allegiance to the Vatican" at the Synod of Whitby in 664. In ignoring this feast day, Holgate was loyally following recent royal legislation scraping a number of holy days. Angry at its omission Hallam leapt up in church and with the support of the rest of the congregation forced Holgate to announce the feast day.[357] On one of the days following these events, Hallam went to Beverley and heard an account of the Lincolnshire uprising from the delegates who had come from Lincolnshire. He had sworn himself in and received letters which he used to raise his own neighbours in rebellion. Whether or not Hallam was actually "so cruel and fierce a man among his neighbours that no man durst disobey him"[358] or whether this was just a slur to discredit him for his role in the uprising, it is clear that in 1536 there was plenty of material to fuel discontent. Local disputes could come together with wider political questions to encourage rebellion.

Writing in 1904, the historian Edwin Gay noted that the question of enclosure "played an appreciable part" in the Pilgrimage, but "it was not the characteristic inclosure of the period, that of the open fields, which is most prominent, but the much older and long-continued inclosure of commons". Gay continues:

> During the greater part of the Pilgrimage of Grace the spirit of opposition to the inclosures or 'intacks' from the common waste, which was embodied in one of the demands of the rebels at Doncaster, made little noise and was easily held in check by the gentlemen leaders of the insurrection.

But this agrarian radicalism was blunted by the "gentlemen leaders" who ensured that "the council of the rebel leaders at York took order against the 'casting down of inclosures of commons'".[359]

Robert Aske

At this point in the story of the Pilgrimage of Grace we meet one of the key figures of the whole rebellion, Robert Aske.

Aske was from a long-established line of Yorkshire gentry. Unlike the vast majority of the gentry who were involved in the Lincolnshire rebellion and the Pilgrimage of Grace, he appears to have been entirely committed to the events once he was captured. Aske's first encounter with the uprising was on 4 October when he was returning with three nephews to London, where he was employed as a lawyer. Just after crossing the River Humber, he was stopped by a party of Lincolnshire rebels who swore him "unwillingly" to the cause before letting him move on. Finding that everywhere he went was in revolt, Aske was eventually captured by a second group of rebels. His nephews were let go, and Aske seems to have immediately joined attempts to raise nearby towns and villages along the river.[360]

At about the time that Beverley was rising in revolt and Stapleton was trying to hold them back, Aske was in Yorkshire, having been back and forth to Lincolnshire multiple times. Initially wary of starting a rebellion in Yorkshire he wanted to wait till he had heard the king's response to the petition from Lincolnshire. In order to ensure that there was no rising,

Aske left detailed instructions. For instance the people of Howdenshire were told that they should not ring their bells till they had heard the bells of Marshland, but in Marshland Aske told them the reverse. In other words, neither town would ring first! Unfortunately this plan unravelled when Howdenshire saw a beacon burning and sounded the alarm. Marshland followed and once they had risen Aske put himself at the head of the rebellion.[361]

A letter sent out by Aske, and signed by other captains, called on the commons to assemble:

> Masters, all men to be ready tomorrow and this night and in the morning to ring your bells in every town and to assemble yourselves upon Skipwith Moor and there appoint your captains Master Hussey, Master Babthorpe, and Master Gascoigne and other gentlemen and to give warning to all beyond the water to be ready upon pain of death for the commonwealth and make your proclamation every man to be true to the king's issue and the noble blood, to preserve the church of God from spoiling and to be true to the commons and their wealths and ye shall have tomorrow the articles and causes of your assembly and petition to the king and place of our meeting.[362]

Holye argues that the importance of this letter is that it places the Lincolnshire articles as the key reason for Aske's revolt.[363] His conversion to the rebellion was precisely because he had read the articles "at a poor man's house at Whitgift". Having been himself converted to the rebellion by reading the Lincolnshire articles, Aske naturally wanted potential recruits to hear them as well. The problem for Aske was that the Lincolnshire articles had been produced by the gentry there to demobilise and delay. They were not subscribed to them, whereas Aske saw them as a political programme that he could support. The other problem was that at precisely the time that Aske was bringing together the different forces in Yorkshire, the Lincolnshire movement was disbanding. Thus Aske found himself at the head of a new rebellion.[364]

On Monday 16 October 1536, Aske led his rebel army into York. It was en route to the city that Aske told two messengers "they were pilgrims and had a pilgrimage gate to go to". This was the first use of the word "pilgrimage" in association with the rebellion. Aske was keen to portray the rebellion as being specifically about religious questions and the role of those around the king.[365]

York capitulated without a struggle, though the authorities had no choice. Aske's army was perhaps 20,000 strong and the city itself had limited defences, as well as a population that was sympathetic to the rebels. At York Aske must have heard the news of the disbanding of the Lincolnshire rebellion. Rather than leaving him demoralised, he seems to have risen to the challenge. He proceeded to make a number of declarations to emphasise the peaceful nature of the rebellion, banning looting and insisting that goods obtained by the rebels should be paid for. He also had a bill posted on the door of York Minster allowing the restoration of suppressed religious houses.[366]

It was at York that the rebellion received its full name, the "Pilgrimage of Grace", Aske using the title to identify the movement as separate from that in Lincolnshire and to give it coherence "as the arbiters of the true church".[367] During this time Aske also wrote an oath to be sworn by all the rebels, which includes the words

> Ye shall not enter into this our Pilgrimage of Grace for the commonwealth but only for the love that ye do bear unto almighty God, his faith, and to holy church militant... Ye shall not enter into our said Pilgrimage for no particular profit to yourself, nor to do any displeasure to any private person but by the counsel of the commonwealth, nor slay nor murder for no envy, but in your hearts put away all fear and dread, and take afore you the cross of Christ and in your hearts his faith, the restitution of the church, the suppression of these heretics and their opinions by the holy contents of this book.[368]*

From York, Aske proceeded to drive the rebellion on, advancing to Pontefract and capturing the castle there.

Captain Poverty

Eventually the revolt of October 1536 engulfed much of the north of England. But it did not spread from a single centre, rather there were a number of places where it began, sometimes inspired by other risings. The rising that began in Richmondshire, a large area of north Yorkshire, was simultaneous with the other risings of the Pilgrimage of Grace and has many similarities with it. But there are a number of noteworthy differences, particularly in terms of the demands of the rebels. The rebellion here was particularly shaped by existing discontent. The Richmondshire

---

* Note that, as Hoyle discusses, this oath contains an ambiguity in its use of the word commonwealth. The first use distances the Pilgrimage from the wider concerns of the commons, particularly the question of taxation, that are identified in the Lincolnshire articles. The second use of "commonwealth" seems to refer to the collective of the rebels, suggesting that actions should only take place if agreed by the Pilgrimage itself. See the discussion in Hoyle, 2001, p206.

rising quickly spread to nearby villages and towns and then accelerated across England until it had reached Scarborough in the east, Penrith and Carlisle in the north-west, Kendal and down towards Lancaster in the west. Rebellion spread up into County Durham as far as Spennymoor, with the rebels eventually mustering on Pontefract in the south, some travelling via Skipton.[369]

The main preoccupations of the Richmondshire rebellion were, once again, the fear that church goods would be confiscated, the dissolution of abbeys and monasteries and increased or extra taxes. But there are indications that there were wider issues behind the discontent. Contemporary reports refer to leaders of the commons, going by the name of Lord Poverty or Captain Poverty, and in one account of the demands of the rebels there are references to what Hoyle describes as an "agrarian programme", opposing entry fines, high rents and tithes.[370]

As the rebellion spread the rebels captured or chased members of the gentry, many of whom tried to escape. Some headed for Scarborough Castle; others like Sir Francis Bigod from Mulgrave near Whitby tried to get a boat to London, but it was blown back to shore and he had to evade the commons waiting in Hartlepool, before being captured back at his starting point.[371]

As with the rest of the Pilgrimage, local disputes fed into national questions, though often the disputes were very local indeed. Dr John Dakyn fled the revolt in York back to his parish near Richmond. Captured there, he was threatened by a man called Tomlinson, "whom Dakyn had excommunicated in a matrimonial cause". Tomlinson threatened Dakyn and demanded £40. This specific reasons aside, Dakyn was also accused of being an "institutor of the new laws and a putter down of holidays" by the crowd who had captured him.[372]

Others hid until they were captured or forced to come in, often because the commons threatened their families or property.

One example of this was the capture of the Adam Sedbar, the abbot of the extremely wealthy Abbey of Jervaulx. Having initially fled the commons and hidden on the fells with his father and a boy, Sedbar returned to the abbey each evening when the rebels had left. Eventually the commons had had enough and instructed the monks to choose an alternative abbot or face the burning of the abbey. Unable to decide, the monks sent for Sedbar, who was assaulted, abused and made to ride bareback to a meeting of the commons.[373] Sedbar ended up playing a key role in the rest of the Pilgrimage and paid for it with his life. Once again though, the role of the gentry in the rising was ambiguous. Individuals being forced into a leadership position against their will and then trying to use that position to hold back the commons.

Take Marmaduke Neville, a younger brother of Lord Latimer and a servant of the Earl of Westmorland. A delegation of gentry already sworn to the rebellion failed to get the earl to support the rebellion, but told Neville to join them.[374] He tells his own story in a disposition while imprisoned after the revolt.

> First, after the commons came to Spenymore, two miles from Branspathe, Robt. Bowes, William Conyers, of Maske, and Roland Place came and moved my lord of Westmoreland to come to them, but he refused. They also said to me I should lose my goods unless I came. The night before Robt. Bowes' coming, or after, I forget which, my brother Danby came to move my said lord to come forth, and advised me to come, as neither "my lord my brother" nor any other could help me. Then, through Sir William Evre, I got my lord of Westmoreland's licence to depart to save my goods and wife, and came to the commons about 10 o'clock. Upon further motions, my lord came forth the same night and met the commons at Spenymore next morning. Then all the townships were summoned, and, by my lord and the commons, I was appointed to guide certain townships of Richmondshire.[375]

The gentleman who became most associated with the Richmondshire rising was Robert Bowes. He was from a wealthy family with large estates around Barnard Castle. On Sunday 15 October, the castle was surrendered without a fight and on the same day, at a huge meeting of 10,000 in Richmond, Robert Bowes was elected captain of the commons.[376]

Right from the start Bowes made it clear that the commons had to follow his lead. In this he was successful, John Dakyn said that:

> Mr Robert Bowes might have done the most of any man in those parts. He is greatly esteemed for as soon as he come in amongst them, I, being there, perceived that all things he devised to the going forward took effect. Marry, how they would have been ordered if he had persuaded the contrary I cannot tell, but I think Richmondshire men had not gone into the bishopric had not he moved them to, for he did most and spoke most of any man at that time.[377]

This esteem was to prove important in the days ahead, not least for Bowes's ability to restrain the movement. However concerned with agrarian issues the movement may have been previously, after the meeting at Richmond it, according to Hoyle, "may be that Bowes's seizure of the initiative diverted the Captain Poverty movement in Richmondshire away from agrarian warfare".[378] Certainly the rebels did restore religious houses including one at Coverham, the canons here being so pleased that they sang matins in the middle of the night instead of the traditional dawn.[379]

Once the Richmondshire rising was spreading, Lords Aske and Darcy in Yorkshire sought to unite rebel forces. Letters called the rebel forces to Pontefract. One wing of the Richmondshire force went directly; the others took a more roundabout route via Skipton where they laid siege to the castle for several days. The Earl of Cumberland, who defended the castle, won only a pyrrhic victory when Robert Aske summoned the besiegers away to Pontefract; the earl's tenants had looted his other houses.[380]

The Earl of Cumberland had already met rebels, but these were ones from North Craven where a wing of the Richmondshire rebellion had spread. On 12 October the movement that had spread out of Richmondshire into North Craven restored the monks at Sawley Abbey, but further musters of the commons had taken place on 20 October, after bills were posted on doors. A delegation had been sent to Skipton to urge the earl to join their cause, but he had refused. Following this, the delegation rejoined the North Craven rebels who were spreading south-westward. Then the movement seems to have run out of steam, until it had to reconvene to deal with the first threat to the rebels from royal forces.[381]

The Earl of Derby had been instructed by Henry to mobilise against the Lincolnshire rebels, but that changed when Henry heard that the monks of Sawley Abbey had returned to their monastery. The king's orders give the earl freedom to violently repress the rebellion:

> We lately commanded you to make ready your forces and go to the earl of Shrewsbury, our lieutenant to suppress the rebellion in the North; but having since heard of an insurrection attempted about the abbey of Salley [Sawley] in Lancashire, where the abbot and monks have been restored by the traitors, we now desire you immediately to repress it, to apprehend the captains and either have them immediately executed as traitors or sent up to us. We leave it, however, to your discretion to go elsewhere in case of greater emergency. You are to take the said abbot and monks forth with violence and have them hanged without delay in their monks' apparel, and see that no town or village begin to assemble. We shall remember your charges and service.[382]

Derby agreed to attack on the 28 October,[383] but the pre-warned commons occupied his planned base. Just as a major battle seemed likely, Robert Aske wrote to the commons instructing them to disband their forces and Darcy wrote to Derby asking him to respect a truce recently agreed at Doncaster. Derby agreed and also disbanded.

There is no space here to detail the events of the rebellion further to the north-west around Kendal. Events here were linked to the Pilgrimage and clearly the rebels here had some contact with Robert Aske (when 3,000 rebels arrived in Lancaster they described themselves as a "pilgrimage"). Yet these movements were also one stage removed, rising in part out of fear of events elsewhere. When the Dent commons rose they received a letter from nearby Kendal telling them not to "meddle" in their affairs.[384] But eventually, after both groups met for a mass meeting, the combined forces marched on Lancaster.[385]

Nor do we have space to consider in detail the rebellions that took place in Westmoreland and Cumberland. Here the movement spread westwards out of Yorkshire. Events here began in a church in Kirkby Stephen on 15 October when St Luke's Day was left out of the service. The population had heard of the risings to their east and from this grew a movement which spread northwards. Centred on Penrith, where the movement's captains where dubbed "Charity, Faith, Poverty, and Piety", it eventually reached as far as Carlisle. It was significant in size; one mass meeting at Broadfield Oak had 15,000 or 20,000 attendees.[386] Despite the separation from the wider rebellion, the Penrith rebels certainly saw themselves as part of a larger movement. A delegate was sent to Yorkshire from Westmorland and returned with news of the truce at Doncaster. A petition was then also produced and taken to Darcy in November. This highlighted various complaints to do with tithes, entry fines and rents.[387]

The demands that were raised during the rebellion linked national and local issues and were shaped by anger and concern over religious changes, but also sought to deal with wider economic worries. Take this selection of rebel demands:

9. That the lands in Westmoreland, Cumberland, Kendall, Dent, Sedber, Fornes, and the abbey lands in Mashamshire, Kyrkbyshire, Notherdale, may be by tenant right, and the lord to have, at every change two years' rent for "gressom," according to the grant now made by the lords to the commons there. This to be done by Act of Parliament.

10. The statutes of handguns and crossbows to be repealed, except in the King's forests or parks...

13. The statute for inclosures and intacks to be put in execution, and all inclosures and intacks since 4 Hen. VII., to be pulled down 'except mountains, forests, and parks'.[388]*

The revolts that grew from the Richmondshire rising had many different focuses and causes. They also differed in the way they progressed, particularly in the role of the gentry. Hoyle summarises this:

> In its heartland this movement was captured by the gentry and the influence of the common's captains, who may have preached social revolution, was curbed; it was likewise, in the movements in the North Wolds and around Malton. As in the Lincolnshire movement, the gentry outmanoeuvred the common's petty captains by offering a superior leadership. Elsewhere the movements remained immature because they never acquired gentry leaders. The commons laid themselves open to manipulation because of their strong instinct to capture gentry and incorporate them into their leadership.[389]

But Hoyle also notes the importance of what he describes as "the solidarity of the 'commons'". When one area rose, its neighbours tended to follow and if they did not, the rebels in arms demanded their solidarity. This ability to organise and spread the revolt over very large geographical areas represented "a political organisation which existed independently of the gentry". This was why the role of the gentry, in putting themselves at the head of the movements was so important. It enabled an alternate leadership to blunt the more radical demands of the commons and "Captain Poverty" and divert the struggle down a path that was less threatening to the status quo.[390]

The end of the Pilgrimage
As the end of October approached there were tens of thousands of rebels in arms in northern England and almost everywhere, with the exception of a few isolated islands of royal supporters, was under their control. Almost all of the rebels looked towards Robert Aske as their leader, their "Grand Captain". At the other end of the country the king lacked a strategy. Having disbanded his troops and prematurely cancelled the military muster at Ampthill in Bedfordshire when the Lincolnshire rising ended, he lacked a force in the field capable of challenging the rebels. Henry clearly underestimated the threat. In part this was due to the delay in communication as letters had to travel with messengers on horseback.

---

* Gressom was a feudal tax on a tenant taking over a property.

The king received a letter from Darcy sent on 17 October which outlined the scale of the threat—there were 60,000 rebels, 20,000 of them in York. Many members of the gentry had been captured and forced to take leadership roles in the rising and such was the support for the rebellion locally that there was no one left who could be part of a counter force.[391]

Far away in London Henry could not comprehend the problem. The king was not known for his strategic thinking and likely did not understand the depth of the discontent in the north. Indeed, one of the great frustrations that helped fuel the uprising was the north's belief that it was neglected by the court. We can get a sense of the despair of those hiding in Pontefract Castle from a letter sent on 15 October to the Earl of Shrewsbury, who had advised them to stay there:

> And, our good lord, after your advice, here we tarry. And if we should sparpill [disperse] and depart, by our faith where to go to be in surety we know not. And twice I the said Lord Darcy with the assent of the others have written to the king's grace declaring truly the feebleness of this castle and for aid, money, ordnance, artillery, powder, and gunners, for here there be none, and of it none answer nor remedy therein. And without speedy succour or comfort from his grace or from you, herein we plainly reckon us all in extreme danger.[392]

Two days later the Earl of Shrewsbury reported that it was no longer possible to get messages into the castle because of the siege.[393]

Aske travelled to Pontefract Castle on 19 October and met with "Lord Darcy, Edward Lee, Archbishop of York, and forty or so knights and gentlemen" who were sheltering there.[394] Two days later the castle surrendered and those inside joined the Pilgrimage. Aske now wrote to the other rebel hosts urging them to congregate at Pontefract.

Two of the gentry, Lord Darcy and Sir Robert Constable, who had been hiding in the castle now became important leaders of the rebellion. As an example of the contradictory role that these members of the ruling class were playing, it is worth noting that Robert Constable, who was executed for his role in the Pilgrimage of Grace, had been knighted by Henry VII on the battlefield at Blackheath in 1497, having played a key role in putting down the Cornish uprising.[395]

As the pilgrims debated what to do, some of the royal forces led by the Earl of Shrewsbury and the Duke of Norfolk were arriving south of Pontefract. "Contradictory government orders" meant that Norfolk's plan to hold a defensive line to block further rebel advance was not put into place. Recognising his weak position, Norfolk wrote to the rebels asking for four representatives to meet him south of Pontefract at Doncaster to explain their rising.[396]

We shouldn't underestimate the inadequacy of the royal forces at this point. Shrewsbury estimated the rebel army to number 40,000, though he only had 7,000 men and Norfolk had 5,000.[397] So why didn't the rebels simply crush the enemies while they had the time? Hoyle persuasively argues that the reason they didn't lies in the fact that the leadership of the Pilgrimage was now concentrated in the hands of Robert Aske. There was no collective "cohesive leadership", in fact, as Hoyle argues:

> Aske appears to have expected to surrender the leadership of the move-ment into the hands of the nobility at Pontefract, and was disappointed when they declined to accept it. But according to [Archbishop] Lee's account of the first meeting at Pontefract...Aske himself was uncertain of what he sought from the nobility and gentry who had fallen into his hands. 'We desire to have you and my Lord Darcy that you may be mediators to the king's highness for our requests and for your counsel.' As Lee pointed out, the two were incompatible: 'if you would have us mediators to the king's highness for you, then convenient is that we remain as we be and not join with you, for if we join with you, we shall be no meet mediators.'[398]

Aske had the loyalty of the rank and file. Yet he seems to have had no desire to lead them into a battle that might well plunge the country into civil war. Later, in prison, when he had every reason to portray himself as a restraining force on the rebellion, he wrote that if battle had taken place, a victory for the rebels would have meant the gentry were "attained, slain and undone and the country made a waste for the Scots", but a victory for the king's army would have ultimately led to "carnage of the nobility".[399]

So four representatives, Sir Ralph Ellerker, Sir Thomas Hilton, Robert Bowes and Robert Chaloner, were sent to meet the Duke of Norfolk on 27 October. Robert Aske was not part of the negotiations; instead he stayed with the rebel army which was massed nearby as a reminder to those in discussions of the massive force that the Pilgrimage possessed. From his discussions with the four representatives, Norfolk would have known inside out what the rebels were thinking, as well as their strengths; they also would have discussed what to do about Aske himself.[400] Norfolk tried to get the gentry to break with the commons, but they refused. Later, Darcy explained that he refused to do so precisely because "he that promysseth to be true to one, and deseyveth hm, may be called a treator: which shall never be seyd in me for what is a man but is promysse".[401]

Darcy's refusal to break his oath to the Pilgrimage may have been an act of honour, but the presence of 40,000 armed rebels must also have helped sway his principles.

Agreement was made that there should be a truce and that Ellerker and Bowes would take a petition from the Pilgrimage to Henry. Crucially, both the rebel and royal armies were to disband. The petition taken to London on the basis of this agreement was very general and essentially repeated earlier demands of the Pilgrimage, such as the punishment of people like Cromwell, the repeal of unpopular laws and the protection of the church's freedoms. They also asked for a pardon.[402]

The rebel representatives went to London with the Duke of Norfolk and both armies broke up. That the rebels had forced Norfolk to the negotiating table was a sign of their strength. That they were so willing to break up in the face of future concessions from the king is a sign of their enormous weakness—a willingness to believe that Henry would grant them concessions. But it was also a failure of leadership. Despite the reluctance of "wild people" among the rebels to disperse, no forces from within the rebel rank and file arose that were capable of challenging the leadership of Aske and the other gentry.[403]

It was almost a month before Bowes and Ellerker returned to meet with the gentry and the commons. The truce held, though both sides continued with attempts to strengthen their hand. The rebels kept signal beacons ready and watched the roads, and complained about the royal soldiers who did not leave. The royals kept up the pressure on the rebel gentry, trying to widen the gap between them and the commons. But as time passed, and the delegates to London did not return, it became harder and harder to maintain the truce.[404]

Henry's response to the rebels was begun even before Bowes and Ellerker arrived at court. A proclamation of pardon was written which, in a similarly belligerent tone to the one used for the Lincolnshire rebels, began by denying the rumours that had sparked the rebellion. A letter written after Bowes and Ellerker had presented their petition took a similar line, of denial and pardon, followed by a demand that the uprising's ringleaders should be surrendered. However the king repeatedly changed tactics. The message that was eventually taken back to the rebels by Bowes and Ellerker failed to answer any of the Pilgrimage's demands, merely suggesting further negotiations between 300 pilgrims and the Duke of Norfolk.[405]

On Tuesday 21 November, a conference of the Pilgrims' council together with 800 commons met in York and heard further reports from

Ellerker, who assured them he was convinced by the king's goodwill. Though a captured letter from Cromwell was also read which gave a very different picture, promising that the rebels would be destroyed if they did not end their rebellion. After intense discussion it was agreed that there would be nothing wrong with meeting with Norfolk, but before this the rebels agreed to further, mass, meetings at Pontefract and Doncaster. Stung by the king's accusation that the petitions presented by Bowes and Ellerker had been "dark, general and obscure", they planned to clarify exactly what their demands were. It is worth noting that many different people were involved in penning what turned into a "twenty four article manifesto".[406] The result was a confused document which reflects the wide input from different sources.[407] It was, however, agreed by the different groups of pilgrims, indicating the solidity of the cause despite the length of time since the truce had been agreed with Norfolk.

On Wednesday 6 December, a delegation of 20 knights and esquires and 20 commons met with Norfolk in Doncaster. They had been selected from a larger group of lords and 300 delegates who had gone to the city. A much bigger group remained at Pontefract. At this meeting Norfolk informed the delegates that a pardon would be granted, as would a meeting of a future parliament which could discuss the detail of the 24 articles. Aske then rode to Pontefract to announce the agreement. On hearing the decision at a mass meeting at the market cross, the "commons were then very joyous thereof and gave a great shout in the receiving of the same".[408]

Superficially this looked like a victory, but very few of the pilgrims' demands had been granted. Aske had to work hard to get this accepted by the majority of the movement; indeed there is some suggestion that it might have come to a physical fight between those who accepted the agreement and those who saw its limitations. Nonetheless, the pilgrims had won an agreement that their articles would be discussed at a future parliament. Aske and the other rebels formally knelt before Norfolk, the representative of the king, and removed their badges. It must have seemed like victory, though the king did nothing to finalise the agreements. Aske was even invited to London where he spent Christmas as a guest of Henry.[409]

The real victor at Doncaster was Norfolk. His deft manoeuvring meant that the gentry and delegates had accepted an agreement that would disband their forces. Aske had been Norfolk's tool in getting this acceptance. But the king had little interest in coming to any sort of compromise with the rebels. He was waiting for his opportunity to annul the agreements. In the New Year, this arrived out of the blue.

Space precludes a detailed description of what took place in the first months of 1537. On the 16 January a new uprising began in the East Riding, driven by popular discontent with the king's failure to act on the agreements made in December. This rising was led by Sir Francis Bigod and John Hallam, a captain of the commons. Their plan failed and they were captured, but it did provoke further risings in the West Riding, Lancashire, Cumberland and Westmoreland and elsewhere.[410]

This time, however, there was no involvement of the gentry and despite raising relatively large forces, these commons' armies were stopped. An army of 6,000, for instance, laid siege to Carlisle, but was defeated by a strong force which captured between 700 and 800. The Duke of Norfolk came to Carlisle, declared martial law and proclaimed that all those involved in the attack should come forward to submit. Some 6,000 came, many because they feared execution, the punishment of their families or the loss of property. Some 74 were chosen to stand trial and many executed. The executions took place in the victims' own villages as an example to the rest of the population.[411]

Henry now had the excuse he needed. There was systematic suppression of the new uprisings, with rebels being punished by hanging. It is worth noting that Bowes and Ellerker now acted, under the supervision of the Duke of Norfolk, to try the rebels. A total of 144 executions were carried out, though the government was careful to only base their charges on events after the pardons had been granted. Sir Thomas Percy, Lords Darcy and Hussey, Sir Robert Constable and Sir Francis Bigod were executed. Henry's revenge was violent and wide-ranging. He had Margaret Cheyney, the wife of Lord Bulmer, burnt at the stake because her husband was implicated in discussing further rebellion in January 1537. He even executed Lancaster Herald, a royal representative who had been utterly loyal and central to undermining the rebellion, because he reported to the rebels their numerical strength over the king's forces.[412]

Bigod's rebellion provided the opportunity to remove those who Henry saw as traitors from the previous year. That men, such as Darcy, who were essentially loyal to their king, lost their lives reveals the arbitrary nature of justice under Henry VIII. Darcy went to the scaffold proclaiming his innocence. Letters to the king and Cromwell were ignored despite protestations that "I have served above fifty years the king's majesty and his father and should not in my old age enter rebellion with the commons". Henry himself was too inflexible to understand the role played by the gentry in saving his throne. But Henry also used the opportunity to strengthen his own position, giving lands to those who had been loyal and with the execution of Sir Thomas Percy, removed a perceived threat to his throne from the north.[413]

The one remaining figure is Robert Aske. Aske led the rebellion, though he was not the leader of a conspiracy among the gentry that some have suggested. He took his chance to lead the commons to press for reforms, without any desire for fundamental change. He failed to understand that the king had no interest in changes that challenged his personal ambition and political project. Aske paid for this with his life on 12 July 1537 at Clifford's Tower in York when in front of the Duke of Norfolk and members of the Yorkshire gentry, including his elder brother, he was executed and his body left hanging in chains as a warning against rebellion.[414]

Discontent continued across the north, but Henry's violent suppression of the Lincolnshire rebels and pilgrims meant that it rarely evolved into rebellion, though there was a small uprising in 1541 which was crushed with the execution of 15 of those involved. So complete was Henry's revenge that it is notable that the north did not rise with other parts of the country in 1549.[415]

The story of the Pilgrimage of Grace is usually remembered as the story of a Catholic rebellion of the gentry. The reality is different. This was a movement of a mass of ordinary people across the north of England. In different regions there were different causes. But in general discontent arose from the political and economic policies pursued by Henry VIII. These policies challenged the commons' view of the world, as well as impoverishing them and their families. The failure of the revolt lies not with a lack of bravery on the part of ordinary people in 1536; indeed, there were plenty of occasions when the commons wanted more militant action than the gentry were willing to allow. While few people were actually killed during the rebellion, the rebels were prepared to engage in a major military confrontation to win their demands.

In their swearing of oaths, their lighting of beacons and ringing of church bells, Captain Poverty letters, bills stuck on doors and through mass meetings, the rebels used a multitude of methods to mobilise the population. They were incredibly successful, bringing tens of thousands of armed people into the field.

The Achilles heel of the movement was the reliance on the gentry for leadership. The commons failed to develop their own leadership which would have allowed the rank and file to push forward where the gentry hesitated. On occasion this came close, as when, in the Chapter House at Lincoln Cathedral, the commons insisted on checking the reading of the letter from the king and turning on the gentry when they were betrayed. Some of the rebels drew this conclusion themselves, but too late. In prison, Captain Cobbler is supposed to have declared: "What whorsones were we that we had not killed the gentlemen, for I thought always that they would be traytors".[416]

This lack of leadership is understandable among what was essentially a network of loosely connected peasant communities across the north of England. Fantasies that there was an anti-monarchy conspiracy among the gentry arise because some historians find it difficult to imagine the capacity of ordinary people to organise. In 1536 the population of the north of England nearly brought down one of England's most famous kings. This struggle, with all its complexities, should not be forgotten.

4

1549—The "Commotion Time": A year of peasant rebellion

THE YEAR 1549 was one of chaos for the English ruling class. Two large-scale revolts took place. In the south-west, the rebellion in Devon and Cornwall is often known as the Prayer Book Rebellion or Western Rising; that in Norfolk is known by the name of its leader, Robert Kett. There were many smaller rebellions in counties across England and it often took extensive military operations to suppress them. One study suggests that, outside of Devon and Cornwall, 25 counties, "in effect, all lowland England" except for London, was affected.[417]

Hundreds of rebels lost their lives in the aftermath; though the defeat of the rebellions was not inevitable. Lacking a standing army the government had to rely on European mercenaries to quell the discontent. This, combined with tactical mistakes by the rebel leaders, probably saved the regime. Rather than marching on the capital, the rebels often set up camps, which is why the uprisings are sometimes known as the "Camping Time". This localised the protests and helped stop them spreading.*

The scale and co-incidence of some of the risings and the camps has led some historians to suggest that the uprisings must have been planned across the country. Anthony Fletcher and Diarmaid MacCulloch wrote of the protest camps that arose in July 1549 that they showed "unmistakable signs of coordination and planning right across lowland England".[418] It is impossible to prove this for certain, but the rebellions took place in the context of a changing agrarian world, with the rural commons facing a time of uncertainty. Andy Wood has identified a growing tendency during this period by labouring people to see events in the context of social conflict, a struggle between the poor and better-off sections of society. As one account of the rebellion in Yorkshire in 1549 has it, the rebels were motivated by "a blind and a fantasticall prophesie...that there should no king reigne in England, the noblemen and gentlemen to be destroyed".[419]

---

* Excluding the Western Uprising and Kett's Rebellion, at least 18 other camps took place; we know of nine petitions in addition to the six from Devon and Cornwall; Fletcher and MacCullock, 2008, p67.

In 1549 there were uprisings in the Thames Valley, the Home Counties and the Midlands, as well as multiple rebel camps in East Anglia. Some of these protests were short-lived but others were on a larger scale. One at Melton in Suffolk had over 1,000 rebels who required enormous amounts of provisions, one foraging expedition returned with a haul including 320 sheep and 4,000 rabbits.[420]

Like the Pilgrimage of Grace, the 1549 rebellions had complicated, but interlinked causes. A key grievance was the agrarian question. Edward VI, who was only 12 at the beginning of 1549, wrote that the cause of the rebellions were "because certain commissions were sent down to pluck down enclosures".[421] We have already seen that enclosure, in its different forms, particularly the growing importance of sheep at the expense of traditional farming, was causing poverty and discontent. One historian of 1549 describes the decade as one of "acute crisis", a crisis to which the land question was central.[422] But Edward VI was oversimplifying, there were other factors, not least the ongoing Reformation which, particularly in the west, was a key source of discontent.

Since the death of Henry VIII England had been ruled by a council. Henry had specified the makeup of this council, which was to rule during the minority of the new king, Edward VI. But in the immediate aftermath of Henry's death, the Earl of Hertford, Edward Seymour, effectively seized power by ensuring he was made Lord Protector. Henry's council was an idealistic solution to the minority of Edward VI, as it was unlikely to survive a decade until the king was old enough to rule. When the council first met, it upheld Seymour's claim with little opposition, probably because those present knew that anything else would lead to civil war. Seymour himself was in a strong position to become Protector. He was the brother of Henry VIII's third queen, Jane Seymour, who was the mother of Edward VI. As well as being the uncle of the new king, the earl was also head of one of the richest families in England, with extensive estates in Wiltshire, Yorkshire and Somerset. His military service, riches and membership of the Seymour family had made him a central figure in Henry VIII's court and difficult to oppose as the new Lord Protector. To ensure others on the council were supportive, and to help reduce dissent, a number of peerages were conferred. The Earl of Hertford, Edward Seymour, became the Duke of Somerset.

Somerset's administration attempted to introduce agrarian reforms. These did not stem from any particular interest in improving the lot of those who worked the land, rather they were:

Designed mainly to preserve the traditional framework of society, they served equally to protect the 'oppressed' aristocrat. He [the Duke of Somerset] was, none the less, genuinely worried about the effect of depopulation on the stability of the state, but in the long run his real concern was to eliminate grievances before they could interfere with his cherished Scottish project.[423]

Somerset's "Scottish project" was his attempt to militarily unite England and Scotland. In 1547 he had invaded Scotland and afterwards had formed garrisons to try and hold the country in the face of a French army sent to fight the English. This attempt at top-down unity required vast amounts of money and men and was the reason for the presence of foreign mercenaries on English soil in 1549.

Agrarian problems, however, were significant. In the minds of many at the time the two key issues, enclosure and inflation, were closely linked. The logic was that the profits from sheep farming were such that they reduced the amount of land available for farming, which in turn created food shortages and price rises. Somerset seized on this argument as it detracted from an explanation that argued that the cause of inflation lay in his own debasement of the currency to fund military intervention in Scotland.[424]* Somerset's enthusiasm for agrarian reform caused discontent from other landowners and was widely understood as sympathy for rebellion. A letter sent to him from one of his advisers, William Paget, on 7 July 1549, just before the outbreak of Kett's Rebellion, shows how sections of the ruling class were frustrated by Somerset's reforms.

> I told your Grace the trouthe, and was not beleved: well now your Grace seithe yt...the King's subjects owt of all discipline, owt of obedience, caring neither for Protectour nor King, and much lesse for any other meane officer. And what is the cause? Your owne levytie, your softnes, your opinion to be good to the pore... I knowe, I saye, your good meaning and honest nature...yt is pitie that your so muche gentleness shuld be an occasion of so great an evell as ys now chaunced in England by these rebelles.[425]

The MP John Hales tried to introduce a number of reforms, says Julian Cornwall, to "restore tillage, to enforce the keeping of cows in addition to sheep, and prevent dealers in victuals manipulating the markets".[426] Parliament was dominated by landowners and Hales's reforms failed,

---

* Stephen K Land highlights that Somerset's policies were also about protecting a key aspect of the basis for the feudal system. The king's military strength depended on the ability of lords to raise troops from those who farmed their land. Sheep farming drastically reduced the numbers of men available when compared to normal farming and was thus a security threat.

but in mid-1548 the government did issue a proclamation condemning enclosures. Commissions were appointed to examine the state of the countryside, though only the one headed by Hales took place. It found "numerous offences", such as in Cambridge where Hales found, according to Julian Cornwall:

> Two cases of farmhouses which had been severed from their land, and two more which had been allowed to fall down, as well as four almshouses. Six closes had been made out of common land, while in eight cases baulks and pathways had been ploughed or stopped up. A certain Mr Braken was found to be keeping upwards of 600 sheep on the common...crowding out the animals of other tenants.[427]

Robert Crowley, a contemporary writer, publisher and reformer knew exactly what caused the uprisings. Writing in 1550, he said:

> If I should demand of the poor man of the country what thing he thinks to be the cause of Sedition, I know his answer. He would tell me that the great farmers, the graziers, the rich butchers, the men of law, the merchants, the gentlemen, the knights, the lords, and I cannot tell who; men that have no name because they are doers in all things that any gain hangs upon. Men without conscience. Men utterly void of God's fear. Yea, men that live as though there were no God at all! Men that would have all in their own hands; men that would leave nothing for others; men that would be alone on the earth; men that be never satisfied. Cormorants, greedy gulls; yea, men that would eat up men, women, and children, are the causes of Sedition. They take our houses over our heads, they buy our grounds out of our hands, they raise our rents, they levy (yea, unreasonable) fines, they enclose our commons![428]

In April 1549, the government received news of small, localised "disturbances among the peasantry in many parts of the country", these were not particularly unusual, but by May things were getting more serious. On Sunday 5 May, 200 men "mostly weavers, tinkers and other workmen" in Frome, Somerset, had destroyed hedges and fencing. The men said they believed that what they had done was legal, following on from the recent proclamations. Suggesting this was the work of "agitators", rather than reflecting wider discontent, the local bishop encouraged the participants to disband and put their complaints in writing. But those who did so were imprisoned when they handed their petitions in. This sparked "unlawful assemblies" all over Somerset and Wiltshire, more fences and hedges were torn down and troops from Wales, led by Sir William Herbert, who had lost his park and deer to the rebels, had to be used to put down the rising, killing many of the rebels.[429]*

Similar events took place in other areas of the country: Hampshire, Kent, the Midlands, Leicestershire, Rutland and Lincolnshire and Norfolk. These were mostly dispersed without any violence, though in Kent, Sir Thomas Wyatt hanged three "rioters" and deployed cannon to intimidate would-be rebels.[430] But the first of 1549's two great uprisings could not be dispersed so easily. It began on Thursday 6 June, in Bodmin, Cornwall.

The Western Rising or the Prayer Book Rebellion

The date that the Western Rising, or the Prayer Book Rebellion as it is also know, began is significant. It was the anniversary of the execution of Martin Geoffrey, who had led a local rebellion the previous year and of whom we will hear more shortly. More significantly it was three days before the new *Book of Common Prayer* was to be first used in the local church of St Petrock.[431]

Published in January 1549, Thomas Cranmer's new prayer book replaced the existing services, part of the Duke of Somerset's "renewed protestantisation of the church of England".[432] It was illegal for a priest to refuse to use it, for anyone to criticise it, or prevent its use. The Prayer Book itself was a significant step in the ongoing Reformation. While appearing to keep much of the structure of worship in place, it made major changes to how it was practised. Eamon Duffy, a historian of the Reformation, explains how it

> set itself to transform lay experience of the Mass, and in the process eliminated almost everything that had till then been central to lay Eucharistic piety. The parish procession, the elevation at the sacring, the pax, the sharing of holy bread, were all swept away...and the book clearly envisaged that in the foreseeable future, most of those present at the parish Mass would be onlookers, not communicants.[433]**

These changes were not simply about presentation, they went to the heart of church doctrine. Many old feast and saints days disappeared from the religious calendar as well as other regular services. Latin was abolished and services were to be conducted in English which, as Duffy

---

* Sir Herbert's park had been created through the razing of a whole village, Cornwall, 1977, p10.
** Sacring is the repetition of the Latin words which are supposed to bring about the miracle of transubstantiation in the bread and the wine during the mass. Duffy, 1992, is an essential book for understanding traditional religious practice and the impact of the Reformation.

notes, "immediately rendered obsolete the entire musical repertoire of cathedral, chapel and parish church". Perhaps more importantly the use of Latin in prayers and books gave these an "element of mystery [which] gave legitimacy to the sacred character of Latin itself, as higher and holier than the vernacular".[434] In other words, the bedrock of much of religious practice was being undermined.

It is difficult to comprehend the shock of these changes for the English population. Much that had been held sacred was suddenly taken away. Deep-rooted traditions, practices and beliefs were being destroyed and rendered illegal. We have already seen how similar changes, or rumours of changes, had provoked uprisings, so it is no surprise that people in the south-west of England responded to the introduction of the *Book of Common Prayer* with rebellion. A greater surprise is perhaps that the religious changes did not form part of the motivation for uprisings elsewhere in 1549.

Today, the Prayer Book Rebellion is usually seen as an uprising motivated by religion—as we shall see the restoration of traditional forms of worship were central to rebel demands. In 1549, John Hooker, who was in Exeter during the rebels' siege, was clear that this was a religious rebellion, "only concerning religion which then by Act of Parliament was reformed".[435] Some of the Reformation's changes had a disproportionate impact on the Cornish when compared to the rest of England. One of these was language. Few Cornish people understood Latin, but it was the traditional language of religion and replacing it with English, which few Cornish spoke either, was seen both as a blow against tradition and a new imposition from the ruling elite. Elsewhere in England this might have been welcomed as an opportunity for people to understand religion in their own language, but this did not apply in Cornwall.

But to see the Western Rising as solely about religion is to misunderstand the nature of religion itself, as well as the role it played in the 16th century. To understand this, let us look at another aspect of the Reformation, the dissolution of the chantries. It was common for people to make donations or endowments in order for priests to say prayers or mass for the souls of the departed. Under the Act, these endowments now went to the crown. By removing this right it was no longer possible to actively try and reduce time spent in purgatory for a deceased loved one. As the historian A G Dickens explained:

> if a man really believed that the ministration of a chantry priest shortened
> the bitter years of Purgatory for himself and his dearest departed relatives,

then the Dissolution gave him great spiritual offence and became a matter for his passionate concern.[436]

The threat to introduce taxes on christenings and marriages meant that the poorest would face the risk of their children, in the words of historian M L Bush, "being condemned, by virtue of their parents' poverty, to spend eternity in limbo"[437] and in an era when many children died young, the Prayer Book's suggestion that baptism should only take place on Sundays and holy days, meant that, in the belief of most people, their child might never be saved. The Reformation challenged such fundamental beliefs of the common people, but these changes were also closely linked to their everyday lives.

The dissolution of the chantries also confiscated money that had been given to provide for other, more earthly, reasons. Ashburton in Devon, for instance, lost control of its market, money endowed to its school and funds for looking after the sick, providing water and supporting its clergy.[438] The money that had been given to these funds went to the crown, or as historian Andy Wood points out, "a vague class of 'rich oppressors'".[439] The rich got richer at the expense of the poor's religious and material well-being. Because everyone understood society through their religious beliefs, the Reformation was thus understood as an assault on every aspect of their lives.

Simply because the rebels of Cornwall and Devon raised few demands concerning more traditional economic or political grievances does not mean that their rebellion was not inherently a social one. Andy Wood has noted, in the context of 1549, that a key part of the ideology of Tudor rebellions was the belief that "outside forces" threatened the "destruction of the commons". Given the way that Henry VIII and the protectorate that followed after his death had prosecuted the Reformation, this was hardly a surprising conclusion. The wealth of rural towns and villages was literaly being stripped away and given to the rich. The fabric of their society was being torn apart.[440]

Thus the rebellion that began in early summer 1549 in Bodmin did not come from nowhere. It had its origins in ongoing social changes. Indeed, rebellion had already raised its head in previous years, when anger exploded against a corrupt local representative of the government, William Body.

Body was close to Thomas Cromwell and had become rich through being granted some 20 religious offices.[441] In 1548, Body went to Cornwall with a mission to destroy church images. His speeches provoked uproar and in Helston on 6 April Body was confronted by a crowd of people from Helston and surrounding villages. They were led by Martin Geoffrey, the parish priest of St Keverne, the village that had initiated the Cornish Rising of 1497. The crowd, made up of "fishermen, farmers, tinners, agriculturists—some thousand men in all, armed with assorted weapons, swords, staves, sticks, hauberks, bows and arrows"—dragged Body into the street where he was killed.

In the face of such numbers the local authorities could do little. The crowd gathered in the market place and John Resseigh, a yeoman from Helston, spoke saying that:

> they would have all such laws as was made by the late King Henry VIII and none other until the King's Majesty that now is accomplished the age of xxiv years, and that who would defend Body or follow such new fashions as he did, they would punish him likewise.[442]

The ringleaders were hunted down and executed the following month, including Martin Geoffrey, who was taken to London and executed there.[443] The collective punishment was designed to cow the population, but discontent simmered until it exploded almost exactly a year later in Bodmin.

Bodmin

On 6 June 1549, the Mayor of Bodmin, Henry Bray, began the day with a town meeting. While the new Prayer Book had yet to be used in church, its contents were undoubtedly known to him and other key figures in the town. Julian Cornwall suggests that at the meeting Bray and others passed resolutions condemning the new Prayer Book; this would eventually become a central demand of the Rebellion.[444] With the town's leadership agreed, the next step was to muster the local population.

Julian Cornwall argues that because of the relative lack of wealth of the Cornish gentry, ordinary people tended to equip themselves with "harness" as the gentry could not afford to maintain equipment for a large military force. This contrasts with the 1536 rebellions, which often required the gentry to provide weapons and other equipment. This meant that relatively quickly a large crowd of well-armed men gathered at Bodmin.

The gentry in Cornwall were wary of the rising when it came. Many of them went into hiding in the local strongpoint of St Michael's Mount rather than risk getting caught up in events. Humphry Arundell, the commander of St Michael's Mount, was at nearby Helland where his wife was about to give birth. Hearing the news of the rising, he and two other gentlemen went into hiding. Within a few days, Arundell was called from his hiding place by an urgent message from his wife to her bedside. While there, Arundell was overpowered by rebels and taken away. In the aftermath of the revolt, Arundell claimed he did not want to take part in the Rebellion, in fact the rebels allowed him to write to the former High Sheriff, Sir Hugh Trevanion, asking what to do. The response was "to tarry with the rebels and to be in their favour to the intent to 'admittigate' their outrageous doings". Following this, Arundell joined the leadership of the Rebellion. He was a well-off member of the gentry, probably one of the richer Cornish landowners, but was he merely a victim of the rebels? Sir Trevanion denied ever giving Arundell advice and his reputation did not help. He was often involved in lawsuits and "charged several times with forcible entry on the lands of other men" and had a family history of involvement with rebellion against the king. It is unlikely we will ever know Arundell's motivations, but in the aftermath of 1549 few thought his story plausible. He was one of only two gentleman involved in the Rebellion, the other was John Winslade of Tregarick.[445]

Arundell's importance to the rebels was his military experience. Gathering his forces at an old earthwork outside Bodmin, Arundell set about training his new army. A small force was sent to St Michael's Mount, which was captured easily. The rebels carried bundles of hay to protect themselves from archers as they crossed the causeway. The garrison quickly yielded and many prisoners were taken. These, and other gentleman from around Cornwall, were imprisoned, initially at Bodmin and later in Launceston.

Some 6,000 people welcomed the fighters back to Bodmin. Here at their camp, the rebels drew up their demands, which were sent to the king. Other than a demand for relief from the sheep tax, the articles were all related to religion.[446]

Sampford Courtenay[447]

News of events in Bodmin must have spread rapidly, though we do not know whether or not they directly inspired the rising that began in Sampford Courtenay in Devon a few days later. The immediate cause was the use, on Whitsunday, 10 June, of the *Book of Common Prayer*. The following day the villagers forced the priest, William Harper, whom they accosted before he arrived at the church, to defy the government and not use the new services. John Hooker wrote at the time that the priest "yielded to their wills and forwith ravessheth [clothed] himself in his old popish attire and sayeth mass and all such services as in times past accustomed".[448]

News of these events spread rapidly. The Whitsun Festival that began after Whitsunday was an opportunity for celebration and traditionally villages visited each other to sample specially brewed ales, which provided the perfect opportunity for the rebellion to spread.

Hearing news of these events, Sir Hugh Pollard and several local justices rode to the village to calm the people down, but John Hooker tells us that the villages were "so addicted and wholly bent on their follies... that they fully resolved themselves willingly to maintain what naughtily they had begun".[449] According to Hooker, with their retreat the justices unwittingly fuelled the rebellion:

> as a cloud carried with a violent wind and as a thunder clap sounding through the whole county is carried and noised abroad throughout the whole country: and the common people so well allowed and liked thereof that they clapped their hands for joy and agreed in one mind to have the same in every one of their several parishes.[450]

Sampford Courtenay also saw the first victim of the rebellion. William Hellyons was a respected yeoman. He spoke out against the rebels, and was taken to the church house. There, after continuing his criticisms, he was attacked and killed. Hellyons was quickly buried, but William Harper ensured that he was buried lying north to south, indicating he was a heretic.[451] This suggests that the local priest was sympathetic and clergy were to join the rebellion in large numbers. Within a few days of their initial rebellion, hundreds of rebels were gathering at Sampford Courtenay. We do not know exactly when they joined with the Cornish rebels, though eventually they formed a massive army.

Following banners which depicted the Five Wounds of Christ, the same image used on banners and badges during the Pilgrimage of Grace, Arundell led the rebels on a march to London. The image of the five wounds was associated with acts of charity for the poor and was also closely associated with traditional religious beliefs and so became "a popular expression of the people's loyalty to the whole Catholic belief and practice".[452]

Perhaps between 2,000 and 3,000 relatively heavily armed men marched with Arundell. In particular, there were Cornish archers with their powerful longbows and Hooker tells us the rest of the force was heavily armed with "swords, shields, clubs, cannons, halberds, lances and other arms, offensive and defensive".[453]

Arundell's army marched eastward, capturing strong points and the city of Plymouth, though not its castle. On the way to Plymouth, the castle of Richard Grenville was besieged. Grenville had been one of the local lords who had tried those arrested for the killing of William Body in 1548 and was an important prize. His castle couldn't be breached so the rebels tricked him into leaving it for a parley and captured him. Their successes at Plymouth brought more arms and rebels to Arundell's army, which continued its march to the town of Crediton. Arundell owned a house near here, which he used as his headquarters.[454]

By now, the governing council in London was aware that discontent in the west was reaching dangerous levels. Two camps developed, the majority urging rapid and violent repression. There were 4,000 German mercenaries available and Sir William Paget told the Duke of Somerset to use them and other troops. "Should the rebels come peaceably to justice, let six be hanged of the ripest of them without redemptions, the rest to remain in prison" argued Paget. But Somerset wanted to avoid open repression so Sir Peter Carew and his uncle, Sir Gawen, both owners of land and property in the south-west were sent with a mission of "appeasing of this rebellion; quieting the people and pacifying the country; and to cause every man to return quietly to his home and to refer the causes of their grief and complaints, if they had any, to the King and Council".[455] The wording of this instruction implies that the council still had little idea of the scale of the discontent that they faced, a problem that was to dog the Carews as they faced the rebels in Devon.

After riding day and night, the Carews arrived in Exeter on 21 June. Here they met with local magistrates and, learning that the rebels were nearby at Crediton, Sir Peter decided that they would immediately set out to confront them. But the rebels,

> having secret intelligence of these resolutions, determined not to recede
> in the least from what they had before agreed upon; and therefore with
> all imaginable speed armed themselves; digging trenches in the highways,
> and fortifying a mighty rampart which they had made at the town's end,
> as also the barns next adjoining thereto; in which they put men and muni-
> tion, having pierced the walls that their shot might go through them.[456]

When the "gentlemen" arrived at Crediton, they found their way barred and proposals for a conference were rejected. Hooker blamed the intransigence of the rebels on temporary madness ("the sun being in cancer, and the midsummer moon at full"), but Julian Cornwall suggests that a bigger problem was that the rebels had no one who could confidently negotiate with the gentry.[457] More likely the rebels did not want the enemy in their camp and felt confident enough to keep them outside behind their defences. Hooker tells us that "greatly irritated" the gentlemen tried to force themselves in, but were prevented from doing so and were forced to retire "with the loss of some and the hurt of many". What happened next was to have a profound impact upon events in the south-west.

> In this distress a certain servingman named Fox, belonging to Sir Hugh Pollard, suddenly set one of the barns on fire; this not only obliged those who were therein to quit it, but those upon the rampart also fled. By this means the gentlemen got over the rampart into the town; where they found only a few poor old people, those who opposed their entrance, trusting more to their heels than their arms, having fled.[458]

News of the burning of the barns at Crediton spread rapidly across the region, helping to encourage the belief that the Council intended the destruction of the rebellion and a collective punishment of the local population. While Hooker tends to blame "artful wicked persons" for spreading the story, there is no doubt that the rumours stoked the very fires that had led to the rebellion in the first place. Hooker writes:

> These rumours put the people into a great rage; so they assembled them-selves in great troops in different parts of the country, entrenching and fortifying themselves, as if an enemy was ready to invade and assail them. This was done, among other places, at a village called St Mary Clyst, belonging to Lord Russell, distant about two miles from Exeter, which they began to fortify for their defence and safety.[459]

Clyst St Mary was to become one of the focal points of the rebellion. Its inhabitants were spurred into fortifying their town by an incident, related by Hooker, which gives us an insight into the way that the common people were thinking. An elderly woman walking to church was accosted by a gentleman, Sir Walter Raleigh, who, seeing her counting her prayer beads, began an argument with her about religion and its reform. He tried to persuade her that "it was her duty, as a good Christian and a good subject, to pay all due obedience...telling her at the same time, that there was a punishment appointed for her and all such as should refuse to yield proper submission to the law". Unsurprisingly, the woman was frightened and angered by this and on arriving at church spoke to the congregation telling them that a gentleman had threatened that unless she gave up her beads and stopped using holy bread and water all their houses would be burnt.[460]

As Wood has argued, this was not simply about religion but was understood as "an attack upon the physical and cultural fabric of the parish church itself". The encounter and the aftermath described by Hooker is an example of "an important aspect of the ideology of popular rebellion in Tudor England: the willingness to believe that outside forces intended the 'destruction' of the commons".[461]

Messengers spread out from Clyst, urging local villages to send assistance. Raleigh himself was captured by a party who had gone to nearby Topsham to take guns from ships there. Raleigh would likely have been killed but was rescued by a group of sailors. His relief was brief, a few days later he was captured again and imprisoned for the duration of the rebellion.

Hearing the news from Clyst, Sir Peter Carew decided once again to ride out. So on Sunday 23 June, they arrived at Clyst St Mary and found the bridge blocked. Carew decided that he would be able to talk to the rebels, and dismounting walked towards the barricades. John Hamon, one of the villagers "an alien, and a smith", was about to shoot Carew but at the last moment he was stopped. Carew retreated and eventually the villagers agreed to meet with three gentlemen, Sir Thomas Dennis, Sir Hugh Pollard and Thomas Yarde. John Hooker tells us that they spoke the best part of a day without persuading the rebels to disband. As the long day drew on, those outside began to get restless and considered an attack, several men going so far to test the depth of the river, which caused an outcry among the defenders who saw it as a breach of trust during the negotiations. Having failed to achieve anything through discussion, the gentlemen rode back to Exeter, telling Sir Peter Carew that:

> The Commons has promised to keep themselves in peaceable order for the future, and attempt nothing further, provided the king and his council would not alter the religion of the country but suffer it to remain in the same state King Henry VIII left it, until the king himself came to full age.[462]

This was not the answer expected and despite the delegates telling Carew that they had done their best, recriminations and accusations grew. Carew argued that Dennis, Pollard and Yarde had effectively encouraged the rebels by failing to stand up to them. The meeting broke up and the next day, Carew left to find Lord Russell, who had been sent to take over. The others speedily left Exeter, "every one shifting for himself".[463]

The commons immediately took the opportunity to strengthen their hand: they blocked the roads, digging trenches and cutting down trees. As a result many gentlemen were quickly captured and imprisoned where they "endured very great hardships". Having met Lord Russell, Carew was sent to London to report to the king and his council. The king took the news badly as other rebellions were breaking out and he knew that the forces that had been raised to attack Scotland had to be deployed against the rebellion. Carew was blamed for "exceeding his commission" but gave a resolute defence of his actions, arguing that he was acting within his remit. At least some of the council seemed to agree and Carew was allowed to return to Devon to assist Russell. Carew found Russell at Honiton, 20 miles from Exeter, where Russell waited for weeks for promised arms, money and soldiers.[464]

Russell was woefully under-prepared to take on an insurrection on the scale that was now taking place. He hadn't even been sent with an army, but rather with preachers to argue for the Reformation. As late as the end of June, the Council was suggesting that Russell could calm the rebellion down by explaining that the peoples' fears about the Reformation were unfounded. This was despite the whole of the south-west being in uproar and thousands of rebels barricading their villages and setting up camps. Finally realising that military force would be needed, the Duke of Somerset sent detailed plans to Lord Russell, including the suggestion that agent provocateurs should be used to encourage the rebels to action and that cannon be used against barricaded villages. These detailed instructions, and the associated suggestion to torture selected rebels, still failed to grasp the scale of the insurrection (the rebels were about to lay siege to Exeter) nor the fact that Russell had almost no troops and was unable to raise any from the surrounding countryside.[465]

The siege of Exeter

John Hooker tells us that the rebels had an army of 10,000. Julian Cornwall's detailed analysis of the rebellion suggests that they had "3,000 first line troops with perhaps twice as many light armed men in support"—still a formidable force. Despite the city having a reputation as Catholic and a "hotbed of disaffection", the city council had refused to surrender and on 2 July, the rebels began the siege of Exeter.[466]*

Whether or not to lay siege to Exeter was Arundell's first great tactical test. The city was a strongpoint, dangerous to leave unguarded in the rear if the rebel army continued on to London, but big enough to require a

---

* The camps around Exeter likely had strong support from surrounding villages. In his forensic study of the village of Morebath, about 25 miles north of Exeter, Eamon Duffy shows how the parish paid for five men to go and join the camp. In the repression after the rebellion, the parish priest, Christopher Tychay, tried to erase reference to the camps from his accounts. Note that the inclusion of reference to the camps in the official accounts by the priest is used as evidence by Duffy that the rebellion would not have been seen as such by the participants at the time. See Duffy, 2003, pp135-140.

major force to capture it. The rebels could justifiably believe that there were also many within the city who would join their cause and they certainly would also have wanted the stores of arms and food. But a siege would bring delay, and that would only help the government gather its forces. Arundell decided to try and capture Exeter quickly before moving eastwards. Had Arundell continued his march to London the outcome of the rebellion might well have been different. There was no standing army between them and the capital and he could have got to London with a formidable force, perhaps bringing down the council and leading to the end of Somerset and Edward.[467]

But Exeter did not surrender quickly and Arundell's force never got to London. The city council quickly organised the defences and the distribution of provisions. In particular, aware that there was sympathy in the city for the rebels, they organised to make sure that everyone had enough food to reduce discontent.

Hooker, who was in Exeter at the time, explains how this was organised:

> But a scarcity of victuals being severely felt, the people began to wax weary... However, the magistrates...having special regard to their duty towards the king and a love to the commonwealth, did everything in their power to quiet the people, and keep them steadfast in their obedience to the established laws of the land, as also to resist the enemy to the utmost; at the same time relieving their necessities very liberally (as far as the circumstances of the times would permit), and using many fair speeches, the people readily agreed with them, and with one consent resolved to abide every hardship patiently hoping...they would soon be relieved.[468]

Hooker overstates Exeter's unity; later during the siege there were attempts to let the rebels in and despite the rationing the diet was poor. The main food was bran, mixed with meal, moulded into loaves in cloths as the mixture wouldn't stick together.

Arundell understood well the art of siege warfare and destroyed bridges and blocked roads with trenches and tree trunks. Lead water pipes that fed water to the city were dug up to deprive the rebels of water and to be melted down for ammunition.[469] Eight different rebel camps were set up around Exeter. Siege technology in the 16th century had begun to use huge guns to batter down walls, but the rebel army did not have access to these. Instead they set up smaller cannon that could "sweep the streets" from higher ground. The defenders put cannon on the walls and at every gate, and two enormous cannon, 12 feet in length with a 12-inch bore, were hidden behind Exeter's South and West Gates. Last used during the siege of 1497 these were powerful weapons and were used again to devastating effect. One strategy employed by the rebels was to load carts with dry hay and push them against the gates to try and set them alight. On one occasion, Hooker recounts that the gates were secretly opened and the huge cannon, loaded with dried flints and "hail-shot", were fired point blank at the attacking rebels. The carnage must have been appalling and Hooker drily notes that those who survived "had but little stomachs left to come again".[470]

Lacking firepower the rebels had to use other resources and one of their best weapons was the skills of those who supported them. The Cornish tin miners who had joined Arundell's force set to work digging under the West Gate and packing the space with barrels of gunpowder. Unfortunately for the rebels, another tin miner, John Newcombe, was trapped in Exeter, and he recognised the noise of the miners under the ground. Having dug a counter-mine, his own team spotted the explosives ready to be detonated and then ingeniously he got every person who lived in a street that had a slope towards the gate to simultaneously empty tubs of water from their doorways. The water streamed into Newcombe's excavations and thence into the rebels. Helped by "the great Goodness of God", who Hooker tells us simultaneously sent a huge rainstorm, the rebels' attempt to mine the West Gate was "disappointed".[471]

Hooker's account of the siege of Exeter is fascinating for the insight it gives into siege warfare in this era. The rebels tried everything to capture the town. There were regular attacks and attempts to storm the walls with ladders and from the nearby high ground a Breton gunner was able to kill many with carefully placed shots. This same gunner also came up with a plan to burn the city with an incendiary bombardment. The rebel leadership was keen and the plan was on the point of being enacted when Robert Welsh, a vicar who was highly respected among the rebels, rushed up and urged:

> Do what you can by policy, force, or dint of sword to take the city, I will join with you and do my best, but to burn a city, which shall be hurtful to all men and good to no man, I will never consent thereunto, but will stand here with all my power against you.[472]

As a result of the intervention, the city was not burned, but as we shall see this did not save Welsh.

Despite the setbacks for the besiegers, life in Exeter was getting hard. Food was short and sorties were organised to try and catch cattle that came close. The council worked hard to try and clamp down on discontent. Hooker describes how the council tried to play it softly to avoid the outbreak of rebellion:

> In the time of this famine, if any wrong had been done even to the meanest of the common people, upon complaint made they found redress; but if any of them committed disorders or riots, the same was winked at, and the most gentle and courteous words given to them; praying them not to be guilty of the like again, and begging they would patiently hold out somewhat longer.[473]

This gentle approach by the city's rulers was purely because if rebellion had broken out in besieged Exeter, the odds were against the authorities.

> In the city there were two sorts of people; one of which (by far the greatest number) was of the old stamp, ie of the Romish religion. The other party (who was to a man of the reformed religion) endeavoured to conform themselves in all things to the religion and the laws then established by the king and parliament. The first was so bigoted to their own opinions in matters of religion that they could not bear the thoughts of suffering any change...but being wholly of the opinion of the rebels, would therefore have no reformation of religion.[474]

Those sympathetic to the rebels kept up secret communications with the army outside, smuggling letters in and out through messengers or by firing them attached to arrows. The rebels outside tried to fan any flames they could, organising truces to try and encourage the city to join the cause. There were several plans to open the gates and on one occasion a member of the council, John Wolcot, a merchant and "a man of unblemished character", actually left the defences while captaining the watch and visited the rebel camp with two friends, taking the keys with him. After a long discussion with the rebels they appear to have disbelieved his story and sent him packing, perhaps thinking he was leading them into a trap.[475]

Without relief from outside, the fall of Exeter was inevitable given the strength of the army outside. The question was whether the city could hold out long enough for assistance to arrive.

The rebel demands

Unable to march on the capital, the rebels sent a messenger to the king with their demands. These concentrated on political and religious issues. There are various versions, with one demanding "four lords, eight knights, twelve esquires and twenty yeoman" as hostages until the king and parliament had granted their demands.[476]*

The rebel demands began by demanding a return to how things had been before the reforms of Somerset and Cranmer: "We will have all the general councils and holy decrees of our forefathers" and "we will have the laws of our sovereign lord King Henry VIII concerning the six articles to be used against as in his time they were".[477]

As with earlier rebellions, and crucially with the near contemporary rebellion in East Anglia, the rebels did not see themselves as such, but rather as "rallying to communal values, not challenging the monarchy or legitimate government".[478] The articles that the rebel camp produced at Exeter make this clear.

Articles 3 to 10 were explicitly about religious changes. They ranged from demanding "We will have the Mass in Latin as it was before, and celebrated by the priest without any man or woman communicating with him" (4) and "We will have holy bread and holy water made every Sunday, palms and ashes at the times accustomed, images to be set up again in every church" (7) to "We will have every preacher in his sermon, and every priest at the Mass pray...for the souls in purgatory as our forefathers did" (9). They also demanded that the English bible and books of scripture were "called in" and the return of practices such as the hanging of the sacrament over the altar. The language question was central to demand number 8, "we Cornishmen...utterly refuse the new English".

Articles 11 and 12 dealt with the treatment of Catholic prisoners and the pardon of Cardinal Pole, an exiled representative of the pope whom the rebels wanted admitted to the king's council.

Article 13 has been the subject of much discussion both at the time of the rebellion and since. It reads:

> We will that no gentleman shall have any more servants than one to wait upon him, except he may dispend of a hundred marks in land, and for every hundred marks we think it reasonable that he should have a man.

Some of the confusion stems from the fact that normally the gentry were considered to under-employ servants, thus increasing unemployment in the countryside and keeping their wealth to themselves. This seemed to demand the opposite and should be understood as an argument by the rebels to reduce the military strength of the gentry who would customarily

---

* There are several versions of the articles, Hooker, 1765, pp51-52 lists only eight demands for instance. Julian Cornwall notes that the hostage demand (article 16) is found in only one version of the articles and may have been a verbal addition. Cornwall, 1977, p114.

arm their servants when needed. Philip Caraman sees this specifically as intended to reduce the ability of the gentry to use force to enclose land.[479]

Article 14 called for the creation of places where the devout could pray for the king and commonwealth through the repossession of "half part of the abbey lands and chantry lands in every man's possession". This would have saved the key abbeys in the south-west of England.[480]

These demands received multiple responses. In addition to one from the Lord Protector, there were two other challenges, one from Archbishop Cranmer and the other from Nicholas Udall, who had been commissioned to write an "independent" critique by the council.[481] Somerset responded in detail in a conciliatory tone, though his answer ended with a threat:

> We have condescended out of love, to write rather than war against you as rebels, but unless you repent we will extend our princely power and draw the sword against you as against infidels and Turks.[482]

The response took up each rebel demand in turn. For instance, in defence of the new mass, the Lord Protector wrote on behalf of the king:

> For the mass, we assure you no small study and work hath been spent by all the learned clergy, and to avoid all contention thereof, it is brought even to the very use as Christ left it, as the apostles used it, and holy fathers delivered it: indeed somewhat altered from that which the popes of Rome, for their lucre, brought it to.[483]

But much of the reply was a defence of the existing order; the right of the king to rule and the subservience of those who were demanding change.

> And dare any of you, with the name of a subject, stand against an Act of Parliament, a law of the realm? What is our power, if laws should thus be neglected? Or what is your surety if laws be not kept? Assure you most surly, that we of no earthly thing under the heaven make such reputation as we do of this one, to have our laws obeyed, and this cause of god to be thoroughly maintained.

The answer also attempted to undermine the rebel demands by arguing that the changes were being introduced with the full authority of an adult king, not one who had yet to reach majority.

> If you would suspend and hang our doings in doubt until our full age, ye must first know, as a king we have no difference of years, but as a natural man and creature of god we have youth, and by his sufferance shall have age. We are your rightful king, your liege lord, the sovereign Prince of England,

not by our age, but by god's ordinance; not only when we shall be one and twenty years of age, but when we were ten years. We possess our crown not by years, but by blood and descent from our father, King Henry the Eighth.

Clearly the authorities were concerned that any retreat on their religious reforms would undermine their position because they would undermine the king and his council. That the rebels, in the words of Hooker, "persisted in their wicked rebellion" after receiving the king's response meant the uprising had to be stopped or risked threatening much wider upheaval.

Lord Russell's counterattack

Russell received the various responses at Honiton for distribution. He was stuck there awaiting reinforcements and being bombarded from London with instructions to deal with the rebels quickly. London still believed that the rebellion was small perhaps only a few hundred and he was short of money and weaponry. Morale was low and some, including the West Country gentleman who had rallied to his cause, were leaving. At one point Russell too wavered, hearing rumours of the fall of Exeter and further uprisings behind him, he and other Dorset gentry bolted, but were brought back by Carew, who used the opportunity to get himself and his uncle appointed to the council of war.[484]

Without a standing army, mobilising against rebellions like this was a slow process in Tudor times. But unusually, because Somerset was preparing for an offensive against Scotland, there was a large European mercenary force available. However, using these forces posed political problems for Somerset. Firstly, mercenaries had a reputation for barbarity. Using them to put down his own subjects could harm the king's reputation. It would also mean delaying Somerset's planned attack on Scotland and placing this powerful force in the hands of someone who might use them against him.[485]

Eventually, despite misgivings, Somerset agreed to send mercenaries to Lord Russell. On 8 July Russell had demanded 2,000 infantry from the council. But Somerset was stretched, he had to divert Lord Grey to Oxfordshire and Buckinghamshire with 1,500 troops to deal with a rising there. Details about events in Oxfordshire are limited, but it seems that, as in Cornwall and Devon, events were linked to religious questions, though there had been "agrarian disorders" in Buckinghamshire in the summer of 1548. Lord Grey easily suppressed the Oxfordshire rising killing many rebels and executing its leaders.[486]

With rebellion growing elsewhere in England (rebellion had broken out in Norfolk in early July) the need for swift action was clear. In mid to late July Russell finally received the troops he had been demanding. Some of them came from the mercenary troops sent from London—150 Italian arquebusiers under the command of Paolo Batista Spinola, a nobleman from Genoa.* Russell was also able, finally, to raise troops locally: three Exeter merchants, trapped outside the besieged Exeter, provided the cash needed.[487] Getting troops gave Russell confidence and he decided on his first foray towards Exeter with the aim of sizing up the enemy forces. Unfortunately for Russell, the rebels were prepared for him and he quickly found his way barricaded. Fearing ambush, Russell made his way to Ottery St Mary, planning to get closer to Exeter the following day. But once again he was thwarted by roadblocks. In anger and frustration, and in a sign of what was to come, Russell burned down the village and any houses he passed on the way back to Honiton.[488]

Arundell now made a mistake. He decided to try and defeat Russell's forces before further reinforcements arrived. On 28 July, Russell received news that some of the rebel army had advanced from Exeter to within two miles of Honiton, to the village of Feniton. On 29 July, Russell decided to engage the rebel troops. The rebel army had an excellent defensive position at Fenny Bridges, just east of Feniton. Here the River Otter branched and the rebels were able to strongly fortify the bridges, with their main forces waiting in the fields behind the bridges. After repeated attempts to storm the bridges had failed, Russell launched an all-out assault, supported by cannon fire. His troops finally broke through the defences and engaged the rebels beyond. Despite coming under heavy fire from archers, Russell's forces were militarily superior and were able to chase off the rebels after a bloody battle.[489]

Mercenaries fight for pay and loot and as the rebels fled the battlefield, they fell upon the dead and dying, stripping their bodies of any valuables. They were then caught by surprise as a counter-attack by about 200 Cornish tin miners who crept upon them under cover of the meadow's hedges and killed 30 or 40 of Russell's men, who "paid dearly for their wares".[490] Hooker pays his respects to the Cornish rebels in his account of the second fight and its aftermath. The battle

> was very sharp and cruel. For the Cornishmen were very lusty and fresh and full bent to fight out the matter: nevertheless in the end they were overthrown and their captain whose comb was cut, showed a fair pair

---

* An arquebus is an early firearm, a forerunner of the rifle.

of heels and fled away. In these two fights there were reported to be slain about three hundred rebels which were very tall men, lusty and of great courage and who in a good cause might have done better service.[491]

Russell may have lost 100 men in total, the rebels some 300. Russell chased the rebels for three miles, until he was brought to a halt by his fool who warned him that the country behind had risen. The evidence for this was the ringing of bells in nearby churches. The fool was mistaken, but Russell panicked and returned to Honiton.[492]

It must have been frustrating for those besieged in Exeter that Russell didn't press home his advantage. Food shortages were critical and those sympathetic to the rebels were gaining a hearing. A rebellion inside the city was organised, and on Sunday 4 August, when most were at church, a crowd of people gathered to try and seize the town. The only reason they were starving, they argued, was that the leaders of Exeter were too fearful of losing their wealth to the rebels. They chanted:

Come out these heretics and two penny book men! Where be they? By God's wounds and blood! We will not be penned in to serve their turn. We will go out and have in our neighbours; they be honest good and godly men.[493]

But their forces were too small and they lacked confidence. The mayor was able to make them disband and return home and the rebellion evaporated.

In the aftermath of his victory, Russell wrote to Exeter's mayor telling him that relief was on its way, though, according to Hooker, some in the city seemed to take Russell's promises with a pinch of salt, his relief being so long in coming. On 3 August, the day before rebellion nearly broke out in Exeter, Russell left Honiton reinforced with new troops from London. This included further Italian mercenaries and Lord Grey with 250 horsemen. Grey was an experienced soldier and his presence would have given confidence to Russell. Hooker suggests that the force was 1,000 men, but more recent studies suggest it was much larger, over 3,000 including 1,462 foreign mercenaries.[494]

Camping overnight near a windmill, the army had advanced rapidly and was close to capturing the key strategic bridge at Clyst St Mary. Knowing this, the rebel commanders urged their own forces forward and a major battle took place. Hundreds of rebels were killed and, in thanksgiving for their victory, Russell ordered a sermon to be preached by Miles Coverdale, his army chaplain and future Bishop of Exeter. It is not known how the foreign troops responded to this. Many of them were Catholics themselves and some of them had apparently requested that as part of payment for their involvement they should be taken to Rome where they could receive absolution for fighting against fellow Catholics.[495]

In the midst of Coverdale's sermon, further alarms were raised as news of the main rebel army entering Clyst was received. Figures are unclear, but there may well have been several thousand in the rebel army which set about fortifying the town.[496]

The battle at Clyst St Mary was a "very fierce, cruel and bloody fight".[497] According to Hooker, up to 1,000 lost their lives. There was hand-to-hand fighting through the streets, but the battle was not without farce. After breaking into the defences, the royalist troops were confused by the sounding of a trumpet and drum. Assuming that there was a force behind them, they stopped their advance, causing men to crash into each other. In the confusion, panic broke out and the attackers ran headlong out of the village they had just captured, leaving guns, armour and everything else behind them. In reality, all that had happened was that Sir Thomas Pomeroy, one of the rebel leaders, had found himself trapped behind enemy lines with a trumpeter and drummer and ordered them to sound a charge.

The chaos was enough to make the troops retreat two or three miles before regrouping and realising they were not being pursued. While the rebels had quickly helped themselves to the discarded weaponry, this was not enough to turn the tide. The government troops were simply too numerous and heavily armed. Bloody hand-to-hand fighting turned into a massacre as buildings were fired to kill those hiding inside. Many defenders tried to swim the river to escape, drowning as their armour pulled them under.

While the horsemen could ford the river, the bridge at Clyst was the only way to cross for the main body of the army. Barricaded with trees and defended by a lone cannon, Lord Grey offered 400 crowns reward to anyone who could capture the gun. A volunteer "more respecting the gain than forecasting the peril" tried to earn the prize.[498] He was blown to pieces, but the gunner was killed before he could reload and the way was clear for the troops to cross.

If the battle of Clyst had been marked by farce, tragedy now followed. Riding to the top of a nearby hill, Lord Grey thought he could see an army gathering behind them, their armour flashing in the sun. Warning Russell about this new threat to the army's rear, they decided that their weak point was the large number of rebel prisoners they had captured. In the event of an attack, their rationale was that the prisoners would join with the attackers. So Grey and Russell agreed to massacre the prisoners.[499]

The army now camped on Clyst Heath, while Arundell ordered every man from the Exeter siege to reinforce his position, setting up a new defensive position. The next morning they fired their cannon at the royalist army. The king's army split into three forces and encircled Arundell's forces. Hooker tells us the rebels were caught on all sides

> and must either yield or fight. The one they would not, and in the other they prevailed not; tho' indeed they fought most stoutly, nor would give out as long as life and limb lasted; so that few or none were left alive. Great was the slaughter, and cruel was the fight; and such was the valour of these men, that the Lord Grey declared, that he never, in all the wars that he had been, knew the like.[500]

No doubt the rebels knew that surrender would lead to their deaths. While the victorious army marched towards Exeter, camping at Topsham, the rebel besiegers melted away from outside Exeter. Those gentry like Walter Raleigh, who had been imprisoned since the early days of the rebellion, brought news of the ending of the siege to the city's sentries. Hundreds rushed out of the gates and ransacked the rebel camp for food. Russell finally arrived at Exeter the following day, 6 August. The soldiers then set about pillaging the surrounding countryside for food and provisions, which they sold to the inhabitants of Exeter at a "good price". Lord Russell engaged in another form of pillage, distributing land that had belonged to known rebels to those who had helped win his victory. In addition to confiscated land, Russell gave out "prisoners, bodies, goods and lands" but also "commanded gallows to be set up...within the city, as in sundry parts of the county; and caused many of the most forward and busy ringleaders to be executed".[501]

One of these, Hooker tells us, was Robert Welsh, the vicar who had prevented the rebels from burning Exeter to the ground. Hooker could not understand why a man "descended of good and honest parentage" and with "many good things in him" could have become a respected leader of the rebels. Welsh was charged with three "heinous" crimes: "first, that he did not only persuade the people to condemn and reject the reformed religion, and to keep and observe the Romish religion; but did also use the same in his parish church. Secondly that he was a captain, and principle ringleader...thirdly, that he caused one Kingwell, a tinner of Chagford...to be hanged because he had secretly conveyed letters between Lord Russell and his master".

For this Welsh was condemned to death and his sentence carried out in a way that was designed to be as humiliating as it was barbaric. Welsh was hanged from gallows erected on the top of his church's tower, wearing his vestments and hanged with "a holy bucket, a sprinkling brush, a small bell, a pair of beads, and other Romish articles". His body was left there as a warning.[502]

Lord Russell believed the military campaign was over. He began writing letters back to London describing the victory and distributing prizes, including land, to those who had helped lead the king's army against the rebels. Russell himself did well out of the rebellion, being made Earl of Bedford and being rewarded with land worth £300 a year.[503] But that was in the future, for the moment, Russell had to face one last trial. Given that he thought the uprising was at an end, it must have come as a shock to him when on 16 August he received news that a rebel army of about 1,000 had formed under Arundell's leadership at Sampford Courtenay. Russell eventually marched on the rebels with up to 8,000 men. The rebels fortified themselves in the village, but Russell's forces were able to overwhelm them. Heavy fighting in the village was followed by a rout as the rebels fled onto the moors and were pursued by Russell's cavalry. Perhaps 700 rebels lost their lives and there were as many prisoners. The rebel leaders, including Arundell, were captured in Launceston, from where they were taken back to imprisonment in Exeter Castle. As John Sturt has pointed out in his account of the uprising, the trek from Launceston to Exeter would have passed through villages, many of them already with the body of a rebel hanging from a gibbet.[504]

Post-rebellion repression now followed. Russell put Sir Anthony Kingston in charge. No records remain of the scale of the repression, but it was severe. "Parsons were hanged from one end of Cornwall to the other" as were town officials. The accounts that remain indicate that Kingston took personal enjoyment in his role, an enjoyment that bordered on sadistic behaviour. On one occasion Kingston visited Bodmin and met the mayor, Nicholas Boyer. According to Cornwall's account, Boyer "was a moderate who tried to steer the best course open to him in circumstances of great difficulty". When Kingston arrived in Bodmin he sat down to dinner with Boyer, but before it started, he instructed the official to have some gallows erected to punish some rebels. When the meal was over, he took Boyer to view the gallows. Asking Boyer if they were strong enough, and receiving the reply that they were, he told Boyer to climb up and be hanged, "You have been a busy rebel, and therefore, this is appointed for your reward". Kingston's pleasure in punishing rebels even extended to those who had done nothing but serve those who had rebelled. In one village the local miller was wanted for rebellion and he asked his servant to pretend to be him when Kingston came looking for him. When the servant was taken away and protested who he really was, Kingston had him hanged, declaring to those watching that the servant had never done "a better service [to his master] than to hang for him".[505]

Some prisoners were ransomed and others had their property seized and sold. But ten rebel leaders, including Arundell, were taken to London. Five were released and one may have died in prison. The remaining four were imprisoned in the Tower, and, on 27 January 1550, they were taken to Tyburn and punished with a traitor's death. Hanged until almost dead, they were cut down, suffered "their entrails ripped out and burned before their eyes", before being beheaded and quartered.[506]

By this point, Lord Somerset himself was in prison in the Tower. This rapid turnaround in fortunes had everything to do with the crisis that engulfed England in 1549. To understand the scale of this, we must turn to the huge agrarian rebellion that took place almost simultaneously with the Western Rising, at the other end of the country in Norfolk, and its famous leader, Robert Kett.

Kett's Rebellion

On the surface, Kett's Rebellion seems very different to the Western Rising. Many accounts of events in Norfolk in 1549 highlight the lack of a religious aspect to the rebels' demands. In his account, author Stephen K Land writes that: "religious doctrine was not a factor in the eastern rising". Instead, he locates the causes of the uprising in the transition from a manorial system to a "capitalist economy". Similarly, Julian Cornwall writes that the programme of Kett's rebels "has been well summed up as an attempt to cut back the growth of rural capitalism".[507]

Cornwall continues that the Rebellion and the "articles" it produced were "essentially populist...unmistakably conservative... It contains no hint of the egalitarian rumblings that were to be heard here and there. The significance of calls to decimate the gentry and equalise the distribution of wealth is debatable. So far from reflecting considered opinion, they stand on record as intemperate outbursts in pubs or slogan shouted by rioting mobs... The articles accepted the social structure, seeking merely to restore the status quo by reversing the recent deterioration in conditions".[508]

Thousands of people took part in Kett's Rebellion. To dismiss their mass action, which included two military assaults on Norwich and almost two months of mass camps outside the city as "intemperate outbursts", is to misunderstand the dynamic of change taking place in the countryside. These changes may well have been the beginnings of a process that would result, centuries later, in a capitalist economy. But they were experienced by those living and working in England as an assault on their way of life. Reaction to the Reformation was not even a peripheral part of the demands of the rebels in Norfolk. But religious questions were part and parcel of the changing world they inhabited and formed the backdrop to their rebellion.

In their camps on Mousehold Heath the rebels used, without discontent, the new Prayer Book. But they were unlikely to be, as Eamon Duffy has pointed out, "convinced evangelicals". Duffy notes, for instance, that the rebellion began at a two-day festival which celebrated the (illegal) "feast of the translation of St Thomas Becket's relics", an event that would have been viewed with horror by anyone who supported the Reformation. That said, Anthony Fletcher and Diarmaid MacCulloch note the "explicit and whole-hearted adaptation of the language and practice of the emerging evangelical Reformation which Somerset's regime was helping to forward".[509] The rebel demands drawn up on Mousehold Heath contain several references to religion, demands closer to those of the Reformation, and attempts to link Kett himself to more traditional religious practices are limited.[510]

The problem with this analysis is it tries too hard to separate religion from wider social, economic and political questions. As we have seen, in the mid-16th century, the Reformation was commonly seen as part of a plot to destroy or impoverish the commons. So while events in Norfolk lack overt religious demands when compared to the Western Rising, there were certainly actions that reflect anger at the consequences of religious changes. One example of this is the harbour in Great Yarmouth which had been built with money raised from the sale of items confiscated from churches and was destroyed by rebels as a result.[511]

Kett's Rebellion began as a protest movement against local enclosures around the village of Wymondham, about ten miles south-west of Norwich. Initial anger was directed against Sir John Flowerdew, a prominent local landowner. Local hatred against Flowerdew was shaped by a dispute that the villagers had over their beloved local church. The church building had been shared with Wymondham Abbey and there had been disputes between the villagers and the monks over the use of the building and the location of the bells. These complex disputes were important because when the abbey was dissolved, the building became the property of the crown. Most abbeys were demolished, but in this case it would have destroyed the church. The man responsible for over-seeing the demolition was Flowerdew. The parishioners petitioned Henry VIII to retain the parts of the buildings that were structurally important to their church. This was granted in 1540 and probably deprived Flowerdew of personal income, so he continued his demolition, taking the lead and some of the stone. The parishioners' leader was Robert Kett, the largest landowner in Wymondham.[512]

The beginning of July was the time of the annual fair and festival that celebrated the feast of the Translation of St Thomas of Canterbury. This festival brought people together at Wymondham from all around Norfolk and in 1549 there was no doubt much discussion of current affairs. Anger at enclosures broke out the day after the festival, on 8 July 1549, and Flowerdew was one of the first landowners to be targeted. He intervened and urged the small crowd to attack the fences of Robert Kett, giving them a small bribe. This the villagers did, until Robert Kett himself arrived and declared that he would lead them against the landowners. After helping organise the destruction of his own hedges, he led the crowd back to Flowerdew's land and organised the destruction of the enclosures there.[513]

The beginnings of Kett's Rebellion thus lie in a personal dispute between two relatively wealthy landowners, shaped by centuries of disagreement between the villagers and the monks of the local abbey. This was brought to a head by Henry's dissolution of the monasteries, but the throwing down of hedges also brought an economic aspect to the protest, one even more politically charged because of Somerset's stated opposition to enclosures.

On Tuesday 9 July, Kett led the crowd towards Norwich, throwing down fences and hedges on the way and gathering support. But discontent was springing up elsewhere, no doubt fuelled by discussions that had taken place at the two-day festival. In Norwich the local population had opened up the Common Close on the same day as Kett began his march and provoked a panicked response from the town authorities, who sent messengers to the Duke of Somerset and other local gentry. By 10 July, Kett was camped at Bowthorpe, west of Norwich, but this was inadequate and Kett decided to move to Mousehold Heath east of the city.[514]

Kett sent a message to the mayor of Norwich, Thomas Codd, in the hope his band might be allowed to pass through the city. Unsurprisingly, Codd refused and the band began to move around Norwich to the north on 11 July. En route they met a second member of the gentry, Sir Roger

Woodhouse, who tried defusing the growing movement with a three cartloads of food and beer. Woodhouse's gifts were taken, but he was pulled off his horse, stripped naked and thrown in a ditch before being taken prisoner.[515]

On 12 July, the rebels continued to march towards Mousehold Heath, stopping to pull up hedges and fences and in one key incident destroyed the dovecote of a lawyer, John Corbet. Dovecotes were hated because the birds would destroy crops (it should also be noted that this dovecote was huge—up until two years before it had actually served as a chapel).[516] The banning of dovecotes was part of the rebel demands drawn up later.

Kett made his headquarters on Mousehold, then a large open heath. He commandeered Surrey House, putting his prisoners inside. This was a much better site for a rebel camp; the hill provided a stronger defensive position and the area was deforested as the rebels took wood for shelter and fuel. The ringing of church bells and the lighting of beacons summoned further people to the heath, where 16,000 eventually camped.[517]

For the council of Norwich, the camp was a major threat. Their first problem was that they had no armed forces to resist an assault and it was technically illegal for them to raise such a force without royal permission. The second was that there were significant numbers inside the city who had sympathy with Kett. In 1549 Norwich was England's second city with a population of 13,000. But it was in a bad economic state, with high unemployment and a decline in its principle trade, the cloth industry. In 1525 some 35 percent of the population was too poor to pay the minimum tax rate of four pence.[518] These people were Kett's natural constituency, as angry at the gentry as their compatriots outside the city walls.

The town authorities compromised. They decided to wait for a response from London and to retain relations with Kett and the rebel camp. In hindsight it seems strange, but Kett's men appear to have been able to come and go from the city and people from Norwich, including the Mayor and other leading figures, regularly visited the camp. This informal truce seems to have lasted until 21 July when Kett attacked the city.[519]

While there seems to have been little alternative for Norwich's council, in the aftermath of the rebellion they were considered by some to have effectively aided the rebel cause. In John Cheke's pamphlet, *The Hurt of Sedition*, written in the aftermath of rebellion, the contrast between Norwich and the resistance of Exeter was highlighted:

How much and how worthily may Exeter be commended, which being in the midst of siege, did nobly hold out the continual and dangerous assault of the rebels? Etc. Whose example if Norwich had followed, and had not rather given place to traitor Kett, than to keep they duty, and had not sought more safeguard than honesty, and private hope more than common quietness, they had ended the rebellion sooner, and escaped themselves better, and saved the loss of the worthy Lord Sheffield.[520]

This is unfair on Norwich's leaders. The western rebels were openly hostile to Exeter from the start, whereas Kett had tried to maintain cordial relations. Norwich was far from defendable in the same way as Exeter was and anyway once the rebel assault began, Norwich did resist.

Norwich might have seemed like a military city, but its defences, particularly its castle, were in a state of disrepair. Stephen K Land notes that the castle was located more to intimidate the citizens than protect them from external assault and the rebel camp was too distant to hit with its cannon. Norwich's walls were in a better state, but they needed more troops than were available to guard them and crucially the section of the city facing Mousehold Heath had no walls.[521]

Robert Kett did not sit idly in the camp at Mousehold Heath. He created a council with "two deputies from each of the 22 Norfolk hundreds and one of Suffolk" and set out to provision his army. To do this, Kett issued "warrants" in the name of the king.[522] One read:

We, the King's friends and deputies, do grant license to all men to provide and bring into the camp at Mousehold all manner of cattle and provision of victuals, in what place soever they may find the same, so that no violence or injury be done to any honest or poor man, commanding all persons as they tender the King's honour and royal majesty, and the relief of the Commonwealth to be obedient to use the governors and to those whose names ensure.

Robert Kett [and two delegates from each hundred]

These warrants, with their implied threat of violence, may not have brought food to the camp. But bands of rebels certainly did, bringing in, Cornwall says, "3,000 bullocks and 20,000 sheep, to say nothing of pigs fowls, deer, swans and thousands of bushels of corn...in a few days".[523]

The gentry were targeted for food and money and many were captured and brought back to Norwich and Mousehold. Money and supplies were obtained from nearby towns and country homes. Cannon were brought from Lynn and Yarmouth, Paston Hall was made to provide guns and

Norwich supplied the gunpowder which, Land points out, was eventually used to destroy its own walls![524]

Kett carefully tried to mimic the political and legal makeup of the existing state. His officers carried commissions penned in the name of the king (though these had no legal power). A captured lawyer, Thomas Godsalve, was made to write the required documents to give these an air of validity. At this stage of the rebellion, Kett saw himself as being on the side of the king and had no fear of invoking the king's name to justify his actions. Kett tried to make sure that the camp followed the workings of a legal state and to provide discipline and justice he created a "court" at the Oak of Reformation. Here food and supplies were distributed and disputes settled by Kett and his officers. Prisoners were also tried there, and one (hostile) account describes this:

> And the gentlemen they took they brought to the tree of reformation to be seen of the people to demand what they would do with them: where some cried 'Hang him' and some 'Kill him' and some that heard no word cried even as the rest...and indeed they did press their weapons to kill some of the gentlemen brought to them.[525]

Land points out that there is no record of violence against the prisoners, most of whom escaped during the battle that marked the end of the Rebellion. More importantly though, Land sees in the actions of Kett and his army on Mousehold an attempt not to supplant English law and its institutions, but instead to "imitate and preserve them".[526] Anger was directed at injustices and particular individuals, but it was not manifesting as general discontent against the system as it stood. It is notable, for instance, from the demands drawn up on Mousehold and forwarded to the king that Kett hoped that those who had stood with him would be paid for their time.

The Mousehold Articles

The 29 demands that were drawn up by the rebels and signed by Robert Kett, together with Mayor Codd and Alderman Aldrich, give further insights into the motives of the rebels. That Codd and Aldrich were signatories should not in any way lead us to believe they supported the Rebellion. They did have seats on Kett's council, but they were unwilling participants in a situation over which they had no control. The articles themselves are a mixture of specific demands and general grievances.

Andy Wood sees in the articles "a desire to limit the power of the gentry, exclude them from the world of the village, constrain rapid economic change, prevent the over-exploitation of communal resources, and remodel the values of the clergy".[527]*

Some of these demands are specific to the region, for instance the first article demands the protection of existing enclosures of saffron, an important local crop, but said that no more shall be enclosed. Article 19, asks that "poor mariners and fisherman may have the whole profits of their fishings as porpoises, grampuses [orcas], whales or any great fish".[528]

But the majority of the demands form an agrarian programme that challenges the behaviour of the gentry and protects the interests of the ordinary rural population of Norfolk. Some, like articles 5 and 6, are demands to protect rents and prices: "We pray that reedground and meadowground may be at such a price as they were in the first year of King Henry VII" and "We pray that all the marshes that are held of the King's majesty by free rent or of any other, may be again at the price they were in the first year of King Henry VII" and article 14 calls for rents to be reduced to earlier levels.

Other articles would limit the powers of the gentry or curb their money grabbing behaviour. For example, article 25 states: "We pray that no manner of person having a manor of his own shall be no other lord's bailiff but only his own". Article 21 prohibits the conversion of freehold land to copyhold: "it be not lawful to the lords of any manor to purchase lands freely and to let them out again by copy of court roll to their great advantage and to the undoing of your poor subjects". Article 3 demands that lords shall not use the commons and article 10 that no one beneath a knight, or esquire, be alowed to have a dovecote unless they had a traditional right to one.

Others protected the interest of the commons, such as article 17 which argued that "rivers may be free and common to all men for fishing and passage". Article 18 stopped the poorest (whose land was worth £10 or less) from being called in front of officials who had the power to rule on land ownership, thus protecting them from expensive legal cases.

The clergy were not excluded from these demands. Article 4 demanded that "priests…shall purchase no lands neither free nor bond, and the lands that they have in possession may be letten to temporal men". Article 8

---

* Diarmaid MacCulloch argues that the Mousehold Articles show that a compromise on the question of enclosure was made between two interests from two different areas of Norfolk. In the "light-soil" region, where a uniquely East Anglican practice of "foldcourse" was common, enclosure was practised by tenants who were barred from owning sheep. Their right to enclose land for crops was protection against lords who wanted to use the land for sheep. This was a reversal of the normal position and MacCulloch suggests that this is why enclosure (despite being the issue that began the rebellion) was "virtually absent from the articles. See MacCulloch, 1979, pp51-53.

demanded that priests should actually be able to preach and if one could not, then the parishioners or lord could chose another.

Article 15 limited what a priest could do: "no priest [shall be a chaplain] nor no other officer to any man of honour or worship but only to be resident upon their benefices whereby their parishioners may be instructed with the laws of God". Article 20 demanded that a parson or vicar on more than £10 a year should have to teach or ensure that someone else was paid to give the children of the poor a religious education.

Brought together the 29 articles were a powerful set of demands for agrarian reform which protected the status quo and, if enacted, would have erected strong legal barriers to prevent the gentry making further inroads into the rights and wealth of the commons. Two other articles stand out. Number 28 demanded that those who had joined the protest should be compensated for their involvement to the tune of fourpence a day and number 16 which said: "We pray that all bond men may be made free for God made all free with his precious blood shedding".

Legally serfdom still existed, but Land suggests only a few hundred in the whole of Norfolk would be classed as villeins and concludes that this is not a general statement on "human dignity" but an objection to an "archaic survival from feudal law".[529] Nonetheless, it demonstrates that while the demands written at Mousehold were mostly aimed at the interests of the small landowner against the wealthy, they also had the interests of some of the poorest in mind. Andy Wood says that this was a radical vision of "autonomous village communities, bound together by the force of the monarch's law". But the villages would be free of interference from the gentry and the clergy would be subject to some democratic control. Wood points out that the articles would also exclude the gentry "from the village economy: 'no lord or no mannor shall common upon the Comons'".[530] It was a radical response to the social and economic changes taking place.

The king's herald and the first capture of Norwich

After Kett and the rebels had camped at Mousehold Heath, an uneasy truce developed between them and Norwich. There were many who sympathised with the rebels and, unsurprisingly, some of those able to afford to fled the city. One eyewitness described the mood:

> The women resorted twice a day to prayer, and the servants...did the
> same. When Kett's ambassadors were sent to any private house, they were
> fain to bake or brew, or do any work for the Camp, else they were carried

as traitors to the Oak. As for trading there was none in the City, people being forced to hide up their choicest goods, and happy were they that had the faithfullest servants. They that did keep open their shops were robbed and spoiled, and their goods measured by the arm's length, and dispersed among the rebels. Their children they sent away for fear of fire.[531]

But on Sunday 21 July, the situation was transformed with the arrival of a messenger from the king. The York Herald arrived in Norwich, was wined and dined and then, putting on his robes he rode to meet the rebels at Mousehold. There, he told the assembled masses (probably numbering over 10,000) that they were rebels, but that the king was willing to offer pardon to those who submitted.

The herald's words were warmly received and many fell on their knees and called out "God save the King". Yet Kett, in a speech to the rebels, proclaimed: "Kings are wont to pardon wicked persons, not innocent and just men; they for their part had deserved nothing and were guilty of no crime; and therefore despised such speeches as idle and unprofitable to their business".[532]

The herald returned to Norwich with those who had decided to take the pardon while they could. Because he had declared on the king's authority that those on Mousehold Heath were rebels, the city gates were now closed. Armed conflict was now inevitable—cannon were turned to face Mousehold Heath and walls and defences were strengthened overnight. Sporadic firing took place the very evening the herald left Mousehold, but battle began the following day, Monday 22 July.

Following a short exchange of cannon fire, which caused little damage, Kett's rebel army attacked the city gates. The defenders fired arrows but this failed to stop the attack, with one contemporary account suggesting that "naked and unarmed" boys ran around collecting spent arrows for the rebels to re-use. The, rather unlikely, account suggests that these boys were occasionally hit and plucked the arrows from their bodies to give to their comrades.[533]

The rebels entered Norwich by swimming the river. There they captured six cannon and "a great number entered houses, robbed shops and did much violence".[534] The York Herald, together with Mayor Codd, re-read the message from the king, but they were scornfully received. The herald decided that discretion was the better part of valour and rode back to London. Having captured the city, most of the rebels remained on Mousehold Heath, where they imprisoned many of the city's leading figures in Surrey House. Keeping most of his army on Mousehold was for Kett a sensible decision. Norwich was clearly difficult to defend and he needed the freedom of manoeuvre. Mayor Codd was released in a form of "open arrest", though with limited powers to run a city under rebel control.[535]

Northampton's mistake

The response to the capture of Norwich was rapid. The herald's report alerted Somerset to the seriousness of the situation and made it clear that the Norwich camp under Kett was not going to bow down simply with an offer of a pardon. Somerset may well have had hopes that this approach would have had more success, the Melton camp, for instance, was successfully persuaded of the sincerity of the offer of pardon and Sir Anthony Wingfield, the council's man on the scene, was sent 100 marks to help complete this in early August.[536]

However, Somerset was also under pressure to respond with force. As we have seen, on 7 July, Sir Paget had advised against a soft response. His letter advised the Protector to respond in the manner of Henry VIII. Where the "commons are become king" Paget thought, "Force is necessary". He continued by drawing lessons from the German Peasant War of 1525, an event well known to ruling classes across Europe:

> In Germany, when similar trouble began, it might have been appeased with the loss of twenty men, or afterwards of one or two hundred...by allowing the matter to run so far it cost one or two thousand lives.[537]

Sir William Parr, the Marquess of Northampton and the brother of the last of Henry VIII's wives, Catherine Parr, was sent with an army of 1,500 troops including some Italian mercenaries. Northampton was responsible for an area that included Norwich and was a significant figure at court, but had little military experience. This, combined with his relatively small military force, was a key reason for the debacle that followed. Northampton rode to Norwich, together with a number of lords and gentlemen, including leading figures of the Norfolk gentry.

On 31 July, Northampton's army arrived outside Norwich and a herald demanded the surrender of the city. It is notable that the demand covered both the rebels and the city's citizens. The mayor was at this time on Mousehold Heath and his representative in the city, Augustine Steward, and several others took the city's sword of state out to Northampton. They only did this after a reply had come from Codd at Mousehold, presumably with Kett's support, agreeing to the surrender. Northampton's army entered Norwich and shut the gates. Northampton thus trapped himself in exactly the same position as the city authorities had been in just a few days previously. This was an extraordinary decision given that Northampton had explicit instructions from the Duke of Somerset not to enter the city, but instead to lay siege to the camp.[538]

As Northampton and the other gentry feasted in the Guildhall, some of the Italian mercenaries ventured out of the city and an officer was captured. This unfortunate captive was quickly executed. Back in the city, Northampton organised the defence of the city and overnight managed to see off a rebel assault which left up to 300 rebels dead. The next morning, a party from the city went out to offer pardon to the rebels. This was rejected and almost immediately afterwards an attack was launched on Bishopsgate. Once again the rebels broke through and there was heavy fighting in the streets. During this encounter Lord Sheffield, a peer of the realm and Northampton's second in command, was unhorsed. Following knightly custom he took off his helmet so that he could be recognised and captured alive for ransom. This might have worked while battling the French nobility, but when fighting rebels who are up in arms against the gentry, it wasn't successful and he was killed. Fulke, the "butcher and carpenter" who killed Sheffield, was later hanged for this piece of class struggle.[539]

Northampton and his forces fled. Both sides had lost about 100 men, but Kett's forces overwhelmed Northampton's smaller army. As the royal army retreated, the rebels stormed Norwich again, burning houses and looting. Augustine Steward recalled climbing to the top of his house and watching the city burn. On coming downstairs he was apprehended by rebels who threatened to kill him unless he told them where Northampton was. Disappointed to have missed the king's commander, they instead looted Steward's home and left when he gave them all his money. Kett's arrival in Norwich seems to have quietened the looting and Kett put Steward in charge of "watch and ward" of the city again.[540]

The revenge of Warwick
The rout of Northampton's army put Kett firmly back in control. But he must have known that this would only bring down further repression. Luckily for Kett the government had no spare troops available and this gave him a breathing space. His first action was to take control of Norwich and "establish a rough duplicate of the administration he had overthrown".[541] His second was to try and further spread rebellion and bring in reinforcements.

Around this time a camp had been set up at Castle Rising near King's Lynn, an important port. Possibly the rebels were influenced by Kett and planned to capture the town, though they were forced to move their camp to Watton, about half way between King's Lynn and Norwich. Land argues that the timing of this move, arriving just before Northampton's arrival and leaving after he had retreated, suggests coordination with Kett's attack. Similarly, a camp was set up at Hingham, between Watton and Norwich. The rebels here were attacked by a small force under Sir Edmund Knyvett from nearby Buckenham Castle. The rebels held him off, but Kett decided that the castle was too strong for his army to attack. We don't know what happened to the Hingham camp after this, but being so close to Norwich they likely joined the main rebel force.[542]

These relatively small camps at Watton and Hingham may have been part of an overall plan by Kett to harass forces coming towards Norwich from London, or they may have been attempts to raise the rest of Norfolk. But Kett had a bigger problem, which was the fishing town of Yarmouth about 20 miles behind him. Yarmouth was Norfolk's second largest town and Kett needed to control it if he was to have hope of keeping the rebellion alive. Yarmouth had refused to join the rebellion in the early days of the rising. Now, on 5 August, Kett ordered 100 men to march to Yarmouth for the "maintenance of the King's town there against our enemies". Yarmouth once again refused to join the Rebellion and sent urgent messengers to London, which elicited a response from Somerset that he was raising an army to subdue the Rebellion.[543]

A further attack on Yarmouth, using cannon from Lowestoft (clearly more supportive of Kett's Rebellion than their compatriots in Yarmouth) was repelled and under cover of smoke from a burning haystack a counter-attack from Yarmouth captured six cannon and 30 rebels. After destroying property around Yarmouth the rebels then retreated back to Norwich, ending Kett's attempt to spread the Rebellion.[544] Kett and the rebels were now on their own.

On 10 August Somerset announced that he was going to lead an army against the Norfolk rebels. But, and we don't know exactly why, this was quickly changed. Instead, the Earl of Warwick would be in command. Warwick headed north with up to 14,000 troops and mercenaries (though the most likely figure from the conflicting sources is 7,500) who arrived at Norwich on 24 August.[545]

John Dudley, the Earl of Warwick, had been a key figure in the court of Henry VIII. A renowned soldier, admiral and a major landowner, he was probably the second most powerful man in England after the Duke of Somerset. Dudley was made the Earl of Warwick at the same time as Seymour and the others promoted themselves. He was one of the landowners who faced losing out if agrarian reforms were passed and hence was opposed to Somerset's policies. His military leadership against Kett's Rebellion would give him an opportunity to dramatically change the government and its direction.

Arriving at Norfolk, Warwick sent a herald to "order the city to receive his army".[546] Meeting with messengers sent out of the city, the herald offered pardon to all except Robert Kett. It seems that both Warwick and Kett might have wanted to avoid a battle, because Warwick ordered the herald to make the offer again. The herald was taken through Norwich to the Bishopsgate bridge and there he spoke to a crowd from Mousehold. Perhaps the rebels too wanted to avoid battle, because they shouted "God save the King!" Battle may well have been avoided, but the herald got the tone wrong. He declared them rebels, guilty of treason and threatened them with an armed response if they did not surrender. This seemed to cause chaos; anger, confusion and rumour spread. Some declared the herald was an imposter, perhaps still believing that Lord Somerset was on their side. The herald, they declared, was dressed up by their enemies (with clothes made from cloth taken from a church) to look like an official and had been "sent only to deceive them, in offering pardon". Kett arrived now, trying to defuse the situation by taking the herald to another part of the crowd. While the herald repeated his speech, the situation fell apart. A boy insulted the herald (and thus the king's authority) by turning and showing his naked backside, then committing a "filthy act". A soldier from Warwick's army was so angry he killed him and the crowd interpreted this as a hostile act and, shouting "treachery", prepared for fighting.[547*]

The herald returned in the direction of Warwick and Kett went with him. Perhaps Kett still hoped to rescue the situation and it is possible he might have avoided battle if he had been able to meet with Warwick. But seeing him go, a band of rebels followed and declared: "Whither away, whither away, Mr Kett? If you go we will go with you, and with you will live and die." Perhaps these rebels thought Kett was deserting them, perhaps they were simply declaring their loyalty or wanting to keep their eye on him. Whatever the reason, Kett left the herald and rejoined his rebel army.[548]

Warwick's attack on Norwich began quickly with the breaking open of the south-western gate. Fighting spread through the streets, Warwick's

* Readers should be wary of the use of the word "boy". It was frequently used to describe an unmarried man, not necessarily a very young person. See Wood, 2009, pp166-167.

troops being assisted by the opening of other gates by Steward from inside. Fighting continued through the day, but the city was quickly in Warwick's hands and he demonstrated this by hanging 49 prisoners in the market square. The maze of city streets that had confounded Northampton also caused problems for Warwick as some of his cannon took the wrong route and were captured by Kett's men. The rebels counter-attacked and had some success, but after heavy fighting, they retreated from the city, taking with them the cannon that they had captured.[549]*

By the end of the day, Warwick had captured Norwich, though this did not necessarily give him an advantage. As we have seen, Northampton's attempt to hold the city had been his biggest mistake. The next day, Kett's men opened fire on the city gates and broke into the city in several places. Once again fighting was heavy and Warwick came close to burning all the bridges across the river to hold off the rebels. Warwick faced a tough decision: leave the city to regroup, and probably let the rebels destroy it, or stay and face a tough battle which it was not clear he would win. Knowing that reinforcements were due the next day, he told the citizens that he had "valiantly answered by God's grace not to depart the city, but would deliver it or leave his life". He demanded that they join him and "made them swear on their swords and by the cross that they would drive Kett out or die". This spurred the citizens of Norwich to finally take sides and according to a contemporary account: "Then did every man take forth his stuff and other things before hidden in places...to minister to the needs of these men [Warwick's troops]".[550]

Kett was now held back and the following day 1,400 mercenary reinforcements reached Warwick, firing their guns in the air to announce their arrival and intimidate Kett's forces. Because of a prophetic rhyme, Kett's men believed they would win a pitched battle with the king's forces. Like all such prophecies, it was ambiguous in its meaning.

> The country gnoffes,
> Hob, Dick and Hick,
> With clubs and clouted shoon,
> Shall fill the vale
> of Dussindale
> With slaughtered bodies soon.[551]**

---

* Those who want to know more about the fighting can follow the course of the hard-fought battle of Norwich in Stephen K Land's book.
** Gnoffes was slang for peasants and "clouted shoon" refers to the patched shoes, or shoes with nail studs, worn by them.

Prophecy aside, Kett must have known he was in an impossible situation. Mousehold was a strong position, but food was short and some rebels had reportedly had no food for three days. The camp was abandoned and burnt, perhaps to signal that the rebels were not returning. Taking with them their prisoners, ammunition and stocks, they blocked the roads behind and marched to Dussindale to make their stand.[552]

Warwick followed with at least 4,000 men, leaving the bulk of the English troops in Norwich. They had borne the brunt of the fighting so far, but perhaps they were not to be relied on for the job that Warwick had in mind. Meeting Kett's army at Dussindale there was a final attempt at ending the rebellion without battle, but the offer of peace and amnesty was met with an emphatic shout of "no". Warwick exhorted his own troops with a message that clearly meant little quarter was to be given.

> They should valiantly invade the enemy, and cast no doubt but repute and take the company of rebels which they saw, not for men, but for brute beasts imbued with all cruelty. Neither let them suppose that they were come out to fight, but to take punishment and should speedily require it at the hands of those most ungracious robbers; that they should lay even with the ground, afflict, punish, and utterly root out the bane of their country, the overthrow of Christian religion and duty. Finally [the rebels were] most cruel beasts, and striving against the King's Majesty with an irrecoverable madness.[553]*

The result was a massacre. Despite attempts to use their prisoners as human shields and an opening shot by the rebels' master gunner which took out Warwick's standard bearer, a volley from the mercenaries and a cavalry charge broke the rebels. The prisoners escaped without injury, but perhaps 3,500 of the rebels were killed. A last stand "that they had rather die manfully in fight, than flying to be slain like sheep" was organised, but Warwick once again offered pardon. Not believing the offer (and given the treatment by the forces ranged against them), the rebels demanded Warwick make it in person. He came forward and the herald read the offer of amnesty, to which the rebels cried out "God Save King Edward" and put down their weapons. One rebel who was not covered by the amnesty was Robert Kett, who fled during the battle. He was found hiding in a barn in Swanninghton and taken to Warwick "hysterical with fear".[554]

---

* Note the attempt to portray the rebels as anti-Christian, perhaps trying to link them with the uprisings against the Prayer Book and the Reformation.

We no longer know the location of Dussindale, but it marked the end of Kett's Rebellion. Perhaps future research will find the site and a suitable marker erected to the rebels who gave their lives fighting for the right to use land and organise their villages as they wanted.

Norfolk's ruling class was enormously grateful. They supplied beer to the returning troops and eventually 27 August was declared a local holiday to mark Norwich's relief from rebellion, a holiday observed until 1667. Warwick remained in Norwich for a fortnight. Despite the granting of amnesty, there was punishment to be meted out. Those who had surrendered when offered pardons were spared. Those captured in battle or at other times were considered guilty.

Nine of the rebels were partly hanged, disembowelled alive and then beheaded. Symbolically the executions were done at Kett's Oak of Reformation. The nine heads were fixed in high places around the city to intimidate future rebels. Total estimates of executions range from 30 to 300. Warwick seems to have tried to stop a general collective punishment of the commons of Norfolk by the gentry. While some accounts suggest that Warwick acted with magnanimity towards the rebels, he may have also been motivated by economic reality.[555]

> He [Warwick] knew their [rebel] wickedness to be such as deserved to be grievously punished, and with the severest judgement that might be. But how far would they [the gentry] go? Would they ever show themselves discontented and never pleased? Would they leave no place for humble petition? None for pardon and mercy? Would they be ploughmen themselves and harrow their own land?[556]

The uprising was over. But its echoes would last for some time. On 21 September, Robert Burnham was accused of declaring: "There are too many gentlemen in England by five hundred". When Burnham was imprisoned, William Mutton was put in the pillory with his ears nailed to it, for criticising the mayor. Another labourer, Edmund Johnson, was also tried for saying that if Robert Kett was executed, another thousand lives would be lost.[557] These, however, were the fantasies of a defeated class. Kett, and his brother, were taken to London for trial and punishment.

Both Robert and his brother William Kett were imprisoned in the Tower of London, the traditional destination for traitors awaiting trial and execution. On 14 October, however, they were joined in the prison by the Lord Protector, the Duke of Somerset. Somerset's policies of agrarian reform and his less than emphatic response to the Norfolk rebellion had angered others on the royal council. While the rebellions were in progress the ruling elite showed a united front. But once the rebels had been defeated the cracks in their policies reappeared. Mutterings against Somerset grew. He was alleged to have lined his own pockets, spending lots of cash on lavish building projects including Somerset House in London and a new family residence named Wolf Hall after the Seymour's historic home. Somerset's brother, Thomas Seymour, was also executed for treason for an alleged plot to capture the king.[558]

But Somerset's agrarian policy was the key problem. It had always set a large section of the landowners against him and the rebellions of 1549 proved to them that Somerset's policies were dangerous. Returning to London from Norwich with much of his army intact, the Earl of Warwick was now in a powerful position, as was Lord Russell in the west, who still commanded the forces used against the rising there.

Somerset had two cards left. One was the king, whom he had personal responsibility for. The other was the loyalty and support of ordinary people. Calling on the latter would prove his unsuitability for the role of Lord Protector in the eyes of the rest of the ruling class, so Somerset hesitated in making a general appeal for support. In the end he had to. In early October, Somerset retreated to Hampton Court with the king and called on the commons to protect the king's person. Several thousand responded and preparation was made for defence. As more and more members of the gentry sided with Warwick, Russell, who had earlier sided with Somerset, retreated back from London. Somerset was prevailed upon to surrender, the gentry careful not to provoke a general uprising in London and its surroundings. Somerset was imprisoned, but fully pardoned a few months later.[559] The Ketts were not so easily forgiven.

Their trial was held on 26 November 1549 and both men pleaded guilty, offering no defence. The court declared both guilty of raising rebel armies and making traitorous proclamations, to "levy open war against... the King". Together they were charged that

> during all that 20th day of July, and the six weeks then next ensuing, to carry out their traitorous intention aforesaid, together on Mousehold Heath...and in divers other places in the same county of Norfolk, with the aforesaid force of arms, assembled themselves, confederated and conspired together, by war and in warlike manner to destroy the people of our said Lord the King...and very many faithful subjects of our said Lord the King that now is, viz Knights, esquires, and gentlemen of the said county of Norfolk...did they feloniously and traitorously imprison; and in that

prison for a long time feloniously and traitorously detain them, crying and shouting out with these words: Kill the Gentlemen.[560]

The two brothers stood no chance. They were found guilty and sentenced to be hanged, drawn and quartered. They were delivered into the hands of the Sheriff of Norfolk, Sir Edmund Wyndham, and taken to Norwich. William Kett was executed by being hanged from a tower of Wymondham Abbey. His brother, Robert Kett, the acknowledged leader of the mass rebellion, was drawn on a hurdle through the streets of Norwich and hanged from the castle walls.[561]

Kett's Rebellion ended here, as did the great year of rebellion. While dominated by the concerns of the rural poor, those who took part in the Norfolk uprising were from a wider cross-section of the urban and rural population. In Stanley Bindoff's classic study of the uprising he notes that a list of 47 of the "rank and file" of the uprising includes, 17 husbandmen, seven butchers, four tailors, two labourers, two tanners, two fishermen, two millers, two coopers, two shoemakers and an inn-keeper, a mason, a baker, a waterman, a hatter, a mercer and a rat-catcher. While many of these would have been town and city dwellers, some would also have often had their own plots of land. Indeed, the initial uprising by Kett was met enthusiastically by the population of Norwich who protested at the enclosure of common land near the city. Bindoff summarises that "1549 was a rising of the common man, the man in the street as well as the man in the field".[562]

The Midland Rising of 1607

After 1549 there was only one major agrarian rising—the Midland Rising of 1607—though there were uncountable protests and risings against local injustices, enclosures and the like, such as a rising of Buckinghamshire peasants in 1552.[563]

The rising of 1607 involved a significant number of peasants protesting "against the depopulating inclosure of the common fields". It is also notable for the use of the words "diggers" and "levellers" to describe the rebels, names that would later become popularised by radical movements in the English Civil War.[564] Events in 1607 involved thousands of peasants beginning in Northamptonshire at the very start of May and spreading to Warwickshire and Leicestershire. Mass protests took place, involving 3,000 at Hilmorton in Warwickshire and 5,000 at Cotesback in Leicestershire.[565] In a declaration produced during the revolt, *The Diggers of Warwickshire to all other Diggers*, the authors write that they would prefer to "manfully die, then hereafter to be pined to death for want of that which those devouring encroachers do serve their fat hogs and sheep withal".[566]

Edmund Howes, who updated the *Annals of England* originally written by John Stow, described events.

> About the middle of this moneth of May, 1607 a great number of common persons, sodainly assembled themselves in Northamptonshire, and then others of like nature assembled themselves in Warwickshire, and some in Lecestershire, they violently cut and brake downe hedges, filled up ditches, and laid open all such enclosures of Commons, and other grounds as they found enclosed, which of ancient time hadde bin open and imploied to tillage.[567]

The causes of the rising were rooted in the agrarian changes taking place in the Midlands. Steve Hindle writes that: "Many open-field communities…experienced rapid and sometimes complete enclosure in the decade or so before 1607. Among these villages were Cotesbach (Leicestershire); Ladbroke, Hillmorton and Chilvers Coton (Warwickshire); and Haselbech, Rushton and Pytchley (Northamptonshire). Each of these places saw significant crowds of 'levellers' and 'diggers', allegedly as numerous as five thousand, protesting against depopulation in May and Early June 1607".[568]

On 30 May, King James I issued a proclamation instructing the use of arms against the rebels "immediately to suppresse them by whatsoever meanes they may, be it by forces of Armes, if admonitions and other lawfull meanes doe not serve to reduce them to their dueties." At Newton near Kettering in Northamptonshire, where 1,000 men and women had assembled to destroy enclosure hedges and fences, a force led by the local gentry broke up the crowds, killing 40 or 50 peasants.[569] John Reynolds, the local leader of the rising, had a "great leather powch" which he told his followers contained "sufficient matter to defend them against all commers". As with many other rebel peasants of the time, he claimed that he was fighting in the king's name and he "had authoritie from his maiestie to throwe downe enclosures". Sadly Reynolds's talisman did not protect his rebellion and when he was captured it was searched and found to only contain a piece of "greene cheese".[570] Reynolds and other leaders of the risings were hanged.

The rebellion clearly scared James I who followed up his earlier proclamations by promising reform (claiming that the enclosures were made under previous monarchs and were not his responsibility). On 24 July he also granted pardons to those that would admit their involvement. Actual reform was very limited, but a series of commissions were sent to the affected counties to examine evidence about enclosure and the depopulation it was causing. Yet when parliament met it decided not to introduce legislation against enclosure, which, as Andy Wood concludes, was an "important victory for the pro-enclosure lobby".[571]

As soon as the 1549 rebellions ended they became the subject of debate. For those who took part and survived there were often fond memories of a time of rebellion, such as John Oldman who recollected: "It was a mery world when we were yonder eating of mutton", though others did not have such fond memories. Just as earlier protests had inspired the rebels in 1549, the year became a touchstone for those who still dreamed of social justice in the countryside. The ruling class, however, worked hard to ensure that the events were remembered differently. Alexander Neville's 1575 account of events in Norfolk was a warning against the folly of rebellion.[572] The translation of this into English from Latin by Richard Woods helped cement Kett's Rebellion as the key event of 1549 in the historical narrative. This emphasis on Norfolk was immensely important to the ruling class as an alternative narrative, one that downplayed the countrywide rebellion and emphasised the uniqueness of events in Norfolk.[573]

Following Karl Marx, Andy Wood argues that the "economic basis" of the struggles of 1549 lies in the "emergence of capitalist relations of production in the countryside" and that it was a "dispute between lord and tenant over relations of production and modes of exploitation".[574] The rural discontent in England existed because of the economic and social changes taking place in the countryside. These changes themselves fundamentally altered social relations within rural communities, which meant that rebellions would not occur again in the same way. As Wood explains:

> as the sixteenth century drew to its close, social changes in agrarian regions increasingly divided rich from poor. The consequence of this was to fracture the social alliance upon which the tradition of late medieval popular rebellion had rested. Wealthier villagers had increasingly little in common with the social complaints of their poorer neighbours; indeed, in some communities, they became the target of popular opprobrium.[575]

The wealthier villagers were beginning to form a new class in the English countryside, one with its own set of interests. Over time this would lead to a challenge to the whole social order and the creation of a new world. We will now examine this process in more detail.

5

From feudalism to capitalism

ANDY WOOD concludes his study of the events of 1549 by arguing that English rural society was fundamentally changing, "the yeomen elite of communities...had long ago distanced themselves from the interests of their poorer neighbours".[576] The end of the 16th century saw a growing gap between the richer and poorer inhabitants of rural communities. This had huge implications for society's ruling class, who had ideologically justified their position on the basis of an unchanging world.[577] These better-off farmers, yeomen, increasingly saw their wealth deriving from the employment of waged labour. The gentry, in turn, found that they too could get richer by leasing land to yeomen, rather than continuing to exploit the peasantry.

To understand who these yeomen were and where they came from we need to look at some of the long-term trends taking place in the economy of the English countryside, what that meant for the people who lived there and how they got their wealth. We have seen how the classic feudal society, with a lord exploiting peasants through a system of obligated labour, began to break down in the aftermath of the Black Death and the Peasants' Revolt. In England, there was no formal ending of serfdom and, as we saw reflected in the demands of the rebels on Mousehold Heath in 1549, there were small pockets where the existence of "bondmen" persisted.

Production under feudalism was for immediate use either by the lord or by the peasants, though the latter would often only receive enough from their work to ensure that they could continue labouring and raising their families. This is why feudal lords were interested in land—it was the source of their wealth and power. Under feudalism, merchants who traded goods did so by trying to "buy cheap and sell dear"; they helped to keep the system going by providing goods that were needed by the lord or peasantry.[578] The exchange that they took part in was, however, peripheral to the peasants' production for use that dominated the feudal economy.

This is not to say that lords were uninterested in developing trade or increasing their wealth in gold and silver. Encouraging merchants to visit the lord's area was a sensible idea as it would improve the income from the land. This is why over 1,000 charters were issued in the 13th century for markets, mostly to lords who wanted to encourage merchants to come to their towns. If a town or village became prosperous from its market, the lord had additional opportunities for income. He might build homes and warehouses to rent to merchants, but it is important to note that the rent from towns was "no more than a useful supplement to their main income from rural manors".[579]

But gradually this began to change. Instead of production for immediate use, what was becoming important was production for exchange—to trade for money. This was in part stimulated by the population changes in England following the Black Death in the latter half of the 14th century. In the immediate aftermath of the plague, wages (relative to food prices) declined because the price of corn remained high due to bad weather. But in the longer term, in the 1370s and 1380s, wages reached a new high point: the decreased population reduced demand for food, which lowered prices, lowered rents and caused a labour shortage (in part because there was land enough for former labourers to become small-holders).[580]

In the last two decades of the 14th century, the low price of grain meant that it was far more profitable for lords to rent their lands. As a result, the lords "did not suffer a catastrophic fall in income" and demand for land by the mass of the population also rose. The majority could now afford better food and drink, better clothing and more and higher quality goods. While some "industry", such as wool exports, did suffer a fall, by the year 1400 things had much improved.[581] Christopher Dyer summarises what happened after the defeat of the Peasants' Revolt:

> Lords gave up their role as direct producers, and the peasants cautiously accumulated larger holdings. As the masses, including those depending mainly on wages, spent their new wealth, the urban and commercial economy regained some of the lost ground and grew once more. The low population also failed to produce predicted effects because there were many other forces for change, such as innovations in the organisation of production.[582]

Agriculture too was beginning to see changes that slowly began to improve productivity. Throughout the 15th century there were improvements, with new crop rotations, fodder crops and an increased use of manure as the number of animals grew. In particular this led, in some parts of the country, to a turn towards pastoral farming.[583]

The gradual recovery of the population led to an expansion of the area under cultivation. Lack of land, or the impossibility of further dividing tenancies, meant that there tended to be labour migration out of the villages towards the towns. This helped stimulate agriculture as fewer people grew their own food. These slow and gradual changes began to shift the economy towards a new way of organising. At first this took place in rural areas, as Karl Marx explains:

> The original historic forms in which capital appears at first sporadically or *locally, alongside* the old modes of production, while exploding them little by little everywhere, is on one side *manufacture* proper (not yet the factory); this springs up where mass quantities are produced for export, for the external market... Manufacture seizes hold initially not of the so-called *urban trades*, but of the *rural secondary occupations*, spinning and weaving, the two which least requires guild-level skills, technical training.[584]

Marx was arguing that it was rural manufacturing that was easiest to turn towards the "characteristic" of "manufactures" because they required much less in the way of the development of production than those in urban areas.

Not all towns thrived, but nor did they all suffer in this period. Some, like Hull, declined as a result of a nationwide decrease in wool exports. Other towns as geographically varied as York, Leicester, Lincoln, Yarmouth and Nottingham declined or stagnated as well. Still others, however, became newly wealthy, or renewed their prosperity. Gloucester, Coventry, Salisbury, Norwich and Bristol all prospered in this period. Bristol's cloth industry in the town and the surrounding countryside enabled it to strengthen its trade with Europe and even expanded exports as far as Iceland.[585] The decline or success of different towns had everything to do with the growth of production for the market, but while there was a growing demand for goods some towns were not able to relate to this. As Chris Harman commented, "the very spread of the market...meant the fortunes of individual towns were accident prone".[586]

Towns provided a market for the products of the countryside, in turn further stimulating agricultural production. Some of the products of the towns also made their way into rural communities, helping to improve the lives of the newly wealthy peasants and farming methods. As Harman explains when discussing similar changes on the continent, a "contributing factor to the economic advance of Bohemia in the century before the Thirty Years War was the circulation of books detailing the most productive agricultural methods".[587]

Towns formed complex relationships with the rural areas around them. This hinterland, of six or seven miles, reflected the distance that the local population was able to travel to market. Markets in different towns were arranged on different days so that they did not clash, which encouraged traders to move between towns through the week. Traders might visit different villages and towns in turn, buying up stock to sell at the region's largest markets. The larger the town, the more varied the products produced. Some commodities, particularly luxury goods, might be traded great distances. In the medieval era, agricultural products could also travel long distances to market in the towns. In the case of animals, this caused problems as cattle would lose weight the further they walked to market, a problem that could not be solved until the invention of canals and railways. Nevertheless, some Welsh cattle eventually ended up as far away as London. London, being the largest city, pulled in food from a large hinterland with grain coming from as far as 50 miles away.[588]

As late as the 1520s, only 20 percent of the English population lived in towns, a roughly similar figure to that of 1377. London's population was around 60,000 by the 1520s. Its growing suburbs contributed to the city's size and importance, making it the political and economic hub of the country. Most imports came to the capital and were then distributed around the country. London manufacturing was also some of the most important in the country and had a reputation for quality, so frequently manufacturers of luxury or specialist items might buy from London instead of closer alternatives. The huge London market itself was also controlled by the local merchants, usually to the detriment of outsiders and, most importantly, London clothiers controlled exports to the continent.[589]

By the early 16th century, some towns across England were beginning to show the specialisations that would identify them in modern times. These often reflected the local availability of natural resources. For example, Stourbridge was associated with the iron industry and Newcastle was building on its long association with coal, which even in the 14th century saw it sending thousands of tons of fuel to London.[590]

Between 1350 and 1520 the "urban scene changed significantly". There was a drop in the total number of towns and overall fewer people lived in towns, but while there had been changes in trade and industry, the picture in 1520 was roughly the same as it had been in 1350.[591] However, as Christopher Dyer concludes,

> In parts of England the urban system had reached maturity. Wales and particularly Scotland were not so stable... Of course, individual town dwellers went through hard times as their town shrank or their trade failed, and they fell into poverty or moved out, but most townspeople were enjoying a higher standard of living than their predecessors.[592]

Towns grew out of the need for rural lords to find places to sell the produce from their lands. The growing surplus from agriculture stimulated manufacturing in the towns. In turn, this led to a further growth in trade and the strengthening of those who made their wealth from this. But the towns also rested entirely on agricultural production in the surrounding areas, as well as immigration from the countryside.

Because the productivity of urban manufacturing increased much more rapidly than agricultural production, it was possible for those who owned manufacturing workshops in towns to get richer faster than the existing landowners outside the urban areas.[593] This begins to shift the balance of power away from rural landowners. But we should be wary of seeing the growth of manufacturing in towns through the eyes of modern capitalism. This was manufacturing based on small enterprises of individuals or a few craftsmen. One effect of the growth in manufacturing was that it encouraged "commodity production" through the stimulation of the market.

Alongside the growth in manufacturing there was also a growing need for manufacturers and merchants to organise to protect their interests. Successful merchants often protected their wealth by buying land, which helped give them a say among the establishment. This gave the successful merchants a stake in the system which led them, as Chris Harman points out, to play a somewhat conservative role, standing for "moderate reform" in the coming revolutions against feudalism in the 17th and 18th centuries.[594]

A small number of manufacturing enterprises could grow to sizes comparable to later factories. So in the 1500s, John Winchcombe of Newbury was supposed to have employed 200 weavers in one room, plus hundreds of other apprentices, as well as women in "carding" and children. But this was very unusual; other "clothiers employing hundreds of spinners and weavers employed them in their own cottages, sending the wool and taking away their cloth".[595]

The growth of manufacturing and trade did not mean a new economic order had arrived. Feudalism had not yet been replaced by capitalism. The existence of "profit maximising" or trade in a society is not proof of the existence of the capitalist mode of production. For capitalism to arrive much more fundamental changes had to take place.[596]

However, the changes that were taking place—new methods of manufacturing, the adoption of new technologies, the growing use of the promissory note, or the way that "merchant of the Calais staple would receive for their wool letters of payment, by which a continental merchant would give them written authority to receive the money from a third party, often in London"[597]—collectively point towards fundamental changes at the heart of the English economy, which ultimately could lead to a new order. Christopher Dyer points out how "public efforts to control disruptive and idle behaviour, and...discriminatory policies adopted towards the poor" also demonstrate new ways of looking at economics. He notes that there were new emphasises on privacy and an encouragement of thrift, as well as discouragement of idleness.[598]

The countryside had also seen dramatic transformations. As we have seen, some of these changes, such as the enclosure of land, had inspired rural struggles. Others reflected wider changes. So, for instance, from the 14th century onwards more and more barley was grown because of increased demand for beer; crops such as beans, peas and vetch increased as they were used to feed growing numbers of animals. From 1470 to 1520 "most lords increased their revenues" principally because of an increase in the livestock prices, but also a "more assertive, even more predatory style of profit-seeking entered into the mentality of the officials of the great estates of this time... The royal estate...was run more efficiently, with surveyors appointed who had instructions to gain the maximum return from leases".[599]

J L Bolton also notes that the 15th century was one of "quiet prosperity" for the mass of the population. He argues that in order to provide the capital for the farming equipment (and animals) needed to expand agricultural production, the peasants had to find money. One way to do this was to refuse to pay rents. Bolton shows that the Bishop of Worcester lost a twelfth of his income annually in this way. Other tenants would threaten to leave the area if rents were not reduced. Money lending (including, for example, the rental of cattle) was also common. Increasingly, money was becoming central to the agricultural economy. By the 15th century, every village had a group of wage labourers who received most of their income from working for others and still others who would work in other rural industries. Land was increasingly being leased by lords to tenants, helping reduce costs to landowners by putting the onus for maintenance on the tenant. It also meant an end to "direct management" by the lord and his officers of the agricultural work of the village, though they still enforced the law through manorial courts.[600] Enclosure in particular was seen as a way of making more money. The yeoman farmer Henry Best believed his enclosed pasture had increased in value threefold. In the mid-1650s Joseph Lee wrote a pamphlet extolling the virtues of enclosure as increased profits and more efficient farming with higher yields.[601]

The growth of capitalistic production in both rural and urban areas fed each other's development. Some Marxist historians, following Robert Brenner, have argued that the key development was "agrarian capitalism". However, agrarian capitalism developed in a symbiotic relationship with developments in the towns. As Chris Harman explains:

> This period [in the aftermath of the crisis of the 14th century] also saw in certain towns the growth of new industries, organised on capitalist lines in a much more sophisticated way than previously... It also saw the spread of the organised market system (controlled by merchants, big or small) which encouraged better off peasants to employ wage labour to produce much more than they needed for their own immediate consumption, so encouraging some feudal lords to protect their revenues through leasing lands to such peasants rather than feudal dues.[602]

Thus fully fledged capitalism arises not just from "merchant capitalism" or "agrarian capitalism" but out of the interactions between rural and urban areas.*

But the growth of the market and the transformation of the economy to one where money was key brought problems. Harman says that despite "Money being the measure of everything...the official values of society were still those embodied in the hierarchy of the old feudalism". He continues:

> The impact of technical change and new market relations between people within feudalism led to a 'mixed society'—'market feudalism'—in which there was an intertwining but also a clash between capitalist and feudal ways of acting and thinking.[603]

As we have seen, the dominant ideology in medieval times was provided by the church. The tensions inherent in the growth of new social relations brought with them a need to justify and explain the new methods of production and the values associated with them. Here lies the importance of the Reformation. Protestantism reflected the interests of an emerging section of society. The figures associated with the new protestant ideas, men such as Martin Luther or Jean Calvin, did not set out to transform society but were motivated by what they saw as the

---

* This is a very short summary of a complex debate. For Brenner's original paper see Brenner, 1976. A recent reassertion of Robert Brenner's position is in Dimmock, 2014. Counterpoised to this is the Pirenne-Sweezy position which emphasises the importance of merchant capitalism. Chris Harman's essay *From Feudalism to Capitalism*, first published in 1989 and collected in Harman, 1998, (also online at the Marxists Internet Archive), is the most accessible critique of these two positions and my argument here is heavily indebted to it. Harman's *People's History of the World* (1999) has an invaluable summary of the development of capitalism.

corruption or limitations of the old Catholic Church. The failings of the church and the greed and corruption of its central figures led masses of people to flock to the new ideas.[604]

The Reformation led to mass movements and rebellions, enormous military campaigns and much of Europe saw decades of fighting as rival factions of the ruling class fought to extend and entrench their positions. While these struggles were often fought along religious lines, it would be crude to suggest that all protestants were "emerging capitalists" and those who adhered to Catholicism were feudal lords. Instead different people took different things from the radical preachers. As Harman summarises:

> Those who were most radical in their religious reinterpretation of the world tended to be those who wanted it changed most—whether, as with the radical Hussites or the Anabaptists, to an egalitarian classless society, or, as with the more sober minded Calvinists, to a society based upon commodity production and the relentless attempt to accumulate capital.[605]

But the growth of the market also brought with it problems. Production for profit meant sections of the population would lose out. This also led to struggle by the producing classes to defend conditions and fight for an improved share of their labour.

Rural artisans and riots in the Western Rising of 1626-1632

One of the consequences of the changes taking place in the English countryside was a growth in importance of "artisans". In some areas of the country, rural industry such as cloth making and mining were of great importance; these industries were not new, mining, for instance, had taken place for centuries. Other industries were developing too. In 1612, the Earl of Pembroke was granted permission to build four blast furnaces and three forges, known as the King's Ironworks, in the Forest of Dean.[606] There has been much discussion about these artisans. Some historians have argued that those engaged in these industries were predominately engaged in agriculture and cloth making or mining were "by-employments". In his detailed study of the rural communities in the west of England and their riotous response to enclosure and disafforestation,* the historian Buchanan Sharp has concluded that artisans were a distinct, landless grouping in certain areas of England:

---

* Disafforestation is the legal process changing former royal forest into land that could be rented for farming etc. Note that in this period, the word forest did not mean a heavily wooded area as it does today, but an area of open land, including wooded areas.

Whatever the state of artisans in those parts of England where agriculture provided the main source of the livelihood...there can be no doubt that in the industrial areas of Tudor-Stuart England—the broadcloth centres in the South and forested West, the East Anglian new-drapery, and mining and metallurgical locations such as Dean and Kingswood—the skilled as well as unskilled work force was overwhelming propertyless and dependent on wages. Although these artisans obtained important supplements to their wages through grazing a few beasts on an acre or two of pasture...or through communing in forests and other wastes, they had ceased to be peasants.[607]

These cottagers, who, as Sharp points out, were lucky if they owned a few animals and a couple of acres, were highly dependent on the forest commons. Thus when, in the early 17th century the king found himself short of revenue and decided to disafforest some of its crown forests, this provoked what has become known as the Western Rising or the Disafforestation Riots between 1626 and 1632.*

This Western Rising was not a continuous event, but rather a series of mass riots that took place across a region in response to multiple enclosures of forest. They began in Gillingham in Dorset. The land had been granted to Queen Anne in 1603. In 1625 a commission was organised to disafforest Gillingham.[608] What then took place was a process that was repeated in a number of other areas. The commission worked to arrange the disposal of the land. As Sharp has concluded, these enclosures were not arbitrary, simply forced upon an unwilling population. They were actually examples of "enclosure by agreement" and the process that took place exposes the class differences of the English countryside in the areas concerned.

Those who had land, "freeholders and copyholders", were asked to grant their consent to enclosure and the consequent loss of common rights. In return tenants would receive compensation. The commissions would also organise allotments and roads/paths through the forest to ensure access. This process took place in court which, after negotiation, would be made legal.

The Crown was interested not in defining rights of common but in extinguishing them so that the demesne waste of the forest could be

---

* The 1626-1632 Western Rising should not be confused with other events with this, or similar titles. We have already looked at the Prayer Book Rebellion of 1549 which shares this name. The Duke of Monmouth's rising against Charles II, sometimes know as the Wessex Rising or the Revolt in the West, involved artisans from south-west England. Sharp, 2010, p170 notes that support for this latter rising had roots in ongoing social and economic problems that predated the Civil War.

enclosed and improved. In return for their agreement, freeholders and copyholders were offered considerable compensation.[609]

At Gillingham this compensation totalled 400 acres and tenants of Mere also received 100 acres as common land. Further land was granted for access roads and a road through the forest and 250 acres were allocated to the poor of Gillingham Manor. The remainder was sold to Sir James Fullerton, Groom of the Stole, who received "2,408 acres free and clear of all claims of common...along with the herbage and pannage of Gillingham Park" in 1628 for the annual rent of £131.8s. Over the next few years Fullerton renegotiated this and was given a further 753 acres.[610]

Rioting against enclosure started in 1626 and continued for two years. Riots in 1626 resulted in four men being fined in the Star Chamber. In 1628, riots broke out on a larger scale when the enclosure commission had finished and workmen were fencing off sections of the forest. Soldiers from near-by Shaftesbury destroyed enclosures, probably encouraged by local people, which led to three more individuals being fined. Throughout 1628, riots destroyed enclosed lands and fences, deer were killed and "threats were made against the lives and property of Fullerton's labourers in an attempt to force them to stop the work of enclosure. At least two messengers of the Chamber sent to serve process on the rioters, were assaulted (according to one account they were tied to a post and whipped) and their prisoners rescued". In response to this, in late 1628, local sheriffs were sent to arrest over 100 people suspected of riot. The sheriff of Dorset, however, retreated finding his forces outnumbered by "numerous, well-armed, and resolute" local people, who had declared: "Here were we born and here we will die".[611]

Similar events took place elsewhere on a scale that paralysed local government. In Dean, a 30,000-acre forest, the size of the riots terrified the authorities with up to 3,000 people taking part in a series of riots against enclosure intended to allow the development of mining for iron ore. On 25 March 1631, for instance, 500 men "with two drummes, two colulers and one fife in a warlike and outrageous manner assemble themselves together armed with gunnes, pykes, halberds and other weapons" proceeded to destroy enclosures belonging to Tristam Flower, then marched to Mailescott Woods, where they destroyed hedges and ditches and assaulted the workers digging in ore pits (which they filed in). They fired at the house where the agent of the owner, Lady Villiers, lived, burned an effigy and outside of the agent's house "made an Oyes and commanding silence said that if this deponent [the agent] would make the like worke against May

Day next they would be ready to doe him the like service and dared him to come out of his house which he feared to doe". On 5 April, 3,000 rioters marched again with drums and banners and broke the enclosures in much of the rest of the forest and burned houses. By the end of the month all the enclosures in Dean that had been decreed in 1628 had been destroyed.[612]

These riots approached, at least in the eyes of the authorities, insurrectionary scales and terrified the government. The king and his councillors worried that they would spread if not dealt with firmly. Officials in Gloucestershire, for instance, were told to "use all possible diligence to resist and suppresse these exorbitaunt outrages rather in the nature of a Rebellion than a Ryott." One fascinating aspect to this response is that the government became obsessed with the belief that the riots were organised by a countrywide network of agitators. They focused on three men—Henry Hoskins and John Phillips from Gillingham and John Williams—who were local leaders, but the government was convinced they were organising across the country.

This, combined with the belief that the "lower orders" were unable to organise themselves and there must be "persons of quality" behind the riots, caused confusion for the government in their attempts to deal with the rioting. This latter belief was common at the time and is expressed in Francis Bacon's essay *On Sedition*, where he writes:

> If poverty and broken estate in the better sort be joined with a want and necessity in the mean people, the danger is imminent and great: for the rebellions of the belly are the worst." But this required leadership "for common people are of slow motion, if they be not excited by the greater sort".[613]

Some of the confusion for the government in trying to find a leadership conspiracy among the riots stems from an interesting aspect to the Western Rising, the role of "Skimington". Some of the riots at Braydon Forest were led by men wearing women's clothes calling themselves "Lady Skimington". It was alleged that Henry Hoskins had urged "Lady Skimington"—that is, the riot leaders—to come to Gillingham and destroy enclosures there as well. The patterns of the riots sometimes mirrored a traditional, community protest known as Skimington, which was often used to show collective disapproval or punishment of individuals in a locality for behaviour considered unacceptable, such as adultery. The Skimington involved the humiliation of the individual, often a woman "who had gained notoriety as a scold or as one who had cuckolded her husband", through the beating of drums or pots and pans while villagers paraded dressed up in unusual clothes or outfits to mock the victim and the eventual ducking of the victim or the destruction of them in effigy.[614]

The government's obsession with a conspiracy and belief that there was leadership from the "better sorts" in rural society was not grounded in reality. As Sharp has made clear, those who led the riots and who made up most of the rioters were from the distinct class of artisans who relied on the forest for their livelihoods and who were ignored by the disafforestation process because they had little or no land. Studying the backgrounds of those convicted of rioting shows this clearly. In the case of Gillingham, of the 74 found guilty, 45 were artisans, 21 were farmers and eight others. Of the artisans, many were from the cloth industry and many others were artisans who depended on products from the forests for their materials—glovers, tanners, shoemakers, carpenters and so on. The evidence is less conclusive for the riots in Braydon, which lacked widespread artisanal industry, but the three "Lady Skimington" leaders were a tailor, a sievemaker and a gardener.[615] Sharp's comparison of those who took part in legal process around the enclosure of land and those who were tried for involvement in rioting shows that the two groups were almost completely distinct. In the case that led to the confirmation of the enclosure of Dean Forest, there were "forty-one plaintiffs—one knight, thirty esquires and gentlemen, and ten yeomen. Only one of them, a yeoman, is to be found among the fifty-eight known or suspected rioters".[616]

There were two types of people living in the forests that the crown decided to sell off and enclose. Those with some land or tenant rights engaged in a legal process with the government, the remainder, poor cottagers, some of whom engaged in artisanal labour, who relied on the forest for their livelihoods tended respond to enclosure with riot.[617] The crown made an attempt to compensate the poorest:

> And his Majestie being very tender of the welfare of the inhabitants and borderers about the said forest and that the poorer sort of them who had noe right of common at all but yet had used to common might no bee left destitute but might in some reasonable measure bee provided for mearely out of his Majesties compassion and grace.[618]

Yet this compassionate act was negligible when divided among all those who would lose the access to land they had used for generations. This could affect significant numbers of people. One study of Brigstock Village in Rockingham Forest, Northamptonshire, showed that in 1596 only 40 percent of the village had farmland (110 cottages had none). By 1637, 40 new houses, nearly all cottages, had been built.[619] The people who lived in these were reliant on the forest for survival—for game, for wood and for raw materials for their work.

In areas where artisan industry was common the forest was a crucial addition to people's livelihoods. As Sharp concludes:

> The status of the vast majority of rural and small-town artisans suggests that propertylessness was at the root of their involvement in disorders… The outbreak of the Western Rising is to be seen as the result of economic pressure put on the poor cottagers. Disafforestation and enclosure threatened them at least with the loss of income supplements and in some cases with the loss of their livelihood.[620]

Economic problems for the cloth industry in particular forced many to rely increasingly on the forest for survival and this explains the involvement of artisans and the poorest in riotous resistance to disafforestation and enclosure. Ultimately these struggles were mostly ineffective, though they continued for many years. One exception is the Forest of Dean, in which disafforestation "was permanently reversed" by an Act of Parliament in 1668 which "reafforested" it, returning it to an open common to be used by its inhabitants. This success was because of the people who fought, and continued to fight, against enclosure.[621]

Ideas transformed

Henry Best, the yeoman farmer who in the mid-1600s had seen the value of his enclosed land increase threefold, is a fine example of the way that farming for profit was transforming peoples' attitudes to each other. He was "intolerant" of what remained of communal traditions among his fellow villagers, unhappy to contribute to the communal hay stock for winter because "our hay would have been spent in feeding other men's animals". He was vigorous in ensuring that other people's animals didn't stray onto his land (including checks in the middle of the night). Best is a classic example of the individualist farmer, isolated from the wider community because of his desire to maximise his own farm's success. Such a life, and behaviour, would no doubt have alienated Best from the wider community, but it would also have led to a transformation in his views of land, of labour and the world at large.[622]

Men like Best increasingly desired influence and representation within local, regional and national institutions. They wanted to see taxation that benefited their methods of farming or, in the case of those who were making profits from manufacture or trade, from their ways of operating. In England the growth of the gentry meant that there was a corresponding change in the makeup of those sent to the House of Commons. In the 16th century, the House of Commons was still very much a body that advised the king, made up of the nobility and local representatives. But, as George Yerby points out, by the 16th century the "gentry had come to virtually monopolise the composition of the House of Commons...[and] were engineering a substantial increase in the size of the assembly in order to give themselves yet more scope".[623] These gentry were increasingly reliant on income from rents on their estates and the landed class themselves was seeing a remarkable growth, tripling (between 1540 and 1640) at a time when the population "scarcely doubled".[624]

This led to tensions and clashes within the ruling class, much of it linked to the question of taxation and the role of parliament in setting taxes. In 1628, King Charles I demanded taxes to pay for war with Spain and France. Angry MPs refused to grant this money until their "Petition of Right" was acknowledged. The Petition asked that established rights, such as no taxation without parliamentary consent and no imprisonment without cause, be reasserted by the king.[625]

The following year, when parliament met, there were immediate arguments about the collection of "tonnage and poundage" by the king. This was a tax on imports and exports and was obviously disliked by merchants and traders. But the debate was about more than the raising of taxes; it reflected much deeper discussions about whether the king had the right to collect money simply because of who he was, or whether other sections of society, through parliament, had to agree. As Yerby points out, Sir John Eliot said at the time: "tonnage and poundage and other impositions not granted by parliament...[were] a breach of the fundamental liberties of the kingdom, and contrary to...the Petition of Right". Following these arguments Charles decided to rule alone and it was 11 years before parliament met again.[626]* The debates of the 1628-1629 parliament and similar discussions in preceding parliaments underscore that a section of the English ruling class was now thinking and acting in a way that made a confrontation with the existing order inevitable—in 1642 this resulted in full-blown civil war.

Those who went to war on the side of parliament in 1642 against King Charles I did not do so with a plan to end feudal relations and replace them with a new capitalist order. But, as Chris Harman explains, the scale of the crisis meant that those who "did not want a reversion to

---

* Charles's move to personal rule has been described as "tyranny" and certainly it provoked discontent. But it was not unconstitutional and long periods without parliament meeting were not unusual. See Carlin, 2005, p97.

feudalism" had to find a solution that "would steadfastly develop the new forms of production and exploitation as opposed to the old." This effectively meant revolution, as there had to be a break with the old order and, as Harman notes, the areas that were strongest for this were those such as "London, the seaports and those rural areas which produced agricultural and/or manufactured foods for the market".[627] The intensity of the Civil War and the need for an emphatic victory led to Charles being executed in Whitehall in 1649. To win the war Oliver Cromwell had built a coalition of forces that was inherently unstable. In the aftermath of the war he had to rein back the more radical elements, and with his death in 1658 the "revolutionary dictatorship" he had created could not hold, leading "to a series of compromises with the great landowners and merchants [and] the restored monarchy of 1660 and, when this began to show absolutist pretension, the settlement of 1688".[628]

Despite these compromises and the Restoration of the monarchy, the long-term trend towards capitalist development could not be reversed.

In 1656 an Act of Parliament abolished the Court of Wards, the body that fixed feudal dues. In the aftermath of the Restoration in 1660, Charles II's Declaration of Breda was read in the House of Commons. It was designed to move on from the events of the Civil War by issuing a general pardon, religious toleration and the settling of unpaid debts to the army. As soon as the Declaration had been read, parliament moved to reassert the abolishment of the Court of Wards.[629] As Christopher Hill has pointed out, this meant a dramatic transformation in the monarch's powers:

> Its effect was to deprive the crown of a vital means of maintaining its leading subjects in proper subordination; to relieve the landed class of the irritating and erratic death duties which wardship had imposed; and to give landowners…absolute power to do what they would with their own [estates] including the right to settle the inheritance of all their lands by will.[630]

These changes helped encourage further capitalist relations. Michael Žmolek explains: "[t]he market in land was becoming a market in *rents*, and the competitive pressures of the market *compelled* landowners to seek the full value of rents." This is not to suggest that England was now fully capitalist—there still had to be further changes. Žmolek notes for instance, that 75 percent of farms were still unenclosed in 1660 and "a century and a half of struggle over enclosures lay ahead".[631]

Demand for food from the cities increased and this encouraged enclosure (though for cultivation rather than sheep) and there was investment in land and scientific experiments in agriculture. Hill argues that "capitalist society was left to develop unhampered", with the stimulation of industry by the needs of the Civil War leading to "economic trends which could not be reversed". Economic growth was slow, but parliament passed laws that encouraged the industrial economy, such as the 1663 Act that opened the linen industry up to everyone and a 1666 law that decreed the dead were to be buried in wool not imported material. Rights to mine and sell coal were increased, leading to an expansion in that industry. Other laws were passed that reduced the power of the guilds, and apprentices and those thrown off the land through enclosure or the draining of the fens found their way increasingly into urban industry.[632] Hill writes:

> After 1660 the landowning class was secure against social revolt from below. Henceforth a major pre-occupation of governments was to stimulate production and to protect the producer, no longer to safe-guard the consumer or protect the subsistence farmer. This marks a decisive change in outlook.[633]

Capitalism arose out of many, complex, interacting changes within society. But its birth in England in the middle of the 17th century was not inevitable; a section of society had to fight to break with the old order so that the new relations could develop further. This class struggle was at the heart of the English Civil War. Harman summarises it well:

> Caught between the past and the future, the monarchical states facilitated the growth of capitalist forms of exploitation, but also became a drag upon them at key moments in history. Then bitter class struggles alone could determine whether society moved forwards or backwards. And these struggles involved bitter clashes between rival exploiting classes as well as between the exploiters and the exploited classes.[634]

Before capitalism could fully develop in England and spread across the globe, it had to develop further, but it also had to transform the relations that people had with land and labour. This meant an acceleration of land enclosures and the further destruction of common land and "the commodification of all elements of production, including labour".[635] This resulted in bitter class struggle as people in urban and rural areas fought to defend their livelihoods and maintain their land and communities. Before we look at some of those struggles in rural England, we will briefly return to the English Civil War and how the population of the countryside responded to the conflict and organised to protect their interests.

6

The English Civil War and the rural population

THE CRISIS of the English Civil War had its origins in much wider social crises throughout society. The run up to the final collapse in relations between king and parliament was marked in the countryside by discontent at the growth of capitalistic relations. Across the country there were growing attempts to overturn enclosure fences and open up common land that had been previously enclosed.

The outbreak of the Civil War saw rebellion and riot in both rural and urban areas, though there was plenty of cross-over between the two. For instance, in August 1642, a large riot took place in Colchester against the royalist Sir John Lucas. Lucas was a friend of the king and a major landowner disliked by the population because of the "vigour with which he had collected ship money", because of enclosures and his "obstruction of the town's water supply". Up to 5,000 people took part in a riot, pulling down fences in the park, killing deer and eventually destroying Lucas's house and gardens. Similarly, at St Osyth, about 10 miles south-east of Colchester, the estate of Countess Rivers was also destroyed. As well as breaking up her possessions, smashing all the windows and stealing linen, furniture, plate and money and leaving "not a door, nor so much as a bar of a window behind them", the rioters also destroyed her crops and park and stole the cattle. In both cases the rioters appear to have been dominated by artisans. The riot against Sir Lucas was led by a grocer and a brewer; the attack on Countess Rivers' estate was mainly carried out by weavers.[636]

These riots inspired further uprisings along the Essex-Suffolk border, with the cloth-making towns and villages at the heart of events. As Brian Manning has explained, behind these events was a deep economic downturn in the textile industry which stemmed from wider "political uncertainties" due to the conflict between king and parliament. He argues that in these riots "weavers and rural artisans seem to have predominated...with a sprinkling of husbandmen and yeomen", and they involved women as well as men, but few labourers. The riots were not simply about plunder, nor were they "anti-popery riots", though they did target those known or suspected of being Catholic. Manning concludes that protesters targeted "opponents of parliament...and they claimed to have authority from parliament to search the houses of 'malignants' (supporters of the king) for arms".[637]

This was class war. Discontent and economic insecurity, poverty and wider frustrations were coming together with anger at the king. People were taking the opportunity to try and wrest back some of what they had lost, or at least take revenge on those who had oppressed and exploited them. In rural areas the tearing down of fences and the destruction of deer parks were part of people attempting to take control of their lives and communities. Actions like these were common in the early years of the Civil War period and built on existing rural discontent.

The enclosures, draining of marshlands and destruction of common land had already impoverished many. Often peasants took the opportunity to redress the balance. Time and again, villagers destroyed fences and hedges, released their animals onto former common land and defied the sheriffs who came to try and restore order. In the village of Buckden, now in Cambridgeshire, where the Bishop of Lincoln had enclosed land, "hundreds of women and boys, armed with daggers and javelins, in a very tumultuous and riotous manner, entered upon the grounds, threw open the gates, and broke down the quicksets [hedges] of the said enclosure, and turned in great herds of cattle upon the premises". In December 1641, enclosures on the saltmarshes of "North and South Somercotes in Lincolnshire...granted by the king...were thrown down and the inhabitants took over the whole of the marshes as their common again". Again, in Lincolnshire, this time in Stamford, "very poor men" destroyed bridges and water courses feeding the Countess of Exeter's mills. In Burnham Water, fishermen even took oyster larvae from the Earl of Sussex's waters and redistributed them in rivers to which he had no fishing rights.[638]

From the 1620s the Earl of Middlesex had cleared and enclosed forests in Worcestershire, Somerset and Wiltshire, the inhabitants were evicted into starvation and the woodland became the property of the king. No wonder, then, that in October 1642 an uprising killed 600 deer belonging to the earl.[639] Sometimes anti-enclosure riots could be on a huge scale. The Forest of Dean had been enclosed by Sir John Winter in 1639, paying a huge cash sum to a cash-strapped Charles I. Some 4,000 acres of forest were granted as compensation to those who had relied on the woods for common rights, while the remainder, over 18,000 acres, was enclosed. Discontent rumbled until 1641 when the inhabitants of the area destroyed *12 miles* of enclosures.[640]

There are numerous other examples from the period. Buchanan Sharp has assembled many of them in his study of the west of England, where he points out that the people tended to take advantage of the chaos of Civil War to riot.

The inhabitants of Duffield, Derbyshire rioted in 1643, destroying the enclosures in Chevin Ward. In 1642 and 1643, people of Windsor Forest "assembled repeatedly in large groups; they then destroyed the enclosures of the parks, killed many of the deer, and plundered the woods...[a] culmination of longstanding complaints against the large number of deer consuming the vert [vegetation] of the forest and depriving cattle of their pasturage". In Waltham Forest, Essex, between April 1642 and February 1643, "armed crowds" killed 400 of the king's deer. One rioter, when told the riots were against forest laws, responded: "there was noe Lawe settled at this tyme that hee knewe". On a number of occasions troops billeted near to forests took part in riots, encouraged to do so by the locals, though it seems this was less out of opposition to enclosure and more about the extortion of money from landowners. So intense were these riots in the forests of the west, that they have been called a Second Western Rising, continuing until 1651, when a "troop of horse was sent to the forest [Gillingham] to maintain order".[641]

Troops were used on occasion during the Civil War period to quell riots. Often this was simply because soldiers were in the area as part of military action. In May 1643, for instance, parliamentary forces near Gillingham were laying siege to Wardour Castle and the Earl of Elgin got reinforcements to detour to arrest rioters. The four men apprehended were taken to the siege where they managed to escape.[642] Parliament was concerned enough about the disturbances to order forces locally to suppress the riots in July 1643, though nothing seems to have come of this. Local authorities seem to have been divided politically as a result of the war and as a result ineffectual. The end of the First Civil War brought some respite to landowners, with the Earl of Elgin finally getting five rioters in front of the House of Lords in 1648. Despite the riots being described as "open Rebellion", the punishment was minor, with offenders being told to "carry themselves peaceably and quietly". As Sharp explains, this decision was because "the House of Lords, like its predecessor in these matters, the court of Star Chamber, refused to deal with questions of title to land, in this case the right of the defendants to common in Gillingham Forest".[643]

The Fenlands of East Anglia and Lincolnshire were scenes of par-ticularly extensive rebellions. An Act of Parliament in the last years of

Queen Elizabeth's reign had permitted large-scale drainage of the land. These common lands were an important source of fish and birds for the poorest and their loss was a major blow to a way of life, forcing families to depend on wage labour rather than traditional livelihoods.[644] The king was one of the biggest landowners in the country and, as a Lincolnshire landowner, had been involved in the draining of fens and the consequent disputes with those who farmed sheep and cattle there. The population of the fens fought a long and hard battle against the drainage and loss of their land. Brian Manning says this was first "fought constitutionally", but then through "direct action" until when the Civil War started by which point "the whole fenland was in a state of open rebellion".[645]

Peasant tenants served in both the parliamentary and the royal armies. Manning says that while there is "more" evidence for tenants defying their royalist landlords to support parliament, there are examples of the opposite. It was precisely because there was a class war taking place between tenant and landlord at the same time as the fight between sections of the ruling class, that peasants could support either side.[646] David Underdown has also commented that "neutralism...was not always absolute", avoiding involvement in conflict, or desiring a return to normality without further interruption, violence or plundering by one side or the other did not preclude a preference for taking a side in the conflict.[647]

The Civil War itself was marked by the movement of large armies the length and breadth of England. These and the large garrisons, both royalist and parliamentarian, required food and this had to be taken from the land. Armies on the move fed themselves directly from the land, fostering discontent in the countryside. The battles, sieges and the marching of troops caused widespread disruption as markets and industry stopped, prices of materials rose, horses were confiscated and so on.

In Leicestershire, where there were royalist garrisons at Belvoir Castle and Ashby de la Zouch, A M Everitt describes contemporary accounts (by a parliamentarian) of raids into the countryside by royalists "as debased wicked wretches there as if they had been raked out of hell... [They] have three malignant priests there such as will drink and roar... and swear and domineer so as it would make one's heart ache to hear the country people to relate what they heard of them".[648]

This did not mean that rural populations were indifferent to the Civil War; on occasion they did take sides. The very start of the war, in August 1642, was marked by a great rural uprising in the south-west as "husbandsmen and cloth workers" massed in great numbers from north Somerset and the nearby parts of Wilshire and Gloucestershire, armed with "pitchforks, dungpicks, and suchlike weapons". Their rising was against the Marquis of Hertford, who was trying to muster the local population for the king's war. Hertford was forced to flee.[649]

In Yorkshire in December 1642 the king failed to take Bradford after a small parliamentary force sent messengers to outlying areas calling for assistance. Those who came to their aid from Halifax were not experienced soldiers; a few had muskets but most had only clubs or "scythes laid in poles". Together with a party of "club-men" from Bingley, they drove the royalists back. One contemporary account says that a royalist officer, separated from his men and attacked, tried to surrender by giving the traditional call for quarter. Not being military men, his attackers responded that "aye, they would quarter him" and cut him into four. Following this success, Thomas Fairfax "summoned the country" and with 2,000 club-men from the region around Bradford marched on Leeds in January 1643.[650]

These men were clothiers, smallholding farmers who also worked in cloth making. They had a cottage and small piece of land for grazing and predominated around the Bradford/Halifax area. They can be contrasted to those from the Leeds area, where bigger clothiers "employed women spinners and journeymen weavers, took on apprentices, and the biggest employed twenty, even forty, persons... They engaged in farming as a by-occupation but their 'chief interest lay in the production of cloth in larger quantities.'" The smallholders (as with similar small-scale artisans in Birmingham, Manchester and elsewhere) were often vocal supporters of parliament. Leeds, on the other hand, was more supportive of the king. This difference, between the "small clothiers of the Halifax and Bradford area and the big clothiers of the Leeds area, and between the clothiers in general and the merchants of Leeds" explains, according to Brian Manning, "the divergence in the civil war between the fiercer parliamentarianism of the Halifax-Bradford area and the tendency towards royalism in the Leeds area." But this was not just true of Yorkshire. "Smallholding handicraftsmen were the firmest and most radical supporters of parliament". People like this had many motivations, but shared the "hope that parliament would redress their grievances and give them a more secure future...and they were fearful and suspicious of the intentions of all superiors, whether royalists or parliamentarians".[651]

But for A M Everitt the lives of most rural people were not polarised between Cavalier and Roundhead, or king and parliament, because what mattered was "the fortunes of their local community".[652] David Underdown argues that the political positions that rural areas took tended to originate in varying cultures in different regions. The differences between "the chalk and the cheese" areas, the "clubmen most friendly to the royalist forces were those from the 'chalk' – the nucleated settlements of the downlands. Those most friendly to the parliamentarians were from the fen-edge villages of the Somerset levels, from the clothing parishes of the wood-pasture region...and from the 'cheese' area of Wiltshire." Underdown argues, for instance, that communities that were "more independent, more egalitarian, less custom-bound" tended to support parliament.[653]

The 17th century writer John Aubrey explained these differences through a combination of the vegetation (North Wiltshire had "sour and austere plants" which supposedly infected the temperaments of the inhabitants) and more economic explanations. Aubrey believed for instance that in the arable areas people worked too hard to be diverted by politics, but in the cheese country they had time which "set their wits a-running and reforming".[654]

Reality is much more complex. But it does seem that the different economic paths of the rural regions played a part in the development of local ideology which influenced whether or not an area was likely to be pro-parliament or royalist during the Civil War. Underdown explicitly rejects a simple "reductionist resort to economic determinism".[655] There are, after all, plenty of counter-examples, if you look at individual villages. But viewed on a larger scale, there are some general trends which can only be explained by differing economic conditions shaped primarily by the way that different agrarian approaches altered the general cultural outlook of communities. Underdown explains that in the three counties he studied, Somerset, Wiltshire and Dorset, he

> Identified marked contrasts in the distribution of allegiance...marked variations of outlook that were regional rather than narrowly parochial in character. Those contrasts...are connected with the relatively advanced stage of social polarisation reached in the clothing districts, and with the survival of a more homogeneous, paternalist society in the arable regions... The 'fit' between pre-war culture and civil war allegiance is not exact, but it is close enough. The downlands and Blackmore Vale were very different in social structure, economic life, and settlement patterns. But they were both strongholds of cultural conservatism, and they were both royalist in the civil war. In all areas we find an attachment to localism: the cultural differences explain why the localism of some regions produced a preference for Parliament, of others for the King.[656]

Precisely how rural populations reacted to the Civil War depended on a complex interaction of economic development, local experience and the role of the local elite (churchmen, landowners and so on), but people did react. It is not enough to say that most rural people remained neutral. They may not have actively engaged in events (though many did) but they certainly had opinions and beliefs, and most of them took sides.

During the Civil War, ordinary people suffered greatly.* Conscription to either side was possible and both armies were happy to seize property and food. Taxes were also increased to pay for the war. Not surprisingly, rural populations in areas controlled by both parliament and the king organised to resist these impositions. There were risings against conscription and taxation in 1644-1645 against both sides. In early 1645, for example, people in the countryside near Hereford rose against violence, conscription, taxes and requisition of crops by the royalist garrisons. This led to a major uprising on 19 March 1645 when up to 12,000 peasants, mostly armed with clubs, began a siege of Hereford demanding compensation for the families of those who had died and the withdrawal of soldiers. Eventually, Prince Rupert sent troops against those who refused to disperse and 200 "clubmen" were arrested and their leaders hanged. Interestingly, an attempt by a parliamentary leader to organise the Herefordshire clubmen as a military force against the royalists was rejected.[657]

Thousands of rural people joined such movements, known as the "risings of the clubmen". These, however, were not simply spontaneous affairs, but were highly organised, often involving mass meetings of thousands. The risings took place mostly in Wilshire, Dorset and Somerset. Manning has pointed out that the name clubmen refers most obviously to their weapons, as they lacked firearms, but also to the "clubs or associations" that they formed. The clubmen described themselves as "associates" indicating their own organisation and at one meeting in Wiltshire in June 1645 they agreed to "assist one another in the mutual defence of our laws, liberties, and posterities against all plunderers, and all other unlawful violence whatsoever".[658]

Ronald Hutton has highlighted the difficulties with seeing the clubmen as a universal phenomenon, pointing to the varied responses of the different groups to the authorities. In royalist Worcestershire, for instance, he notes that the clubmen's leagues were a "sensible" response to the Civil War, setting up "workable local mechanisms for the preservation of the

---

* As a proportion of the English population, the Civil War resulted in more deaths than either the First or Second World War.

countryside from plunder, operating the rules agreed by the Royalist leaders themselves". Contrast this with the experience in the neighbouring counties of Shropshire and Hereford which both had clubmen movements that were prepared to confront royalist authorities more directly. We have already noted events in Hereford. In Shropshire, in December 1644, there was a rising demanding the reposting of a "hated officer" and the "evacuation of two local garrisons". This was only partially successful: the officer was removed but the garrisons remained.*

If the clubmen represented localised responses to the depredation of the Civil War, it was a reactive response. Let us know look briefly at attempts during the period to shape a radical agrarian alternative to the dominant forms of rural society.

Winstanley's Diggers[659]

The English Revolution, the time of Civil War and its aftermath, saw a great flowering of radical ideas and organisations. Some of these movements, particularly the Levellers, became central to driving the revolutionary movement forward until the execution of Charles I and the establishment of a republic. In the aftermath, the alliance that Cromwell had created to defeat the king fell apart and the Levellers were suppressed.[660]

Gerrard Winstanley was a key figure in a smaller, but more radical, group, the Diggers, which attempted to put into practice a new, communal agrarian society in the years of the English Revolution. He was born in Wigan in October 1609. At the age of 20 he moved to London to be an apprentice in the cloth trade. In 1638 he set up his own business and described himself as a "strict goer to church...and a hearer of Sermons".[661]

In 1640 he married Susan King, whose family owned a small estate in Cobham, Surrey. When his business failed in 1643, they moved to Cobham and settled there. The rural community was very different to London and Winstanley was forced to earn a living as a labourer, eventually becoming a householder who earned a living from farming. Nonetheless the failure of his business had a lasting influence on him:

> For matter of buying and selling, the earth stinks with such unrighteous-nesse, that for my part, though I was bred a tradesman, yet it is so hard a thing to pick out a poor living, that a man shall sooner be cheated of his bread, then get bread by trading among men, if by plain dealing he put trust in any.[662]

---

* Note that while these counties border each other, there is no evidence of interaction, Hutton, 1979, p45 and pp44-46.

In 1646 he, along with five other locals, had been fined for digging peat on the common. The struggles over land and common rights, as well as the growing radicalism and experiences during the Civil War (Winstanley was always a supporter of the parliamentary cause) shaped his ideas. As Winstanley's biographer John Gurney explains, we "cannot know for certain the precise religious path that he followed in the 1640s, but we can tentatively see him as moving from orthodox Protestant to Baptist, Seeker and finally Digger".[663] The questioning of established religion and his own explorations of ideas led him to some radical conclusions, as well as conflict with the established church. Many of these would later be seized upon to portray him as a pre-Communist thinker. His writings certainly confirm his radicalism and his originality of thought:

> The Spirit Reason, which I call God, the Maker and Ruler of all things, is that spiritual power that guides all men's reasoning in right order, and to a right end…and knite every creature together into a oneness, making every creature to be an upholder of his fellows; and so everyone is an assistant to preserve the whole. And the nearer man's reasoning comes to this, the more spiritual they are; the further off they be, the more selfish and fleshy they be.[664]

Here, in 1648, Winstanley is arguing for the central importance of the relationship between the individual and the wider world. It is the beginnings of the ideology that would form the basis for Winstanley's, and those that followed him, experiments in radical communal living and ownership; ideas that Winstanley would later write out in detail and form some of the first examples of how a society of equals might work.

In a number of his works Winstanley laid out in detail how society could be organised to ensure that everyone received the full fruits of the earth's bounty. These ideas are surprisingly detailed, and are rooted in Winstanley's own experiences of the rural communities he lived and worked in.[665]

Some selected points from Winstanley's 1652 "Law of Freedom in a Platform: Or True Magistracie Restored" illustrate his vision.[666]

> Every Family shall come into the field with sufficient assistance at seed time, to plough, dig and plant, and at harvest time to reap the fruits of the Earth, and to carry them into the Storehouses… If any refuse to assist in the work, the Overseer shall ask the reason; and if it be sickness or any distemper that hinders them, they are freed from such service; if mere idleness keep them back, they are to suffer punishment according to the Laws against Idleness.

In every Town and City shall be appointed Storehouses for flax, wood, leather, cloth and for all such commodities as come from beyond seas. These shall be called General Storehouses whence every particular Family may fetch such commodities as they want, either for their own use in their house, or for to work in their trades, or to carry into the Country Storehouses.

If any do buy and sell the Earth, or the fruits thereof, unless it be to or with strangers of another Nation, according to the Law of Navigation, they shall be both put to death as Traitors to the Peace of the Commonwealth. Because it brings in Kings Bondage again, and is the occasion of all quarrels and oppressions.

He, or she, who calls the Earth his, and not his brother's, shall be set upon a stool, with those words written in his forehead, before all the Congregation, and afterwards be made a Servant for twelve months under the Task-master.

The Storehouses shall be every man's subsistence, and not any ones.

No man shall either give hire or take hire for his work; for this brings in Kingly Bondage.

But for Winstanley theory and practice could not be separated and in April 1649, in the midst of growing radical discontent following the execution of King Charles I, Winstanley and his followers, known as the Diggers, put their ideas to the test. On 16 April, Henry Sanders sent a report to the Council of State describing the arrival of the Diggers on St George's Hill in Surrey. They

began to dig on that side the hill next to Campe Close, and sowed the ground with parsnips, carrots, and beans. On Monday following they were there again, being increased in their number, and on the next day...they fired the heath, and burned at least forty rood of heath, which is a very great prejudice to the town. On Friday...[they] wrought all day at digging... They invite all to come in and help them, and promise them meat, drink and clothes. They do threaten to pull down and level all park pales, and lay open, and intend to plant there very shortly. They give out they will be four or five thousand within ten days, and threaten the neighbouring people there, that they will make them all come up to the hills and work: and forewarn them suffering their cattle to come near the plantation; if they do, they will cut their legs off. It is feared they have some design in hand.[667]

The Council of State was concerned about these events, less because of the activity of planting crops and preparing farmland and more because of what might happen as a result. They asked that a military force be sent to Surrey to find out what was happening in case "that conflux of people may be a beginning whence things of a greater and more dangerous consequence may grow, to the disturbance of the peace and quiet of the Commonwealth."

Captain John Gladman was sent to investigate and reported back to Lord Fairfax and arranged for Gerrard Winstanley and William Everard, a radical and one of the founders of the settlement on St George's Hill, to meet him to explain their actions. A contemporary newspaper account reports what Everard said:

> there had lately appeared to him a vision, which bad him arise and dig and plough the earth, and receive the fruits thereof. That their intent is to restore the Creation to its former condition. That as God had promised to make the barren land fruitful, so now what they did was to restore the ancient community of enjoying the fruits of the Earth, and to distribute the benefits thereof to the poor and needy, and to feed the hungry and to clothe the naked.

The Diggers did not plan to break down enclosures, nor interfere with other peoples land and labour, but only to use "what was common and untilled, and to make it fruitful for the use of man". They believed that others would join them, giving up their own lands:

> And for all those that will come in and work they should have meat, drink and clothes, which is all that is necessary to the life of man; and that for money, there was not any need of it, nor of clothes more than to cover nakedness.

These were very radical ideas that challenged the new republican order. Christopher Hill argues that "similar ideas were arising simultaneously... in more or less sophisticated forms, in various parts of the country".[668] Hill suggested that St George's Hill was only the "tip of the iceberg of True Levellerism".[669] Indeed, similar camps to Winstanley's in Surrey were also set up at locations in Northamptonshire, Kent, Barnet, Enfield, Dunstable, Bosworth and Nottinghamshire, possibly in Buckinghamshire and Gloucestershire.[670]

The number of Digger camps is impressive, though we know very little about most of them, but they reflected wider discontent. The call for the enclosed land, or that which had been given to the crown, to be returned for the use of the poor became a "standard radical demand".[671]

The camps appeared at an unfortunate time for those who had just executed the king. No doubt they were hoping for a period of calm so that they could entrench their rule; instead discontent was growing, particularly within the army. Radicals were disappointed with events since Charles's execution; hunger was an issue even in London and in April Leveller mutinies took place in the army after soldiers refused to serve in Ireland as part of a military campaign organised by Cromwell. These spread to other regiments around the country and eventually Cromwell and Thomas Fairfax, the commander of the New Model Army, executed leading Levellers at Burford on 14 May 1649.

But Hill points out that despite the growth of radical ideas, many leading figures in the radical movement were keen to disavow Winstanley's "Communism". In September 1648 a Leveller petition had "repudiated any idea of abolishing property", though it was in favour of destroying recent enclosures. In April 1649 a Leveller "manifesto" declared that they "never had it in our thoughts to level men's estates, it being the utmost of our aim that...every man with as much security as may be enjoy his property".[672]

Events at St George's Hill became the focus for national media scrutiny. Newssheets from across the political spectrum discussed, with varying degrees of "accuracy and seriousness", what was taking place.[673] Fairfax himself visited St George's Hill and talked to the Diggers, including Winstanley, at length. While there was no outright military repression of the Diggers, it does seem that groups of soldiers may have harassed the Diggers. More problematic was the response of the local rural population. They had destroyed the Diggers' fields from early on and by May Winstanley's group was facing systematic and violent resistance. Not surprisingly, the locals wanted access back to their commons and, as a result, the Diggers themselves became the victims of traditional forms of rural protest. On 11 June, a group of local men, dressed in women's clothes, attacked a small party of Diggers. After this, legal action was taken against the Diggers which encouraged other forms of action against "Diggers' livelihoods away from St George's Hill". Winstanley, for instance, lost cattle and had his crops destroyed.[674]

A broad alliance formed against the Diggers which held protest meetings and economic boycotts, eventually forcing Winstanley and his comrades to retreat to Cobham. But the abandonment of the camp at St George's Hill was not the end of Digger experiments. By the spring of 1650 the Digger colony at Cobham had grown. Four houses had been built and several acres of corn planted. We know this from a letter written by Winstanley and circulated by a group of Diggers who travelled around asking for funds for the colony's survival.[675]

However, the Diggers' experiments were soon to be ended. In April 1650, 15 Diggers were indicted for riot at St George's Hill and four were charged for illegally building houses in Cobham. Violence was still directed against them as well: homes were burnt, crops were destroyed and men and women beaten. This was the end of the Cobham colony and others did not last much longer. Winstanley was defeated, but his hopes and dreams continued.[676] He firmly believed in his cause and his methods, and remained

> Assured of the righteousnesse of the work, and it shall take root in one place or other, before many years passé over Englands head, I can set no time, but I wait for the consolation of Israel to Arise up, and break forth in others, as I have a taste of him in my self.[677]

Winstanley's experiment in communal living was defeated and Winstanley spent the rest of his life in obscurity and disappointment. His writings came in a very short burst of just a few years—he rose with the English Revolution and went down with its decline. But his vision of an egalitarian society based on common ownership of the land continues to inspire.

> Take notice, That England is not a Free People till the Poor that have no land have a free allowance to dig and labor the Commons, and so live as comfortably as the Land Lords that live in their Inclosures. For the people have not laid out their monies and shed their blood that their Land Lords, the Norman Power, should still have its liberty and freedom to rule in tyranny, but that the Oppressed might be set free, prison doors opened, and the Poor People's heart comforted by an universal consent of making the Earth a Common Treasury, that they may live together united by brotherly love into one spirit, and having a comfortable livelihood in the Community of one Earth their Mother.[678]

7

Enclosure and the English countryside transformed

AFTER THE end of the Civil War and the establishment of the Commonwealth, protests continued "in the forest and fen regions" because government policies essentially remained the same.[679] In 1653 and 1654, parliament ordered the sale of remaining royal forests, provoking resistance. The draining of the fens also continued with "An Act for Drayning the Great Level of the Fens" passed in May 1649.[680] Opposition to the draining reappeared and in some areas it was successful. For instance, in the northern fenland "both the drainers and the Crown were permanently dispossessed of their shares in the fen". In 1699, 1,000 men destroyed works at Deeping Fen in Lincolnshire, delaying the draining there, and elsewhere compromises were reached as a result of protests that meant only partial drainage took place. Protests against enclosure and loss of common land continued across England, for instance, between 1650 and 1700 there were repeated riots in Coventry.[681]

The period also saw continuing protests against deer parks. As the historian Andrew Charlesworth has noted, forest communities "opposed the presence of deer parks, they were resisting the social and economic repercussions of landscapes created for pleasure and social prestige". They were targeted precisely because they represented "aristocratic power". These protests and riots included the "destruction of fences, the cutting down of trees and the killing of deer". In the 1720s there were widespread protests against deer parks in "Windsor Forest, the Farnham area of Hampshire, Alice Holt Forest, Woolmer Forest, Waltham Chase, the Forest of Bere...Enfield Chase and Richmond Park".[682]

E P Thompson notes that "there are better population statistics for the deer in Windsor Forest than for the human denizens", reflecting the interests of the aristocracy in the use of their lands. The sheer scale of the forests (Windsor had over 3,000 deer in 1607) made them targets for a disgruntled local population. During the Civil War and Commonwealth period, mass hunting ensured there were no deer in Windsor Great Park by 1649. Despite restocking the forests after the Restoration, numbers never recovered.[683]

This was highly illegal and dangerous, so poachers adopted disguises or painted their faces, leading to it being known as "blacking". As we have seen, forests and land had always been sites of class struggle as communities fought to use the resources instead of them being limited to the rich landowners. Medieval laws already existed against "blacking" and in the late 17th century these were strengthened. Under a 1661 law imposed by Charles II, poachers could be fined £20 or face a year in prison. In 1691, laws were extended by William and Mary to target "deer stealers". Thompson notes that the 1691 Act referred to the collective nature of deer hunting, with poachers organising as "a brotherhood and fraternity". The penalty for killing or wounding deer was increased to £30 but the Act was clearly intended to encourage individuals in rural communities to oppose poaching—"One third of the fine was to go to the informer (generally the gamekeeper or his servant), one third to the poor of the parish and one third to the owner of the deer".[684]

Laws against poaching became much harsher through the 18th century. The Game Act of 1719 made deer stealing a crime that could be punished by transportation and the infamous Black Act of 1721 made poaching and other offences a capital crime. Over time, hunting was transformed into a privilege for the rich while the poor faced draconian penalties. A law of 1671, explains Christopher Hill, "prohibited all freeholders with land worth less than £100 a year...from killing game, *even on their own land*" (my emphasis). Those who met the property qualification could "hunt where they pleased". After 1671, evidence from a single witness was enough to find someone guilty.[685]

Unsurprisingly, resistance was "widespread". In the second half of the 18th century, for instance, some 800 poachers were "dealt with" on Cannock Chase, near Stafford, alone. Opposition to game laws led to the mass involvement of whole communities and the deployment of large numbers of gamekeepers against them. Sometimes this would lead to confrontations on the scale of pitched battles.

In his detailed study of poaching on Cannock Chase, Douglas Hay recounts how popular anger at the Earl of Uxbridge's extension of rabbit warrens led to mass protests half way through the 18th century. Uxbridge's rabbits "occupied about 3,500 acres of the Chase" numbering about 15,000 animals. The rural commoners were suffering "serious losses" as the rabbits had the best grazing. After appeals to the earl and legal proceedings failed, between 200 and 300 men spent two weeks destroying the warrens, leaving only the one they believed Uxbridge had a right to. All the rabbits were killed, valued at over £3,000. After a lengthy court case, a judge eventually ruled for the earl, declaring an ordinary person could not "destroy the estate of the lord, in order to preserve his own small right of common".[686]

There was an enormous expansion in laws designed to stop poaching. Rural historian Pamela Horn points out that "in the first 60 years of the 18th century there were only six acts directed against the ordinary poaching of small game. In the next 56 years 33 such acts reached the statute book" and that it was over the question of the hunting of game that the "greatest ill-feeling and friction arose between rich and poor in rural society".[687] For some, poaching was a supplement to their livelihoods but for others it was a source of income far greater than they would ever receive from their day jobs, for instance, John Lightwood made £12 selling 80 hares he had killed in 1764, "probably as much as he earned in a year as a labourer".[688] Draconian punishments for poaching were pursued with great zeal, thousands of people were convicted under the game laws, many of whom must have broken them in order to feed their families or protect their crops.

In the 1840s as many as one in four convictions in Suffolk were for poaching and as late as the 1880s it made up 22 percent of cases in parts of rural Oxfordshire. In England in 1843, 7.5 percent of all convictions were made under the game laws; in 1870 there were 10,580 prosecutions and the number of prosecutions peaked at almost 12,400 in 1877.[689]

For those agricultural workers for whom the occasional rabbit or bird supplemented their diet, the game laws were more than an inconvenience; they were a major hardship. The legal changes that meant that only some could enjoy the full fruits of the countryside were well summed up by the leader of the National Agricultural Labourers' Union, Joseph Arch. In 1873 he gave evidence to a parliamentary select committee on the game laws:

> The plain truth is, we labourers do not believe hares and rabbits belong to any individual, not any more than thrushes and blackbirds do... To see hares and rabbits running across his path is a very great temptation to many a man who has a family to feed...and so he may kill a hare or a rabbit when it passes his way, because his wages are inadequate to meet the demands on them, or from dire necessity, or just because he likes jugged hare as well as anybody else.[690]

Game laws were not simply about restricting hunting to the wealthy, or protecting their assets from the hungry poor. It was part of a process that was transforming the countryside through capitalist property relations.

The countryside was being parcelled up into quantifiable pieces of land. Alongside this, the animals that lived on, under or flew over the land were also taken away from the poor. Private property was sacrosanct and even the casual hunting of animals became a crime that had to be punished in order to enforce the new order. Christopher Hill, quoting a historian of poaching laws P B Munsche, points out that game effectively became the private property of "an entire social class". Hill continues by arguing this is associated with a transformation of the nature of labour. Game laws, according to Francis Bacon would "prevent persons of inferior rank from squandering that time which their station in life requireth to be more profitably employed". In other words poaching had to be stopped because it helped the lower classes avoid their real social role—labouring for the wealthy.[691] As we shall see, there were a whole number of traditional supplements to rural incomes that had to be similarly broken as part of the development of capitalism.

Enclosure and resistance

One history of enclosure defines it as:

> Land reform which transformed a traditional method of agriculture under systems of co-operation and communality in communally administered holdings, usually in large fields which were devoid of physical territorial boundaries, into a system of agricultural holding in severalty by separating with physical boundaries one person's land from that of his neighbours. This...disintegration and reformation of the open fields into individual ownership...declared void for all time communal obligations, privileges and rights.[692]

As a definition of what took place, this is adequate, but it doesn't explain what enclosure meant to communities—how it broke people from their traditional use of the land, destroyed communities and forced people off the land, turning them into wage labourers. As we have seen, enclosure took place in a variety of different ways, for different reasons. But from the 17th century onwards, enclosure took place for the benefit of landowners. From 1700 onwards, enclosure tended to occur through Act of Parliament, rather than the "enclosure by agreement" that had dominated previously.[693]

The outcome of the swath of enclosures that took place in the 150 years after the English Civil War was the transformation of British farming. Small farms continued to be an important part of agriculture up to the mid-19th century, but, as Michael Turner notes, this "obscured the other important feature of British farming, the emergence of 'the large farm using hired labour and working wholly for the market', that is the emergence of capitalist farming and the existence of a substantial rural proletariat".[694]

Karl Marx noted the "whole series of thefts, outrages and popular misery that accompanied the forcible expropriation of the people, from the last third of the fifteenth to the end of the eighteenth century". He poured scorn on those that could only see this as being about the improvement of land and noted how at the end of the process the "very memory" of the link between agricultural labourers and communal property had been destroyed. Marx went on to highlight the contemporary violence of similar processes in Scotland, collectively known as the Highland Clearances, which, like the enclosures in England, cleared people from the land.[695] Many of those forced off the land in Scotland ended up farming poor coastal soils, emigrating to the colonies or, like their English brethren, working in factories.

Enclosures took place on an enormous scale. Between 1793 and 1815, 2.9 million acres of land were enclosed by Act of Parliament—8.9 percent of England.[696] There were a variety of reasons why individual landowners might decide to enclose land. The general growth of the market for agricultural products encouraged the process, but there was also an ideological aspect to enclosure. The British ruling class saw the economic benefits, but also they saw it as having a modernising and improving effect on rural areas. In fact, for them it was similar to how they understood the role of the British Empire in "civilising" the globe. In 1803, Sir John Sinclair, President of the Board of Agriculture, made this explicit when he said: "Let us not be satisfied with the liberation of Egypt, or the subjugation of Malta, but let us subdue Finchley Common; let us conquer Hounslow Heath, let us compel Epping Forest to submit to the yoke of improvement".[697]

The sheer number of Parliamentary Acts is, according to E P Thompson, "testimony not only to the rage for improvement but also to the tenacity with which...fellows blocked the way to enclosure by agreement, holding out to the last for the old customary economy".[698]

Enclosure encouraged further enclosure. As people lost access to common land, or lost their own smaller farms, they became more dependent on the market for food and this further increased demand. While enclosed farms would not automatically have higher yields or lower costs than non-enclosed land, they allowed the owner more control over their agriculture and, as Micheal Žmolek has written, "enabled the tenant-farmer to escape the jurisdiction of customary law...to assert absolute individual rights of property over the land...to respond directly to market compulsions".[699] Enclosure too tended to favour larger land-owners—costs of enclosure (such as the erection of fences) were higher per unit of land the smaller the land being enclosed.[700] Thus enclosure was both a product of the development of capitalist agriculture and furthered that process, even if it was costly and its benefits were not as great as expected.

The loss of the historic rights and the ending of customary law were contested. Time and again, the length and breadth of the British Isles, men and women signed petitions, made collections to pay lawyers, pro-tested, burnt property, tore down hedges and fences and destroyed crops.

The rest of this book will look at the struggles of ordinary people in a rural world very different to that which had existed in England before the Civil War. This was a world where production was now dominated by the interests of a new bourgeois ruling class who were driven by the desire to maximise profits.

In 1688 William of Orange became King of England. His victory over James II was, in the words of Duncan Hallas, the "decisive culmination of the English bourgeois revolution". The next 150 years, Hallas continues, saw "the establishment of maritime English supremacy around the world, the conquest of India, the conquest of North America, and the first British Empire. But more than that, it was the period that saw the destruction of the English peasantry, to borrow Stalin's phrase, their liquidation as a class." For E P Thompson, 1688 was the date when the gentry "gained the day".[701]

Society was now fundamentally different to the old feudal order. As Hallas points out, William was king but his position was fundamentally different to the monarchs that had preceded the English Revolution.

> William's position in England was essentially not different from that in the Netherlands. He had to rule in collaboration with the existing ruling classes, he could not rule against them, he had no other base of support. In this peculiar way the bourgeoisie was established as the ruling class in a coherent sense. But the vast majority of MP's in the parliaments under William and right through to the first half of the nineteenth century were landowners.[702]

By 1850, agriculture had ceased to be the British economy's dominant form of industry. The change had been relatively rapid; according to Pamela Horn, in 1811 agriculture, forestry and fishing combined were responsible for over a third of gross national product, but by 1851 the same industries accounted for a fifth. Instead, "manufacturing, mining and building now held the lead". Manufacturing, particularly in the north, became increasingly dominated by larger scale enterprises, powered by water and, later, steam. The growth in rural manufacturing, based on the home or small workshop that took place in the 17th and 18th centuries was eventually undermined and destroyed by larger-scale factory manufacturing.[703]

One unusual example of this comes from the "free miners" of the Forest of Dean, who fiercely protected their communities from outside influence while paying the monarch fees for the right to mine coal and use the forest.[704] In the early 17th century, the miners had set down their rights in the unusually named "Book of Dennis". This listed their rights to make roads to facilitate their mines, or use timber for fuel and building materials. Outsiders, known to the mining communities as "foreigners", found it difficult to join, having to work a seven-year apprenticeship as opposed to a year and a day for someone born of a free miner. The miners also had the right to enforce their own laws through a Mine Law Court. This was exclusive to the forest and made up only of people from within the forest. This prevented the exploitation of the people and resources of the forest by capital and so, from the early 19th century onwards, the state began to undermine these rights. There was resistance, including the destruction of fences and hedges that enclosed forest land.[705] This reached a peak in 1831 at a time of widespread struggle for social reform, with mass protests. A notice issued to call free miners to a meeting was published by Warren James, the leader of the resistance. It was "for the purpose of Opening the Forest, and the Right of Common" and warned those who had opened up the forest for grazing "contrary to the Rights and Privileges of the Miner" that they had to "remove the same [animals] forthwith otherwise they will have their stock impounded without further notice".[706]

These protests were in defence of traditional rights against gradual attempts to open up lands to stock grazing in the interests of capitalist farmers. They involved thousands of people, including women and children and men who did not work as miners but lived in the forest.[707]

Over four days in June 1831, some 60 miles of fence were levelled and the miners let their own animals roam the previously enclosed lands. I have mentioned this example of resistance for several reasons. It shows the way that attempts to reassert or protect traditional rights were used to resist changes. It also shows the way that landowners and capitalists would use parliament to legislate away, or undermine, traditional and customary rights. The first Mines Act of 1838 subtly changed who could be a miner in the forest, for instance. But most importantly the example of the Forest of Dean shows how resistance to enclosure, and other associated changes, were often mass affairs involving hundreds, if not thousands. In 1831 in the Forest of Dean, Warren James divided his protesters into groups of between 50 and 300 and "accompanied by carts carrying provisions and cider" they dispersed into the forest to take down enclosures. This involved an enormous amount of labour, as this contemporary description shows.[708]

> Their mode of proceeding was this; they took a few yards at a time, which a large body rushed on, and by mere muscular strength overthrew. This appears still more worthy of note, from the thickness of the walls, which were mostly composed of clayey earth, in some places seven or eight feet think. Gorse of many years growth had strengthened these boundaries by shooting down roots into the earth of a prodigious size, and interlacing its branches in such a manner on the top, that it appeared to a spectator to require a work of time to effect its overthrow, and not that of two or three days. They first cut away some of the strongest of the roots and then proceeded in the way mentioned, tearing down all before them, and at the fall of each fresh piece giving loud and repeated cheers.[709]

The development of capitalist agriculture and capitalist relations in the countryside was fought at every step of the way and even when the vast majority of the rural population had become wage labourers working in an agriculture driven by the market, their resistance or the struggles to improve their conditions was often defined by the idea of customary rights. The struggles against enclosures themselves were often highly localised and frequently almost forgotten. E P Thompson, for instance, makes note of a "substantial" enclosure riot at Maulden in Bedfordshire involving 200 poor people, which is only known because of a letter mentioning it in War Office records.[710]

Such opposition was widespread and often violent, but was eventually defeated. In some areas the battles were successful, though these were often in urban areas. It is notable that almost all of the green areas that exist in London today for public enjoyment are the result of battles to defend the commons in the 18th and 19th centuries.[711]

The battles over customary rights—rights held to have been accepted locally from the distant past—were widespread. Whether against enclosure or access to common land or similar rights, these battles were extensive and frequently violent. In his *Customs in Common*, E P Thompson noted the way that these customary rights became a site for struggle between differing interests within which each participant would battle for their own advantage. Thompson writes: "Agrarian custom was never fact. It was ambience...a lived environment comprised of practices, inherited expectations, rules which both determined limits to usages and disclosed possibilities, norms and sanctions both of low and neighbour-hood pressures".[712]

Thus it would be impossible to sum up the whole range of customary rights covered, but they might include the right to graze an animal; to collect wood; to, as in the case of the Forest of Dean free miners, hold court on the behaviour of individuals within a community; or a right of way. These rights overlapped one another and were sometimes in conflict, and might benefit different sections of a community to a greater or lesser extent.

Take an early 18th century example from Loughton, near Waltham Forest in Essex. Here a petition came from the poor about their right to chop firewood from trees. This right was not disputed, but had been restricted to Mondays, which by coincidence was also the day the poorest "generally let themselves to work with the farmers that employ them for the whole week". The poor also complained that the lord and lady of the manor were cutting trees down, selling wood, overstocking the woods with animals (including creating rabbit warrens) and ploughing up land.[713] In other words, the landowners were doing what they wanted with the land, but the poor's traditional right to use it had been restricted to the only day when they were least able to use it.

Thus customary rights were part of the day-to-day struggle of rural life, even beyond the general trend of changes in the countryside introducing laws in the interest of capital. The rich had the law and lawyers to protect them and could call on the army or the militia if needed. The poor could petition or try to raise money for legal representation, but they could also use their force of numbers to break open gates and push over fences, kill animals, burn buildings and join mass protests. Both strategies were sometimes successful in defending rights and slowing the process of enclosure. Even the legal system and parliament could occasionally also be used to the advantage of ordinary people, however limited their resources, as this description from the *Annual Register* in 1767 quoted by John and Barbara Hammond demonstrates:

> On Tuesday evening a great number of farmers were observed going along Pall Mall with cockades in their hats. On enquiring the reason, it appeared they all lived in or near the parish of Stanwell in the county of Middlesex, and they were returning to their wives and families to carry

them the agreeable news of a Bill being rejected for inclosing the said common, which if carried into execution, might have been the ruin of a great number of families.

Records show that petitioners against the enclosure of common land at Stanwell were numerous, involving representation from 11 parishes across Middlesex. They claimed the commons and wasteland in Stanwell were part of Hounslow Heath over which they had right of pasture. The total land covered amounted to 2,126 acres, a significant area. While the petitioners were successful in 1767 with the second reading of the Bill, seeing it defeated 34 to 17 votes (the occasion of the march down Pall Mall), it was only a delay. Stanwell was enclosed 22 years later in 1789.[714]

Other rights were also tested in court. In 1788 the Court of Common Pleas judged that no person had a right to glean. However this did not make gleaning illegal; where it could be claimed as a local, customary right of the manor or village, it could continue. But the judgment made it easier for landowners who wanted to restrict the right, particularly when combined with the enclosure of land.[715]

Enclosure had other, less obvious impacts. For instance, the loss of land associated with cottages or the commons meant that families were no longer able to keep animals, particularly cows. This had a major impact on diet as milk was no longer easily available, particularly in the corn areas of south and south-eastern England. Any milk that was produced was sold to urban areas, for, in William Cobbett's words, "the idlers, the thieves, the prostitutes who are all taxeaters in the wens of Bath and London".[716] One consequence of the lack of milk was an increase in the consumption of tea, which provoked anger from rich commentators who saw the poor wasting their money on what was seen as a luxury product. It does not seem to have occurred to them that the tea drunk in a poverty stricken village was very different to that imbibed at a party in the wealthier parts of London. As one contemporary commented, tea drinking was not the cause, "but the consequence, of the distresses of the poor".[717]

It would be impossible to describe here the full range of protest that took place across the country through the 18th century against enclosure. As I have already noted, many of these were localised protests that involved hundreds of people but made little impression on the historical record. They cannot be separated from other protests against general trends in the countryside, such as attacks on deer parks and battles against gamekeepers by poachers. In Charnwood Forest between 1748 and 1751 there were sustained riots against the landowner's claims to "free warren", basically the right to hunt in the forest area. In Hampshire there was mass stealing of wood from forests.[718]

In the Midlands industrial workers often joined protests against enclosure such as in Leicester in 1754 and Burton upon Trent in 1771-1772. In 1757, people came out of the town at Shaw Hill in Wiltshire to level enclosures and at North Leigh Heath (1761), Warkworth (1765), Redditch (1772) and Malvern (1778) and there was mass opposition to the drainage of the fens in Lincolnshire from 1768 to 1773.[719]

Andrew Charlesworth concludes that for the period 1780-1831, in England,

> Despite the fact that the enclosure movement reached its peak during this period, only certain communities were prepared to take direct collective action, and then most of these protests occurred before 1800. There were protests that harked back to the collective action of the commoners and peasantry of the seventeenth century; in the fenland and its borders in East Anglia, enclosure in particular was opposed... In Oxfordshire from 1786 to 1831 the men of Otmoor opposed all attempts at enclosing and draining the moor. The most dramatic episode in the struggle over the moor was the '"possessioning" and demolishing every fence' on 7 September 1830 and the riot at St Giles Fair in Oxford...when the prisoners taken by the troops at Otmoor were rescued.[720]

We have already noted the large anti-enclosure protests by the free miners of the Forest of Dean in 1831, which should be supplemented with accounts of other workers who also fought for their rights and against enclosure, such as quarrymen at Headington near Oxford who "resisted the enclosure of a traditional passageway to the village burial grounds", fishermen who rioted in Suffolk and workers squatting on the fells in County Durham who attacked enclosure commissioners.[721] Battles over town fields continued in some areas well into the 19th century and I have already mentioned the struggles for London's parkland.

The 18th century did not see a mass, nationwide uprising by the rural population against the changes to their lives. The nature of enclosure, which took place village by village, area by area, common by common, encouraged localised struggle. While some areas did manage to defend customary rights, by and large, for the vast majority of the population, enclosure was a slow, but near unstoppable process.

Karl Marx saw this process as part of the "primitive accumulation" which laid the basis for the capitalist system. It did so by breaking the historic relationship that existed between people and the soil. As he summarised:

the theft of the common lands, the usurpation of feudal and clan property and its transformation into modern private property under circumstances of ruthless terrorism, all these things were just so many idyllic methods of primitive accumulation. They conquered the field for capitalist agriculture, incorporated the soil into capital, and created for the urban industries the necessary supplies of free and rightless proletarians.[722]

The development of capitalism transformed the lives of the original producers. They were driven from their lands and lost their homes and rights. Those that remained in the countryside became wage labourers. This is the context for the struggles that are described in the remainder of these pages.

Food riots

The transformation of the English countryside into a capitalist economy meant that for the first time in English history communities found that their needs might not be met by traditional means. Those who grew grain, ground it into flour and baked bread might no longer be willing to sell it to those closest to them, however hungry they might be, but instead sold it elsewhere for a higher price. Bulk buyers might have already paid for the crop and be looking to sell it in the city or even abroad.

Food riots to protest high prices or the export of food became increasingly common during the 18th century. According to Andrew Charlesworth, they were the main form of collective struggle by "town artisans and proto-industrial and industrial, that is non-agricultural workers". Rural labourers did take part in food riots, but usually only when they were initiated by other groups. Instead they tended, certainly in the later part of the 18th century, to focus their struggles around the question of wages rather than food prices. In part this was because farmers employing agricultural labourers avoided increases in wages because price fluctuations meant they might have to reduce wages quickly; wages tended to be supplemented through charity or the Poor Law. Thus struggles for wages became a key issue for the growing agricultural workers movement.[723]

As E P Thompson points out in his classic study of the "moral economy" and how people responded to this new situation, the "breakthrough of the new political economy of the free market was also the breakdown of the old moral economy of provision".[724] This is why we cannot understand the food riots of the 18th century simply in terms of hungry people demanding food for themselves and their families, nor were they simply criminal behaviour. We must also understand them in terms of a response to economic changes and a struggle for a fair relationship between producer and consumer. This was not simply about prices (though that was frequently a large stimulus to riots), but also about how and where food was sold.

This is not to suggest that before the development of capitalism food riots did not take place; people frequently did riot from hunger, from anger at profiteering and so on.[725] The question of the food riot and its causes was a perennial issue for Tudor and Stuart governments.

Successive monarchs had attempted to manage food distribution. For example, in 1587, legislation was passed under Queen Elizabeth I to deal with food shortages in England. This was an attempt to manage food distribution and avoid riots and disturbances. It was supposed to ensure that local authorities knew who had grain and where it was stored. The idea was to make sure that those who needed it—for food, brewing and so on—could access it. Strict regulations covered the sale of grain: only in open market and while supervised. The first hour was reserved for the poor, after whom those who needed larger orders (greater than four bushels) could buy. Other rules governed the type of bread and the quality that could be baked, prevented the buying and reselling of corn and parishes that were short could call on their neighbours for help. In part this latter agreement was to prevent people leaving their village and labour to find food. These rules also targeted those who were considered the root cause of the problem: "engrossers of corn be carefully seen unto and severely punished according to the law". Repeat offenders were threatened with "severe punishment for the better ensample [example] of others".[726]

Until the 1770s, there was a "paternalist model" of food sales. In this, sales were supposed to be direct to the consumer. Food should only be sold in the market where the exchange could be managed. The poor went first, then the larger purchasers. Millers and bakers were seen as "servants of the community, working not for a profit but only for a fair allowance".[727] This model began to break down through the 18th century with farmers finding ways to try and get around the older regulations. Thompson quotes a 1766 letter about practices at Chippenham:

> He himself sent to market for a quarter of wheat, and though there were many loads there, and it soon after the market bell rang, wherever his agent applied, the answer was "'Tis sold"...to avoid the penalty of the law, they bring it to market, yet the bargain is made before, and the market is but a farce.[728]

As Thompson points out, this could provoke riot as in 1757 when the population of Oxford "seized and divided" up corn "suspected to have been bought by sample, and only brought to the market to save appearances".[729] In Salisbury in 1795 an anonymous letter to the mayor showed how people were angry at the profiteering of the farmer and merchants:

> Gentlemen of the Corporation I pray you put a stop to that practice which is made use of in our Markits by Rook and other carriers in your giving them the Liberty to Scower the Market of every thing so as the Inhabitance cannot buy a single Artickel without going to the Dealers for it and Pay what Extortionat price they think proper and even Domineer over the Peopel as thow they was not Whorthy to Look on them.

The letter continues by complaining of the butchers' practice of taking away whole carcasses of meat and selling them later, instead demanding that they "cut it up in the Markit and sarve the Town first".[730] This example combines a struggle for a more traditional organisation of food distribution with righteous class anger at those who "domineer" over the people. There are many examples of anonymous letters that threaten the wealthy with violence of one form or another designed to force charity and other support in hard times. Some of these letters display an unexpected venom:

> Lord Buckingham...who died the other day had Thirty Thousand Pounds, yearly For setting his Arse in the House of Lords and doing nothing. [Norwich, 1793]

> We don't care a Dam for them fellows that Call Themselves Gentlemen Soldiers But in our opinion they[y] Look moore like Monkeys riding on Bears. [Odiham, Hampshire, 1800][731]

We shall see similar examples later from the era of the machine breakers. The gentry were supposed to benevolently look after the poor in their times of need but, as these letters show, the poor were not naive enough to believe that. While the threats might have been designed to force action to deal with hunger, or high prices, they were only part of a process. Thompson points to the "counter-theatre" of some of the protest actions such as people parading around the markets or "rough music". In one case a fisherman, John Hart, carried around a market by several hundred people in Harwich who were "drumming a ridiculous Tune of Roundheaded Cuckolds &c... [Hart] came to the Mayor's...door and made signs with his hands intimating that We might kiss his Arse".[732]

Readers will note here similarities with the traditional village "Skimington" collective punishments mentioned earlier. But when such theatrical protests were not enough, the crowds were not afraid of taking direct action—burning machinery or buildings, destroying crops, completely smashing roof tiles on homes, all formed part of mass protests. Thompson suggests that these actions formed part of a "gentry-crowd reciprocity" whereby the majority of the poor population were prepared to resist and riot if they needed to, but were unlikely to go beyond "the parameters of gentry hegemony".[733]

Direct action like this might not have been about simply forcing the rich to provide for the poor. Crowds frequently took things a step further by confiscating goods and reselling them at what was considered a fair or moral price. Again, we need to distinguish this from simple criminal behaviour; many examples exist of events like this where the money raised, and sometimes even the sacks that held the grain or flour, were returned to the owner. In other words, food rioters did not steal food and distribute it for free, but rather they took it and sold it at what they considered a fair price. Sometimes this meant the crowd actually acting to enforce the law itself, or at least an interpretation of the law, in the absence of action from the authorities. Thompson quotes an example from 1766 in Gloucestershire, reported by the sheriff, a "gentleman clothier". Rioters

> went...to a farmhouse and civilly desired that they wou'd thresh out and bring to market their wheat and sell it for five shillings per bushel which being promised, and some provisions given them unasked for, they departed without the least violence or offence.

But such protests might include different forms of riot, sometimes considerate to the owners, others less so. The same sheriff reports later a mob raised by the "blowing of horns" and involving the "lowest of the people", who cut open bags of flour, gave it away and destroyed corn. But then he could say about the very same crowd:

> They visited Farmers, Millers, Bakers and Hucksters shops, selling corn, flower, bread, cheese, butter and bacon at their own prices. They returned in general the produce [the money] to the proprietors or in their absence left the money for them; and behaved with great regularity and decency where they were not opposed, with outrage and violence where they was: but pilfered very little, which to prevent, they will not now suffer Women and boys to go with them.[734]

On other occasions though food rioters did not compensate the owners or punished them in other ways:

> There was great rioting here on Friday last [September 1766]... They took a wagonload of cheese out of one of the storehouses to the market cross and began to sell it by weight, but that was very soon over, so they sold large cheeses for 1s 6d and 1s per cheese, but that also soon ceased, for the mob took it without money or price: they carried a cartload of cheese away and only carried the owner three shillings for it. It was all deposed of at the open cross. There were more wagonloads of wheat at the cross on that day than ever I saw at any one time before, and oats also for I gave 10s for one bag of Poland oats.[735]

Near Wolverhampton in 1800, a dairyman taking butter to market was stopped by a group of women who asked the price he was charging for butter. When hearing it was 18 pence a pound, "they immediately seized him and besmeared him all over with his butter and then rolled him in a ditch".[736]

In the view of those who celebrated it, the new capitalist order was supposed to prevent shortages and hunger. The free market was supposed to internally compensate for problems—abundant crops in one part of the country would supply areas of shortage through rising prices. Farmers might hold back some of their crop to sell when prices were higher, effectively rationing the food through the year. All of this could only be facilitated by removing state intervention.[737]

In his classic of free market capitalism, *The Wealth of Nations*, Adam Smith specifically uses corn as an example of how the free market, correctly used, can feed a hungry population and ensure good profits. It is in the interest of the corn merchant, writes Smith,

> to raise the price of his corn as high as the real scarcity of the season requires, and it can never be his interest to raise it higher. By raising the price he discourages the consumption, and puts everybody more or less, but particularly the inferior ranks of people, upon thrift and good management... If by not raising the price high enough he discourages the consumption so little that the supply of the season is likely to fall short of the consumption of the season, he not only loses a part of the profit which he might otherwise have made, but he exposes the people to suffer before the end of the season, instead of the hardships of a dearth, the dreadful horrors of a famine.[738]

Yet the reality was not the rational planning of prices and distribution but a rush to maximise profits. Those who were hungry acted in their interests and fought the logic of the market. They did not simply riot against high prices, but also organised to prevent food leaving the areas where it was needed. As one 1783 notice in Carlisle chillingly warned two corn dealers:

> Peter Clemeseson & Moses Luthart this is to give you Warning that you must Quit your unlawfull Dealing or Die and be Damed your buying the Corn to starve the Poor Inhabitants of the City and Soborbs of Carlisle to send to France and get the Bounty Given by the Law for taking the Corn out of the Country but by the Lord God Almighty we will give you Bounty at the Expence of your Lives you Damed Roagues.[739]

The years 1795 to 1800, says Thompson, "saw the efflorescence of a regional consciousness once more... Roads were blockaded to prevent export from the parish. Wagons were intercepted and unloaded in the towns through which they passed. The movement of grain by night-convoy assumed the proportions of a military operation... Threats were made to destroy the canals... Ships were stormed at the ports. The miners at Nook Colliery near Haverfordwest threatened to close the estuary at a narrow point".[740]

Historians have often argued that food riots were led and organised by women. Thompson concluded, for instance, that: "Initiators of the riots were, very often, the women." In their famous history, *The Village Labourer*, the Hammonds called 1795, a year of great food shortages and large-scale food riots, the "revolt of the housewives".[741] Many accounts of food riots do highlight the central role of women. Taking examples from 1795 quoted by the Hammonds, at Aylesbury, "a numerous mob, consisting chiefly of women, seized on all the wheat that came to market, and compelled the farmers to whom it belonged to accept of such prices as they thought proper to name." In Fordingbridge Sarah Rogers served three months hard labour for taking butter to sell at a cheaper price. In Bath women stormed a boat carrying wheat and flour and refused to let the ship sail with the food. The Hammonds also noted a contemporary report of a riot that "destroyed two mills" as having such a great number of petticoats" that men were likely taking part, dressed as women.[742]

Thompson's famous article on the moral economy from which his conclusion about women initiating food riots is taken was followed by a critical piece by John Bohstedt, a historian of riots. Bohstedt argued, in contrast to Thompson and the Hammonds, that "food riots were not a distinctly feminine province"..."women typically joined men in food riots. Since food riots were the chief form of plebeian politics in such towns, women's co-operation with men is much more significant than the monopoly suggested by the older view".[743]

In Bohstedt's view, women and men (and children) "all acted together in food riots because they all acted together in household production. Men were expected to defend their families' living-standards as much as women".[744] This, he argues, is because the dominant form of production in pre-industrial societies was the household economy in which both genders took part in production (within the household and in small manufacturing workshops) so that both women and men took part in riots. To quote Bohstedt: "Women's essential role in winning family subsistence gave them the status to join men in defending it".[745]

This position was vigorously critiqued by Thompson who defended his original essay. He describes food riots as evolving events that might be initiated by a particular group, which others join and some leave. There would be all sorts of factors governing how an individual event would run its course, such as how the authorities responded to the riot, for instance. Discussing the "Guildhall riots" of 1740, Thompson points out that:

> Women contributed to both physical and verbal episodes of violence, breaking into granaries and one woman going down on her knees in front of magistrates and crying out 'Blood for blood!'. The authorities came down most heavily upon the women who had unloaded wheat from a boat in Stockton, whereas in Newcastle they selected the pitmen for indictment and passed over the women.
>
> This shows whole communities in action, with one sex or the other coming into prominence as each assumes a different part.[746]

Thompson concludes that the prominent role of women within certain riots was certainly to do with their role in the household economy, but also because one of the key roles of women in the household was purchasing and producing food so they were "especially sensitive to price and quality". In other words, their involvement was heightened because of their gendered labour, "not because gender roles were almost indistinguishable". Thompson continues to critique Bohstedt for downplaying this role, over-emphasising the role of women within the household manufacturing economy. But this, concludes Thompson, leads to Bohstedt suggesting that "women expressed their solidarity with men" rather than being key figures that initiated, led food riots and were frequently punished by the courts for their roles.[747]

The food riot was a key part of the struggles of both rural and urban workers throughout the 18th century. But as the century progressed, there was a gradual change in where and how food was sold. The market became less important and food riots declined. This affected the involvement of women in these battles, but Thompson still concludes that: "no other issue commanded women's support so wholeheartedly and consistently".[748]

The rise of the capitalist mode of production increasingly meant that communities had to struggle to ensure that they had food in times of shortages and that the food for sale in the market was at an acceptable price. Women were absolutely central to those struggles and frequently faced heavy fines or imprisonment for their actions. On occasion, they faced down armed forces sent to protect the profits and private property of the manufacturers and farmers. They were part of creating an alternative to the new world of profiteering without regard for the needs of communities and people. This alternate "moral economy" is, in the words of E P Thompson, "summoned into being in resistance to the economy of the 'free market'."[749]

The decline of the food riot as a key form of class struggle at the end of the 18th century is associated with the growth of other forms of collective resistance, such as wage negotiations, strikes and the formation of trade unions. This can be linked to the "onset of industrial cycles not related to bad harvests and stoppages due to wartime blockages of trade but to the inner transformations of capitalist development".[750]

The rural world too was changing and there were new forms of struggle beginning to take centre stage. The scale of the change for the mass of the rural population is summed up well by comments from a French traveller to England in the 1860s, Hippolyte Taine, who wrote:

> The large property increases, and the small one diminishes. At the close of the last century, Arthur Young wrote: "I do not know a single cottage to which a piece of land is not attached." Moreover, the poor villagers had some fowls, and a pig on the common. But, by the Enclosure Acts, the commons are being constantly reduced in size; hence the peasant has no longer the resource of fowls and pigs; having sold his bit of land, he can count upon his arms alone, and he lets them for hire. In the purely agricultural districts it appears that the wages are from seven to eight shillings a week, and not twelve, as I have found them here. To add to this, the villager lets for hire the arms of his wife and of his children: one sees bands of them hoeing root-plants, of which the culture extends itself unceasingly. Agriculture being conducted on a large scale, and having become a scientific form of industry, has had the counter-effect of introducing into the country districts the rule, the monotony, the miseries of manufacture.[751]

8

The rise of the rural proletariat

BY 1800 English agriculture was in the words of the Hammonds, "capitalist and specialised".[752] As we have seen, the process of enclosure had robbed the rural poor of their land and their support mechanisms. Rights were taken away at the same time as the wealthy congratulated themselves on making the poor less lazy. The right to glean was taken away in 1788, mostly because the judges believed that it encouraged the poor to be lazy or to steal. Studies suggest that gleaning meant far more to the rural population than a few extra loaves of bread; in one example quoted by the Hammonds, it was the equivalent of six or seven weeks' wages. Yet the loss of these rights and the ability to get food and materials from common lands was in no way compensated for by increases in wages.[753]

Village labourers now relied entirely on wages to feed and support their families, but these had a lower purchasing power than the wages he had "supplemented by his own produce". One estimate of wage changes is that between 1760 and 1813, wages rose by 60 percent, but the price of wheat rose by 130 percent.[754] Poverty and hunger were commonplace in rural England. The greatest minds of the time debated earnestly how to deal with the question. All sorts of plans were concocted to alleviate poverty, including dietary improvements, a minimum wage system and attempts to reduce time spent in the tavern through the provision of allotments.

The wealthy, particularly the large landowners, worried that increased wages would be impossible to reduce in the future. As the rich and powerful struggled to come up with an answer that fitted their needs and ensured that labourers and their families were able to buy enough bread to be fit for work, or to survive until harvest time, a meeting in a pub came up with a solution that fitted the needs of the ruling class.

In May 1795, local magistrates met in the Pelican Inn in Speenhamland, Berkshire, now part of Newbury. There they came up with a solution which was to be generalised across the country. It is notable that this meeting took place in the same year that food rioting was at a peak—it was not the result of altruism, but rather the country-wide struggle being waged by the hungry population. The execution of Louis XVI, King of France, in the Revolution the other side of the channel a few months previously no doubt also focused minds in the Pelican.

Simply put, the meeting agreed that wages should be linked to the price of food, particularly bread. Farmers would increase or decrease wages as the price changed and any shortfall was to be made up by the parish. In theory it was a great idea, but in practice farmers used the opportunity to keep the wages as low as possible and make the parish subsidise wages. The Act was passed nationally as an amendment to the pre-existing Poor Laws, but was implemented in various ways. Some parishes offered free or subsidised food to top up workers' wages.

Poverty was being made worse in rural communities not simply as a result of the move towards wage labour, but also because technological developments were changing the nature of work. If you read accounts of agriculture in 19th and early 20th century England a constant theme is the loss of traditional knowledge as machinery transforms much rural work. There were still times where large amounts of labour power were needed—such as harvest time—but at other times there was a perennial problem with unemployment, under-employment and seasonal labour. One effect of this was that landowners could rely on a pool of unemployed to undermine strikes or replace troublemakers. As with all the changes to the rural economy, the question of technology was also contested. Workers, as we shall see, frequently destroyed machines to defend jobs. But this was rarely successful for any length of time. Nor was the issue simply agricultural work—changes hit rural industries as well. Inventions such as the flying shuttle (1733) or the spinning jenny (1765) would transform the cotton industry. In the 18th century, cotton weaving was a rural cottage industry:

> The workshop of the weaver was a rural cottage, from which when he was tired of sedentary labour he could sally forth into his little garden, and with the spade or the hoe tend its culinary productions. The cotton wool which was to form his weft was picked clean by the fingers of his younger children, and was carded and spun by the older girls assisted by his wife, and the yarn was woven by himself assisted by his sons.[755]

By 1830, the skilled work of hand-spinning had all but disappeared and while some weaving was still done in homes, increasingly, along with all the preparatory processes, weaving was being done in factories with power-looms, often using child labour.[756]

The vast majority of workers who were forced from the countryside into urban factories were not skilled. In part the Luddite revolt and similar protests were against the de-skilling that replaced skilled workers with less-skilled ones (often including women and children) using new technology. Indeed, mill owners deliberately sought out cheap, unskilled labour like this to maximise their profits. At Quarry Bank Mill near Manchester, more than half of the workers between 1784 and 1840 were children. They were recruited from the poorhouse and worked there for seven years, often facing brutal punishments for transgressions such as stealing an apple. In 1833, according to a historian of the cotton industry, "36 percent of workers in Lancashire cotton factories were younger than sixteen".[757]

At the end of the 18th century the British state acted to strengthen its repression of workers' struggle and to restrict the ability of workers to organise. In 1795, the year of the food riots, gatherings of 50 people or more were made illegal. In 1799 and 1800 the infamous Combination Acts banned trade unions and between 1792 and 1815 the government built 155 barracks to better police the workers.[758]

Machine breaking

The destruction of private property had a long tradition in rural communities protesting against changes to their circumstances. The destruction of enclosure fences and hedges was often part of mass protest action involving hundreds if not thousands of men and women. Poaching, the burning of hayricks or barns, the dismantling of equipment and even the maiming of animals were also tactics used by groups of rural workers who wanted to send a message to the local landowner and authorities.

At two points in the 19th century the systematic destruction of machinery by crowds of workers reached levels that terrified the authorities. Machine breaking was not new, but in the years after 1811 and again in the 1830s it reached new heights. Machines were seen as taking away jobs, but they had other impacts as well. As John Archer has noted, machinery also limited the opportunity for labourers to steel grain during the harvest—a Suffolk folksong makes the point: "the old sow will mourn the throshin machine".[759] Farmers also liked machines that reduced waste, though the labourers would know this meant less left behind for gleaning.

There were drastic responses from the government including the deployment of the army to the towns and villages of England and the mass punishment of hundreds of workers, urban and rural, who were part of the protest movements. Today, these movements are best known by names of the imaginary figures who led them—General Ned Ludd and Captain Swing.* While these names were unlikely to have belonged to any single figure, threatening letters bearing their signatures, confessions from prisoners or overheard whispers reported by spies were enough to convince the authorities that countrywide rebellion was taking place. In the atmosphere after the French Revolution, and during the wars with Napoleon, as well as the later movements for political reform, this seemed an all too real possibility.

Luddism, which began in 1811, was a far more urban movement than the Swing rebellion, which the Hammonds called the "last labourers' revolt". As such we will only briefly look at the story of Luddism in order to understand the context to the mass rural machine-breaking that took place nearly 20 years later.

Luddism

> The poor cry aloud for bread
> Prince Regent shall lose his head
> And all the rich who oppress the poor,
> In a little time shall be no more,
> With deep regret, I write these things,
> They'll come to pass in spite of Kings.[760]

One of the great tragedies when trying to understand the Luddites is that the name has become synonymous with the rejection of technological innovation. This was certainly not how the workers who took part in this resistance saw it. By and large their actions were driven by the need to protect their conditions and their jobs.

The context of the Luddite rebellion was a huge squeeze on workers' living conditions. The movement peaked in 1812, which, like the three preceding years, was marked by a wet summer and a poor harvest. Prices rose accordingly, with 1812 seeing wheat's "highest annual average...during the Napoleonic Wars". In addition, the population was growing rapidly— by 14 percent between 1801 and 1811, from 10,472,048 to 11,911,644.[761]

This, along with changing technological practices in manufacturing, was putting pressure on workers and their jobs. This provoked protest and

---

* The origin of the names is unclear. In 1811, the *Nottingham Review* claimed that Ned Ludd was an apprentice who refused to work hard and was whipped, so he destroyed his knitting frame with a hammer in retaliation. Hammond and Hammond, 1995c, p259. An excellent resource for Luddite history is the website created for the 200th anniversary, www.luddites200.org.uk

eventually the destruction of equipment in defence of conditions.* These protests were not opposing machinery in general, but specific changes that would increase unemployment or reduce wages. Take the example of the wool industry. Wool had been a staple of the economy of the British Isles for centuries. Its manufacture and processing involved tens of thousands of workers across the country. The development of mechanised spinning machines helped to improve production, because spinning was a slow point in the process of turning raw wool into material. As the historian Robert Reid has pointed out, when the process was entirely without machinery, "a skilled weaver could weave in a day as much yarn as twenty spinners could spin by hand in a day". So spinning machines, and other technologies such as the foot treadle, which allowed "five spinners to supply one weaver", were invented to fill this gap. Other machines swiftly followed, such as Edmund Cartwright's power loom, which enabled smaller numbers of workers to produce larger volumes (of often lower standard) cloth.[762] Inventions like these helped usher in the factory system as tens, then hundreds, of spinning machines were brought together in single buildings.

However it is produced—by hand or by machine—woollen cloth needs to be finished to make it comfortable to wear. This was a highly skilled task, which involved the combing of the material and the trimming of the raised "nap" of wool. Traditionally this final, delicate task, was done by skilled workers using huge pairs of metal sheers that might weigh 50 pounds, the larger and heavier the shears, and the stronger and more skilful the labourer, the better the finish. The sheers were also used to crop the cloth, cutting it to size. Changes to the shears in the 17th century made the work much easier, but it was the mechanisation of the process that transformed the industry. As Reid points out, in the case of cropping it drastically reduced the total work: "One of these new machines could now crop in eighteen hours what a skilled cropper using hand shears took eighty-eight hours to do." Similarly, the amount of work raising the nap a skilled man had previously done in a week of 88 hours, was now done by "a man and a boy in twelve hours".[763]

Karl Marx wrote about how resistance to machinery was part of the fight against capitalist exploitation:

> The struggle between the capitalist and the wage-labourer starts with
> the existence of the capital-relation itself. It rages throughout the period

---

* It should be emphasised that this did not begin with the Luddites. For instance, a proposed 400-loom steam powered factory in Manchester had barely begun having the machines installed before it was destroyed, two decades before the Luddites. See Žmolek, 2014, p456.

of manufacture. But only since the introduction of machinery has the worker fought against the instrument of labour itself, capital's material mode of existence. He is in revolt against this particular form of the means of production because it is the material foundation of the capitalist mode of production.[764]

In his discussion on machine-breaking, Marx notes various examples of this sort of class struggle, including the destruction of a water-powered wool-shearing machine by 100,000 workers in 1758, but then points out that it would take the experience of Luddism, and other similar rebellions, before workers "learnt to distinguish between machinery and its employment by capital". Marx continues by noting the "chronic misery" for the workers forced into competition with machinery.[765]

The Luddite risings began in February 1811 in the Nottinghamshire village of Arnold with an attack on knitting frames. Key parts of the machinery were removed and "hidden in local churches". Similar events against particular employers continued throughout the year with hundreds of frames broken at dozens of villages throughout 1811 and the following year in Nottinghamshire and the Midlands. Of 30,000 frames in England, 85 percent were in the Midlands.[766]

The protest movement reached new heights in November when a mass attack, led by some calling themselves "Ned Lud", was made against a manufacturer, Edward Hollingsworth. Hundreds of workers, from several villages, attacked his house and workshop. Hollingsworth had barricaded his house and fired on the attacking crowds who were trying to break the doors down. Shots were returned from the crowd, and one worker, John Wesley, was killed. Once they had broken in, they did not kill Hollinsgworth or any other defenders, instead only destroying knitting frames. Rather than random destruction, the crowd targeted specific machines, the wider frames that produced "broader, cheaper cloth". Wesley's funeral became an occasion for a mass, peaceful protest demonstrating the general support that there was for the Luddites in towns and villages.[767]

Similar events took place repeatedly over the next weeks and eventually the government was forced to station thousands of soldiers in the Midlands, in addition to local militias, to try and keep the peace. The *Leeds Mercury*, an important newspaper for workers in the period whose reports were often read aloud in workshops, commented in December 1811 that: "The insurrectional state to which this country has been reduced for the last month has no parallel in history, since the troubled days of Charles the First".[768]

The start of 1812 saw the unrest spread into Yorkshire, Lancashire and Cheshire. Threatening letters were sent to manufacturers and factory owners and while many protests targeted individual, small workplaces, there were also large attacks.

A sense of the level of organisation of the Luddites can be obtained by the following account from the *Leeds Mercury* of an attack on 22 February 1812 in Marsh, near Huddersfield. The Luddites

> assemble with as much privacy as possible, at the place marked out for attack, and divide themselves into two parties, the more daring and expert of which enter the premises, provided with proper instruments for the work of destruction, which they accomplish with astonishing secrecy and despatch. The other party remain conveniently stationed at the outside of the building, to keep off all intruders or to give the alarm... As soon as the work of destruction was completed, the Leader drew up his men, called over the roll, each man answering to a particular number instead of his name; they then fired off their pistols...gave a shout and marched off in regular military order. They do not appear to have done any mischief besides breaking the machinery; and one of the party having asked the Leader what they should do with one of the Proprietors, he replied, not hurt a hair of his head; but should they be under the necessity of visiting him again, they would not shew him any mercy.[769]

On 11 April 1812, hundreds of workers attacked the Rawfolds Mill owned by William Cartwright, in the Spen Valley in Yorkshire's West Riding.[770] The Hammonds describe Cartwright as "a man of courage and resolution, but of a cold and unsympathetic temperament". He certainly prepared his defences well and the attackers were fought off, sustaining serious injuries. The battle was intense: cries from the attacking workers of "Bang Up!", "Murder Them!" and "Pull Down the Door" were met with a barrage of gunfire. Some 140 musket balls were fired at the workers in what must have been a terrifying 20 minutes of fighting. Cartwright had even prepared containers of sulphuric acid to use. The attackers included workers from "Halifax, Huddersfield, Liversedge, Heckmonwike, Gomersal, Birstall, Cleckheaton" and elsewhere; reinforcements from Leeds arrived late but were scared off by the sound of gunfire.*

Two injured workers were left behind, Samuel Hartley, a 24-year-old cropper, and John Booth, a 19-year-old apprentice. Both were in agony from serious wounds. Cartwright seized the opportunity to quiz them

---

* One soldier who refused to fire was court-martialled and received 300 lashes in punishment.

about Luddite organisation and leadership, hoping to break the wall of solidarity that existed in support of the machine-breakers. Cartwright refused medical assistance for the wounded until a crowd gathered hours later and he allowed them to be taken away to the Star Inn at Roberttown, where soldiers prevented an angry crowd from entering. The *Leeds Mercury*'s account claims that help was given "with all possible despatch", yet this was long after the fighting had stopped.

The men's cries when they were eventually treated by a surgeon (Booth's leg was described as being "shattered to atoms" by a bullet and had to be amputated) led many to believe that they were being tortured for information. Whether this was true in this case is not known, but we do know that other suspects were beaten by the militia and the army.

Neither Booth nor Hartley would survive their wounds, but neither broke their vows of silence or gave any information away. Famously Booth was supposed to have called a parson, Hammond Roberson, over. The Reverend Roberson had arrived late on the scene of the battle and was probably keen to help the authorities with information. "Can you keep a secret?" Booth asked Roberson. When Roberson responded "I can", Booth replied "So can I" and died without betraying his comrades. Hartley also died the next day.

The *Leeds Mercury* felt justified in adding a comment addressed to the Luddities following its account of the attack on Rawfolds Mill:

> Let them reflect deeply on the fate of Hartley and Booth—let them recollect that they themselves may be the next victims, and let them stop in this desperate career before it is too late.

The *Mercury* then reported that a coroner's inquest had recorded a verdict of justifiable homicide in the case of Hartley and Booth and noted that none of the other wounded had been found. Despite offers of £1,000 for information, no one came forward. In the weeks following the Rawfolds attack there were major disturbances in cities such as Manchester and Sheffield, including food riots and breakages.

Across the north and the Midlands thousands of workers were taking part in riots, protests and machine-breaking. All in all, thousands of frames and other machines were destroyed. They had the support of the vast majority of their communities and the local authorities were unable to do anything to prevent the attacks. Few in government understood the reasons for the disturbances. In part they were distracted by events on the continent, where England was fighting a war with Revolutionary France.

On 27 February, the young Lord Byron made his maiden speech in the House of Lords on the occasion of the first reading of a bill making machine-breaking punishable by death. Byron's theme was the failure of the government to address the root cause of the rebellion: poverty. His words were spread to the affected areas.

> But all the cities you have taken, all the armies which have retreated before your leaders, are but paltry subjects of self-congratulation, if your land divides against itself, and your dragoons and executioners must be let loose against your fellow-citizens. You call these men a mob, desperate, dangerous, and ignorant; and seem to think that the only way to quiet the 'Bellua multorum capitum' [the many-headed monster, that is the mass of ordinary people] is to lop off a few of its superfluous heads. But even a mob may be better reduced to reason by a mixture of conciliation and firmness, than by additional irritation and redoubled penalties. Are we aware of our obligations to a *mob!* It is the mob that labour in your fields, and serve in your houses—that man your navy, and recruit your army—that have enabled you to defy all the world,—and can also defy you, when neglect and calamity have driven them to despair. You may call the people a mob, but do not forget that a mob too often speaks the sentiments of the people. And here I must remark with what alacrity you are accustomed to fly to the succour of your distressed allies, leaving the distressed of your own country to the care of Providence or—the parish… And at this moment, when thousands of misguided but most unfortunate fellow-countrymen are struggling with the extremes of hardship and hunger, as your charity began abroad, it should end at home. A much less sum—a tithe of the bounty bestowed on Portugal…would have rendered unnecessary the tender mercies of the bayonet and the gibbet. But doubtless our funds have too many foreign claims to admit a prospect of domestic relief—though never did such objects demand it. I have traversed the seat of war in the peninsula; I have been in some of the most oppressed provinces of Turkey; but never, under the most despotic of infidel governments, did I behold such squalid wretchedness as I have seen since my return, in the very heart of a Christian country.[771]

Few others in parliament cared. The scale of the rebellion was enormous, and the government's use of force was overwhelming, after all as, one mill owner said: "If more military is not sent into the country…they will not be called upon to protect it, but will be required to reconquer it".[772]

Thousands of soldiers were sent to the rebellious areas with unprecedented powers. General Maitland, who had overall command, declared that what was needed was "Fear, and Fear alone".[773] Small groups of "commandos" were set up, cavalry forces or light infantry that could swiftly deploy to villages and terrorise anyone organising or protesting.[774] In addition, networks of spies were deployed. These men often played roles closer to that of an *agent provocateur*, encouraging the signing of illegal oaths, spreading news from elsewhere and, perhaps most problematically for the workers, encouraging a belief that there was a widespread, well-organised and well-funded revolutionary movement that was planning to overthrow the government.

Paying their informants well for information, and receiving further embellished tales in return, the ruling class became convinced that there was indeed a revolutionary plot. In part this explains the severity of their response to the Luddities and the heavy punishments inflicted. But despite the best efforts of their informers and spies, the authorities were not able to find definitive proof of any such plan. Clearly there were individuals drawing revolutionary conclusions, and no doubt some hoped to make this a reality. In early May 1812 posters in Nottingham "spoke of making 'foul blood, run clear and fine of Tyrants great and small!' and included the line 'Make [Prime Minister] Perceval your aim'".[775] But these were isolated incidents. The government was not able to find the stockpiles of weapons it had been told about and while it was true that there was some level of networking between different areas, this was not the action of a concerted group of revolutionaries planning an uprising.

This is not to underestimate the scale of the crisis for the ruling class. While there is some truth in historian Malcolm Thomis's description of Lancashire Luddism as a "shapeless protest movement [which] lacked the precise aims to permit the registering of measurable success", this downplays the levels of organisation that did exist.[776] With a major war in Europe and war brewing with America, economic downturn and enormous anger among the working classes, the situation was ripe for an uprising. Tens of thousands of workers were part of Luddite actions, food riots or other protests. Petitions for the reform of parliament or economic relief were popular and there was a degree of passive support from small manufacturers who were threatened by the growth of large workplaces.

On 16 January 1813, 14 convicted Luddites were executed outside York Castle. In his summing up at the end of the trial the week before, the judge was concerned with the way that the accused had used the swearing of illegal oaths to build a network of activists who could lead machine-breaking protests. He found one of the accused, John Eadon, guilty of being "long practised in administering these oaths. To the person whom you administered it, you gave instructions to get that oath by heart, that he might qualify himself to be the administrator... you fully explained to what it was intended to bind the parties, not scrupling to admit that the intention of it was to overturn the very government of this Country".[777]

The trials at York included charges for a number of crimes, including the administration of illegal oaths, the destruction of property, the taking of arms or money and the murder of William Horsfall, a woollen manufacturer. Those found guilty of illegal oaths were sentenced to seven years' transportation. Seventeen others, found guilty of the other crimes, were sentenced to death at York, including five for the attack on Rawfolds Mill. The three found guilty of killing Horsfall had already been executed, so the remaining 14 were hanged together the weekend after the trial. The judge, Baron Thompson, is supposed to have joked when asked if they all should be hanged on one beam that "they would hang more comfortably on two".[778]

The death sentence was used both as punishment and to terrorise others who might consider swearing oaths to form confederations and protest in the future. As the judge said:

> It is of infinite importance, however, that no mercy should be shown to any of you... It is of importance also, that the sentence of the Law for such evil works should be very speedily executed, and it is but right to tell you that you have but a very short time to remain in this world. It is to be hoped that the forfeit of your lives, which you are about to pay, may operate as an example to all who have witnessed your trial and your condemnation, and to all without these walls, to whom the tidings of your fate may come, to be cautious how they engage in any such illegal confederacies, as you have unfortunately entered into. For they may rest assured, that it never will be in their power to say... 'Hitherto will I go, and no further.' They cannot stop in that career, in which they shall have once engaged, till death shall overtake them, in the shape of punishment.[779]

The *York Herald* reports that the day before their execution, a Reverend Brown preached to the condemned "Be not deceived, evil communications corrupt good manners". The writer notes that the prisoners expressed "a degree of regret for their crimes" and points out that their families were not allowed to join them in the chapel. A week after the 14 were hanged, the *Herald* reported that an "immense" crowd had gathered to watch the hangings and, no doubt, to the authorities' relief, did so with the "greatest decorum". In anticipation of an attempted rescue, soldiers had been deployed but they were unnecessary.[780]

In May and June 1812, further mass trials took place, aimed against those who rioted and broke machines in Chester and Lancashire. At Chester, 28 were found guilty and 14 received the death sentence, though only two were hanged. At Manchester, 58 were tried for a number of crimes, including food riots, arson and illegal oaths. Eight received capital punishment and 17 were transported, others were imprisoned and 20 acquitted. Those acquitted included a number of young workers aged 15 or 16. Age did not save everyone—Abraham Charlson, a boy aged 16 "called on his mother for help...thinking she had the power to save him" but was hanged. In August, 38 further prisoners were tried and escaped punishment because the prosecution relied solely on the evidence of a spy, Samuel Fleming, whose courtroom evidence was inconsistent and contradictory. The jury decided the evidence was not strong enough and freed the men who had already spent three months in prison.[781]

The harsh punishment of the Luddites was designed to behead and demoralise the radical movement. It cannot be doubted that this had some success. The military occupation of the north and the punishment of known Luddite activists had an impact on the movement. A slightly improved economic situation by the end of 1812 meant some workers at least had better wages and hours, which helped undermine the need for further action. And some employers did abandon, at least temporarily, the use of machinery or granted small pay rises. In terms of machine destruction, the successes of Luddism were short-lived. In Yorkshire between 1806 and 1817, for instance, the "number of shears operated by machinery [increased] from 100 to 1,462" and of "3,378 surviving croppers 1,170 were totally and 1,445 partially employed".[782]

The Luddite movement effectively ended with the suppression of 1812-1813. Its defeat, however, did not prevent other protests as the working class grew in size and confidence. Nor did it prevent the next outbreak of machine-breaking which was to shake rural communities less than 20 years later.

East Anglia 1816 and 1822[783]

Before looking at the major outbreak of rural rebellion in 1830, we will briefly examine two smaller revolts that took place in East Anglia. There had been a long tradition of rural protests in these areas, including food riots and protests against the enclosure of the fens. In 1816 agricultural labourers protested together with "townsmen, industrial workers, cottagers, [and] fenmen". Charlesworth identifies three types of protest which depended on location—town events, fenland events and events in "the strong loam and clay lands of Essex, Suffolk and Norfolk". Almost all the first type of protest were food riots and barely involved agricultural workers at all, as was common in riots of this type. In the second group of protests, which were "over the use of mole ploughs and threshing machines and over the demand for higher wages", agricultural workers were "at the centre" of events. The third group of fenland protests involved a cross section of fen society, agricultural labourers, "small tradesmen and artisans" a "peasant society" who depended on the fens in some way plus "a new group of workers attached to the drainage of the fens and the maintenance of the drainage schemes".[784] This diversity reflected the transformation of the fenlands themselves. The authorities responded with a mixture of repression and conciliation. However, the "dramatic breakdown of law and order" in the fenland resulted in the Home Secretary, Lord Sidmouth, deploying the army through Norfolk and Suffolk and taking to task "magistrates who had bought time by making concessions". As a result, the wave of protests was halted.

The mixture of those involved in the 1816 protests can be contrasted with 1822 when protest took place on a much larger scale in East Anglia, but was concentrated in a smaller geographical area south of Norwich. In 1822 the protesters were almost entirely agricultural workers. In February, in the area around Diss and Eye between Bury St Edmunds and Norwich, labourers broke threshing machines. Arrests of some of those involved provoked further protests and smashing of machinery. The labourers "parading round their villages either attempting to persuade farmers to put aside their threshing machines or when this failed actually destroying the machines themselves".[785]

While the protests, fires and threatening letters of 1822 were concentrated in a small area of rural East Anglia, it is worth noting that newspaper accounts show that there was support for the labourers from urban areas.

The *Norfolk Chronicle*, on 16 March 1822, describes the scene a few days after the end of the protests on 7 March.

> On Monday & Tuesday 17 prisoners, convicted of breaking thrashing machines, &c. were removed from the [Norwich] Castle, escorted by detachments of Major Harvey's squadron, to Aylsham and Wymondham bridewells; on their root to the former place the escort was assailed in Magdalen-street, by a number of disorderly people, who pelted them with stones; one of the cavalrymen received some injury. At St Faith's the inhabitants (chiefly women) assembled & threw bread & other provisions into the van, in which the prisoners were riding.

The *Chronicle* also reports on the use of the yeomanry to break up protests:

> In consequence of the serious disturbances of a misguided peasantry in the breaking of Thrashing Machines and destroying the property of many respectable Farmers in the neighbourhood...the Hingham Troop of Yeomanry...were called out by the Magistrates to assist the Civil power in apprehending the rioters... They made a strong muster and rode off to Wymondham, the scene of the depredations, but only arrived in time to assist in arresting two of the rioters, (notorious characters) the rest dispersing in all directions as soon as they heard the Yeomanry were in pursuit.

Another troop of yeomanry was stoned by a crowd as they escorted prisoners through Norwich, resulting in them threatening to fire on the protest "for their own preservation".[786]* The heavy use of troops like this, and the mobilisation of special constables made up of "respectable people", made public protest impossible and instead "a series of arson attacks followed".[787]

Captain Swing

The movement that is today known by the name Captain Swing is usually said to have begun on the 28 August 1830. That evening, in the village of Lower Hardres near Canterbury in Kent, 57 people destroyed a threshing machine. Later a smaller crowd continued to a farm at Eastleigh and broke two more machines there.[788] But four days earlier, a machine had been broken in the parish of Elham and both Hobsbawm and Rudé note repeated fires in June in Orpington, which may or may not have been directly connected to the Swing events that followed.[789]**

This confusion of dates illustrates a problem with telling the history of the Captain Swing events. Accounts tend to parcel the story together as a single outburst of anger by agricultural labourers which focused on threshing machines. But to see Swing like this is to misunderstand the wider context of the uprising, which was to eventually lead to almost 2,000 people being put on trial, 481 transportations and 19 executions.

Instead Swing must be understood as a high point in decades of rural class struggle. This struggle rose and fell, and had a number of peaks,

---

* Bridewell refers to a prison. Readers may note that Wymondham, mentioned twice in this report, was the market town where Kett's Rebellion began 273 years previously.
** Incendiarism had a long tradition in rural communities as protest, for settling scores or other criminal activity. Janet Gyford's pamphlet, *Men of Bad Character* (1991), looks at a series of fires in Witham, Essex, in the 1820s. It has a detailed explanation of legal processes that would have been used in the 1830s.

such as the East Anglia protests of 1816 and 1822 and the Swing events in 1830. Machine-breaking, riots or other protests were endemic to rural communities in the early 19th century. As A J Peacock pointed out when writing about East Anglia, "years like 1816, 1830-32, 1835-36 were exceptional only in the amount of violence that took place".[790] As we can see from the numbers prosecuted for their involvement, the Swing rebellion was of an unprecedented size and stands out as "the greatest machine-breaking episode in English history".[791]

The main reason for rural discontent was poverty caused by unemployment, or under-employment. In addition to the displacement of the population as a result of enclosure and other agricultural improvements, the permanent workforce on farms was being reduced. Increasingly, labourers were hired on a casual basis at times when the need for extra work was high, such as seeding or harvest. The Poor Law system also aggravated things. Under this, the parish was liable to support those with no income, either through unemployment, old age or sickness. But this was only true in the parish where the person was born and so there was no incentive for labourers to move to areas in search of work as there was no guaranteed income. As Roger Wells notes: "The social security system therefore encouraged workers in the South and East to remain put and become part of the growing pool of underused labour. Here under-employment and periodic unemployment began to assume serious proportions in the late 1760s and 1770s." Later, he goes on to say that by the end of the 18th century, "the word 'poor' became synonymous with agricultural labourer".[792]

Additionally, the end of the Napoleonic Wars led to 400,000 soldiers being demobbed and looking for work, further saturating the labour market. During the Napoleonic wars the impossibility of trade with the continent and poor harvests had caused massive increases in the prices of grain. Farmers did well out of wartime conditions "while their labourers hovered on the verge of starvation, and succumbed to famine conditions".[793] But after 1813, wheat prices crashed and remained low until 1835.[794]

All this took place at a time when, in the words of Hobsbawm and Rudé, the "labourer was peculiarly denuded of protection".[795] This encouraged a number of forms of resistance by workers attempting to improve their wages and conditions. One response was the food riot; another was crime, such as poaching; there were "isolated attempts at strike action";[796] and finally there was machine-breaking and arson. Threatening letters, which today we associate mainly with Swing, were common in the late

18th century, with a "marked" increase in the 1790s.[797] These would threaten destruction, usually the burning of hayricks or buildings if wages were not improved.

Protests were not always directed at wealthy employers or landowners. They might also target those seen as taking work away. One target for this was seasonal migrant agricultural workers, especially, though not always, Irish labourers. Large groups of workers moved around the countryside and were often seen as taking away local employment. Historians have differed on the importance of this to sparking revolt. In their account Hobsbawm and Rudé say that protest at the Irish was "of no general importance, though the press made something of it".[798] More recently, the historian Carl Griffin has argued that attacks on migrant labour and those who employed it were of "critical importance" in helping start the Swing movement, a view shared at the time by the radical William Cobbett who wrote that attacks on Irish labourers on the Isle of Thanet in Kent were "Swing's first real manifestation".[799]

The blaming of outsiders was not new. In East Anglia in 1815, for instance, a group of Irish labourers was attacked by locals who tried them in a "mock court" and "sentenced" them to death by drowning in a drainage ditch.[800]

Cobbett wrote:

> The millions have, at last, broken forth; hunger has, at last, set stone walls at defiance, and braved the fetters and the gallows; nature has, at last, commanded the famishing man to get food. All the base and foolish endeavours to cause it to be believed that the fires are the work of foreigners, or of a conspiracy, or of instigation from others than labourers, only show that those who make these endeavours are conscious that they share, in some way or other, in the guilt of having been the real cause of the mischief.[801]

The rapid spread of Swing indicates the existence of myriad local grievances that inspired revolt, in the context of widespread and deep rural poverty.

The Swing movement that began in Kent at the end of August 1830 and quickly spread across the core parts of the English agricultural countryside utilised many of the existing methods of struggle—in particular arson and letter writing—but did so publically. Instead of covert acts, the labourers in 1830 frequently took part in mass protests, occasional strikes, and collective destruction of property while marching from farm to farm destroying machinery. There were literally hundreds of incidents[802] and to describe them all here would be impossible. Instead I intend to give an overview of the spread of the movement, examine the often complex dynamics that took place in villages and give some sense of what took place, before looking at the violent repression that the state inflicted.

As we have seen, Captain Swing began in Kent. Hobsbawm and Rudé describe the pattern of protest in that county:

> First, fires in the north-west, reaching into the neighbouring county of Surrey; second, the wrecking of threshing machines in East Kent around Dover, Sandwich and Canterbury; third, late in October, wages meetings accompanied by Radical agitation against sinecures, rents and tithes around Maidstone; in early November, wages meetings and machine-breaking in West Kent, reaching into the Sussex Weald, and after mid-November, a further round of fires, tithe-riots and machine-breaking in East Kent.[803]

The machine-breaking groups were not enormous, often numbering 20 or 30 individuals, but they did a lot of damage. On occasion these events also reflected wider radical ideas. The French tricolour was raised on a number of occasions, sometimes with a black flag. Hobsbawm and Rudé note that these were sometimes linked to the path taken by a "band led by an evidently Jacobin and Republican naval deserter, Robert Price".[804] Kent had many links to France and Belgium, and it is no surprise that news of the European Revolutions and political influence crossed the Channel with traders and refugees, as well as smugglers and fishermen. In November 1830, the *Maidstone and Kentish Advertiser* noted that the anti-slavery campaigns had also been active in the region.

Fear of revolution coloured the authorities' response to Swing. In mid-September 1830, the *Kent Chronicle* carried a brief report of a meeting held to discuss the situation, even before the Swing uprising had reached its peak:

> A meeting was held at the freemason's hall...'to take into consideration the best mode of rationally educating, employing and uniting the people, in order to prevent the necessity for the depressing occurrences which have lately taken place in France, as well as to give a new and beneficial direction to the enormous mechanical power which is now reducing the greater part of the population to poverty and misery'...a committee was nominated, at the head of which were the Duke of Wellington and the Archbishop of Canterbury, to carry the 'emancipation' of the human mind, as proposed by the philosopher of Lanark [Robert Owen], into effect.[805]

As the movement spread, workers gained confidence—with attacks in the daytime and the numbers involved growing. Demands were raised for higher wages—2s 3d in winter and 2s 6d in summer. The crowds were also demanding farmers and landowners give "contributions in money or in kind".[806]

There are numerous accounts of the movement that illustrate how organised the workers were. Here is one newspaper report of a labourer's meeting at Sutton near Maidstone in Kent in late October 1830:

> About 5 o'clock we were visited by about two hundred men and lads, more or less, armed with sticks. Their object appears to have been merely to get refreshment at the several public houses of the town. They conducted themselves peaceably and orderly, and were dismissed by a sort of leader, who spoke to them, as I am informed, in a sensible manner, and desired for them to go to their respective homes without doing mischief by the way, and to meet him in the morning at this place,—to come with a good heart or not at all.
>
> I was concerned to know what these men aimed at in thus assembling together, and enquired of two labourers not of that party...if they could inform me what were the grievances these men wished to get redressed. I find, if correctly informed, that they wish to have more wages, and not to be obliged to apply to the parish for relief; two shillings per day...in the winter, and two shillings and sixpence in summer. But to be reduced to twenty pence a day seems the object of their dread.[807]

The same paper reports on fires and attacks around Kent and notes the confidence of the workers:

> Many of the farmers are so terrified of the appearance of the rioters, who are represented as having marched about in great numbers, breaking the machines in open day, many of them being armed with hatchets, hammers, saws, and even guns, which they discharge in the midst of cheering when their work of destruction is accomplished.

There was "so much terror" the newspaper reported, that the 7th Dragoons were deployed to Sittingbourne to contain the rising. The labourers who fired the machines, barns and ricks were often described as standing about watching attempts to tackle the blazes, "actually smoking pipes". Another group of labourers, 300 strong, marched from Lenham to other villages carrying a banner inscribed "starving at 1s 6d a week". On many occasions these groups compelled other workers to join them, or forced them to take part. These roving protests have a semblance of more contemporary flying pickets and events on occasion seem more like a strike wave than riots:

> At Ash, where several tumultuous assemblages have already taken place, the labouring men have struck, determined that no married man shall go to work unless he receives half a crown a day for his labour.

The last few examples of protests and strikes come from a single newspaper describing events near Maidstone in late October. It is a mark of how intense the struggles were that there is so much material condensed into one locality. But Captain Swing was spreading much further afield.

Hobsbawm and Rudé note that in Kent from early November onwards the focus was much more on wages than machines. This also meant demands being raised around the question of tithes and taxes.[808] Here we see another important aspect of the Swing insurrection. Surprisingly, many farmers supported the labourers and on numerous occasions facilitated the destruction of their machines (particularly as they were often hired equipment). They also readily agreed to raise wages and frequently handed over cash or other payments in kind, such as food or beer, to the protesters. This reflects a reality of 19th century rural life. The smaller landowners and farmers were being squeezed themselves. In particular, the payment of the tithe, a tenth of their income, to the church was a source of anger. Hence they often agreed to pay labourers wage rises on condition that the labourers also protested against tithes.

Other related issues became part of the growing movement. We get a sense of this from a letter delivered on 15 November during a mass meeting of about 150 labourers to Lord Gage, the main landowner near Ringmer in Sussex. It shows questions of wages and poor relief becoming key to protests. The letter was not handed to Gage, it was thrown from the crowd so that no individual risked being exposed for future victimisation:

> We the labourers of Ringmer and surrounding villages, having for a long period suffered the greatest privations and endured the most debasing treatment with the greatest resignation and forbearance, in the hope that time and circumstances would bring about an amelioration of our condition, till, worn out by hope deferred and disappointed in our fond expectations, we have taken this method of assembling ourselves in one general body, for the purpose of making known our grievances, and in a peaceable, quiet, and orderly manner, to ask redress; and we would rather appeal to the good sense of the magistracy, instead of inflaming the passions of our fellow labourers, and ask those gentlemen who have

done us the favour of meeting us this day whether 7d a day is sufficient for a working man, hale and hearty, to keep up the strength necessary to the execution of the labour he has to do? We ask also, is 9s a week sufficient for a married man with a family, to provide the common necessaries of life? Have we no reason to complain that we have been obliged for so long a period to go to our daily toil with only potatoes in our satchels, and the only beverage to assuage our thirst the cold spring; and on retiring to our cottages to be welcomed by the meagre and half-famished offspring of our toilworn bodies? All we ask, then, is that our wages may be advanced to such a degree as will enable us to provide for ourselves and families without being driven to the overseer, who, by the bye, is a stranger amongst us, and as in most instances where permanent overseers are appointed, are men callous to the ties of nature, lost to every feeling of humanity, and deaf to the voice of reason. We say we want wages sufficient to support us, without being driven to the overseer to experience his petty tyranny and dictation. We therefore ask for married men 2s 3d per day to the first of March, and from that period to the first of October 2s 6d a day: for single men 1s 9d a day to the first of March, and 2s from that time to the first of October. We also request that the permanent overseers of the neighbouring parishes may be directly discharged, particularly Finch, the governor of Ringmer poorhouse and overseer of the parish, that in case we are obliged, through misfortune or affliction, to seek parochial relief, we may apply to one of our neighbouring farmers or tradesmen, who would naturally feel some sympathy for our situation, and who would be much better acquainted with our characters and claims. This is what we ask at your hands—this is what we expect, and we sincerely trust this is what we shall not be under the painful necessity of demanding.[809]

In Brede, Kent, on 5 November, a meeting of labourers had started a movement against the overseers of the poor. This peaked with a meeting of 50 paupers who took their revenge on the notorious assistant overseer, a Mr Abel, who was responsible for introducing a parish cart and sometimes those requiring poor relief were made to pull it in harness. It is not surprising that the "labourers were determined to have a reckoning with him". The Hammonds explain what happened:

> The labourers went to Mr Abel's house with their wives and children and some of the farmers, and placed the parish cart at his door. After some hammering at the gates, Mr Abel was persuaded to come out and get into the cart. He was then solemnly drawn along by women and children, accompanied by a crowd of five hundred.

He was dumped on the parish boundary and the crowd returned to celebrate, each adult treated to a half pint of beer by one farmer and another who donated a barrel. Following this, the farmers asked their labourers to help reduce the tithes, the labourers were to protest but not to take violent action in order to "get a little of the tithe off". The protest was successful, with the labourers demanding a reduction in the tithe and a school for the poor children. The agreement was met with cheers and bell ringing.[810]

The successes of the workers of Brede inspired other villages in the neighbourhood. Carts were used to dump several overseers out of the parish and protest meetings reduced wages and tithes. Workhouses were also targeted. The workhouses at Headley and Selbourne were destroyed and others threatened. As Carl Griffin points out, many of these actions were highly symbolic of the poor's hatred for the Poor Law schemes. At a "pre-arranged" meeting between farmers and workers at Ringmer workhouse (mentioned in the letter to Lord Gage), the grindstone on which the unemployed were made to work was pulled down.[811]

West Sussex

By mid-November the Swing movement had spread to West Sussex, Swing letters being received in Horsham, and there were "disturbances" and fires in the area. Hobsbawm and Rudé speculate that "Horsham and Brighton, centres of radicalism anxious to spread the agitation against aristocracy and corruption, may have acted as relay stations" spreading the movement, though it is clear that what had happened already in Kent was well known. On the same day as Lord Gage met his labourers, threshing machines were destroyed in Arundel, Bersted, Bognor, Felpham and Yapton, alongside demands for a 4s weekly rise in pay. As in Kent, the protests involved marches and riots, and demands for cash and payment in kind (usually food and drink). On 16 November a mass protest of 1,000 labourers met the "justices and principal farmers" at Chichester's market day.[812]

On 22 November, the *Sussex Advertiser* lamented that the destruction of private property had become more frequent. They reported on huge meetings of workers demanding wage increases, the arrest of several ring-leaders and dozens of fires and other attacks, including the forcing of parish figures to reduce tithes. The *Advertiser* points out the workers success:

> Similar meetings have been holden at Wadhurst, Hellingly, Eastborne, Cuckfield, Rotherfield, Herstmonceux, Uckfield, Barcombe, and at several

places in the western part of the County...on Monday, the labouring class assembled at Bognor, and repaired to their employers, requesting more wages: which after some delay, was promised to them, and they returned to their work. Almost every parish in this neighbourhood has followed their example: in some cases the men's grievances have been redressed; but in some others they have been left in uncertainty and refused.[813]

Hampshire

Having spread into West Sussex, the movement crossed the county quickly into Hampshire and the West Country. Here Hobsbawm and Rudé say the movement reached its "greatest momentum" and focused more on machine-breaking and protests around wages, with less arson and concerns about tithes and rents. Once again there are dozens of examples of machine-breaking and rioting. On occasion these events reached insurrectionary levels. In the small town of Andover, Hampshire, riots took place for several days from 19 November. According to Hobsbawm and Rudé, a local magistrate wrote to the Home Secretary: "the peasantry have not only dictated a rate of wages, not only destroyed all agricultural machinery, and demolished iron foundries, but have proceeded in for-midable bodies to private dwellings to extort money and provisions—in fact, have established a system of pillage". The labourers also destroyed a threshing machine, leading to the arrest of one of their number, whom they released by forcing open the prison gates. The day after this, a crowd travelled two miles to Tasker's Waterloo Foundry, which made parts for threshing machines, and destroyed machinery valued at £2,000 (over £200,000 in 2018 prices). "Peace and penitence" was restored in Andover only when cavalry troops arrived a few days later.[814]

Another newspaper report gives a sense of the mood in Hampshire, describing events in the town of Overton, a few miles east of Andover, on 25 November:

> Early in the morning several labourers assembled and paraded in the streets, demanding from the affrighted inhabitants money or food, and saying that they had been starving with their wives and families long enough on potatoes and bread; that their sufferings were at length past all endurance; and if they could not get more wages...they would take that which they could get without working at all. Many of the neighbouring farmers, their masters, came into the town, and used every endeavour to pacify them, and to persuade them to return peaceably to their homes and their work, by promises that their wages should be raised and their

wants relieved. This appeal induced them to disperse, but not till they had extracted from the shopkeepers and other inhabitants money and food. During the night, a very large and valuable rick of seeds, belonging to farmer Longman, of Bourne, was set on fire, and burnt to the ground.[815]

Other factories were destroyed on 23 and 24 November at Fordingbridge near the border with Dorset, when 300 labourers destroyed machines and then destroyed about £1,000 worth of machinery at two mills that made sacking and threshing machines. The workers were led by James Thomas Copper, an ostler known as "Captain Hunt", who rode a white horse. He was later executed for his role. This was the last major event in Hampshire, but it is worth mentioning a report from Lymington: "there has been what is termed a 'strike for wages' in almost every village hereabout but unattended with anything like outrage".[816]

Wiltshire and the West Country

In Wiltshire[817] the Swing rising took off with similar patterns to elsewhere: Swing letters were sent, and protests and fires took place leading to over 300 people being tried. The radical orator Henry Hunt, who was travelling through Wiltshire at the time, recorded that labourers told him: "We don't want to do any mischief, but we want that poor children when they go to bed should have a belly full of tatoes instead of crying with half a belly full". Wiltshire wages were "notoriously low" and Swing took off in this county with as much energy as anywhere else. After relatively low-level beginnings, riots took off "with explosive force" on 22 November in the east of the county in a "score" of villages. The next day 25 villages are recorded as having riots. In Salisbury, reports were that all nearby threshing machines had been destroyed and there were fears that the iron foundry would also be destroyed, the owner having "already received threatening letters".

It is worth recording a major engagement a few days later west of Salisbury, when 400 labourers armed with "bludgeons and crowbars" smashed threshing machines including one at Pyt House, in Tisbury, owned by John Benett. Benett told the rioters that if any one of them would inform on ten others, they would get £500 reward (an astonishing amount of money for rural workers at the time). No one claimed the money and his machines were destroyed. Immediately after this, a "troop of yeomanry cavalry" arrived and a battle took place in which the labourers fought with "hatchets, hammers, pick-axes, sticks and stones" against muskets. One worker was killed, several injured and 25 arrested. The same day, another troop fought a battle with a crowd who had blocked the road to Warminster to rescue their comrades who were being taken there as prisoners.[818] With these events, Swing peaked in Wiltshire, though there were isolated fires and skirmishes in the days following.

Swing spread from Wiltshire into Dorset and even Devon, where there was a "scattered crop of outbreaks". In Dorset Mary Frampton wrote in her journal that "the plentiful harvest, good potato crop, remarkably fine autumn weather without frost to impede the labours of husbandry, appeared to have no effect in lessening the murmurs of discontent". Her husband, the local magistrate, James Frampton, was a leading figure in opposing the labourers. Mary's account tells how he grabbed a protesting worker by his smock, but the worker slipped out, leaving Frampton holding nothing but the man's clothing. Allegedly, Frampton's role "went to his head", which helps explain his later zeal in prosecuting the Tolpuddle Martyrs. The further west the movement went, the more the movement was reduced to local incidents, but it is worth noting that even in Cornwall there were events, including food riots, in November.[819]

Few English counties seemed to be immune from Swing. In Worcester there had been riots by Kidderminster carpet weavers in August and there was machine-breaking at Redditch and a few other isolated locations. A placard posted in Evesham hints at links between these "urban and rural movements", according to Hobsbawm and Rudé: "Be not afraid of Evesham new police for they're nothing but thieves and robbers. Down with machinery and A free trade in Corn".[820]

A Swing letter sent to a farmer in Whitney, Hereford, on the border with Wales, is testament to how far the message of rural rebellion had travelled. Its author was punished by transportation to Australia.

> Remember in Kent they have set ("with fire") all that would not submit and you we will serve the same for we are determined to make you support the Poor better than they have been soppored yet for they are all starving at present so pull down your Thrashing Maschine or else Bread and Fire without delay. For we are 5 thousand men and will not be stopt.[821]

Berkshire, Oxfordshire and Buckinghamshire[822]

As well as spreading westwards, the movement also spread north from its origins in Kent. In November, Berkshire experienced riots over wages and the burning of machines. Threatening letters were sent in a number of locations, but crowds of labourers marched from village to village destroying equipment. There were reports of crowds of between 800 and

1,000 marching in the villages around Reading, destroying machinery.[823] At Colthrop, a paper mill was destroyed, but the movement was halted by a militia of "tradesmen and constables" who read the Riot Act and arrested 11 rioters. At Hungerford there was a "violent wave of rioting", including the breaking out of a beggar who had been imprisoned for abusing a magistrate who had denied him poor relief. Machines were broken and money demanded from farms, and £260 (over £20,000 today) worth of machines destroyed at an iron foundry in Hungerford. The authorities called a meeting with labourers' delegates at the Town Hall and agreed a "12s weekly wage, a reduction in house rents and the destruction of all machines". With this, the Hungerford delegates dispersed, but some from Kintbury who had arrived "armed with hammers and bludgeons", wanted more. Their spokesman, William Oakley, a wheelwright, demanded more money and declared:

> You and the gentlemen have been living upon all the good things for the last ten years. We have suffered enough, and now is our time and we will now have it. You only speak to us now because you are afraid and intimidated.[824]

Since "they departed with £5 in their pockets" William Oakley clearly spoke the truth to a frightened local authority. But this did not stop the Kintbury workers who now joined with comrades from other localities who clearly wanted what the Hungerford workers had won. Riots spread, and the destruction of machines became highly organised. Francis Norris, a bricklayer, was appointed treasurer and was responsible for the monies demanded from farmers after their machines had been destroyed (usually 40s). When arrested he was found to have £100. The Kintbury workers were quickly arrested. But this failed to stop Swing's momentum, with the movement continuing to get new life as other villages heard of their successes.[825]

The movement spread into Oxfordshire on 21 November. Here there were some links to anti-enclosure protests. But events were dominated by protests against machinery and for higher wages. Unusually, in Oxford, there was an instance where protests began in an urban area, spreading outwards. This was in Banbury and crowds marched outwards to nearby villages.[826]

The county adjacent to Oxfordshire and Berkshire, Buckinghamshire, had its own Swing events at the end of November. In addition to threats to destroy machines, buildings and crops, another target was paper mills, with unemployed paper workers protesting about their conditions. On 26

November, a mass meeting of paper workers marched on the hall where "justices and householders were assembled and turned their meeting into a bedlam. The Riot Act was read to no avail and the presiding magistrate was even persuaded to send the Buchinghamshire Yeomanry Cavalry away in order to appease the crowd".[827] The local paper mill's machinery was destroyed on 29 November, despite shots being fired and "four gallons of vitriol" being thrown at the attackers (the person who threw this was "ducked in a pond"). After the successful riot, the protesters returned to the town and "levied contributions" from shopkeepers. The rioters were eventually suppressed by local yeomanry and a militia of gentry wearing their huntsman's red coats (though Hobsbawm and Rudé point out that the rioters were "exhausted" at this point, and many were drunk after stopping at the Red Lion pub). Elsewhere in Buckinghamshire, there were "lower key" attacks on threshing machines at the same time as these events. Swing riots also spread into the Midlands at the end of November.[828]

East Anglia, Essex, Cambridgeshire and Lincolnshire

As we have seen, from Kent Swing moved west and north-west, but it also spread northwards into East Anglia.[829] I have already noted that this area had a history of agrarian disturbance. Hobsbawm and Rudé argue that this "long standing antagonism of farmers to tithe was strongly reflected in the East Anglian movement" which was dominated by "tithe-and-wages riots". They also explain that here labourers and farmers "collusion" was closer than anywhere else and noted by commentators at the time.[830]

In Norfolk in early November haystacks were burnt, a small number of farms attacked and protests took place. But the movement proper began in the remote north-east of Norfolk on 19 November when 70 men marched to a meeting of the local justices in North Walsham, demanding "all threshing machines in the district be destroyed or laid aside". That evening (after visiting a pub) they proceeded to take matters into their own hands. Over the next few days machines were broken over a wide area. At the end of the week, the *Norwich Mercury* could report numerous attacks, including arson but mainly of machine destruction. They described "a great number of labouring people, men and women" marching around joining with other groups to destroy machines.

> On Wednesday and Thursday [24-25 November 1830] large bodies again assembled in the neighbourhood of Reepham, and the reports of their having broken many threshing machines have reached our office... Several gentlemen who had received threatening letters, mustered their

tenants and neighbours, and a party of dragoons were posted on the Lynn road, near Taverham, to be at hand...information has been sent us that at Hempnall there was a large assembly of the peasantry, who insisted on the farmers withholding their tithes, from the appointed collectors on Thursday, and they were under the necessity of returning without the tithes.

The newspaper gives a sense of panic at events spiralling out of control, with local landowners being sworn into the militia, troops stationed on key roads, and protest and riot spreading rapidly. The *Norwich Mercury* claimed that for the previous 12 years it had called for action on rural poverty and complained at the lack of action by the government and that events had "vindicated" them. Warning that the country was bordering "Civil War", the journal called for action and, while protesting against the destruction of property, demanded that the government respond not with "conflict" but "conciliation", that "owners, occupiers and clergy, immediately together offer a rise of wages—grants of land and constant employment even at a loss" until the government could bring about general relief for the labourers. Such liberal views, however, were tempered by the newspaper's urging that the mobilisations of labourers be met with associations of the masters and inhabitants of local towns. Quoting the MP and philosopher Edmund Burke it concluded: "when the bad conspire, the good must associate".[831]

Nonetheless, conciliation was part of a response by the authorities in Norfolk. While arrests of rioters proceeded, magistrates and landowners understood that the disturbances arose from the widespread use of threshing machines and low wages. Hobsbawm and Rudé reproduce a remarkable notice from North Walsham on 24 November urging landowners to discontinue the use of machines:

> The Magistrates therefore beg to *recommend* to the Owners and Occupiers of Land...to *discontinue the use of Threshing Machines, and to increase the Wages of Labour*... The Magistrates are determined to enforce the Laws against all tumultuous Rioters and Incendiaries...at the same time they feel a full Conviction that *no severe measures will be necessary*, if the proprietors of Land will give proper employment to the Poor.[832]

Hobsbawm and Rudé point out that this was not "an isolated... opinion". From the north-east, machine-breaking spread south towards Norwich and paper mills were also broken near the city. In early December there were riots by workers in the city itself when weavers "cut the silk in twenty-six looms". But this was unusual; Swing in the region was dominated by the breaking of machines on dozens of farms through the month.

Dozens of examples exist of villages where mass protests by labourers challenged the local authorities. In Haddiscoe, the Reverend Thomas Elliston was "besieged in the Crown Inn, where he had gone to receive his tithes, by an 'assembly of persons' carrying a red flag and blowing a horn, who said 'that they wanted a reduction of the tithe, so that their masters might pay them more wages.'" When Elliston refused, he was imprisoned until he agreed to the labourers' demands. At Forncett, protesters failed to catch the minister, so they "partly pulled down" the local poor-house.[833]

From Norfolk the protest movement spread into eastern Suffolk, with similar protests taking place across villages. Hundreds of examples exist and readers wanting to know more should consult the detailed accounts in Hobsbawm and Rudé's book.[834] One incident is worth highlighting though, which is the arrest in Stradishall, south-west of Bury St Edmunds, of a man believed to be Captain Swing.

John Saville was a "well-dressed, middle-aged straw-plait merchant from Luton". He was found to have travelled across the eastern counties carrying £580 in cash and a large number of "'inflammatory' notices all signed 'Swing.'" Saville had been seen travelling through the village of Stradishall in Suffolk and dropping notices behind him. He claimed to have travelled 1,200 miles doing this because he was a Methodist and motivated by scripture which "denounces woe to the oppresser". A radical and "ranter", but not the "Captain Swing" the authorities wished he was, Saville's notices are fascinating in their content: "Will you farmers and Parsons pay us better for our labour, if you wont we will put you in bodily fear". As Hobsbawm and Rudé suggest, he was probably using the situation for his own reasons rather than actually being a leader of events, but such were the times that he was fined £50 and sentenced to 12 months' imprisonment, a sentence reduced by reports of Saville's good character.[835]

Early December saw fires and wage riots in Cambridgeshire, beginning in areas closest to counties that had already experienced Swing events. Fears of a "general rising" in Cambridge on 4 December failed to materialise, but two days later labourers in nearby villages marched demanding higher wages. A fortnight after these riots, more took place in the village of Fowlmere where labourers struck and a policeman was assaulted; for this five people were arrested. The final outburst of Swing in Cambridgeshire was the breaking of machines as late as September 1832, leading to the arrest and sentencing of 15 workers.

Lincolnshire saw a few threatening letters and arson but no widespread disturbances during the Swing rising. Other counties saw limited events: threatening letters were reported in "Staffordshire, Derbyshire, Lancashire, Shropshire, Cheshire, Nottingham, Yorkshire and Cumberland". Many Midland counties saw rick burning and as far north as Carlisle, letters were sent in the name of Swing and ricks burnt, but Hobsbawm and Rudé say that this had "nothing to do with the labourers' movement" but note that it points to the "pervasive influence of 'Swing'".[836]

What was Swing?

Captain Swing's influence was felt the length and breadth of England, but its focus was the key agricultural areas in the south and south-east of the country. Here, motivated by anger at years of poverty, low pay and unemployment, thousands of rural workers were engaged in extended direct action to try and improve their conditions. In the short term they were frequently successful. Farmers often drastically improved wages in the face of strikes, protest, riot and arson. Threshing machines, which became the key target of the movement, were destroyed in their hundreds and work was undertaken, at least in the short term, by hand.

Local conditions mattered. This was a national movement, but it was not nationally led or shaped. In some areas machine-breaking was a key part of the struggle. In others, protests about wages and arson dominated. The question of tithes was frequently important, but the extent to which there was association between labourers and farmers varied from place to place. In a few locations labourers widened the scope of their movement to target workhouses or particularly disliked landowners. Confidence was frequently high—bands of hundreds of men and women roamed from farm to farm demanding money, smashing equipment and destroying property.

Despite the hopes of predominately urban-based radicals, the movement failed to take up wider political demands in relation to the then growing movements for political reform. Indeed, Swing might be seen as the final peak of the last expressions of the old traditions of rural class struggle before the development of trade union consciousness in the 1860s and 1870s.

Yet Swing came at a time when the British ruling class was experiencing a difficult period. Its scale and rapid spread terrified the government. Swing raised the spectre of revolution, particularly in the context of revolution in France and Belgium. At a critical period for the British ruling class— Wellington's government fell (15 November 1830) and was replaced by the Whig government of Lord Grey—large parts of the country were in open rebellion. Grey's government went on to pass the Great Reform Act in 1832 and while Swing had little role in this, the fear of rebellion was a key driver of reform. As Grey himself put it in the House of Lords on 22 November 1830, while Swing rioters were still making their protests known: "The principle of my reform is, to prevent the necessity for revolution".[837]

Other, relatively minor, legislation had some of its origins in the 1830 events. The Poor Law Amendment Act of 1834 was based in part on the work of commissioners who collected much material related to rural conditions, including events in 1830. Thus Swing had a part in shaping that, as well as the Tithe Commutation Act of 1836, which, together with other legislation, helped reduce the rights of clergy to collect tithes. In addition, Allotments Acts of 1831 and 1832 were in part passed because a frequent suggestion for solving rural poverty was the creation of allotments for workers to grow food on.[838]

In the short term wage rises won by labourers in 1830 were kept. Sometimes the wage rises won were significant. In one location in Sussex which had "notoriously poor living conditions", 100 labourers demanded 2 shillings per day for married men and an extra 2 shillings a week, for every child after the second. This was granted.[839]

In the longer term though, the situation did not improve dramatically, though the legacy was there. In 1833, in Norfolk a labourer could say: "If we had never had any fires our wages would not have been more than 10s a week". A curate in Kent wrote to the Poor Law Commission "them there riots and burnings did the poor a terrible deal of good".[840]

Threshing machines did not return to the English countryside in any great numbers until the 1850s. This was not just because of Swing, but also because they offered limited profit at great investment, particularly to smaller farmers. Yet as Hobsbawm and Rudé conclude, it was the action of the labourers in 1830 that removed them from the fields, without this there would likely have been no movement to return to manual labour.[841]

However the resistance of the labourers did not disappear with the end of 1830. Despite the enormous and violent repression of the movement, confidence did not vanish. In some cases this was shown by what happened when farmers tried to reduce wages the next year, but it also manifested itself in continued protests and strikes over wages, as well as further machine-breaking. Carl Griffin has highlighted a number of examples of this that demonstrate that the old idea that Captain Swing was broken by repression is not true.[842] Just as Swing did not appear "out of the blue", it similarly did not simply vanish in the aftermath of repression and defeat.

The aftermath

The repression, however, was unprecedented. At the beginning the response was relatively lacking in severity. The Home Secretary, Robert Peel, described this as "unparalleled lenity" and it certainly helped encourage further protests.[843]

In the aftermath of the first machine-breaking events at the end of August 1830 near Elham in Kent, the authorities arrested key figures from the protests. On the advice of a local vicar, who told them they were less likely to be convicted if they confessed, "Fifty men came forward, many of whom claimed to have been press-ganged into taking part in the machine-breaking... Some had been bribed...with beer, while others had been genuinely under the impression that it was not illegal to break threshing machines".[844] When the time of the trial came, however, seven prisoners were released with minimal sentences; they were jailed for three days. The magistrate, Sir Edward Knatchbull, hoped that "the kindness and moderation evinced this day...would be met by a corresponding feeling among the people".[845]

Robert Peel was unimpressed: "I should have thought a severe example in the case of Destruction of farming property would have had a much greater effect than the unparalleled lenity shown to the Destroyers of Thrashing Machines".[846]

As a result of Peel's objection more encouragement was given to those trying to find those who were responsible for the destruction of property. Police were sent from London to assist magistrates, special constables were sworn in to break up protests, the yeomanry was reformed and, following growing demands from the regions, troops were used. Troops of cavalry were stationed around rural areas ready to mobilise at short notice. In Hampshire, for instance, Griffin explains, "military support to civil forces in arresting 'ringleaders', forcing all other protestors to flee, and duly escorting the prisoners to gaol proved effective throughout the county".[847]

Punishment for those found guilty was heavy. As we have seen, 2,000 people were tried, 481 transported and there were 19 executions. The Hammonds detail at great length the work of the Special Commissions and the many injustices that arose. To take just one example, in Salisbury, the prisoners were unable "to see their attorney except in the presence of the gaoler or his servants". In one capital case, that of James Lush who was accused of "extorting money in a mob", his confession was obtained because his legal adviser had to hand over a copy of statements made confidentially. Yet Lush was so poor that when he came to trial he was "without legal advice or assistance". Perhaps inevitably he was sentenced to death. The lack of justice for those accused of participation in Swing is apparent in the Hammonds' account of trials at Salisbury:

> Batch after batch of boys and men in the prime of life were brought up to the dock for a brief trial and sentence of exile. Such was the haste that in one case at least the prisoners appeared with the handcuffs still on their wrists, a circumstance which elicited a rebuke from the judge, and an excuse of over work from the gaoler. Amongst the first cases eight prisoners, varying in age from seventeen to thirty, were sentenced to transportation for life for doing £500 worth of damage at Brasher's cloth mill at Wilton. Thirteen men were transported for seven years and one for fourteen years for breaking threshing machines on the day of the Pyt House affray.[848]

In these trials, evidence about poverty and distress was inadmissible and repeatedly ruled out of order. This was, on occasion, to stop evidence coming out that some farmers had assisted the labourers in their protests, but usually it was considered irrelevant to proceedings. The Hammonds continue:

> The proportion of charges of extorting money was smaller at Salisbury than at Winchester: most of the indictments were for breaking machines only. In some instances the prosecution dropped the charge of robbery, thinking transportation for seven years a sufficient punishment for the offence. Three brothers were sentenced to death for taking half a crown: nobody received this sentence for a few coppers.[849]

The commission judges had a great deal of leeway in prosecution and the fate of prisoners often depended on character references by local landowners. The Hammonds note that those who were not agricultural labourers (they give the example of a shepherd and a bricklayer) tended to receive much harder sentences. The reasoning of the judge was that threshing machines had nothing to do with their jobs, unlike the labourers, and their involvement in the destruction was thus a far worse crime.[850]

Many death sentences were commuted to transportation, though this was as final for the friends and family of those found guilty. Many villages lost significant numbers of their young men, and, as this account from *The Times* makes clear, the horror was enormous:

> Immediately on the conclusion of this sentence a number of women... set up a dreadful shriek of lamentation. Some of them rushed forward to shake hands with the prisoners, and more than one voice was heard to

exclaim, "Farewell I shall never see you more"... The car for the removal of the prisoners was at the back entrance to the court-house and was surrounded by a crowd mothers, wives, sisters and children, anxiously waiting for a glance of their condemned relatives. The weeping and wailing of the different parties, as they pressed the hands of the convicts... was truly heartrending.[851]

Hobsbawm and Rudé's *Captain Swing* has a chapter detailing the lives of some of those who were deported 12,000 miles from home. Few ever came home; Hobsbawm and Rudé were only able to find two who returned to England when their sentences were over. Of these one, John Tongs, a Hampshire blacksmith, returned home and then returned to Australia in 1843 with his wife and children.[852] Despite the numbers exiled to Australia in the aftermath of Captain Swing, they brought no radical traditions with them and most lived peacefully as agricultural workers and farmers on the new continent, albeit cut off from their friends, family and previous lives. But Swing left a more immediate impact on the workers' movement back in England, as this account by a participant helps to explain:

> In the years 1831-2, there was a general movement of the working classes for an increase of wages, and the labouring men in the parish where I lived (Tolpuddle) gathered together, and met their employers, to ask them for an advance of wages, and they came to a mutual agreement, the masters in Tolpuddle promising to give the men as much for their labour as the other masters in the district. The whole of the men then went to their work, and the time that was spent in this affair did not exceed two hours. No language of intimidation or threatening was used on the occasion.[853]

When the labourers learnt that other labourers in the district were to get 10 shillings a week, they had every expectation that they would earn the same. After all, the local minister had sworn that he would ensure they received this. The author of these lines, George Loveless, was delegated to meet the chief magistrate of the locality, James Frampton, and raise the promised wages.

Frampton told the labourers' delegation that they "must work for what our employers thought fit to give us, as there was no law to compel masters to give any fixed sum of money to their servants".

Disappointed, Loveless returned to Tolpuddle. There, he and others, "knowing it was impossible to live honestly on such scanty means", decided to "form a friendly society among the labourers". George Loveless became the acknowledged leader of the Tolpuddle labourers. James Frampton, the man who framed the "Tolpuddle Martyrs" in 1834, said that both George and his brother James had been "very active in the riots of the winter of 1830".[854]

Thus the legacy of Captain Swing had direct links to the most famous struggle for agricultural workers' rights in British history. As we shall see, the fact that Captain Swing's near insurrectional movement remains relatively ignored while the struggle of the Tolpuddle Martyrs is widely celebrated, is a product of the interests of a section of the British labour movement.[855]

9

Tolpuddle: The victims of Whiggery

God is our guide no sword we draw,
We kindle not wars battle fires,
By reason, union, justice, law,
We claim the birthright of our sires.
We raise the watchword Liberty,
We will, we will, we will be free.
We raise the watchword Liberty,
We will, we will, we will be free.[856]

THE CASE of the Tolpuddle Martyrs is the most well known example of
rural trade unionism in the United Kingdom. When the six Martyrs—
George Loveless and his brother James, James Brine, James Hammett,
Thomas Standfield and his son John—were found guilty of making illegal
oaths and sentenced to seven years' transportation in 1834, their case
rapidly became a cause célèbre. Within a week up to 10,000 attended a
protest meeting in London,[857] followed by meetings and demonstrations
up and down the country. By the end of the campaign an estimated
800,000 people had signed petitions to parliament in their support.

Today the example of the Martyrs, the campaign to free them and their
eventual, triumphal return, have entered the pages of trade union folklore.
Their struggle is marked by a major annual festival which transforms the
small village of Tolpuddle every year. The sycamore tree where the Martyrs
met is protected, the village has numerous plaques commemorating sites
related to Loveless and his comrades and even the local pub is called
the Martyrs Inn. The Martyrs' museum is itself housed in what was the
common area of six cottages specially built by the Trades Union Congress
to mark the centenary of the trial, to house retired agricultural workers.

That such an enormous industry has arisen out of the Tolpuddle
Martyrs' case is somewhat surprising, as while they experienced very real
injustice, it was in reality a relatively minor example of rural protest. The
scale of the contemporary response and today's historical remembrance has
less to do with the facts of the Martyrs' case and more to do with it occur-
ring at a seminal moment for the nascent British trade union movement.

The story of the Martyrs is simple enough. As George Loveless explained, in the years following the Swing movement, agricultural labourers in Tolpuddle and surrounding villages protested to farmers for higher wages. The Dorset village of Tolpuddle was no different to thousands of other villages around England at the time and the refusal of the farmers to increase pay led to Loveless and others deciding to form a union.

Contrary to popular belief, the Tolpuddle labourers were not tried and transported for the crime of setting up or joining a trade union. The Combination Acts, which had historically banned unions, were repealed in 1824 as a result of lengthy campaigning, but this in turn was amended in 1825. The result was legal confusion with, as we shall see, a number of additional laws that the government could use against those organising at work. This led to a situation where, as one historian of the early union movement explains, "trade unions, if not yet exactly legal, were no longer explicitly illegal".[858]

It is precisely because trade unions were flourishing in this environment that the individuals involved in setting one up in Tolpuddle could call on the assistance of others. Following George Loveless's arrest, one piece of evidence found in his home was a "printed paper headed Flax and Hemp trade of Great Britain" produced by the Flax Dressers Trades Union in Leeds. This had been obtained by George from his brother John who worked in that trade near Tolpuddle. George also received information from a Robert Loveless, who lived in London and had contacts with trade unions there. As a result of this network of contacts, 40 local labourers met with two activists from the London trade union movement in Tolpuddle.[859] These delegates are often said to have come from the Grand National Consolidated Trades Union (GNCTU). But the GNCTU was formed a few weeks later, though it was building on existing foundations. Already there were many different union bodies, organising different workers and trades. Many of these acted as friendly societies or were simply about supporting members in times of difficultly.

Workers getting organised were already thinking about the land and agriculture. For instance, about a fortnight before the Tolpuddle meeting, a "Friendly and Protective Agricultural Association" was set up, headquartered in Covent Garden in London. One aim of this body was to help members in distress by resettling them on the land. Whoever the delegates who came to Tolpuddle were, they would have been able to speak confidently of the growing union movement and the forthcoming creation of the GNCTU. The growth of unions worried the ruling class and the agricultural aspect was part of this. In November 1833, an open letter in the press warned Lord Melbourne, the Home Secretary and future Prime Minister, that rural trade unions would soon threaten to make "the whole landed property of the country change hands". This was an exaggeration, but there were a number of such organisations beginning, and not just in Tolpuddle.[860]

The meeting that took place in late 1833 with representatives from London and local workers was a significant event. Tolpuddle then was a small village—there were only 175 males recorded in the census, over half of whom were children. Even allowing for the fact that people probably attended from nearby villages, this meant a substantial proportion of the Tolpuddle working class took part in the union meeting. The meeting took place in Thomas Standfield's cottage and included the reading of the new society's rules, which included provision for the setting up of a committee that would be elected every three months. Plans were made for lodges (or branches) that would be set up in nearby areas, each with seven elected officials, including two guardians, "outside and inside". These two reflected the concerns of the time as their role was to guard entrance to meetings. Each lodge would have a password: Tolpuddle's was "Either Hand or Heart". The rules of the union included fee payment when members were in work. Two crucial rules included what would happen if a worker had wages reduced (the members were to finish the work in hand and immediately leave together with other members) and if a man was to be sacked for joining a union (this required an immediate end to work). The final rule of the union was "that the object of this society can never be promoted by any act or acts of violence, but on the contrary, all such proceedings must tend to injure the cause and destroy the society itself. This order therefore will not countenance any violation of the laws." In addition, there were a number of other prohibitions during meetings such as banning swearing, drinking and discussing political and religious issues.[861] These somewhat conservative rules in part reflected the need to protect the union from accusations of radicalism. But they also reflected the moral values of some of the key figures. George Loveless and most of the other Tolpuddle Martyrs were Methodists, George being a well-known local preacher. He and the others saw the struggle to improve workers' conditions as a moral action, not one that meant challenging the state.

The meeting concluded by agreeing to set up a "Friendly Society of Agricultural Labourers" in Tolpuddle, with plans to expand outwards into the wider Dorset area. Following this meeting, individuals were initiated into the union. Today joining a union is as simple as filling out a form online and agreeing to set up a direct debit. In 1833 the action was still, despite the legality of the movement, fraught with potential problems. While the union movement was coming out of illegality, it inherited traditions from its time underground that were still very useful. One of these was the swearing of an oath to the union and comrades.

This oath was to assume great importance in the prosecution of the leading figures in the Tolpuddle case, so it is worth recording in full. This was one of the items found after searching George Loveless's house following his arrest.

> I do before Almighty God and this Loyal Lodge most solemnly swear that I will not work with any illegal man or men, but will do my best for the support of wages, and most solemnly swear to keep inviolate all the secrets of this Order, nor will I ever consent to have any money for any purpose but for the use of the Lodge and the support of the trade; nor will I write or cause to be wrote, print, mark, either on stone, marble, brass, paper, or sand, anything connected with this Order, so help me God, and keep me steadfast in this my present obligation. And I further promise to do my best to bring all legal men that I am connected with into this Order; and if I ever reveal any of the rules, may what is before me plunge my soul into Eternity. And may I be disgraced in every Lodge in the kingdom.[862]

At the trial, further details of the ritual oath taking were revealed, though the witness accounts are slightly confused. Potential union members seem to have been blindfolded and made to kneel while a reading was made, probably a text from the Bible. The blindfolds were removed and the initiates were shown a large image of Death or Father Time, while James Loveless said "remember thine end". After this, the new members were blindfolded again, there were further readings and the oath taken followed by the kissing of the Bible.[863] While seeming strange to us today, these actions were common to unions of the time as they helped bind members to one another at a time when exposing membership of a trade union could be very dangerous. Unfortunately, in this case two of the 50 people who joined the Tolpuddle Union broke their oaths and gave evidence against their comrades.

On 24 February 1834, George Loveless and the five other men who were to become the Tolpuddle Martyrs were arrested and made to walk seven miles to Dorchester. A few days earlier, placards had appeared in the area around Tolpuddle signed by the local magistrates warning people that taking an unlawful oath could result in serve punishment. We know that George Loveless had seen this, as he had a folded copy in his pocket when arrested.

Again, it is worth quoting this at length, as this was the basis for the prosecution of the Tolpuddle labourers. It began by noting that "mischieving and designing persons" were trying to get others "to enter into Illegal Societies or Unions to which they bind themselves by unlawful oaths".

> Any Person who shall become a Member of such a Society, or take any oath, or assent to any Test or Declaration not authorised by law—Any Person who shall administer, or be present at, or consenting to the administering or taking any Unlawful Oath, or who shall cause such oath to be administered, although not actually present at the time—Any person who shall not reveal or discover any Illegal Oath which may have been administered, or any Illegal Act done or to be done—Any Person who shall induce, or endeavour to persuade any other Person to become a member of such Societies, will become guilty of Felony and liable to be transported for seven years.[864]

This placard was the result of months of work by the presiding magistrate of the area, James Frampton. We have already met Frampton as an enthusiastic prosecutor of action against Swing labourers. He was a wealthy local landowner from a family of country gentlemen who lived at nearby Moreton House and very much part of the local establishment. He was well connected with the rich in London, where he regularly spent time. Frampton had been in France in the early years of the French Revolution and likely had a fear of the masses threatening the wealth and power of his class. This is why he spent time and energy in hunting out information on the nascent union movement around Tolpuddle.

Letters between Frampton and Earl Digby show that he had already found out a lot about union activity in January 1834. They show that he knew that "nightly meetings" were taking place, that oaths were being sworn and that strikes were planned. In addition to Tolpuddle, he knew that "persons of Addpuddle, Britantspuddle and Turnerspuddle" were involved. Frampton also wrote to Lord Melbourne to get official backing. A reply from Melbourne's secretary agreed with Frampton's strategy in "employing trusty persons to endeavour to obtain information regarding the unlawful combinations".[865] Following this reply, a close correspondence developed between Frampton and Melbourne, who was regularly apprised of developments and offered advice in return. While Frampton was zealous in taking forward the prosecution of the Tolpuddle Martyrs, it was Melbourne who was to offer legal strategy for prosecution.

The cautionary placard was posted on Saturday 22 February 1834. We can assume that the magistrates were hoping that it could be used as evidence that the Tolpuddle trade unionists had been clearly warned of the dangers of their actions. There were two problems with this. Firstly, the men were arrested very early on the following Monday—hardly enough time for them to have done anything about the union, even if they had wanted to. Secondly, the caution clearly referred to "illegal societies or a union" which, as we have seen, was not strictly illegal.

Whatever the intention of the caution posted by Frampton and the other magistrates and however George Loveless felt when he read it, it is unlikely that he or any of the other Tolpuddle trade unionists believed that they had done anything wrong. In fact, when arrested they all walked to Dorchester without coercion. They had no idea that it would be many years before any of them saw their homes again. On arrival at Dorchester, George Loveless and the other trade unionists were questioned by a local magistrate, Mr Woolaston, and James Frampton. George records that he answered: "We are not aware that we have violated any law; if so, we must be amenable, I suppose to that law".[866] It is hardly a spirited defence and reflects, perhaps, a certain naivety on the part of Loveless and the others.

In his account of the trial and transportation, Loveless emphasises several times that the whole experience is new to him. In fact only Hammett had ever been in trouble with the law previously, for a minor crime which had earned him four months' hard labour. The prisoners had their heads shaved and were locked in a room before being moved to a prison cell a week later.

Once the prisoners were committed to trial, officials tried to get information out of them to enable wider prosecutions. Loveless tells how an attorney met with him alone and tried to get him to become an informant:

> [He] called me into the conversation room, and, among other things, inquired if I would promise the magistrates to have no more to do with the Union if they would let me go home to my wife and family? I said, "I do not understand you." "Why," said he, "give them information concerning the Union, who else belongs to it, and promise you will have no more to do with it." "Do you mean to say I am to betray my companions?" "That is just it," said he, "No; I would rather undergo any punishment".[867]

To their credit neither Loveless nor any of the others gave in to attempts to make them break their promises. This extended to their arrival in Australia, when pressure was again put on them to give further information on the union movement. Since it must have been becoming clear to all of them that they were facing serious punishment, it was remarkable that they did not break. It contrasts heavily with those, such as Edward Legg, who did scab on the movement and testify against the Martyrs. It is worth also noting that had George Loveless broken, the results could have been catastrophic for dozens of families as the authorities had the membership records and knew the names of those who had joined the union and probably only needed to prove that they had sworn an illegal oath—for which they would have needed a witness like George.

The pressure from all quarters didn't let up. Loveless recalled:

> The same day [as his meeting with the attorney] we were sent to the high jail, where we continued until the assizes. I had never seen the inside of a jail before, but now I began to feel it—disagreeable company, close confinement, bad bread, and what is worse, hard and cold lodging, a small straw bed on the flags, or else an iron bedstead—"and this", said I to my companions, "is our fare for striving to live honest".

The chaplain arrived "to pour a volley of instruction in our ears, mixed up...in the cup of abuse. After upbraiding and taunting us with being discontented and idle, and wishing to ruin our masters, he proceeded to tell us that we were better of than our masters, and that government had made use of every possible means for economy and retrenchment to make all comfortable."

Loveless replied that he could not believe the masters were less well off than the labourers when he could see "them keep such a number of horses for no other purpose than to chase the hare and the fox." After further pointing out that "gentlemen wearing the clerical livery...might do with a little less salary", the clergyman left saying he believed that the court would "make an example of you".[868]

The details of the trial will not detain us here, though readers who want to know more can find accounts based on contemporary newspapers in most histories of the Tolpuddle Martyrs,[869] but there is no doubt that the court set out to make an example of the men.

The plan had been concocted in detail by Lord Melbourne in correspondence with James Frampton and leading legal figures. On 10 March, Melbourne wrote to the "Attorney and Solicitor Generals" explaining that there were, throughout the country, societies with the object of increasing wages, whose members had sworn "secret oaths". Melbourne asked whether people were committing a crime by being members of such societies, and whether the societies themselves were illegal. If this was the case, Melbourne wanted to know, how he could proceed to punish those taking part.[870]

We know the reply he must have received, because, as Joyce Marlow explains,

> The 1817 Act made the members of societies taking oaths not required by law guilty of belonging to unlawful combinations within the meaning of an earlier Act, 39 Geo. III, c 79. This had been passed in 1799 'for the more Effectual Suppression of Societies Established For Seditious and Treasonable Purposes'...and it was a section of this 1799 Act that had originally made members taking secret oaths guilty of unlawful combination.[871]*

The 1799 Act, however, was based on an earlier act, 37 Geo. III, c 123, passed in 1797. This was a very specific piece of legislation ("An Act for More Effectually Preventing the Administering or Taking of Unlawful Oaths") that was passed at a moment of panic for the government during the Spithead and Nore mutinies. These mass strikes over wages by sailors in the Royal Navy involved crews on dozens of ships and led to the raising of radical political demands, giving events the name of the "Floating Republic". The 1797 Act was specifically designed at preventing mutinies in the armed forces and would have been irrelevant to the Tolpuddle case were it not that in addition to mentioning military personal it included the words "and others of His Majesty's subjects".[872]

This was enough to ensure that the Dorchester Labourers, as they were known at the time, were found guilty. At this time, defendants were not allowed to speak in court to defend themselves, but George Loveless gave a short statement in writing to the judge, who read it aloud to the court:

> My Lord, if we have violated any law, it was not done intentionally: we have injured no man's reputation, character, person or property: we were uniting together to preserve ourselves, our wives, and our children, from utter degradation and starvation. We challenge any man, or number of men to prove that we have acted, or intend to act different from the above statement.[873]

The judge read it out, but so indistinctly that Loveless complained that he couldn't understand it, even though he had written it. It made no difference for, in Loveless's words, the jury was selected from "landowners, the petty jury, land renters" who would have no trouble condemning

---

* Note that the nomenclature "39 Geo. III, c 79" is called the chapter number, describing when British parliamentary Acts are passed. In this case, the 79th act passed in the 39th year of the reign of George III.

the six men. This they duly did after only 20 minutes' discussion. A few days later, on 19 March, six men were sentenced to transportation for a period of seven years, the maximum permitted by the law for this crime. As Baron Williams, the trial judge, was to explain when passing sentence, "The object of all legal punishment is not altogether with the view of operating on the offenders themselves, it is also for the sake of offering an example and a warning...the crime...is of that description, that the security of the country, and the maintenance of the laws, on the upholding of which the welfare of this country depends, make it necessary for me to pass on you the sentence required".[874]

After sentencing, Loveless scribbled down the words to the song printed at the start of this chapter and threw them to the crowd. It was to become a rallying cry for the movement that sprang up almost immediately to get the labourers returned from abroad.

The *Dorset County Chronicle*, which reported in detail on the men's case, left in no doubt that they saw this as preventing the spread of trade unions:

> The extent to which these combinations in defiance of the law have lately existed, and the rapidity with which they are spreading, rendered it absolutely necessary that such examples of due severity should be set; that men should know that the laws of England are not to be defied with impunity... After such an instance as this...individuals who may be induced to assist in the purposes of these combinations, and the band themselves together in secret opposition...in self-elected, self constituted clubs, which as was well said by the learned Judge..."are calculated to shake the foundations of society, and bring the country into extremely perilous circumstances"—they can no longer plead ignorance.

The *Chronicle* continued gleefully to celebrate the men's punishment:

> They will be doomed to a long and wearisome exile from their native land, severed from their families, friends and connections, and wearing out their days in a state of slavery of the most pressing and laborious kind.[875]

It is interesting that the *Chronicle* chose to use the word "slavery" to describe the reality of transportation. In the months after the Tolpuddle Martyrs were found guilty and a campaign grew to get them freed, radicals and activists frequently used the term to describe the experience. In 1833 the Slavery Abolishment Act had been passed ending slavery through most of the British Empire. This had been the result of years of campaigning and at the time the Martyrs were transported was still an emotive issue. In his best selling pamphlet, *The Victims of Whiggery*,

George Loveless described his own experiences, and those of other transportees. Loveless was sent to Van Diemen's Land, now the Australian island of Tasmania.

> I worked on the roads with the chain-gang in the day, and slept in the barracks at night, without a bed, or covering whether any was allowed for me I cannot say, I had none. On the 22nd of September [1834] I was sent to the government domain farm, New Town, and here for a long time I found it very little better than at the barracks. Eight men, with only five beds, so of course the new comer must go without; and this was my portion, until some of the older hands unfortunately got in trouble, and I was entitled to a bed, having been longer on the farm that others. Our hut was none of the best: in fine weather we could lie in bed and view the stars, in foul weather feel the wind and rain; and this added greatly to increase those rheumatic pains which were first brought on by cold irons round the legs and hard lying; and which, in all probability, will be my companions until I reach the tomb.[876]

Violence was an everyday experience for prisoners who were either employed on government projects or sent to work on farms for settlers who frequently treated them appallingly. Loveless himself was taken before a court for neglect of duty. He was lucky; the magistrate recognised that Loveless simply had too much work to do in a single day and let him off, instead of the 50 lashes he was expecting.

On their return, the accounts of the Tolpuddle Martyrs helped awaken the public to what was happening in Australia. James Brine, for instance, was sent to work on a farm 30 miles from where he had arrived. While walking there he was robbed of all his belongings and had to work for six months "without shoes, clothes, or bedding". His role involved sheep washing, chest high in water. His master refused any assistance, saying he understood that in England, Brine had the "intention to have murdered, burnt, and destroyed every thing before you, and you are sent over here to be severely punished, and no mercy shall be shown you. If you ask me for any thing before the six months is expired, I will flog you as often as I like." Brine points out that this man was a magistrate![877]

The movement for justice for the Tolpuddle Martyrs began almost as soon as they were found guilty. The glee with which the local *Dorset County Chronicle* marked the sentences was not matched by most of the media. Modern trade unionists might be surprised to find that many newspapers, including *The Times*, *Morning Herald*, *Globe*, *Morning Post*, *Sunday Herald* and *Morning Chronicle*, while expressing their criticisms and intense dislike of trade unions, thought that the men had been wronged. Radical newspapers such as the *Republican*, the *True Sun* and Cobbett's *Political Register* supported the labourers wholeheartedly. The *True Sun* in particular became a major supporter of the Tolpuddle Campaign. As early as 20 March, the *True Sun* understood what was to become a major point for the campaign; if the Tolpuddle labourers were guilty, so were large numbers of others.[878]

Public meetings became a major part of the campaign. On 24 March the first such meeting attracted up to 10,000 people in London. Chaired by Dr Arthur Wade, a vicar known as the "chaplain to the metropolitan trade unions", and with a panel including Robert Owen, founder of the "Grand National Consolidated Trades Union", the meeting launched a campaign and petition for the "remission" of the Tolpuddle Martyrs' sentence. Within two days the first petitions were presented to parliament, including one signed by 1,563 people from Oxford, "a city which did not now, nor ever did, contain a single political or trades union". In parliament there was a short discussion on the case, with one MP wanting to amend the 1797 Act and a government spokesperson saying he thought it the intention to recommend mitigation to the king. Parliament then went into recess.[879]

Parliament may not have been sitting, but agitation continued. On 29 March another protest meeting took place in London and on the following day 12,000 people waited while a deputation took another petition to Lord Melbourne. Melbourne told the deputation: "the sentence would not be carried into effect until the petition was in the King's hand". Meetings in Birmingham and Nottingham took place in the next few days. But shortly after these promising events the government decided that Melbourne's assurance was not correct. Instead, they announced that the convicted had left England. This was, in fact untrue. None of the men had left the country and in fact George Loveless was still in Dorchester as he was too ill to travel. The other five were on a convict ship, but it had not yet left. While the others were soon to leave England, Loveless in fact remained in England until the end of May, but campaigners were not to know this. It is not hard to imagine that the government deliberately misled campaigners to try and undermine their campaign.[880]

The campaign, however, was making headway not least in the case of 16 men in Exeter who had been tried on a similar charge to that which had trapped the Tolpuddle men.[881] This Exeter case was dismissed, no doubt because the government did not want to open another front in the struggle.

The movement gathered pace. Protest meetings took place across the country. The politics of Tolpuddle became linked to wider political issues. For instance, in a report of a meeting in Huddersfield, a year after the Martyrs were transported, the *Poor Man's Guardian* reports,

> What the working classes want, is not simply the recall of the Dorchester Convicts, but the disavowal of the principle upon which they were transported. Of what consequence to them that six innocent men are restored, if the power is still to remain to transport as many more as their rulers may find expedient.

This was standard campaign fare, but the report makes it clear that wider generalisations were being made. A motion was passed linking the demand for the Reform Bill to the Tolpuddle case, "if they could carry the Reform Bill, they (the people) could fetch the six poor men back again." To cheers, a speaker made the case: "The great offence of these men was in trying to raise their wages... The cause was their uniting together. He would ask what were monarchies but unions? and what were churches and various other things, but unions...and unions too from which individuals had received thousands of pounds?"[882]

Malcolm Chase points out that in the "Pennine textile region", Tolpuddle was "entwined" with a "volatile local political situation". A general strike in 1834 in Oldham, argues the historian Robert Sykes, "can only be understood in the context of national issues, principally Tolpuddle".[883] Tolpuddle touched a raw nerve in the working class movement. It was clearly a gross injustice against the six men, even sections of the bourgeois press understood this. But it was also clearly about state repression and the rights of workers to organise. As Chase points out, several key working class leaders in the Chartist movement "cut their political teeth" on Tolpuddle.[884]

The behaviour of the ruling class helped fan the flames of indignation. In Tolpuddle, James Frampton refused to allow parish relief to be granted to the families of the transported men. Diana Standfield, who had five children and no income, was informed by the magistrates, "You shall suffer want. You shall have no mercy, because you ought to have known better than to have allowed such meetings to have been holden in your house".[885] This was all reported in the radical press. The response of the trade union movement was to provide support. The account of the Huddersfield meeting mentioned earlier finishes with a report of £3 17s (around £400 today) collected for the Tolpuddle funds, donors include several grocers, members of the cabinet makers' society, a barber, as well as an anonymous donor, who styled themselves "An Enemy to all tyrannical and obsolete Acts of Parliament".

The socialist historian Reg Groves argues in his history of agricultural trade unionism that Tolpuddle became a rallying cry for many not simply because of the injustice but because it was an attack on the right of workers to organise and thus a threat to the whole trade union movement and came at a crucial moment for the young trade union movement which was just beginning to flex its muscles.[886] It is notable that the support for the Tolpuddle men came from trade unionists, radicals and sympathisers on a huge scale. On 21 April 1834 a huge demonstration took place in London, dominated by the working class movement:

> At half past seven about five and thirty banners, fixed to long poles, formed of crimson and blue cotton, each bearing the initials of the different lodges of trades, were arranged in a line along the side of the road… Before eight o'clock, the lodges, preceded by their respective officers, decorated with different insignia and all wearing crimson ribbons, commenced marching on the ground, five and six abreast, with great regularity and almost military precision.[887]

The march led off at half past nine, joined by lodges from across the country, and the *True Sun* reported a "dense mass" of protesters "almost incalculable" in number.

The demonstration itself was the model of respectability. It assembled at Copenhagen Fields, near Kings Cross, which *The Times* described as "the old rendezvous of disturbance". But the newspaper was pleased to report that, while the protest was "most imposing", "utmost decorum prevailed" with a "semblance of military array, discipline and good order". The protest was led by horsemen and leading trade unionists with a carriage carrying an enormous petition on wooden rollers, with between 200,000 and 300,000 signatures.[888]

Despite the respectability, the huge protest must have scared the ruling class. Having previously agreed to meet a delegation, Lord Melbourne changed his mind, saying that he could not accept a petition presented in such a context. The organisers claimed 200,000 joined the march, *The Times* had reporters who calculated that 35,000 took part, a figure agreed by a number of other witnesses, though since they were former military officers in the Junior United Services Club, they might well have downplayed numbers. The radical *True Sun*, however, agreed with this figure as well (though acknowledging it did not include the tens of thousands who watched from the side of the march). Whichever figure was true, this was a massive protest for its time and was used by the radical movement to prove its respectability. With the demonstration, the *Pioneer* newspaper declared of the demonstration: "labour put its hat upon its head and walked towards the throne". Joyce Marlow notes that the *True Sun* thought the demonstration proved that the working classes were fit to vote.[889]

The respectability of 21 April 1834 was a relief to the ruling class and the leaders of the trade union movement. Indeed they must have been very pleased that the original intention for a nationwide strike "a long holiday" did not take place. For those concerned with the respectability of the workers' movement and winning access to parliament, strikes were not the sort of activity that would help. A week later, Tolpuddle was again discussed in both Houses of Parliament. In the House of Commons, Daniel O'Donnell dwelt in part on the legal nature of the convictions, quoting a letter from an eyewitness to the trial who had great concerns about the validity of the convictions, but also argued that trade unions had the potential to be a moral force for good in society. In the House of Lords, however, the Lord Chancellor, Henry Brougham, denounced the trade union movement in no uncertain terms, arguing that secret oaths were "offence most dangerous in itself, and fraught with worse danger still in its more remote consequences; leading to conspiracy,—leading to a violation of the rights of property,—leading to effects the most repulsive to human feelings and the most inexcusable amongst human beings,—leading, as he would emphatically say...even to assassination itself".[890] This was an emphatic statement by the politician whose role it was to oversee the legal system. But it was ironic, because it was precisely on the question of secret oaths that the Martyrs' case was to turn. In the meantime, despite the transportation of the other five Martyrs, George Loveless was still in a prison hulk in Portsmouth. But the government kept this hidden.

Agitation continued and over a year later, on 25 June 1835, Thomas Wakley, the radical independent MP for Finsbury, put a motion to the House of Commons calling for a pardon. He outlined the case against them, their strong moral character and the "conspiracy to entrap the accused" and argued that the union was not illegal, even if the oath was, but that the "oath alone could not make the society illegal". Wakley was defeated by 308 votes to 82, but his side was growing in parliament.[891]

Wakley did not give up. Less than two months later he presented a 5,000-strong petition from Bristol to the Commons calling for a "remission of the sentence". He then turned to something that had become a major question for the establishment and which concerned the Protestant society, the Orange Order. This was not the first time the issue had been raised during the campaign for the Tolpuddle men. Others had highlighted the fact that those who swore a secret oath in the Orange Order where not deported, but George Loveless and the others had been. The difference, as Wakley pointed out, was one of class: "If all those Orangemen thus accused were not prosecuted, the people of England would be satisfied that there was one law for the rich and another for the poor." The problem for the British government and Lord Melbourne (now the Prime Minister) was that the Duke of Cumberland, brother of King William IV, was Imperial Grand Master of the Orange Order![892]

The question of Tolpuddle would not go away. Radicals in parliament and outside agitation meant that it kept being raised. In February 1836, Joseph Hume raised the extent to which the Orange Order was influential in the British Army "tending to sap and undermine its discipline". There were, he said, 200,000 Orangemen in Ireland and 100,000 in England. Despite orders from the king himself that any soldier "who attended any Orange Lodge should be liable to be tried by a court-martial", Hume could point out that because the Duke of Cumberland headed the organisation, this implied that Orangemen "could break the law with impunity".[893]

Facing defeat, Lord Russell, the new Home Secretary, agreed to press the king to take measures to discourage Orange lodges and "all political societies". A few days later, the Duke of Cumberland announced "the dissolution of the Orange Society of Great Britain". Cumberland thus avoided the unlikely scenario of being tried and transported, but having allowed him the opportunity to do this, the government now had to admit that the Tolpuddle men should not have been convicted. Initially the government announced in early March 1836 that the sentences would be commuted, but under pressure from Wakley and further petitions, Lord Russell announced on 14 March 1836, that the king had "been pleased to grant a free pardon" to the Tolpuddle men.[894]

The government had found a way out of its mess. But it had only done this because of the enormous pressure from outside parliament that had meant the issue had not been forgotten. Had this agitation not happened, the question of the Orange Order would never have been linked to the trade union movement and the enormous embarrassment of the king's brother potentially being tried for heading up a secret organisation would never had arisen.

Today it would be a simple matter to send a message to the other side of the world. But in the 1830s communication between England and Australia was enormously slow and letters were frequently lost. Even when news of the pardons reached the authorities in Australia, they deliberately failed to locate the Tolpuddle Martyrs at their places of work. Some of the Martyrs were working a long way from Sydney, but James Loveless and James Brine were working only a few miles outside the town. Even when they learnt of the pardons, officials often failed to tell the men everything. For instance, James Loveless was told he was a free man, but not entitled to free passage home. For months he and James Brine continued to work on the government farm until finally told that free transport had been granted (though the superintendent still tried to delay things by telling them all ships were fully booked for months ahead).[895]

Several of them only found out by accident that they had been released and were hindered in their return by bureaucracy and official lack of interest. Loveless found out in September 1836, from an old newspaper (published in April), of his pardon and wrote a letter to a newspaper asking that the Governor would have the "goodness" to tell him if there were instructions for his return. Loveless refused initially to return to England because he had been persuaded to invite his family to join him in Australia. He didn't want to return home to find that his wife had left already. Only months later, when he received a letter from her, was he willing to travel. He did not leave for England until January and arrived on 13 June 1837.[896]

James Brine, James Loveless and John and Thomas Standfield did not leave Australia until 11 September 1837 and James Hammett was not to return until December 1838 or January 1839 (we don't know the exact date). It is an appalling comment on the British legal system that having been forced to pardon the Tolpuddle men, it took years to release them. They were left ignorant and ignored by officials in Australia and, once they found out the news, had to battle for the right to leave. But they were not forgotten by the working class of England. All of the Martyrs were met with enormous crowds, meetings and processions and tremendous support. The four who arrived together in Plymouth did not return immediately to Tolpuddle but took part in public meetings in that town and in places along the route home. Reunited with George Loveless, they travelled a few days later to London, where the Dorchester Committee had organised a procession and dinner.[897]

As part of the wave of solidarity and sympathy for the Tolpuddle Martyrs and their families, the movement raised a huge collection to buy the six men land so that they could be farmers. The fund was launched after a big demonstration in London at Kennington Common to welcome the men back in April 1838 and enough money was eventually raised to purchase the lease on two farms in Essex, to which the Martyrs moved in August 1838. The five men moved there and as well as running the farms also took part in local Chartist agitation.[898]

In November 1838, after the five men and their families had moved to Essex, a Chartist rally took place on Charlton Down, near Blandford, close to Tolpuddle. John Standfield attended the meeting, being given three cheers by the crowd. The meeting also elected George Loveless, in his absence, to be the Dorset delegate to the "Great Convention" that the Chartists were organising for the following February. Loveless did not go, but it is interesting to see the link between the Tolpuddle Martyrs and the first great mass working class movement in British history.[899]

When Hammett finally arrived back in London the following year, he too was feted, with a large meeting in a London theatre. Proving that their experience had not dimmed their desire for justice, John Standfield made a speech thanking the audience for their support:

> He thanked the Dorchester Committee for their unceasing exertions, and the public for the generosity, and expressed the conviction that whenever any great object was to be attained, they needed nothing but union, a determined union, to achieve it.[900]

At this point the theatre management closed the meeting down.

Hammett returned to Tolpuddle where he lived out his life, though he was no longer a farm labourer, instead working in the building trade. Perhaps he found it hard to get work as a well known trade unionist.

The other five men lived in Essex with their growing families until the 1840s. Then they all decided to emigrate with their families to Canada. Joyce Marlow speculates that the families were worn out by the struggle they had taken part in and by the fact they were assumed to be responsible for "any trade union activity or threat of riot" that happened near their homes.[901] Whatever the reason, the men and their families moved to Canada where they prospered.

Hammett remained in Tolpuddle and as far as we know did not take part in any trade union activity again. However there was one final event that took place which links the Tolpuddle Martyrs to the next and final part of the story of rural class struggle in England. In 1874 there was a rebirth of the agricultural trade union movement, which grew rapidly across the country. The following year, this new union decided to hold a rally at which James Hammett's role in the early years of the movement would be celebrated. On the 41st anniversary of the conviction of the Martyrs, 2,000 people joined a demonstration which marched to Tolpuddle. Rather extraordinarily, it was on this occasion that Hammett confirmed that he had never been at the fateful meeting. Instead he took the blame rather than let his brother John, whose wife was pregnant, be sentenced. James Hammett had never once broken his silence, an amazing act of solidarity. Speeches linked Hammett to other martyrs of the agricultural workers, Wat Tyler and Jack Cade being named. Other speakers called for the need to extend the vote to rural workers. Hammett was presented with a gold watch and a purse of money. Hammett's speech finished when he showed the watch to the audience and said: "Isn't that better than having seven years put on you, and that for a wrong cause? We only tried to do good to one another, the same as you're doing now." Hammett never spoke or wrote about his time in Australia. When asked, he is supposed to have said: "If you'd been sold like a sheep for £1 would *you* want to talk about it?" James Hammett passed away in 1891 in the Dorchester Workhouse. It is fitting that he was part, in a small way, of rural trade unionism's great peak: the revolt of the fields.[902]

Almost from the day of their conviction, the Tolpuddle Martyrs were lauded by the wider trade union movement. This contrasts almost completely with the way that the victims of the repression that followed Captain Swing a few years before have been forgotten. Few memorials stand to them, and no annual festivals commemorate their struggles and sacrifices. In part this was because Tolpuddle coincided with a new spurt of growth of early trade unionism. Just as the organisers of the great London demonstration in support of the Martyrs celebrated its respectability, the trade union movement's leaders wanted to prove their respectability, to the ruling class. They were campaigning for reforms, and in particular the vote.[903] They certainly were not going to celebrate the burning of hayricks and the destruction of threshing machines, however successful a movement that might have been.

Hernhill: "The Last Rising" of the agricultural workers[904]
While discontent at low wages and poverty would continue to lead to sporadic protest and outbreaks of violence in the English countryside for decades after Tolpuddle, there is one final rising, which is almost forgotten today, that we shall note in passing. This is the May 1838 Hernhill Rising that took place in the Swale district of Kent.

The Hernhill Rising has been called the last battle fought on English soil. In reality it was a skirmish between about 150 soldiers of the 45th Infantry Regiment, some local landowners and up to 50 local labourers. The labourers were following their leader, a fascinating figure who called himself Sir William Courtenay. His real name was John Nicholls Tom, and he was a maltster from Truro. Courtenay, or Tom, had a conviction for perjury, had stood for election under his assumed name, had recently been released from an asylum and hoped to become a popular leader.[905] In the early 1830s in Kent, Courtenay set himself up as a "champion of the poor" and his December 1832 election result (379 compared to the 834 and 802 received by his opponents) demonstrates at least some local support. Less successful in a subsequent election (he received four votes), he followed this up with a newspaper aimed at the poor.[906]

A couple of convictions for swindling and perjury brought him into conflict with the authorities. Courtenay faced seven year's transportation, but instead was put in the Kent asylum—he had appeared in court dressed in "full regalia and complete with a small scimitar". In his account of the Rising, Barry Reay makes the point that while Courtenay behaved unusually to our mind, he "makes more sense as a political personality if set in the context of nineteenth-century demagogic and charismatic leadership". Courtenay combined radical rhetoric—in elections and in his newspaper, opposition to flogging in the army and in favour of wage rises—with a "curious mix of religious rambling...with claims he was the King of the Gypsies, Prince of Arabia" and so on.[907]

In May 1838, about 40 men, mostly from the "lower rungs of parish society" who had all suffered as a result of rural poverty, decided to follow Courtenay. As Reay points out, the rising was fuelled by "socio-economic discontent" but driven by religion. Sarah Hills, one of the rioters' wives remembers that another woman had visited her cottage and after drinking ale, showed her and her husband the Biblical passage of Revelations that the Saviour would arrive on a white horse. The following day she saw Courtenay's white horse being led along. Others said Courtenay claimed "the millennium was at hand, and that the reign of the saints was approaching".[908]

On 29 May 1838, Courtenay and a small band marched in military style around the local villages with a loaf of bread on a wooden pole. Many local workers saw them as they passed. Up to 50 people travelled around 40 miles with Courtenay who asked "labourers as they passed to join his ranks, as he would provide them with provisions and money" and "that there was great oppression in the land, and indeed throughout the world, but that if they would follow him, he would lead them on to glory". Fearing that this revolt would spread, the local landowners ordered the local constable to arrest the leaders. The constable, John Mears and his brother Nicholas arrived at Courtenay's base where Nicholas was killed by Courtenay. The military were called and eventually the labourers were cornered by two groups of troops who opened fire "in self defence". Radical newspapers at the time quickly made the point that this was an unnecessary massacre. The labourers had just two pistols and cudgels. The threat to the musket-bearing troops was minimal. Courtenay killed a Lieutenant Bennett and was himself killed, as were eight of his followers. At least one special constable was also killed by the soldiers.[909]*

The Hernhill Rising and massacre was the last of the violent collective uprisings in English rural history. It demonstrated that the ruling class was still fearful of the power of rural workers and had memories of earlier mass protests. They understood that rural poverty had created a tinderbox that could easily explode. Graffiti written on Hernhill's tithe barn door during the revolt reminds us what these labourers fought for:

> If you new ho was on earth your harts Wod turn
> But don't Wate to late
> They how R
> O that great day of gudgement is close at hand
> It now peps in the dor
> Ever man according to his woks
> Our rites and liberties We Will have.[910]

We now turn to the next wave of resistance, the formation of the first national agricultural unions, forged out of a major strike wave.

Between the events of Captain Swing and the rise of agricultural trade unionism, the countryside was hardly quiet. As John E Archer has pointed out in his study of East Anglia between 1815 and 1870, protest was not unusual, it took place *all the time*". He highlights hundreds of examples of fires, assaults and attacks on animals. These acts of resistance and protest were not overtly collective in the sense of the mass actions of Swing, but nor were they simply individual acts of terror. Archer points out that "if one separates the act of starting the fire...from the subsequent reaction which the fire engendered...then the dichotomy does not appear

---

* The 45th Infantry were described as "young and inexperienced". A year later their "inexperience" again led them to kill 20 Chartists during the Newport Rising. Reay, 2010, p76.

to be that great." In other words, the fires provided opportunities for workers to come together and protest in a way that meant they could not be targeted by the authorities.[911] Rural poverty did not disappear with Swing and therefore protest also did not vanish but took on more covert forms. However, these individual acts of protest, even if they were made in the context of wider support, contrast dramatically with the trade union consciousness that would arise in the latter half of the 19th century. Captain Swing represented a peak of struggle, but it was also rooted in the old traditions of rural protest. Tolpuddle had been linked to the emerging urban trade union movement, but it would not be until the 1870s that this found mass expression in the countryside.

10

Joseph Arch: the revolt of the fields and agricultural trade unionism

We won't be idle, we won't stand still,
We're willing to work, to plough and till:
But if we don't get a rise we'll strike, we will,
For all have joined the union.[912]

ON 7 February 1872, in the village of Wellsbourne, Warwickshire, 2,000 labourers gathered around an oak tree. They had come from villages for ten miles around with the intention of forming a union to fight for better wages. Joseph Arch, a local liberal and former labourer, though more recently a carpenter and expert hedgecutter, had been asked to address the meeting. Arch describes the meeting in his autobiography:

By this time the night had fallen pitch dark; but the men got bean poles and hung lanterns on them, and we could see well enough. It was an extraordinary sight... I mounted an old pig-stool, and in the flickering light of the lanterns I saw the earnest upturned faces of these poor brothers of mine—faces gaunt with hunger and pinched with want... My speech lasted about an hour... By the end of it the men were properly roused, and they pressed in and crowded up asking questions... We passed a resolution to form a Union then and there, and the names of the men could not be taken down fast enough; we enrolled between two and three hundred members that night. It was a brave start, and before we parted it was arranged that there should be another meeting at the same place in a fortnight... I knew now that a fire had been kindled which would catch on, and spread...and I felt certain that this night we had set light to a beacon which would prove a rallying point for the agricultural labourers throughout the country.[913]

A fortnight later the crowd was even bigger and Arch comments that "nearly every policeman in the county" was also there. Writing a quarter of a century after events, Arch is even then at pains to make sure the reader knows that he had no intention of them being seen as "red-handed revolutionaries". He "would be a peaceable Wat Tyler of the fields, but I would be no rioting leader of the riotous. Neither I nor they should wear handcuffs and see the inside of a gaol… We had come there to strike off the rusty old fetters that had crippled us…not to forge new ones for ourselves".[914]

Joseph Arch was seen as a natural choice as leader of the local labourers. His radical politics were well known, and he was renowned for his preaching. He was a leading figure in the Primitive Methodists, a sect expelled from the Wesleyan Methodists. They trained working men and women to preach and they often walked miles to do so.[915] As a result Arch was well known through the area.

Too often Arch's autobiography gives the impression that the National Agricultural Labourers' Union (NALU) that grew out of the Wellsbourne meetings was mostly the result of his personal activity. Arch was prone to overemphasise his own role in events and in his later life was left embittered and felt forgotten by the workers he had tried to organise. But as Pamela Horn makes clear in her account of Arch's life, others were doing similar work and there were plenty of villages were meetings took place independently to discuss trade unionism. That said, Arch was one of the key driving forces of the movement. Having agreed to speak at that first meeting, he was driven to build and strengthen the union as much as possible and he travelled the length and breadth of the country at great personal sacrifice to do so.

The countryside was ripe for trade unionism. One of the unusual things about Arch was that he was near untouchable for his radical activities. He owned his own cottage, so would not face eviction by an irate landlord, and he was a very skilled hedgecutter, something that almost guaranteed work. But this was not the case for the majority of agricultural workers.

In 1870 agriculture was still the single biggest employer of male workers in Britain. In 1871 there were 922,024 "agricultural labourers, shepherds and farm servants… In addition, there were 33,513 female labourers and 24,599 farm servants". About a tenth of male workers and a thirteenth of female workers were under 15 (Arch himself began work as a bird scarer at the age of nine, for 4d a day). Economic prosperity and the growth of industry drained workers from the countryside into the cities and increased use of farm machinery was reducing demand for workers. Wages varied dramatically. Pamela Horn quotes one "estimate" for 1869-1870 for Durham at 16s 2d per week, Northumberland 15s 8d, Lancashire 14s 8d, Dorset 9s 4d and Norfolk 10s 5d. Women's wages were lower—in Arch's Warwickshire wages for women varied between 6d and 1s per day.[916]

Readers will note that these figures are scarcely higher than those demanded by the Swing rioters or George Loveless's comrades 40 years earlier. But there was huge variation, especially as agriculture was seasonal. Wages might depend on the length of employment (annual hiring was more common in the north, weekly in the south), gender and age. Wages were sometimes paid in beer or cider, a practice only made illegal in 1887. In 1867 the Gangs Act had made it illegal to employ "gangs" and children under eight. Gangs were usually women and girls who were supplied in large groups to tackle particular jobs, moving around to fill immediate employment needs. Victorian clergy and other commentators worried at how the gang system potentially led to vice and immorality as both sexes worked, and slept, closely together. Rural housing was also appalling. Labourers' homes were often little more than hovels and usually tied to employment. They were frequently overcrowded. The Reverend James Fraser in the late 1860s reported:

> The majority of the cottages that exist in rural parishes are deficient in almost every requisite that should constitute a home for a Christian family in a civilised community... Physically a ruinous, ill-drained cottage, 'cribbed, cabin'd, confined,' and over-crowded, generates any amount of disease...as well as intensifies to the utmost that tendency to scrofula and phthisis which from their frequent intermarriages and their low diet, abounds so largely among the poor.[917]

So it is not surprising that in the 1860s workers began to make moves to get organised. This work was often focused on Methodist chapels. As Reg Groves explains, "their very establishment was often an act of rebellion against squire and parson" and because with each chapel came independent-minded speakers, activists and organisers and the community helped teach reading, writing and encouraged men and women to go out and speak in public.[918]

Early rural trade unionism was often quite different to what we expect today. In 1863 Canon Girdlestone arrived in Halberton, North Devon. He found labourers on 8s or 9s a week, no sick pay and appalling poverty. They also got a daily quart or two of cider, presumably to help them cope with their conditions. Girdlestone used his church as a platform to denounce these conditions, but organised to get families to migrate to areas of England with better pay and as a result some 400 men and their families had moved. This spurred others to copy his practice and clubs, co-operatives and small trade unions were set up around the south-west with similar ambitions.

Other examples of early fledgling unions included the Agricultural Labourers' Protective Association formed in Kent in 1866 and an 1867 strike by labourers in Gawcott, near Buckingham. In Norfolk, a schoolmaster called Flaxman helped found an "Association for the Defence of the Rights of the Poor" which went on to become Flaxman's Eastern Counties Union. In Herefordshire a union formed in 1871 spread around six counties and with the slogan "Emigration, Migration, but not Strikes" helped send "surplus labour" to Yorkshire, Lancashire and Staffordshire "where wages were 6s or 7s higher". In January 1872 a meeting of farm workers in Hagley, Worcestershire, met and agreed to send a deputation to the local farmers asking for a wage rise of 2s 6d a day, which, as Groves says, was "another sign that the labourers were combining".[919]

Given the appalling conditions, it is no surprise that in the countryside there were repeated examples of workers trying to organise. But there were other factors too. Trade unionism in the cities and towns was growing. In 1868 the Trades Union Congress (TUC) was founded and the 1871 Trade Union Act had legalised unions, though the Criminal Law Amendment Act made picketing illegal. The Reform Act of 1867 had extended the vote to male householders and to men who paid rent of over £10 a year. However, while many workers were able to vote as a result, agricultural labourers were still excluded. The Reform Act had been the result of a significant movement and the demand to extend the franchise to agricultural workers was to become a key campaigning point for the rural labour movement. The Labour Representation League, founded in 1869, had begun the long process that would culminate in the founding of the Labour Party. But already the League was helping select candidates for trade union support who stood under the Liberal Party's banner.

So there was a political context to the growth of agricultural trade unionism in the late 1860s and early 1870s, with the working class flexing its muscle, developing its organisations and tackling political questions. However, this was mostly confined to urban areas and there was little belief that workers in the countryside would emulate workers in the towns and cities.[920] But by January 1872, as Pamela Horn tells us, the agricultural trade union movement "had already become established...in a number of counties in southern and central England, including...Herefordshire, North Warwickshire, Lincolnshire and Leicestershire".[921] These precede Joseph Arch's more famous meeting and show that there was a real appetite for union organisation, something that Arch seized upon following his meeting in February. The chapter in his autobiography covering the beginnings of the movement is called "The Call Comes" and Arch had clearly decided to seize the moment: "I felt as if there was a living fire in me. It seemed to me that I was fulfilling a mission".[922] He devoted the next months of his life to travelling around from village to village speaking and organising meetings to set up trade unions. Arch didn't restrict himself to trade unionism, he also spoke on the need for the agricultural labourer to win the vote.

The setting up of the union branches was occasionally followed by strikes as workers were eager to win improvements. The Wellesbourne union leaders recognised that they had to take action soon and put out a demand for a wage increase of 2s 8d a day and fixed hours of work from six to five on a weekday and six to three on Saturday, with overtime rates of 4d an hour. Notice was given that if this wasn't granted, a strike would begin on Saturday 9 March. Confident that this would not take place, the farmers ignored the letter and on 11 March about 200 workers from Wellsbourne and surrounding villagers went on strike. A small number of workers didn't take part as they were afraid of losing their tied cottages and gained a "slight increase in wages" for "loyalty"; nor did the shepherds and carters who earned more than the labourers.[923]

Joseph Arch recalled that the strikers were so unused to having a free day that they did not know what to do with themselves and "hung about idle". But Arch celebrated the strike's unity, "every man who had put his hand to the Union plough meant to stick to it till the Union work was done." With little in the way of funds the strikers had to rely on credit from local shops. Local trade unionists in towns like Leamington quickly formed committees to provide solidarity and supportive articles in the press from journalists writing on the poverty of the countryside helped increase this. Other support came from Birmingham, where Joseph Chamberlain donated money to the Union. Solidarity from workers was also forthcoming, including from Birmingham Trades Council.[924]

The union was rapidly growing. Three weeks after the start of the strike, there were 5,000 members in 60 villages. This helped encourage union growth elsewhere in the country. On Good Friday, 29 March 1872, labourers and their families came together in Leamington for a demonstration. This was also the occasion for the foundation of the Warwickshire Agricultural Labourers' Union, bringing together all the branches under one organisational umbrella. The union's aim was:

> To elevate the social position of the farm labourers...to increase their wages; to lessen the number of ordinary working hours; to improve their habitations: to provide them with gardens or allotments; and to assist deserving and suitable labourers to migrate and emigrate.[925]

Following the setting up of the Warwickshire union, an evening meeting attracted a huge turnout from all around Leamington and joined by the "organised artisans" of the town, they heard Joseph Arch speak. The Wellsbourne strike finished in April; all but 29 of the 200 strikers had been found jobs elsewhere, including in a Liverpool soap factory and at the Gateshead docks, and others had emigrated.[926]

At this time the agricultural unions saw their role as assisting members to find better paid jobs elsewhere, despite this undermining of their own organisation in the long term. A "well attended" open-air meeting in March 1872 at Tachbrooke in Warwickshire, for example, heard from Mr Russell of the union who "made a few remarks deprecating strikes" then talked about the opportunities for those out of work with, for instance, the Midland Railway Company, and said that he would pay travel expenses for those wanting to take up offers. The crowd clearly thought this was good news, cheering when he said that he could find a thousand other jobs. Interestingly, after denouncing the poverty of agricultural workers, he reported that the union had sent £20 to agricultural workers in Ireland who had used it to emigrate to Canada. In Essex, Charles Jay, a leading figure in the new union movement, even brought Mayor Gleig of the Liverpool police down to recruit to the force.[927]

The successes of the union forced a response from the employers and on 5 April a meeting of the Midlands Farmers' Club agreed to resist the "interference of designing political agitators" who were encouraging "dissension between employers and employed" in the region. A lockout of strikers and union members was organised and there were evictions of families. But support for the union was strong and after three months the employers agreed to negotiate with the union and pay rose to 16s a week.[928]

Trade unionism was now spreading rapidly in many areas of the country. In March, the Lincolnshire Amalgamated Emigration and Migration Labour League was formed, led by William Banks, a farm worker. By May there were local unions set up in Cambridgeshire, Shropshire, Wiltshire, Oxfordshire, Kent and many other places. The new union branches were inspired by events elsewhere, but they often had their own flavour. In Old Buckenham, Norfolk, 200 workers met at the White Hart. There were no formal speakers and "Men sat round upon the benches, and each, as he rose to speak, asked for silence. A committee was chosen to send an application to the farmers for an advance in wages, and to raise funds for the continuation of the agitation." The London Trades Council held a delegate meeting to support the agricultural unions and locked out workers and organised a meeting to bring together the different regional unions for 9 April. This was superseded by a call from the Warwickshire union for a national conference in Leamington on 29 May. Warwickshire was "swamped" with requests for assistance from across England and to cope with the demand had agreed to call a conference to which each body could send delegates.[929]

The conference was a huge success. Supported by the radical MP George Dixon, delegates from around the country heard a report of successes so far. Given that the meeting under the Chestnut tree at Wellesbourne had taken place in early February, Warwickshire activists could be proud to have a network of 4,695 members in 64 branches just a few months later. Over the course of its duration the conference and associated public meetings heard reports from across the country, papers on subjects covering allotments, co-operative farming, the state of rural housing and emigration. The end of the first day saw the formation of a national union, and the election of an executive committee of agricultural workers, including Joseph Arch.[930]

The formation of the national union accelerated the growth of workers' organisation everywhere. For instance, take this account of a meeting in Montacute, Somerset, in June 1872 from the *Western Gazette*. The meeting heard from George Potter of the newly formed national union, who argued that the workers

> must take part in the movement going on in all parts of the country, and become members of the National Labourers' Union. He [Potter] advised them to form a branch at once, for wherever there was combination of workmen, wages were reasonable and the hours of labourer were short... Mr Potter said the end of the deep distress of the sons of the soil was drawing nigh. The handwriting was upon the wall; the landlords and the farmers had been put in the balance and had been found want—wanting in generosity to the men they employed.
>
> In times past the oligarchy of the country had monopolised political power, wealth, distribution of places, and sinecures. But that day was gone; and the labourers would no longer be content with cracked and stony floors to their homes; they would no longer be required to have 10 persons sleeping in one bedroom; they would not again go without meat...not more bring up their children in ignorance which led to prostitution, intemperance and crime; but they would strive to be comfortably fed, industriously employed and temperately endowed a people proud of their country, and a country would be proud of her people.[931]

The meeting also heard from George Mitchell, a businessman who had been a labourer and who would put much of his own money and enthusiasm into the movement (though "he was opposed to strikes").[932] But most of the platform represented newly formed union branches and Potter's speech emphasised that this was not a movement of revolution, but one that was demanding improvements in workers' lives in the national interest.

In Dorset, over 2,000 workers joined in the first nine weeks, the centre of the union being Blandford, not far from Tolpuddle. In his account of the union's history, first published in 1948, Reg Groves gives the recollection of trade unionist Bert Wellstead, whose father had heard Joseph Arch speak and had joined the union. At Winterbourne Kingston, halfway between Blandford and Tolpuddle, there was a place still known as "Arch's corner" where the trade union leader had spoken. Wellstead recalled: "Wages were nine shillings a week when Arch came, and hundreds joined his union. When he came to Kingston the farmers turned up in force and pelted him with rotten eggs, but he was soon in a position to deal with them all right and wages went up from nine to twelve shillings a week. And there, they stood till 1916".[933]*

A year after its formation the union had 71,835 members in 982 branches, a formidable total. It had a presence in every English county except "Cumberland, Westmoreland, Yorkshire, Lancashire, Cheshire and Cornwall". A newspaper, *The Labourers' Union Chronicle* (which despite its name was not owned by the union, but supported it), had a circulation of 35,000 at a time when 80 percent of farmer workers could not read.[934]

The two years after the union's formation were ones of hard struggles. Countless small-scale local strikes took place, rarely receiving national coverage. Joseph Arch describes the process: "Union men working for a farmer or two would ask for Union wages. They would give notice on the Saturday that they wanted the rise the next week. If the farmers held out and refused it, the men would leave on the following Saturday".[935]

One that did get national coverage was the July 1872 strike and lockout by 120 men in Wootton, Oxfordshire, after they had demanded a pay rise. National outrage was caused when the farmers used the army to gather in the harvest, despite the Queen's Regulations explicitly saying that this was not allowed if "the employment of the population is not interfered with".[936]

Another strike that made national news was one that showed the role of women. A strike at Ascot, near Chipping Norton, resulted in the

* A visit by Joseph Arch and the formation of a union left a lasting impression on many workers. In his first autobiographical book, *The Distant Scene*, the celebrated author and farmer Fred Archer, who was born in 1915, recalls hearing men talk about the time Arch came and spoke.

farmer bringing in two scabs from a nearby village. A group of women tried to block their entrance to the fields. Although the women were carrying sticks, they did not use them as weapons. Seventeen women were tried for this though Joseph Arch said that in court the two men reported that "far from being set upon with sticks, they had been invited by the women to come back to the village and have a drink". Seven of the women received ten days' hard labour and nine got seven days. The magistrates, who were both clergymen, used the full force of the law, but the decision caused outrage and a riot that evening. Eighty pounds was raised in their support (Arch notes that £5 of it came in pennies) and the women were brought home in style, cheered much of the way as they travelled in a "handsome drag drawn by four thorough-bred horses". The women were presented with £5 each and "a silk dress in the union colours".[937]

By May 1874 the union had grown to 1,480 branches and 86,214 members. Together with the independent unions, some 150,000 farm-workers were now organised. Wages had risen by 2s a week everywhere and by 3s or 4s in some places. It wasn't just the national union though; the independent Lincoln Labour League "fought and won no less than thirteen lock-outs in the year 1873".[938]

It is against the backdrop of growing workers' confidence, countless strikes and a massive union movement that in March 1874 the farmers decided to fight back. At Newmarket in Suffolk, in response to a strike by workers in Exning, the farmers resolved to "not in future employ any men to work for them who are members of the union".[939] Some 1,600 men were locked out. Such "combinations" of farmers and landowners to fight the union were set up in a number of places. The Norfolk-based West Walsham Farmers' Defence Association was founded in March 1873, in May 1873 the Huntingdonshire Farmers' Defence Association was set up and a month later had 100 members representing farms totalling 50,000 acres.[940] The farmers were joined in their struggle against the union by many representatives of the Church of England, whose clergy often preached against the union, though a few were supportive. The church's opposition to the strike led to a "union parody of the church catechism":

What is your name? Clodhopper.
Who gave you your name? My masters, the landowners and farmers, when I was a tiller of the soil, a scarer of birds, a keeper of cows and sheep, follower of the plough, a producer of wealth, that my masters might live in idleness and luxuriousness all the days of their lives.[941]

Nearby workers also went on strike and the employers responded again with a lockout. By April 6,000 were out; 4,000 were in the National Union and the remainder in the Lincoln Labour League. The unions paid strike pay and the members refused to surrender. But the lockout spread. Soon over 10,000 workers in Norfolk, Essex, Cambridgeshire, Bedfordshire, Oxfordshire, Hampshire, Dorset, Warwickshire and Gloucestershire were locked out. Dozens of families were evicted as the employers tried to break the union. In May, two MPs, George Dixon and Sam Morley, managed to broker a compromise in Lincolnshire that meant workers there returned to work and the lockout ended. But elsewhere the farmers remained obstinate.[942]

Thousands of pounds were collected in support of the locked out workers. Much of this came from other trade unions and there were clashes between the national union and the independents as money tended to get sent to Arch's organisation. Delegations of agricultural workers, both men and women, visited towns and raised money. In Manchester on 20 June, "200,000 gathered in the streets and joined in the procession". Ten thousand joined a rally in support in Battersea in July and there were big meetings elsewhere.[943]

The workers held out for five months. But as harvest time approached, many began to return to work or move elsewhere. By July the national union had only 800 men locked out in Suffolk. On 27 July the union executive decided to call off the action, announcing: "That in the face of the harsh and prolonged lock-out in the Eastern Counties this committee cannot feel justified in supporting the labourers in enforced idleness indefinitely; nor can they seek public support continually while the harvest is waiting to be gathered in. The committee therefore resolve to place migration and emigration at the disposal of the labourers or the alternative of depending wholly on their own resources".[944]

It was an inglorious defeat. The union was badly damaged. Andrew Charlesworth argues that, while the struggle was relatively localised, those involved had very high expectations "even millenarian".[945] Many workers were demoralised and the union lost thousands of members. The situation was made worse as the defeat allowed internal arguments to resurface. Arch himself was the focus of much of this. There was some discontent at his pay and the costs to the union of him travelling to North America to see the potential for emigration by English workers. The aftermath of the lockout led to thousands of labourers leaving England, including some of the best union militants. This, and the reality that workers were forced to leave the union to get work (Arch described them as "traitors" despite them having no alternative at all in the aftermath of defeat), meant that the union suffered heavily. By 1877 membership of the National Agricultural Labourers' Union was down to 55,000. But things would get worse. Several years of bad harvests and cheap wheat imports from Russia and America undermined the agricultural economy. Internal arguments and divisions led to splits in the national union.[946]

The union never recovered. In 1881 membership had fallen to 15,000 and by 1889 it had 4,254 members.[947] Arch himself was elected in 1885 as a Liberal MP, the first agricultural worker to enter the House of Commons. Unfortunately his parliamentary career was lacklustre. MPs at the time were unpaid and Arch struggled in this role. It was only the support of prominent liberals who organised an annual stipend for him that ensured he was able to retire back to Barford, where he died aged 92 in 1919, embittered towards the workers whom he felt abandoned him.

But it was the workers who suffered most. It would be almost two decades after the lockout of 1874 before the agricultural workers would rise again, though local struggles continued over the years. In the 1880s and 1890s, for instance, union organisation around East Anglia was strengthened by the influence of radical socialists like William Morris. With the foundation of the Independent Labour Party in 1893, local activists in Norwich made efforts to reach out into the surrounding countryside: "young Socialists would cycle out of Norwich into the surrounding countryside, holding meetings, selling Socialist papers and pamphlets, and urging the rural workers to join trade unions and support the Socialists." The Norfolk and Norwich Amalgamated Labourers' Union had some success in the 1890s; its Norwich branch had 1,000 members at one point.[948] Sadly the brief re-emergence of the union movement in East Anglia was short-lived.

Joseph Arch and the National Agricultural Labourers' Union had proved that trade unionism could be extended into the countryside and that agricultural workers could organise and win. The union's weaknesses reflected, in part, the variations of agriculture across England. The unions tended to be stronger in areas with larger, arable farms and areas with an existing radical tradition. As a result, union membership could be patchy, recruiting a majority of workers in particular villages but not across a county.[949] An as John Dunbabin explains, outside the south of England unionism was weaker as "farm servants were commonly hired on long contracts...hiring fairs generated a distinctive form of labour relations".[950]*

---

* A hiring fair allowed a prospective worker to negotiate directly with their potential employer the conditions for a fixed term contract, usually a year.

The new century saw a rebirth of the agricultural trade union movement. In 1906 a Liberal victory in the general election also saw Labour get 30 seats. In Norfolk, where the labourers voted against the Tories, the farmers "took their revenge". Many labourers thought to have voted liberal or being left wing were sacked and lost their homes. George Edwards, who had been part of the Norfolk and Norwich union in the 1890s, once again found himself at the centre of a new burst of trade unionism. In June 1906 he called a conference, appealing for support from Norwich trade unions and MPs. The Eastern Counties Agricultural Labourers and Small Holders Union was founded in July, but from the start was marked by tensions between the liberals and the more left-wing trade unionists. The emphasis of the founding resolution makes this clear when the conference agreed to found a union "the object of which shall be to enable the labourers to secure proper representation on all local bodies, and Imperial Parliament, protection from political persecution, and better conditions of living". Edwards became a paid organiser for the union and cycled around Norfolk organising hundreds of meetings, leafleting and recruiting. By 1909 the union was well established and tensions between the members, who wanted action, and the Liberal leadership who wanted energies directed towards elections, began to rise.[951]

In Trunch, in April 1910, after several months of tension between farmers and workers, a strike broke out over pay. Supported by the Norwich branch of the Independent Labour Party and ample donations from supporters, the strike lasted several weeks until all but one of the farmers gave in and agreed a nine-hour day at the old wage. The only hold out was a farmer who was himself under notice to leave. The union argued that those locked out from this farm should apply for small holdings on the vacated land. When the land came up for sale, "Edwards was able to persuade the Council to buy it for re-letting in small holdings". By the autumn the land had been divided up and the formally locked-out workers now farmed small holdings on the land, with other workers finding work elsewhere.[952] This illustrates one of the differences between agricultural and industrial trade unionism. Workers on strike in a factory or an office cannot hope to divide the workplace up and redistribute it among the strikers. But this can be possible in agricultural situations were land can be redistributed and, in revolutionary situations, this can take place on a large scale.

The success in Trunch demonstrated that other victories might be possible. Later in May, George Edwards found himself speaking at a meeting of the St Faith's branch of the union.[953] The men wanted "the union to get a rise of 1s a week and the Saturday half-day holiday". Edwards tried to hold the situation back. He was not a militant and was feeling the pressure of the union's executive, who did not want to waste money on strike pay and were more concerned with support for the Liberals. Rather than put the members' demands to the farmers, Edwards wrote to them urging a conciliation meeting. The farmers failed to respond and on 20 May 1910, when the union met again, it was clear that a strike would take place. On Friday 28 May, 105 men went on strike, including 30 from the Trunch area. Scab labour was used by the farmers, housed in purpose-built accommodation and escorted to work by the police. Despite the restraint of the workers and their families, the authorities found reason to prosecute those strikers' wives who "greeted a cartload of strike-breakers and police guards by singing a union song and beating tin kettles and saucepans".

Support was strong. Workplace collections outside Norwich factories ensured the strikers got strike pay of at least 10s a week and extra for strikers with families. The strike went on for six months into the winter, frightening the union executive as there was a general election called in December and they did not want the strike to overshadow the election and undermine Liberal chances. Thus the executive worked to call off the action. They balloted the *whole union* membership. A majority agreed that the executive could enter negotiations, but the St Faith's branch demanded a new ballot arguing that the terms of the negotiations were not clear. A second ballot was much closer: 1,102 for continuation of the strike, 1,052 for ending it "on the old terms, subject to there being no victimisation". Despite the majority, the executive agreed a settlement with the farmers that was total defeat. Forty-three men lost their jobs and the remainder only had their old pay and conditions.

To his credit, George and three other executive members voted against this. On the last day of the strike he took the final strike pay to the workers and some members broke down when they heard the news. Like many trade unionists before and after them, they had been defeated because of their leaders' cowardice.

At the union's next conference, in February 1911, anger at the sell-out of the strike led to the defeat of the old leadership. Two of the St Faith's strikers were elected to the executive and other positions were taken by socialists. Only two of those who had sold out the strike remained in position. Despite this, membership fell as a result of the sell out. But the new leadership took steps to push outwards, and launched the union as a national body, the National Agricultural Labourers' and Rural Workers' Union. By 1913 the union had 12,000 members. A second union, the Workers' Union was also growing.[954]

Between 1910 and 1914 Great Britain was shaken by a massive outbreak of workers' struggle. Dave Sherry summarises events:

> The causes of the Great Unrest...are easy to identify. Trade union membership had trebled since 1889 but real wages fell between 1900 and 1912. 'Everyone in society seemed to have gained in the glittering Edwardian era—except the workers'. Over the next four years a tidal wave of strike engulfed the whole of mainland Britain and colonial Ireland... The Great Unrest centred on huge strikes—first in all the ports, then the railways and the mines. It began in Southampton, then spread into dozens of different industries... The movement involved unskilled and often non-unionised workers. And it directly involved large numbers of women workers.[955]

The movement was much less pronounced in agriculture. But nonetheless there were some big disputes. Between 1912 and 1914 there were "countless small strikes", but in 1913 a strike in Ormskirk in Lancashire showed that the wider discontent was making itself felt in the countryside. Ormskirk's farms supplied the industrial cities of the north-west and the workers here had relatively high wages compared to other agricultural labourers. In May 1913 in response to long hours, and high prices, the workers demanded "a Saturday half-holiday...a minimum wage of 24s a week; 6d an hour overtime and recognition of the union".[956]

Immediately some of the workers were sacked and told to leave their tied cottages. The farmers were confrontational but they had not anticipated the solidarity of the wider union movement. Hundreds of pounds were raised by the urban unions, including dockers and shipworkers. The farmers were hiring scab labour from Ireland, but pickets of boats at Liverpool turned them back. Forced into negotiations, the farmers were intransigent until the National Union of Railwaymen at Ormskirk announced it would not take produce from the strike area to the towns and cities. Alun Howkins has called the railworkers "a new country worker", often from agricultural workers' families but with the "culture" of the trade union movement and "free from the threat of parson and squire". Four days later, the workers had won, securing all their demands except a 24s minimum wage, though they did get between 1s and 3s on top of 20s.[957]

Other strikes by the Workers' Union saw big gains for their membership and the workers and the National Agricultural Labourers' and Rural Workers' Union grew by 8,000 members. By mid-1914 they had 360 branches and 15,000 members. Other strikes and victories took place. Workers on the king's estate at Sandringham gained a promise that labourers there would get 16s and a Saturday half day. The king's agent promised that this would be recommended to all the king's farmer tenants and all cottages should have a six-month tenancy. This somewhat surprising goodwill from the estate shocked his tenant farmers, and probably the labourers, who raised the slogan: "The King's Pay and the King's Conditions". A strike ensured that those farmers who disagreed with the king quickly gave into demands.

In Essex a lockout of union members turned into a strike. In June, a strike brought 400 men out, asking for "16s a week for labourers, 18s to 20s, for stockmen, 20s, for horsemen; a weekly half-holiday and holidays on Christmas Day, Good Friday and Bank Holidays; overtime at 6d an hour; harvest rates at £8 for four weeks and 5s a day beyond four weeks; and for all tied cottages to be held on a three months' tenancy." Again support was strong from urban unions, including the dockers, and many of the demands were won, including an agreement by the farmers to keep their men working (that is, paid) during wet weather. The Essex strike won on 3 August. The following day war was declared between Britain and Germany.[958]

The First World War brought the Great Unrest in town and country to an end. The employers were lucky—thousands of agricultural workers were preparing to strike. Once again, war transformed rural relations. Many young men left to join the armed forces; by July 1915, 243,000 farmworkers had joined up. However after the initial euphoria, the experience of war forced some workers to fight as costs rose but wages did not. Agricultural workers were in a strong position. The pressure was on to produce food at home rather than rely on imports and this, alongside the unions' campaign, led to the Corn Production Act of 1917, which, for the first time, granted a "legal minimum wage for farm workers". The gains were significant for some workers. The first minimum wage, set for Norfolk, was "30s a week, for a fifty-four hour week in the summer and a forty-eight hour week in the winter", good overtime rates and a Saturday half-holiday. But these gains were not implemented until late in the war, or even years after the war in other parts of the UK. Membership of the union also shot up. The Agricultural Labourers' Union had a membership of "170,749 in October 1919 and the Workers' Union said it had over 100,000 in its agricultural section".[959]

The war meant a boom time for agriculture, but in 1921 the government pulled the plug on subsidies. Agriculture went into rapid decline and prices dropped dramatically. The amount of land being farmed also fell enormously. The end of subsidies brought the end of the minimum wage and by 1923 wage levels were lower than in 1914. Unemployment grew dramatically. In 1923 a major five-week strike in Norfolk stopped the fall in wages across the country, but over 1,000 workers were victimised (despite agreements against this). The number of strikers varied as workers were allowed to return to work when farmers were prepared to pay 30s (later 26s) for a 50-hour week. The strike involved 6,000 and sometimes as many as 10,000 workers. Once again, solidarity from industrial unions saw large donations towards the strike funds—"you'll not want for money" railway union leader J H Thomas told the agricultural workers—but this time there was no solidarity action. One historian of the agricultural trade union movement, Renée Danziger, concluded that the strike "was a costly show of the union's strength, which left a cautious reluctance among many members and officials to attempt industrial action again".[960]

The 1930s were difficult years for farm workers. Economic crisis meant lower wages and longer hours. Some 10,000 workers a year moved to the cities for work. Once again, wartime was to see a major change in fortunes for agriculture as the British government ensured that farming was radically expanded. An extra six million acres of arable land were created and the total land available for crops was almost back at the level of its peak in the 1860s. Farmers received a subsidy of £2 for every acre of grassland they brought into cultivation. In some cases the government took over unproductive farms and as thousands of men joined the armed forces, the "Women's Land Army" took over. Farming itself was transformed as motorised equipment was introduced on a massive scale. At the end of the Second World War there were still 545,000 farm horses, but the 56,000 tractors on British farms in 1939 had mushroomed to 230,000 by January 1946. As the historian Angus Calder commented, "Agriculture was dragged...into the 20th century, the ploughman servicing his tractor and the farmer calculating his needs for fertilisers drew closer in spirit and attitudes to the engineers and manager who made, among other things, the new farm machinery".[961]

Agriculture would never be the same again.

Afterword

THOSE WHO worked the land in previous centuries would find 21st century British agriculture almost unrecognisable. The first thing that would be noticeable is how few people work on the land. While 17.2 percent of the British population live in rural areas (about 11 million people), only 1.13 percent of the total working population is employed in agriculture.[962] British farming is almost completely mechanised and highly dependent on artificial pesticides, fertilisers and fossil fuels. One of the reasons for the significantly high environmental impact of agriculture is that farming like this requires high energy inputs, leading to high levels of carbon emissions across the industry.

The National Union of Agricultural Workers, which was founded out of George Edwards' earlier union, became the National Union of Agricultural and Allied Workers in 1968. In 1982 it merged into the Transport and General Workers' Union as its agricultural section.

At the end of the 1940s the National Union of Agricultural Workers had 140,000 members, but despite mergers, by the 1980s its membership remained below 67,000. Increasingly, many of these members were not agricultural workers, but men and women employed in factories associated with food production.[963] The post-war decline in agricultural work did not remove the need for organisation. Trade unions organising rural workers continued the struggle against tied cottages, often fighting evictions in the courts. In his history of the English countryside in the 20th century, Alun Howkins quotes a 1975 account by a Mrs Watts in Hertfordshire describing the reality of tied cottages:

> My husband has worked all his life in farming, the last 20 years as a herdsman. After having been here for 8 years we thought we were settled, and we put a lot of work and money into making the house a permanent home—or so we thought. On 22 March my husband was given redundancy notice and of course along with that, the notice to vacate our cottage on 8 April. The following months were like a nightmare.[964]

Legal changes in 1970s and 1980s helped reduce the number of tied cottages dramatically, but tied accommodation remains a real issue for rural workers. A 1976 Communist Party pamphlet could still complain that around half of farm workers lived in tied cottages. Wages were determined by the Agricultural Wages Board but, as the Communist Party rightly pointed out, the "boards had done little or nothing to lift the incomes of the farm worker to those in other industries". Sick pay and paid holidays were fought for by the agricultural unions but, despite these gains, agricultural workers' wage increases did not match the profits generated by their increased productivity. As the use of machinery and other technologies increased "labour costs as a proportion of all farm production fell" from 20.7 percent in 1964-1967 to 17.9 percent in 1972-1973. Even the gains that workers did get were limited by the interests of the employers—of the three weeks' paid holiday, only two weeks could be taken on consecutive days, as the Communist Party pointed out, the remainder tended to be "taken at the last-minute convenience of the farmer". It continued:

> The change from a labour-intensive industry to a capital-intensive one means that the farm worker is ever more isolated at work. With many villages becoming swamped with commuters and retired persons from the towns the discrepancy between farm pay and the level of wages in other industries is more apparent.[965]

This is not to say there were no gains for agricultural workers. Their trade unions also worked to expose the dangers for workers using the chemicals increasingly being used on fields. A major success was stopping the use of the herbicide 245-T, which had been developed from defoliants used in Vietnam.

In February 1982 a successful strike by 1,200 workers about pay and conditions at a Bernard Mathews poultry plant in Norfolk lasted six weeks and serves to highlight the changes to the agricultural working class. Alun Howkins contrasts this with the trade union overtime ban at the end of August 1984 centred on East Anglia. This, he argues, "was a disaster". Changes in rural employment meant that by "the 1980s and 1990s the average farm worker saw more of his employer during his working time than he did of any fellow worker". This reduced the potential to organise farmworkers collectively and contributed to a "sense of powerlessness".[966]

By the new millennium, one radical socialist analysis of the "crisis in the countryside" noted that:

> The countryside has become a reservoir of low pay, under-employment and deprivation for working families. The closures of coal mining and

many other traditional industries have also left large pockets of working class communities living in 'rural' areas, facing long journeys if they are to find work in local towns.[967]

This "crisis" was in part linked to the outbreak of foot-and-mouth disease that had wreaked havoc across rural areas of the UK in 2001. The spread of this disease was closely linked to changing farming practices, in particular large herds, but also the way that animals were regularly moved from place to place to get the best price. Some 3.9 million animals were culled and the cost to agriculture and rural tourism was estimated at £8 billion.[968]

Yet the predominant response to this crisis was from the right. A network of rural interests had formed in the late 1990s to campaign over "rural issues". But the Countryside Alliance, as it was to become, was certainly not interested in mobilising its wealth and members to improve the lives of ordinary people. Its key campaigning point—the right to hunt with dogs—was an issue that only affected the wealthiest section of the rural population. In July 1997, 100,000 Countryside Alliance members marched through London to protest plans to ban hunting and in March 1998, 250,000 marched. In 2002, when the Countryside Alliance held an even larger protest under the slogan "Liberty and Livelihood", *Socialist Worker* noted that one of its supporters included the Duke of Westminster, whose wealth was estimated at £4 billion yet still received an annual £300,000 subsidy from the tax payer. Despite real poverty in the countryside, *Socialist Worker* noted that the National Farmers Union, which backed the protest, had just withdrawn from the Agricultural Wages Board, which had just recommended a 3 percent increase, taking the basic hourly rate for agricultural workers to £4.91; younger workers received even less.[969]

At the same time, agricultural workers' organisation was declining. In 2007 the Transport and General Workers' Union merged with the Amicus union to become Unite the Union. Further evidence of the decline of the British agricultural working class is that in 2015 Unite's agricultural section merged with the food, drink and tobacco sections.

But the decline in full-time agricultural work has not removed the need for organisation. Casualisation, temporary employment and low wages continue to plague workers in rural communities. This is made worse by high prices for rural housing, something caused by the decision in the 1980s by the Tory government to give those living in social housing the "Right to Buy", which resulted in a sharp decline in available low-cost housing as homes were sold off. In addition, the added pressure of rural properties being purchased as second homes has made it harder for young people to find places to live. Poverty remains a real issue for rural communities—a UK government report showed that in 2014-2015 after housing costs, 16 percent of households in rural areas were in "relative low income", meaning they had an income 60 percent below median income. Another 15 percent of rural households were classed as being in a state of "absolute low income", meaning their income had declined below the "relative low income" level of 2010-2011 when adjusted for inflation. While these figures are actually slightly better than for the urban population, it does mean that thousands of rural families live in low income households.[970]

In the late 1990s and early 2000s, the Countryside Alliance argued that improvements to life in the countryside would come only if the interests of the rich were protected. Despite slogans like "Liberty and Livelihood", they cared little for those who worked and lived on the land. Yet in the absence of a left alternative, the Alliance could look like the only group fighting for rural interests in the face of disinterested government. In 2001 the Labour Secretary of State for the Department of Environment, Food and Rural Affairs, Margaret Beckett, showed no compassion for the reality of life in the countryside when she spoke at the Labour Party Conference:

> Like the rest of the rural economy agriculture is subject to enormous pressure for change... What society as a whole wants from agriculture is changing and probably changing irrevocably... There is no long-term future for an industry which cannot develop in line with market forces. No matter what the industry, its history, or the wider contribution it makes to society.[971]

Beckett's plan to open up agriculture completely to the free market by removing subsidies would only have led to more poverty and unemployment for working people. 15 years later, British agriculture remains highly dependent on subsidies. The British environmental journalist George Monbiot has repeatedly highlighted how agricultural subsidies benefit wealthy landowners because the amount paid is based on land owned. In 2016, for instance, he noted that 80 percent of subsidies go to the richest 25 percent. Many of these people aren't even farmers, but simply own large areas of land. These subsidies also, as Monbiot notes, have the effect of worsening the land's environmental potential in order to receive the money:

Your land just has to look agricultural, which means bare. Among the "ineligible features" listed in Westminster's version of the European rules are ponds, wide hedges, regenerating woodland, reedbeds, thriving salt marsh and trees sufficient to form a canopy. The common agricultural policy is a €55bn incentive to destroy wildlife habitats and cause floods downstream.[972]

If we are to solve the problem of rural poverty and unemployment and make agriculture an industry that produces high-quality food in a sustainable way, we cannot abandon the subsidy system. Instead we need to ensure that money is paid in ways that do not simply benefit the rich, but rather help those most in need. In 1976 the Communist Party pointed out a number of ways that government money could benefit the less well-off farmers. For instance, for some products "the rate of guarantee [guaranteed prices] should be related to the size of the crop; higher for a poor one, lower for a good one... This would have the effect of stabilising farmers' income rather than rate of payment".[973]

Wages should be raised to match those of other comparable industries and be protected. The Agricultural Wages Board, scrapped by the Tories in 2013, needs to be reinstated to ensure that trade unions can engage in national negotiations about salaries and working conditions. Rural housing needs to be built in large numbers and reserved for those on low incomes and money needs to be allocated to ensure that rural poverty becomes a thing of the past. In the past, Marketing Boards, most famously for milk and eggs, guaranteed minimum prices and ensured national standards for hygiene and production. These should be reinstated to help ensure that small farmers and their workers are on a level playing field with larger producers. One key task in the coming years will be to protect and extend the rights of the large numbers of migrant workers who now make up a significant part of the rural workforce. These workers should not be made scapegoats for an agricultural system that drives down wages to maximise profits.

Ultimately, creating a socially just and environmentally friendly agriculture in the UK means challenging the priorities of big business. Despite the relatively small numbers of workers in agriculture (though thousands more work in allied industries like manufacturing and distribution), they will need to be involved in these movements. In 2013 I was proud to stand alongside workers, members of the Bakers and Allied Food Workers Union, at the Hovis plant in Wigan who used militant tactics to protect jobs and pay, as well as giving temporary agency workers equal pay. The dispute was small and local, but it did demonstrate a potential for workers in the food industry to win when facing powerful corporations.

Globally, around 1 billion people work in agriculture, one in three of all workers. Women are more likely to work in agriculture than men and around 60 percent of child labour (129 million children) is involved in agriculture. Despite the rise of large-scale agricultural multinationals, there still remains a significant peasant population; 80 percent of food produced in Asia and sub-Saharan Africa, for instance, comes from small family farms supporting the livelihoods of 2.5 billion people. Yet 75 percent of the worlds "hungry" population live in rural areas.[974]

Farming in the developing world is squeezed by the agricultural multinationals based in the developed world. These companies, supported by massive government subsidies, shape the global demand for food and other products of agriculture. Silvia Ribeiro and Hope Shand explain the negative role of big business in agriculture:

> Corporate concentration in agriculture has allowed a handful of powerful corporations to seize the agricultural research agenda, influence national and international trade and agricultural policy and engineer the acceptance of new technologies as the "science-based" solution to maximising food production. Although frequently promoted in the name of addressing the needs of the world's poor and hungry, the benefits of these technologies typically [accrue] to those who develop and control them.[975]

Neoliberalism has transformed global agriculture in the interests of big business. Food was turned into an international commodity, not something to feed the hungry. The Structural Adjustment Programmes (SAP) of the World Bank and International Monetary Fund of the 1980s and 1990s helped open up developing world economies, reduced the role of the state and encouraged the production of food for international trade. In its 2008 *World Development Report* the World Bank acknowledged:

> Structural adjustment in the 1980s dismantled the elaborate system of public agencies that provided farmers with access to land, credit, insurance, inputs and cooperative organisations. The expectation was that removing the state would free the market for private actors to take over these functions... Incomplete markets and institutional gaps impose huge costs in forgone growth and welfare losses for smallholders, threatening their competitiveness and, in many cases, their survival.[976]

World Bank policies decimated African smallholder and peasant farming in the interests of corporate agri-business. The consequences were appalling, with the rural population displaced and driven into unemployment, underemployment or forced to seek work in the cities.

As neoliberal policies enforce a switch to larger-scale farming at the expense of local, small-scale agriculture, they also have negative consequences for the environment. Even the UK government admitted in 2011 that:

> Many systems of food production are unsustainable. Without change, the global food system will continue to degrade the environment and compromise the world's capacity to produce food in the future, as well as contributing to climate change and the destruction of biodiversity... Nothing less is required than a redesign of the whole food system to bring sustainability to the fore.[977]

A redesign of the world's food system will not come from above. Capitalism is a system in which production is not for need but for profit. As long as it continues, people will starve because they are too poor to buy food. The institutions that have opened up economies to the free market, further impoverished millions of peasants and ensured agriculture is about making profits for giant corporations, will not be able to transform agriculture into a sustainable system that can feed the world's population healthily. Instead, it will be the struggles of ordinary men and women, peasants and workers that will make that change.

Today, millions of peasants and rural workers continue to fight for social justice and an end to poverty. In the face of often brutal repression they fight for the right to live and work the land and enjoy the full products of that labour. Their struggle is about their livelihoods, but it is also a fight for a more rational and sustainable agriculture. They are part of a long tradition of class struggle in the countryside that has taken place in every country in the world. When you take a walk in the British countryside today or look out of a train window, the struggles of Wat Tyler, John Ball, Jack Straw, Jack Cade, Robert Kett, George Edwards or Joseph Arch and countless unnamed and forgotten men and women might seem very distant. But their compatriots in rural communities around the globe continue a struggle that has never been more important.

Bibliography

Anonymous, *Down with the Fences: Battles for the Commons in South London*, Past Tense, 2010.

Arch, Joseph, *From Ploughtail to Parliament*, Hutchinson, 1986.

Archer, John E, *By a Flash and a Scare: Arson, Animal Maiming and Poaching in East Anglia 1815-1870*, Breviary Stuff Publications, 2010.

Ault, W O, *Open-Field Farming in Medieval England*, George Allen & Unwin, 1972.

Bacon, Francis, *History of the Reign of King Henry VII*, Cambridge, 1876.

Baker, Malcolm, *The 'Revolt of the Field' in North Essex 1840-1875*, Baker, 1979.

Ball, Roger, *Tolpuddle and Swing: The Flea and the Elephant*, Bristol Radical History Group, 2010.

Barker, Juliet, *Conquest: The English Kingdom of France*, Little Brown, 2009.

Barker, Juliet, *England Arise: The People, The King and The Great Revolt of 1381*, Little Brown, 2014.

Beckert, Sven, *Empire of Cotton*, Penguin, 2015.

Beier, A L, *The Problem of the Poor in Tudor and Early Stuart England*, Methuen, 1983.

Berens, Lewis H, *The Digger Movement in the Days of the Commonwealth*, Merlin, 2007.

Bindoff, S T, *Ket's Rebellion 1549*, The Historical Association, 1949.

Binfield, Kevin, *Writings of the Luddites*, John Hopkins University Press, 2004.

Bland, A E, Brown, P A and Tawney, R H, *English Economic History: Select Documents*, Bell & Sons Ltd, 1920.

Bloch, Marc, *Feudal Society*, vol 1, Routledge, 1971.

Bohstedt, John, "Gender, Household and Community Politics: Women in English Riots 1790-1810", *Past and Present*, 1988, no 120 (Aug 1988) pp88-122.

Bolton, J L, *The Medieval English Economy 1150-1500*, Everyman's University Library, 1980.

Brenner, Robert, "Agrarian Class Structure and Economic Development in Pre-Industrial Europe", *Past and Present*, 1976, no 70 (Feb 1976), pp30-75.

Calder, Angus, *The People's War: Britain 1939-1945*, Pimlico, 1992.

Caraman, Philip, *The Western Rising 1549: The Prayer Book Rebellion*, West Country Books, 1994.

Carlin, Norah, *The Causes of the English Civil War*, Blackwell, 2005.

Charlesworth, Andrew (ed), *An Atlas of Rural Protest in Britain 1548-1900*, Croom Helm, 1983.

Chase, Malcolm, *Early Trade Unionism*, Breviary Stuff Publications, 2012.

Clayton, Joseph, *The True Story of Jack Cade, Captain of Kent, AD1450*, Frank Palmer, 1909.

Cohn, Norman, *The Pursuit of the Millennium: Revolutionary Millenarians and Mystical Anarchists of the Middle Ages*, Paladin, 1970.

Cornwall, Julian, *Revolt of the Peasantry 1549*, Routledge, 1977.

Coulton, G G, *The Medieval Village*, Cambridge University Press, 1925.

Crown Patent Rolls (CPR), *Henry VI*, vol 5, 1446-1452, HMSO, 1909.

Dallas, R, *Recollections of the Life of Lord Byron*, Charles Knight, 1829.

Danziger, Renée, *Political Powerlessness: Agricultural Workers in Post-War Britain*, Manchester University Press, 1988.

Department for Environment, Food and Rural Affairs, *Rural Poverty Stats*, March 2017 www.gov.uk.

Dimmock, Spencer, *The Origin of Capitalism in England 1400-1600*, Haymarket Press, 2014.

Dobson, R B, *The Peasants' Revolt of 1381*, Macmillan, 1970.

Duffy, Eamon, *The Stripping of the Altars*, Yale, 1992.

Duffy, Eamon, *The Voices of Morebath: Reformation and Rebellion in an English Village*, Yale, 2003.

Dunn, Alistair, *The Peasants' Revolt: England's Failed Revolution of 1381*, Tempus, 2004.

Dyer, Christopher, *Everyday Life in Medieval England*, Hambledon Press, 1994.

Dyer, Christopher, *Making a Living in the Middle Ages: The People of Britain 850-1520*, Yale, 2009.

Eiden, Herbert, "Norfolk, 1382: A Sequel to the Peasants' Revolt", *The English Historical Review*, vol 114, no 456 (April 1999), p370-377.

Empson, Martin, *Land and Labour: Marxism, Ecology and Human History*, Bookmarks, 2014.

Empson, Martin, "Food, Agriculture and Climate Change", *International Socialism* 152, 2016.

Empson, Martin, "A Common Treasury For All: Gerrard Winstanley's Vision of Utopia", *International Socialism* 154, 2017.

Everitt, A M, *The Local Community and The Great Rebellion*, The Historical Association, 1969.

Food and Agricultural Organisation (FAO), *FAO Statistical Yearbook*, FAO, 2012.

Fisher, Chris, *Custom, Work and Market Capitalism: The Forest of Dean Colliers, 1788-1888*, Breviary Stuff Publications, 2016.

Fletcher, Anthony and MacCulloch, Diarmaid, *Tudor Rebellions*, Pearson Longman, 2008.

Froissart, Jean, *Chronicles*, Penguin 1978.

Furley, Robert, *A History of the Weald of Kent*, vol II, part I, Russell Smith, 1874.

Fryde, E B, *The Great Revolt of 1381*, The Historical Association, 1981.

Fryde, E B and Fryde, N, "Peasant Rebellion and Peasant Discontents", 1991, in Miller, 1991.

Gay, E, "The Midland Revolt and the Inquisitions of Depopulation of 1607", *Transactions of the Royal Historical Society*, new series, vol 18 (1904), pp195-244.

Gorgut, Omasius, *Poor Man's Heaven: The Land of Cokaygne and other Utopian Visions*, Past Tense, 2011.

Griffin, Carl, *The Rural War: Captain Swing and the Politics of Protest*, Manchester University Press, 2015.

Griffiths, Ralph, *The Reign of King Henry VI: The Exercise of Royal Authority, 1422-1461*, University of California Press, 1981.

Groves, Reg, *Sharpen the Sickle!*, Porcupine Press, 1949.

Gurney, John, *Gerrard Winstanley: The Digger's Life and Legacy*, Pluto, 2013.

Gyford, Janet, *Men of Bad Character: The Witham Fires of the 1820s*, Essex Record Office, 1991.

Hallas, Duncan, "The Decisive Settlement", *Socialist Worker Review*, no 113, October 1988, pp17-20.

Hammond, J L and Hammond, B, *The Labourer 1760-1832*, Alan Sutton, 1995a.

Hammond, J L and Hammond, B, "The Village Labourer", 1995b, in Hammond and Hammond, 1995a.

Hammond, J L and Hammond, B, "The Skilled Labourer", 1995c, in Hammond and Hammond, 1995a.

Harman, Chris, *A People's History of the World*, Bookmarks, 1999.

Harman, Chris, *Marxism and History*, Bookmarks, 1998.

Harvey, I M W, *Jack Cade's Rebellion of 1450*, Clarendon Press, 1991.

Hay, Douglas and others, *Albion's Fatal Tree: Crime and Society in 18th Century England*, Verso, 2011.

Henry VIII, *Letters and Papers*, Foreign and Domestic, vol 11, 1888.

Henry VIII, *Letters and Papers*, Foreign and Domestic, vol 12(i), 1890.

Hill, Christopher, *The Century of Revolution*, Routledge, 1980.

Hill, Christopher, *The World Turned Upside Down*, Penguin, 1991.

Hill, Christopher, *Liberty Against the Law*, Penguin, 1996.

Hilton, Rodney, "Peasant Movements in England Before 1381", *The Economic History Review*, second series, vol 11, no 2, 1949, pp117-136.

Hilton, Rodney, *Bond Men Made Free: Medieval Peasant Movements and the English Rising of 1381*, Methuen, 1986.

Hindle, Steve, "Imagining Insurrection in 17th Century England: Representations of the Midland Rising of 1607", Autumn 2008, *History Workshop Journal*, no 66, pp21-61.

Hobsbawm, E J and Rudé, G, *Captain Swing*, Lawrence & Wishart, 1970.

Holstun, James, *Ehud's Dagger: Class Struggle in the English Revolution*, Verso, 2002.

Hooker, John, *The Ancient History and Description of the City of Exeter*, Andrews & Trewman, 1765.

Horn, Pamela, *Joseph Arch*, Roundwood, 1971.

Horn, Pamela, *The Rural World, 1780-1850: Social Change in the English Countryside*, Hutchinson, 1980.

Horn, Pamela, *Life and Labour in Rural England, 1760-1850*, Macmillan, 1987.

Howkins, Alun, *The Death of Rural England: A Social History of the Countryside since 1900*, Routledge, 2003.

Hoyle, R W, *The Pilgrimage of Grace*, Oxford University Press, 2001.

Hunter, James, *Set Adrift Upon the World: The Sutherland Clearances*, Birlinn, 2015.

Hutton, R, "The Worcestershire Clubmen in the English Civil War", 1979, *Midland History*, 5:1, pp39-49.

International Fund for Agricultural Development (IFAD), *Rural Development Report*, UN IFAD, 2016.

Jones, E L, *The Development of English Agriculture 1815-1873*, Macmillan, 1968.

Kerr, Barbara, *Bound to the Soil: A Social History of Dorset*, EP Publishing, 1975.

Kesselring, K J, *Mercy and Authority in the Tudor State*, Cambridge University Press, 2003.

Key, Newton, and Bucholz, Robert, *Sources and Debates in English History 1485-1714*, Wiley Blackwell, 2009.

Land, Stephen K, *Kett's Rebellion: The Norfolk Rising of 1549*, Boydell Press, 1977.

Liddiard, Robert, *Castles in Context: Power, Symbolism and Landscapes, 1066 to 1500*, Windgatherer, 2005.

Lindsay, Philip, and Groves, Reg, *The Peasants' Revolt 1381*, Hutchinson, 1950.

Linebaugh, Peter, *Stop Thief: The Commons, Enclosures and Resistance*, PM Press, 2014.

Linebaugh, Peter, *The Magna Carta Manifesto*, University of California Press, 2008.

Lister, John, "We'll Fight them in the Hedgerows: Socialist Answers to the Crisis in the Countryside", *International Socialism* 91, 2001.

Loach, Jennifer, *Edward VI*, Yale University Press, 2002.

Loveless, George, *The Victims of Whiggery* (1837), TUC Publications, (undated).

Loveless, G, Brine J and others, *The Horrors of Transportation* (1838), Tolpuddle Martyrs Memorial Trust, 2005.

Lyle, Helen M, *The Rebellion of Jack Cade 1450*, The Historical Association, 1950.

MacCulloch, Diarmaid, "Kett's Rebellion in Context", *Past and Present*, no 84 (Aug 1979) pp36-59.

Manning, Brain, *The English People and the English Revolution*, Penguin, 1978.

Manning, Brain, *Aristocrats, Plebeians and Revolution in England 1640-1660*, Pluto, 1996.

Marlow, Joyce, *The Tolpuddle Martyrs*, History Book Club, 1971.

Marx, Karl, *Grundrisse*, Penguin, 1977.

Marx, Karl, *Capital Volume 1*, Penguin, 1990.

Miller, Edward, *The Agrarian History of England and Wales*, Cambridge University Press, 1991.

Monbiot, George, "The Shocking Waste of Cash Even Leavers Won't Condemn", *The Guardian*, Tuesday 21 June 2016.

Moorhouse, Geoffrey, *The Pilgrimage of Grace*, Phoenix, 2003.

Morton, A L, *A People's History of England*, Lawrence & Wishart, 1948.

Muskett, Paul, "The East Anglian Agrarian Riots of 1822", *Agricultural History Review*, vol 32 (1984), pp1-13.

Mustin, Graham, "Religion and Revolution in the Middle Ages", *International Socialism* 147, 2015.

Myers, A R, *English Historical Documents, 1327-1485*, Eyre & Spottiswoode, 1969.

Norman, Andrew, *The Story of George Loveless and the Tolpuddle Martyrs*, Halsgrove, 2008.

O'Brien, Mark, *Perish the Privileged Orders*, Redwords, 1995.

O'Brien, Mark, *When Adam Delved and Eve Span: A History of the Peasants' Revolt of 1381*, New Clarion Press, 2004.

Osborne, Harvey and Michael Winstanley, "Rural and Urban Poaching in Victorian England", *Rural History*, vol 17, no 2, 2006, pp187-212.

Owen, Brendon, *One from the Plough: The Life and Times of George Mitchell 1826-1901*, Gazebo, 2001.

Page, Wilf, *Farming to Feed Britain: A Policy for Farmers, Farm Workers and Consumers*, Communist Party, 1976.

Payton, Philip, *Cornwall's History*, Tor Mark, 2013.

Peacock, A, "The Revolt of the Fields in East Anglia", *Our History*, 49/50, Communist Party Historians Group, 1968.

Pollard, A J, *Late Medieval England 1399-1509*, Pearson Education, 2000.

Pound, John, *Poverty and Vagrancy in Tudor England*, Longman, 1973.

Powell, Edgar, "An Account of the Proceedings in Suffolk during the Peasants' Rising in 1381", *Transactions of the Royal Historical Society*, new series, vol 8 (1894), p203-249.

Purkiss, Diane, *The English Civil War: A People's History*, Harper Press, 2006.

Rackham, Oliver, *The History of the Countryside*, Weidenfeld & Nicolson, 1995.

Reay, Barry, *The Last Rising of the Agricultural Labourers: Rural Life and Protest in 19th Century England*, Breviary Stuff Publications, 2010.

Rees, John, *The Leveller Revolution*, Verso, 2016.

Reid, Robert, *Land of Lost Content: The Luddite Revolt 1812*, Cardinal, 1986.

Royle, Trevor, *The Wars of the Roses*, Abacus, 2009.

Scarisbrick, J J, *Henry VIII*, Yale, 1997.

Sharp, Buchanan, *In Contempt of All Authority: Rural Artisans and Riot in the West of England, 1586-1660*, Breviary Stuff Publications, 2010.

Sherry, Dave, *Empire and Revolution*, Bookmarks, 2014.

Smith, Adam, *The Wealth of Nations*, Everymans Library, 1991.

Socialist Worker, "March Ignores the Real Issues", issue 1818, Saturday 21 September, 2002.

Spindler, Erik, "Flemings in the Peasants' Revolt, 1381", in Skoda, H, Lantschner, P and Shaw, R L J (eds), *Contact and Exchange in Later Medieval Europe*, Boydell Press, 2012.

Stone, Lawrence, *The Causes of the English Revolution*, Routledge & Kegan Paul, 1972.

Stoyle, Mark, "Cornish Rebellions, 1497-1648", *History Today*, May 1997, pp22-28.

Stratton, J M, *Agricultural Records AD220-1977*, Baker, 1978.

Sturt, John, *Revolt in the West: The Western Rebellion of 1549*, Devon Books, 1987.

Sutton, Josh, *Food Worth Fighting For: From Food Riots to Food Banks*, Prospect Books, 2016.

Taine, H, *Notes on England*, Henry Holt, 1885.

Tawney, R H, *Religion and the Rise of Capitalism*, Penguin, 1938.

Thomas, Keith, "Another Digger Broadside", *Past and Present*, vol 42, no 1, 1969.

Thomis, Malcolm, *The Luddites*, David & Charles, 1970.

Thompson, E P, *Whigs and Hunters*, Penguin, 1985.

Thompson, E P, *Customs in Common*, Merlin, 2010.

Turner, Michael, *Enclosures in Britain 1750-1830*, Macmillan, 1984.

Underdown, David, "The Chalk and the Cheese: Contrasts among the English Clubmen", *Past and Present*, no 85 (Nov 1979), pp25-48.

Underdown, David, *Revel, Riot and Rebellion: Popular Politics and Culture in England 1603-1660*, Oxford University Press, 2005.

Wells, Roger, A E, "The Development of the English Rural Proletariat and Social Protest, 1700-1850", *Journal of Peasant Studies*, vol 6, issue 2, 1979, pp115-139.

Winstanley, Gerrard, *The Law of Freedom and Other Writings*, Pelican, 1973.

Wood, Andy, *Riot, Rebellion and Popular Politics in Early Modern England*, Palgrave, 2002.

Wood, Andy, *The 1549 Rebellions and the Making of Early Modern England*, Cambridge University Press, 2009.

Woodman, A Vere, "The Buckinghamshire and Oxfordshire Rising of 1549", *Oxoniensia* XXII, pp78-84, 1957.

Yerby, George, *The English Revolution and the Roots of Environmental Change*, Routledge, 2016.

Ziegler, Philip, *The Black Death*, Penguin, 1986.

Žmolek, Michael Andrew, *Rethinking the Industrial Revolution: Five Centuries of Transition from Agrarian to Industrial Capitalism in England*, Haymarket, 2014.

Notes

1   Harman, 1998, p111.
2   Harman, 1998, p112.
3   A good introduction to Chartism is O'Brien, 1995.
4   Sharp, 2010, p25; Henry VIII, 1888, p399; Land, 1997, p141.
5   Quoted in Wood, 2002, p54.
6   Dobson, 1970, pp374-375.
7   Barker, 2014, p217.
8   Fryde, 1981, p7.
9   Fryde, 1981, p10.
10   Fryde, 1981, p11.
11   Fryde, 1981, p11.
12   Hilton, 1986, p64.
13   Fryde, 1981, p9.
14   Hilton, 1986, p227.
15   Hilton, 1986, p228.
16   Quoted in Linebaugh, 2014, p169.
17   Bolton, 1980, p13.
18   Rackham, 1995, pp170-172.
19   Hilton, 1949, p118.
20   Dimmock, 2014, p69. The phrase "caging of the peasantry" originates with the historian Chris Wickham.
21   Quoted in Dimmock, 2014, pp69-70.
22   Bloch, 1971, pp270-271.
23   Harman, 1999, p143.
24   Bolton, 1980, p19.
25   Bolton, 1980, p20.
26   Hilton, 1949, p118 and Bolton, 1980, p21.
27   Ault, 1972, p65.
28   Quoted in Ault, 1972, p83, p86 and p95.
29   Quoted in Ault, 1972, pp167-168.
30   Hilton, 1986, pp35-37.
31   Bloch, 1971, p82.
32   Tawney, 1938, p37.
33   Quoted in Tawney, 1938, p96.
34   Bolton, 1980, p331.
35   Lindsay and Groves, 1950, p16.
36   Morton, 1948, p130.
37   Cohn, 1970, p38.
38   Hilton, 1986, pp207-208.
39   Quoted in Mustin, 2015, p180.
40   For more on this see Mustin, 2015 and Cohn, 1970. For an interesting discussion on the role of visions of Utopian plenty as inspiration for peasant rebellion, as in the mythical land of Cokaygne, see Gorgut, 2011.
41   Dyer, 1994, xiii.
42   Details of this case from the Great Horwood manorial rolls from Ault, 1972, p65.
43   Hilton, 1949, p127.
44   Bolton, 1980, pp117-119.
45   Hilton, 1949, p125.
46   Hilton, 1949, p125
47   Hilton, 1949, p128.
48   Dimmock, 2014, p87.
49   Quoted in Coulton, 1925, p236.
50   Quoted in Coulton, 1925, p237.
51   Ziegler, 1986, p278.
52   Ziegler, 1986, p277.
53   Coulton, 1925, p237.
54   Quoted in Lindsey and Groves, 1950, p34.
55   Linebaugh, 2014, p162.
56   Figures from O'Brien, 2004, p30.
57   Myers, 1969, pp127-128.
58   Lindsay and Groves, 1950, p78.
59   Myers, 1969, p128.
60   Myers, 1969, pp128-129.
61   Lindsay and Groves, 1950, p79.
62   Myers, 1969, p129.
63   Myers, 1969, p129.
64   Lindsay and Groves, 1950, p80.
65   Barker, 2014, p172.
66   Quoted in Lindsay and Groves, 1950, p82.
67   Barker, 2014, pp175-176.
68   O'Brien, 2004, p35.
69   Myers, 1969, p129.
70   Liddiard, 2005, p85.
71   O'Brien, 2004, p36.
72   The appendices to Juliet Barker's book concisely summarise the known evidence about Ball, Straw and Tyler.
73   Myers, 1969, p130.
74   Quotes from Hilton, 1986, pp176-177.
75   Hilton, 1986, pp207-208 and p209.
76   Hilton, 1986, p210.
77   Lindsey and Groves, 1950, p55.
78   This section based on Lindsey and Groves, 1950, p71.
79   Froissart, 1978, p212 and p213.
80   Dunn, 2004, p82.
81   Dobson, 1970, p147.
82   O'Brien, 2004, p37 and Barker, 2014, p421.
83   Dobson, 1970, p270.
84   Dobson, 1970, p270.
85   Lindsay and Groves, 1950, p163.
86   Barker, 2014, p304.
87   Myers, 1969, p130.
88   Lindsay and Groves, 1950, p86. See Barker,

2014, pp292-293 for Ball's trial and the
importance of the letters in finding him guilty.
See also pp429-435 for her discussion of the
letters themselves.

89 O'Brien, 2004, p38. Third letter in Lindsay
and Groves, 1950, p86.
90 Lindsay and Groves, 1950, p84.
91 Froissart, 1978, p214 and Myers, 1969, p130.
92 Myers, 1969, p130.
93 Froissart, 1978, p214. Note that here Froissart
describes the attack on Rochester Castle
as happening after the rebels captured
Canterbury, which is not correct.
94 Quotes in Lindsay and Groves, 1950, p85.
95 Fryde, 1981, p18.
96 Myers, 1969, p131.
97 Myers, 1969, p131.
98 Froissart, 1978, pp216-217.
99 Myers, 1969, p132.
100 Dobson, 1970, p200.
101 Hilton, 1972, p189 and Froissart, 1978, p217.
102 Myers, 1969, p132.
103 Froissart, 1978, p217 and p218.
104 Dunn, 2004, pp106-107, and Myers, 1969,
p132.
105 Dobson, 1970, p169.
106 O'Brien, 2004, p22.
107 O'Brien, 2004, p23.
108 Dunn, 2004, p64 and Lindsay and Groves,
1950, pp56-57.
109 Myers, 1969, p133.
110 Quotes from Dunn, 2004, p108 and p109.
111 Dunn, 2004, p109.
112 Dobson, 1970, p157.
113 Dunn, 2004, p111.
114 Froissart, 1978, p217.
115 Myers, 1969, p135.
116 See Spindler, 2012, p63 and pp65-66; Froissart,
1978, p218; and Myers, 1969, p136.
117 Spindler, 2012, pp66-67.
118 Quoted in Spindler, 2012, p59.
119 Spindler, 2012, pp69-70.
120 Spindler, 2012, p71.
121 Spindler, 2012, p78.
122 Froissart, 1978, p218.
123 Myers, 1969, p134 and Froissart, 1978, p218.
124 Froissart, 1978, p219.
125 Froissart, 1978, p219 and p220, and Myers,
1969, p134.
126 Myers, 1969, p135.
127 Froissart, 1978, p221.
128 Myers, 1969, p135.
129 Froissart, 1978, p221.
130 See Dunn, 2004, p126.
131 Quoted in Dunn, 2004, p125.
132 Quoted in Dunn, 2004, p121.
133 Barker, 2014, pp252-253.
134 Quoted in Barker, 2014, p255.
135 Quoted in Barker, 2014, p255.
136 A point made by Barker herself, p253.

137 Quotes from Myers, 1969, p136.
138 Myers, 1969, p136 and p137.
139 Dunn, 2004, p131.
140 Myers, 1969, p137.
141 Myers, 1969, pp137-138.
142 Dobson, 1970, p207.
143 Dobson, 1970, pp177-178.
144 Myers, 1969, p138.
145 Dobson, 1970, p179.
146 Barker, 2014, p273.
147 Barker, 2014, p280.
148 Dunn, 2004, pp139-142.
149 Barker, 2014, p280.
150 Dobson, 1970, p270.
151 Barker, 2014, p281; Walsingham's account in
Dobson, 1970, pp269-277.
152 Dunn, 2004, p143.
153 Barker, 2014, pp286-287.
154 Dobson, 1970, p275.
155 Barker, 2014, pp285-286 and Dobson, 1970,
p275.
156 Barker, 2014, pp287-291.
157 Dobson, 1970, p277, quoted in Barker, 2014,
p289.
158 Barker, 2014, pp290-291.
159 Details of the historic disputes can be found
in Dyer, 1994, pp221-239. Powell, 1894, is a
detailed study of events in Suffolk which I
have used as the basis for my account here.
160 Barker, 2014, pp298-300.
161 Dobson, 1970, pp244-245.
162 Powell, 1894, p222.
163 Powell, 1894, p224.
164 Barker, 2014, pp328-331.
165 Barker, 2014, p333.
166 Barker, 2014, p327.
167 See Lindsey and groves, 1950, p160-161, and
Barker, 2014, p337 and p341-342.
168 Barker, 2014, pp341-344.
169 Lindsey and Groves, 1950, p161 and p164.
170 Dobson, 1970, p238.
171 Dobson, 1970, p260.
172 Dobson, 1970, pp260-261 and Barker, 2014,
pp349-350.
173 Quoted in Barker, 2014, pp355-356.
174 Barker, 2014, p357.
175 Myers, 1969, p140.
176 Quoted in Barker, 2014, p372.
177 Dunn, 2004, p169.
178 Dunn, 2004, pp169-170.
179 Dobson, 1970, pp373-374.
180 Dobson, 1970, p308.
181 Barker, 2014, p379.
182 Dobson, 1970, p311.
183 Dobson, 1970, pp327-328.
184 Dobson, 1970, p328.
185 Dobson, 1970, p330.
186 Barker, 2014, p386.
187 Barker, 2014, pp387-388.
188 Barker, 2014, p389.

189 Barker, 2014, p398.
190 See Eiden, 1999.
191 Dobson, 1970, p334.
192 Eiden, 1999, p374.
193 Fryde, 1981, p34.
194 Quoted in Key and Bucholz, 2009, p167.
195 Quoted in Fryde, 1981, p34.
196 Quoted in Harvey, 1991, p70.
197 Griffiths, 1981, p628.
198 Harvey, 1991, pp31-32.
199 Quoted in Myers, 1969, p264.
200 Harvey, 1991, pp33-34.
201 Harvey, 1991, p35 and p36.
202 Harvey, 1991, pp44-45.
203 Harvey, 1991, pp45-46 and p47.
204 Harvey, 1991, pp37-38.
205 Harvey, 1991, pp39-41.
206 Harvey, 1991, p42.
207 On Margaret of Anjou, see Barker, 2009, pp317-318.
208 Barker, 2009, pp324-325.
209 Harvey, 1991, p48.
210 Harvey, 1991, p53.
211 Harvey, 1991, pp53-55.
212 Harvey, 1991, p59.
213 Harvey, 1991, p62-63.
214 Harvey, 1991, p63, and Pollard, 2000, p130.
215 Material in this section on Cheyne, Jakes and Winchester from Harvey, pp64-67.
216 Lyle, 1950, p8, and Harvey, 1991, pp68-69.
217 Harvey, 1991, p73 and Griffiths, 1981, p629.
218 Griffiths, 1981, pp631-632.
219 Harvey, 1991, p74.
220 Griffiths, 1981, pp629-630.
221 Lyle, 1950, pp20-21.
222 Lyle, 1950, p7.
223 Griffiths, 1981, p630.
224 Harvey, 1991, pp78-79 and Griffiths, 1981, p616.
225 Harvey, 1991, p79; Griffiths, 1981, p622
226 Harvey, 1991, pp80-81
227 Griffiths, 1981, p629.
228 For the full document, see Harvey, 1991, pp186-188.
229 Harvey, 1991, p80.
230 Griffiths, 1981, pp635-636.
231 Griffiths, 1981, pp624-625.
232 Griffiths, 1981, p611 and p638.
233 Harvey, 1991, pp83-84.
234 Harvey, 1991, pp84-85.
235 Griffiths, 1981, pp613-614.
236 This account of Cade's army in London and the aftermath is based on Harvey, 1991, pp87-98.
237 Harvey, 1991, p87. The account is from a letter written to John Paston, by John Payn one of a famous collection letters of the Paston family. The Payn letter is a fascinating account of events on Blackheath and can be found in Appendix VI of Clayton, 1909.
238 Myers, 1969, p265.
239 Myers, 1969, p265.
240 Harvey, 1991, p97.
241 Harvey, 1991, p97.
242 CPR, 1909, p328.
243 CPR, 1909, p328.
244 Harvey, 1991, p98.
245 Griffiths, 1981, pp616-617 (note Harvey says 10 marks per follower, p98).
246 Material on rebellions after Cade based on Harvey, 1991, pp115-130. See also Fryde and Fryde, 1991, pp806-807.
247 Harvey, 1991, p119.
248 Harvey, 1991, p125.
249 Harvey, 1991, pp126-127.
250 Harvey, 1991, pp127-128.
251 Fryde and Fryde, 1991, pp806-807.
252 Harvey, 1991, p152. On Parmynter's rising, see Harvey, 1991, pp134-137 also Fryde and Fryde, 1991, p807.
253 Harvey, 1991, p152.
254 CPR, 1909, pp460-461.
255 Harvey, 1991, p155.
256 Harvey, 1991, p156.
257 Harvey, 1991, p142.
258 Harvey, 1991, p143 and CPR, 1909, p415.
259 On Wilkyns, see Harvey, 1991, pp162-165.
260 Harvey, 1991, p164.
261 Harvey, 1991, pp165-167.
262 Harvey, 1991, p147.
263 Harvey, 1991, p148, and Pollard, 2000, p133.
264 Harvey, 1991, pp148-149.
265 Harvey, 1991, pp149-150.
266 Harvey, 1991, pp150-151.
267 Harvey, 1991, pp160-161.
268 Harvey, 1991, p170.
269 Harvey, 1991, pp170-171.
270 Harvey, 1991, pp183-184 and Royle, 2009, pp252-269 for the aftermath.
271 Harvey, 1991, p184.
272 Harvey, 1991, p185.
273 Royle, 2009, is an excellent introduction to the Wars of the Roses.
274 Space prohibits a detailed discussion of all Tudor revolts and some are omitted entirely. Some, such as the Yorkshire Rebellion of April 1489, were localised uprisings. Readers interested in finding out more will find Fletcher and MacCulloch, 2008, a very good starting point.
275 Beier, 1983, p5 and p7.
276 Beier, 1983, p9.
277 Cornwall, 1977, p12.
278 Quoted in Pound, 1973, p7.
279 Commission of Inquiry Touching Enclosures, 1517, in Bland, Brown, Tawney, 1920, pp262-263.
280 Bland, Brown, Tawney, 1920, p266.
281 Cornwall, 1977, p16.
282 Cornwall, 1977, p17.

283 Stoyle, 1997, pp22-25.

284 Stoyle, 1997, p24.

285 Stoyle, 1997, p25.

286 Cornwall, 1977, p43.

287 Quoted in Payton, 2013, p23.

288 Bacon, 1876, pp148-149.

289 Stoyle, 1991, p25, and Bacon, 1876, p150.

290 Fletcher and MacCulloch, 2008, pp22-23.

291 Bacon, 1876, p155.

292 Payton, 2013, p23.

293 Bacon, 1876, p155-156.

294 Fletcher and MacCulloch, 2008, p23.

295 Stoyle, 1997, p26.

296 Duffy, 2003, p84.

297 Scarisbrick, 1997, p303.

298 Duffy, 2003, p88.

299 Duffy, 1992, p471.

300 Duffy, 2003, pp89-90.

301 Duffy, 2003, p91.

302 Quoted in Duffy, 2003, p91.

303 Wood, 2009, p177.

304 See Wood, 2002, pp33-35

305 Wood, 2002, p34.

306 Wood, 2002, p34.

307 The detail of my account of the 1536 uprisings is based on Hoyle, 2001 and Moorhouse, 2003. Fletcher and MacCulloch, 2008, contains an excellent summary, together with transcripts of the key documents.

308 Morton, 1948, p174.

309 Scarisbrick, 1997, p342.

310 Moorhouse, 2003, p45.

311 Moorhouse, 2003, p46

312 Duffy, 2003, p75.

313 Fletcher and MacCulloch, 2008, p28; Moorhouse, 2003, p46; and Scarisbrick, 1997, p341.

314 Moorhouse, 2003, pp47-48.

315 Moorhouse, 2003, p48.

316 Moorhouse, 2003, pp48-49.

317 Moorhouse, 2003, p50.

318 Moorhouse, 2003, pp53-54.

319 Moorhouse, 2003, p53.

320 See Hoyle, 2001, p143.

321 Fletcher and MacCulloch, 2008, p29.

322 Hoyle, 2001, p120.

323 Hoyle, 2001, p123.

324 Quoted in Hoyle, 2001, p148.

325 Quoted in Hoyle, 2001, pp116-117.

326 Hoyle, 2001, p117.

327 Hoyle, 2001, p124 and p125, and Moorhouse, 2003, pp56-57.

328 Hoyle, 2001, p125-130.

329 Hoyle, 2001, p144.

330 Quotes from Leche's account in Fletcher and MacCulloch, 2008, pp140-141.

331 All quotes from The Lincoln Articles are from Fletcher and MacCulloch, 2008, p142. The missing words in brackets are from that reproduction.

332 Henry VIII, 1888, p225.

333 Moorhouse, 2003, p64 and p65.

334 Moorhouse, 2003, p65.

335 Hoyle, 2001, p149.

336 Hoyle, 2001, p149.

337 Moorhouse, 2003, p68.

338 Hoyle, 2001, p150.

339 Quoted in Hoyle, 2001, p150.

340 Quoted in Holye, 2001, p150.

341 From Fletcher and MacCulloch, 2008, p30 and Hoyle, 2001, pp150-151.

342 See the discussion in Hoyle, 2001, pp151-152.

343 Hoyle, 2001, pp152-153.

344 Hoyle, 2001, p154

345 Hoyle, 2001, pp156-157.

346 Hoyle, 2001, p174.

347 Henry VIII, 1888, pp302-303.

348 Hoyle, 2001, p175.

349 Moorhouse, 2003, p269,

350 Quoted in Hoyle, 2001, p176.

351 Hoyle, 2001, p178.

352 Hoyle, 2001, pp183-185.

353 Hoyle, 2001, p185.

354 Hoyle, 2001, p187.

355 Hoyle, 2001, pp187-190.

356 Moorhouse, 2003, p78 and p79.

357 Moorhouse, 2003, p79.

358 Hoyle, 2001, pp189-190, and Moorhouse, 2003, p78.

359 Gay, 1904, p196, including footnote 3.

360 Hoyle, 2001, pp122-123

361 Hoyle, 2001, pp192-195.

362 Quoted in Hoyle,2001, p195.

363 See discussion in Holye, 2001, pp195-198.

364 Hoyle, 2001, p197.

365 Hoyle, 2001, p98 and p204.

366 Hoyle, 2001, pp200-202

367 Hoyle, 2001, p206.

368 Quoted in Hoyle, 2001, pp457-458.

369 Hoyle, 2001, p210 – see also Hoyle's map on p211.

370 Hoyle, 2001, p210 and pp217-218.

371 Hoyle, 2001, p219.

372 Hoyle, 2001, p215.

373 Moorhouse, 2003, pp88-89 and Hoyle, 2001, p220.

374 Hoyle, 2001, p221.

375 Henry VIII, 1890, p18.

376 Moorhouse, 2003, pp99-100.

377 Quoted in Hoyle, 2001, p216.

378 Hoyle, 2001, p218.

379 Moorhouse, 2003, p89.

380 Hoyle, 2001, pp222-224.

381 For the spread of the North Craven revolt, see Hoyle, 2001, pp228-231.

382 Henry VIII, 1888, p304.

383 Hoyle, 2001, p231.

384 Hoyle, 2001, p235 and p237.

385 For the details of the movement around Kendal, Dent and Sedbergh, see Hoyle, 2001,

pp233-241

386 Hoyle, 2001, p247 and p250.
387 For the details of the Westmoreland and Cumberland movement, see Hoyle, 2001, pp241-253.
388 Henry VIII, 1888, p507.
389 Hoyle, 2001, p254.
390 Hoyle, 2001, pp253-255.
391 Hoyle, 2001, p263.
392 Quoted in Hoyle, 2001, p265.
393 Hoyle, 2001, p266.
394 Fletcher and MacCulloch, 2008, p34.
395 Moorhouse, 2003, p139.
396 Fletcher and MacCulloch, 2008, p34
397 Hoyle, 2001, p287.
398 Hoyle, 2001, p295.
399 Hoyle, 2001, p297.
400 Hoyle, 2001, p299.
401 Fletcher and MacCulloch, 2008, p35.
402 See what is left of the text quoted in Hoyle, 2001, pp458-459
403 Hoyle, 2001, p304.
404 Hoyle, 2001, pp306-311.
405 Hoyle, 2001, pp311-313, and Fletcher and MacCulloch, 2008, p36.
406 Hoyle, 2001, p329, and Fletcher and MacCulloch, 2008, p37.
407 See discussion in Hoyle, 2001, pp347-353.
408 Hoyle, 2001, p358.
409 Hoyle, 2001, p362, and Fletcher and MacCulloch, 2008, p38.
410 Fletcher and MacCulloch, 2008, pp49-50.
411 Hoyle, 2001, pp392-393.
412 Fletcher and MacCulloch, 2008, pp50-51.
413 Hoyle, 2001, p414 and p415, and Fletcher and MacCulloch, 2008, p51.
414 Moorhouse, 2003, pp344-346.
415 Fletcher and MacCulloch, 2008, p52.
416 Quoted in Wood, 2002, p53.
417 Fletcher and MacCulloch, 2008, p67. See also Land, 1977, pp28-29.
418 Fletcher and MacCulloch, 2008, p72.
419 Wood, 2009, pp170-172.
420 MacCulloch, 1979, p41.
421 Loach, 2002, p85.
422 Cornwall, 1977, p11.
423 Cornwall, 1977, pp35-36.
424 See the discussion of this in Land, 1977, pp10-12.
425 Fletcher and MaCCulloch, 2008, p160.
426 Cornwall, 1977, p36.
427 Cornwall, 1977, p36.
428 Quoted in Linebaugh, 2008, p57.
429 Details of these events from Cornwall, 1977, pp9-10.
430 Cornwall, 1977, p10.
431 Caraman, 1994, p28. Caraman, 1994, pp24-27 is a useful summary of changes brought about by the new prayer book and how they were perceived by ordinary people.

432 Wood, 2002, p55.
433 Duffy, 1992, p464.
434 Duffy, 1992, p465 and p218.
435 Quoted in Caraman, 1994, p29. Hooker's account is the key source for much of the detail of the Rising.
436 Quoted in Caraman, 1994, p10.
437 Quoted in Wood, 2002, p59.
438 Duffy, 1992, p455.
439 Wood, 2002, p59.
440 See the discussion of this in Wood, 2002, pp54-60
441 On Body, see Caraman, 1994, pp12-15.
442 Quoted in Cornwall, 1977, p53.
443 For a detailed account of the killing of Body and the aftermath, see Cornwall, 1977, pp52-56.
444 Cornwall, 1977, p58. My account of the Bodmin events and the start of the rising is based on Cornwall.
445 For Arundell see Cornwall, 1977, pp59-61.
446 Caraman, 1994, p34.
447 My account of events in Sampford Courtenay is based on Caraman, 1994, and Sturt, 1987.
448 Quoted in Fletcher and MacCulloch, 2008, p56.
449 Quoted in Caraman, 1994, p38.
450 Quoted in Cornwall, 1977, p67.
451 Sturt, 1987, pp26-27.
452 Caraman, 1994, p40.
453 Quoted in Caraman, 1994, p40.
454 Caraman, 1994, p42, and Sturt, 1987, p21.
455 Caraman, 1994, pp42-43.
456 Hooker, 1765, pp39-40 I have modernised Hooker's language in these quotes.
457 Cornwall, 1977, p75.
458 Hooker, 1765, pp40-41.
459 Hooker, 1765, p41.
460 Hooker, 1765, p42.
461 Wood, 2002, pp58-59.
462 Hooker, 1765, pp45-46.
463 Cornwall, 1977, p81 and Hooker, 1765, p46.
464 Cornwall, 1977, pp83-84.
465 Cornwall, 1977, pp87-89.
466 Cornwall, 1977, p97 and pp100-101.
467 For a detailed military account of the siege, see Cornwall, 1977, pp101-113, on which this is based. Hooker's account is worth reading as he was in the city for the duration.
468 Hooker, 1765, p50.
469 Hooker, 1765, p69.
470 Hooker, 1765, p71.
471 Hooker, 1765, pp70-71.
472 Cornwall, 1977, pp104-105.
473 Hooker, 1765, p85.
474 Hooker, 1765, pp72-73.
475 Cornwall, 1977, pp109-110.
476 Cornwall, 1977, pp114-116, which includes a summary of all 16 of the rebel articles.
477 Quotes from the rebel articles taken from

Cornwall, 1977, p115-116.

478 Dufy, 2003, p130.

479 Cronwall, 1977, p118 and Caraman, 1994, p57.

480 Caraman, 1994, p57.

481 Cornwall, 1977, p116 and Caraman, 1994, pp71-72.

482 Quoted in Caraman, 1994, p71.

483 Quotes in this section from Hooker, 1765, p60, p62, p63 and p66.

484 Cronwall, 1977, pp118-122.

485 Cornwall, 1977, p124.

486 For the Buckinghamshire and Oxfordshire rebellion, see Woodman, 1957, p80. Cornwall, 1977, pp127-128 gives a sense of the growing rebellion across the country.

487 Caraman, 1994, p82 and Sturt, 1987, p72.

488 Caraman, 1994, p82.

489 Cornwall, 1977, pp162-164 for a description of the battle of Fenny Bridges.

490 Hooker, 1765, p90.

491 Quoted in Caraman, 1994, p84.

492 Cornwall, 1977, p163.

493 Cornwall, 1977, pp165-166.

494 Cornwall, 1977, p177.

495 Cornwall, 1977, pp179-180. For the requirement for travel to Rome, see Sturt, 1987, p71.

496 On the Battle of Clyst, see Cornwall, 1977, pp181-186, on which this account is based. See also Hooker.

497 Hooker, 1765, p94.

498 Hooker, 1765, p95.

499 Cornwall, 1977, p185.

500 Hooker, 1765, p96.

501 Hooker, 1765, p97-99.

502 Hooker, 1765, pp99-100.

503 Cornwall, 1977, p195.

504 Cornwall, 1977, pp198-201, and Sturt, 1987, p99.

505 Cornwall, 1977, pp201-204.

506 Cornwall, 1977, pp231-233.

507 Land 1977, p7, and Cornwall, 1977, p145.

508 Cornwall, 1977, p145.

509 Duffy, 2003, p130, and Fletcher and MacCulloch, 2008, p87.

510 See the discussion in Fletcher and MacCulloch, 2008, p88, and Andy Wood's alternative view in Wood, 2009, pp179-194.

511 See Wood, 2009, p184.

512 The account of this dispute is based on Land, 1977, pp21-23.

513 Cornwall, 1977, p138.

514 Cornwall, 1977, p139-140.

515 Cornwall, 1977, p141.

516 Land, 1977, p47.

517 Cornwall, 1977, p142.

518 Cornwall, 1977, p53.

519 Land, 1977, p50.

520 Quoted in Land, 1977, p51.

521 Land, 1977, p52.

522 Cornwall, 1977, pp146-147. Warrant quoted is from p147.

523 Cornwall, 1977, p147.

524 Land, 1977, p60.

525 Land, 1977, pp60-61. See Cornwall, 1977, pp146-149 for the camp organisation.

526 Land, 1977, p61.

527 Wood, 2002, p66.

528 All references to the rebel articles are quoted from Land, 1977, pp63-66 and his analysis on pp67-72.

529 Land, 1977, p71.

530 Wood, 2009, p164.

531 Quoted in Cornwall, 1977, p152. This section based on Cornwall, 1977, pp151-159 and Land, 1977, pp78-83.

532 Quoted in Kesselring, 2003, p188.

533 Land, 1977, p81.

534 Cornwall, 1977, p157.

535 Cornwall, 1977, p159.

536 MacCulloch, 1979, p43.

537 Quoted in Wood, 2002, p67.

538 Land, 1977, p93 and Cornwall, 1977, p170.

539 Land, 1977, pp95-96.

540 Cornwall, 1977, pp173-174.

541 Land, 1977, p99.

542 Land, 1977, pp101-102.

543 Land, 1977, p104.

544 Land, 1977, pp104-105 and Cornwall, 1977, pp208-209.

545 Land, 1977, pp106-108.

546 Land, 1977, p114

547 Land, 1977, pp114-115; Fletcher and MacCulloch, 2008, p75; Cornwall, 1977, p214.

548 Quoted in Land, 1977, p116.

549 This account is based on Land, 1977, pp116-123.

550 Land, 1977, p120.

551 Quoted in Land, 1977, p121.

552 Cornwall, 1977, pp220-221.

553 Cornwall, 1977, pp221-222.

554 Cornwall, 1977, pp222-223.

555 Land, 1977, pp124-125, and Cornwall, 1977, p224.

556 Quoted in Cornwall, 1977, p224.

557 Cornwall, 1977, pp224-225. See also, Wood, 2009, p210.

558 Land, 1977, p132.

559 Cornwall, 1977, pp226-230.

560 Land, 1977, p139 and p141.

561 Land, 1977, p143.

562 Bindoff, 1949, p20.

563 Cornwall, 1977, p235.

564 Gay, 1904, p196.

565 Gay, 1904, p215.

566 Quoted in Holstun, 2002, p372.

567 Quoted on the British Libraries page for the Midland Revolt in Stow's Annals at www.bl.uk.

568 Hindle, 2008, p23.

569 Gay, 1904, p216.

570 Gay, 1904, p217.

571 Wood, 2009, p239.

572 See the discussion on "memory, myth and representation" in Wood, 2009, pp208-221. Oldman's quote is on p213.

573 Wood, 2009, p231.

574 Wood, 2009, p16.

575 Wood, 2009, p203.

576 Wood, 2009, p207.

577 Wood, 2009, p188.

578 Žmolek, 2014, p22.

579 Dyer, 2009, p147.

580 Dyer, 2009, pp293-295. Note that Dyer writes that "landless workers...almost disappeared", p294.

581 Dyer, 2009, pp295-297.

582 Dyer, 2009, p297.

583 Bolton, 1988, pp243-245.

584 Marx, 1977, pp510-511.

585 Bolton, 1988, pp251-253.

586 Harman, 1999, p181,

587 Harman, 1998, p70,

588 Dyer, 2009, pp191-193.

589 Dyer, 2009, pp303-305 and p307.

590 Dyer, 2009, p309. Yerby notes that by the start of the 16th century, half of the 800 market towns in England were specialising in a particular product. Yerby, 2016, p149.

591 Dyer, 2009, p312.

592 Dyer, 2009, p313.

593 Harman, 1998, pp84-85.

594 Harman, 1998, p88.

595 Žmolek, 2014, pp65-66.

596 See, for instance, the discussion in Žmolek, 2014, pp53-57.

597 Dyer, 2009, p328.

598 Dyer, 2009, pp327-329.

599 Dyer, 2009, p331 and p338.

600 Bolton, 1980, pp240-242.

601 Yerby, 2016, pp78-79 and p250.

602 Harman, 1998, p96.

603 Harman, 1999, p182.

604 Harman, 1999, p183.

605 Harman, 1998, p102.

606 Sharp, 2010, p123.

607 Sharp, 2010, p167.

608 Sharp, 2010, p57.

609 Sharp, 2010, pp86-87.

610 Sharp, 2010, p57 and p87.

611 Information on Gillingham enclosure and riots from Sharp, 2010, pp57-58.

612 Information on Dean riots from Sharp, 2010, pp62-63.

613 Sharp, 2010, p63. For the Francis Bacon quote and background, see Sharp, 2010, pp83-84.

614 For Skimington, see Sharp 2010, pp64-68.

615 See tables in Sharp, 2010, p82. The whole of Chapter 5 of Sharp's book is a study of the class nature of the rioters in the Western Rising.

616 Sharp, 2010, p91.

617 Sharp, 2010, p92.

618 Sharp, 2010, pp92-93.

619 Sharp, 2010, p108.

620 Sharp, 2010, pp111-112.

621 Sharp, 2010, p164.

622 Yerby, 2016, pp249-250.

623 Yerby, 2016, pp138-139.

624 Žmolek, 2014, p118 quoting Stone, 1972, p72.

625 Yerby, 2016, p169.

626 Yerby, 2016, pp170-171.

627 Harman, 1998, p105.

628 Harman, 1998, p108.

629 Hill, 1980, p146.

630 Hill, 1980, p146.

631 Žmolek, 2014, p135.

632 Hill, 1980, pp202-205.

633 Hill, 1980, p202.

634 Harman, 1998, p101.

635 Žmolek, 2014, p57.

636 Manning, 1996, pp44-46.

637 Manning, 1996, p49.

638 Manning, 1978, pp141-142.

639 Purkiss, 2006, pp353-355.

640 Sharp, 2010, pp140-141.

641 Sharp, 2010, pp144-145 and p146.

642 Sharp, 2010, p148.

643 Sharp, 2010, p151.

644 Hill, 1991, p53.

645 Manning, 1978, p139.

646 Manning, 1996, p58.

647 Underdown, 2005, p164.

648 Everitt, 1969, pp12-13.

649 Underdown, 2005, p146 and p166.

650 Manning, 1978, pp232-233 and pp236-237.

651 Manning, 1978, pp234-235.

652 Everitt, 1969, p23.

653 Underdown, 1979, p30 and p37.

654 Quoted in Underdown, 1979, p38.

655 Underdown, 2005, p278.

656 Underdown, 2005, p176.

657 Manning, 1996, p79 and the Clubman Uprisings page, at British Civil Wars, Commonwealth and Protectorate 1638-1660 website www.bcw-project.org

658 Manning, 1996, p80.

659 For an excellent introduction to the life and ideas of Gerrard Winstanley, see Gurney, 2013.

660 For an overview of this see Hill, 1991, and on the Levellers specifically, Rees, 2016.

661 Information of Winstanley's early life from Gurney, 2013, pp12-21.

662 Quoted in Gurney, 2013, p17

663 Gurney, 2013, p22.

664 From *Truth lifting up its Head above Scandals* (1648), quoted in Berens, 2007, p47.

665 I have written further on Winstanley's vision of utopia in Empson, 2017.

666 Quoted in Berens, 2007, pp256-266. These are points 16, 18, 28, 29, 30 and 31.

667 Quotes in this section from Berens, 2007, pp35-38.
668 Hill, 1991, p117.
669 Winstanley, 1973, p30.
670 Thomas, 1969, p59.
671 Gurney, 2013, pp37-38.
672 Hill, 1991, p119.
673 Gurney, 2013, pp57-58.
674 Gurney, 2013, pp65-68.
675 Gurney, 2013, pp79-80.
676 Gurney, 2013, pp82-84.
677 Quoted in Gurney, 2013, p85
678 The True Levellers Standard Advanced, April 1649, Quoted in Berens, 2007, p94.
679 Charlesworth, 1983, p41
680 See www.british-history.ac.uk/no-series/acts-ordinances-interregnum/pp130-139.
681 Charlesworth, 1983, p42.
682 Charlesworth, 1983, pp56-58.
683 Thompson, 1985, pp55-56.
684 Thompson, 1977, pp55-59.
685 Hill, 1996, p101.
686 Hay and others, 2011, p223, p229 and p234.
687 Horn, 1980, p172 and p173.
688 Hay and others, 2011, p203.
689 Example statistics from Horn, 1980, p180 and 181, and Osborne and Winstanley, 2006, p189 and p190.
690 Quoted in Horn, 1980, p181.
691 Hill, 1996, p101 and p103. Bacon quoted in Hay and others, 2011, p191.
692 Turner, 1984, p11.
693 Turner, 1984, p35.
694 Turner, 1984, p71.
695 Marx, 1990, pp888-889. One excellent recent history of the Clearances that shows the social and economic consequences, as well as attempts at resistance, is Hunter, 2015.
696 See table in Turner, 1984, p21.
697 Quoted in Turner, 1984, p23.
698 Thompson, 2010, pp109-110.
699 Žmolek, 2014, pp279-280.
700 Turner, 1984, p56.
701 Hallas, 1988, p17, and Thompson, 2010, p27.
702 Hallas, 1988, p20.
703 Horn, 1987, pp1-2.
704 This section on the Free Miners is based on Fisher, 2016.
705 Fisher, 2016, pp14-15.
706 Quoted in Fisher, 2016, p45. On the Mines Act 1838, see Fisher, 2016, p38.
707 Fisher, 2016, p46.
708 Fisher, 2016, pp46-47.
709 Quoted in Fisher, 2016, p47.
710 Thompson, 2010, p120.
711 See for instance details of the mid-18th century struggle to keep Richmond Park open for public rights of way in Thompson, 2010, pp111-114. See also the pamphlet, Down with the Fences, anonymous, 2010.
712 Thompson, 2010, p102.
713 Thompson, 2010, p102.
714 Hammond and Hammond, 1995a, p55 and pp378-383. Today Stanwell is next to Heathrow Airport.
715 Hammond and Hammond, 1995a, p109.
716 Quoted in Hammond and Hammond, 1995a, p127.
717 Hammond and Hammond, 1995a, pp127-129.
718 Charlesworth, 1983, p48-52.
719 All these examples from Charlesworth, 1983, p50.
720 Charlesworth, 1983, p52.
721 Charlesworth, 1983, p54.
722 Marx, 1990, p895.
723 Charlesworth, 1983, p63 and pp140-141.
724 Thompson, 2010, p258.
725 Sharp, 2010. Chapters 2 and 3 of Sharp's book examine the incidents of food rioting and the development of Tudor and then Stuart responses.
726 Bland and others, 1920, pp374-380.
727 Thompson, 2010, pp193-196.
728 Quoted in Thompson, 2010, p197.
729 Thompson, 2010, p197.
730 Quoted in Thompson, 2010, p216.
731 Both examples quoted in Thompson, 2010, p67.
732 Thompson, 2010, p67.
733 Thompson, 2010, pp69-73.
734 Thompson, 2010, p227.
735 The Bath Chronicle and Weekly Gazette, September 1766, quoted in Sutton, 2016, pp48-49.
736 Bohstedt, 1988, p102.
737 For an extended discussion of the ideological workings of the free market in corn in the 18th century, see Thompson, 2010, pp200-207.
738 Smith, 1991, p463
739 Quoted in Thompson, 2010, p214.
740 Thompson, 2010, p214.
741 Thompson, 2010, p233 and Hammond and Hammond, 1995a, p120.
742 Hammond and Hammond, 1995a, p121.
743 Bohstedt, 1988, p89.
744 Bohstedt, 1988, p93.
745 Bohstedt, 1988, p94.
746 Thompson, 2010, p312.
747 Thompson, 2010, pp321-322. For examples of how women were punished for their involvement see Thompson, 2010, pp325-327.
748 Thompson, 2010, pp322-324.
749 Thompson, 2010, p340.
750 Charlesworth, 1983, p70.
751 Taine, 1885, p162.
752 Hammond and Hammond, 1995a, p166.
753 Hammond and Hammond, 1995a, p109 and p107.
754 Hammond and Hammond, 1995a, p111.
755 From Andrew Ure, Cotton Manufacture of

Great Britain (1836), quoted in Hammond and Hammond, 1995c, p50.

756 Hammond and Hammond, 1995c, p49.

757 Beckert, 2015, pp188-189.

758 Beckert, 2015, pp196.

759 Archer, 2010, p10.

760 Quoted in a letter forwarded 6 May 1812 to Richard Ryder, Secretary of State, see Binfield, 2004.

761 Reid, 1986, p57. For weather records and prices, see Stratton, 1978, pp95-96.

762 Reid, 1986, pp41-42.

763 Reid, 1986, pp43-45.

764 Marx, 1990, pp553-554.

765 Marx, 1990, p557.

766 Reid, 1986, p58. See the chronology of Luddite events in Thomis, 1970, pp177-186.

767 Reid, 1986, pp59-60 and Hammond and Hammond, 1995c, p262.

768 Quoted in Reid, 1986, p60.

769 *Leeds Mercury*, Saturday 29 February 1812.

770 The account here is based on Reid, 1986, pp108-116, Hammond and Hammond, 1995c, pp304-307 and the *Leeds Mercury*, Saturday 8 April, 1812.

771 Quoted in Dallas, 1829, pp213-215 (available at http://lordbyron.org)

772 Quoted in Reid, 1986, p126.

773 Quoted in Reid, 1986, p202.

774 Reid, 1986, pp182-186.

775 Žmolek, 2014, p598.

776 Thomis, 1970, p163.

777 *York Herald*, Saturday 16 January 1813, p2.

778 Hammond and Hammond, 1995c, p332.

779 *York Herald*, Saturday 16 January 1813.

780 *York Herald*, Saturday 23 January 1813.

781 Hammond and Hammond, 1995c, p291-300.

782 Thomis, 1970, p160-164.

783 The accounts of 1816 and 1822 in East Anglia are based on Charlesworth, 1983, p146-151.

784 Charlesworth, 1983, p147.

785 Charlesworth, 1983, p148.

786 The *Norfolk Chronicle*, Saturday 16 March 1822, p2.

787 Charlesworth, 1983, p151.

788 The classic accounts of the Captain Swing movement are in Hammond and Hammond, 1995a, and Hobsbawm and Rudé, 1970. Readers wanting to know more should also consult Griffin, 2015, which builds substantially on earlier work.

789 Griffin, 2015, p87.

790 Quoted in Muskett, 1984, p1. This is also a key point of John Archer's book that looks at East Anglia, see Archer, 2010.

791 Hobsbawm and Rudé, 1970, p17.

792 Wells, 1979, pp118-119 and p120.

793 Wells, 1979, pp121-122.

794 Jones, 1968, p10.

795 Hobsbawm and Rudé, 1970, p72.

796 Wells, 1979, p127. Wells gives as examples the "imprisonment of four Funtingdon labourers" in 1795, and the case of five men from Botley in 1800.

797 Wells, 1979, p129.

798 For non-Irish migrant labour see Griffin, 2015, p57, note 26. Hobsbawm and Rudé, 1970, p85.

799 Griffin, 2015, pp66-67 and p177.

800 Archer, 2010, p9.

801 Cobbet's *Political Register*, 4 December 1830, quoted in Horn, 1987, p83.

802 See for instance nearly 1,000 incidents listed between 24 August and 31 December 1830 in the appendix to Griffin, 2015.

803 Hobsbawm and Rudé, 1970, p97.

804 Hobsbawm and Rudé, 1970, p102.

805 *Kentish Chronicle*, 14 September 1830, p3.

806 Hobsbawm and Rudé, 1970, p102.

807 Quotes from the *Maidstone Journal* and *Kentish Advertiser*, Tuesday 2 November 1830, p4.

808 Hobsbawm and Rudé, 1970, p104.

809 Quoted in Hammond and Hammond, 1995a, pp251-252.

810 Quoted in Hammond and Hammond, 1995a, pp249-250.

811 Griffin, 2015, p174.

812 Hobsbawm and Rudé, 1970, p111.

813 *Sussex Advertiser*, 22 November 1830, p3.

814 Hobsbawm and Rudé, 1970, p116 and pp118-119.

815 *Norwich Mercury*, Saturday 27 November 1830, p4.

816 Hobsbawm and Rudé, 1970, pp121-122.

817 Events in Wiltshire are summarised from Hobsbawm and Rudé, 1970, pp122-126.

818 Hobsbawm and Rudé, 1970, pp125-126.

819 Mary Frampton's account quoted in Kerr, 1975, p101. For events in Dorset, Devon and the remainder of West Country, see Hobsbawm and Rudé, 1970, pp127-130.

820 Hobsbawm and Rudé, 1970, p131.

821 Hobsbawm and Rudé, 1970, p131.

822 Events in these counties are based on Chapter 7 of Hobsbawm and Rudé, 1970.

823 *Norwich Mercury*, Saturday 27 November, 1830, p4.

824 Hobsbawm and Rudé, 1970, p138.

825 Hobsbawm and Rudé, 1970, pp138-139.

826 Hobsbawm and Rudé, 1970, p143.

827 Hobsbawm and Rudé, 1970, p144.

828 Hobsbawm and Rudé, 1970, p145.

829 Events in East Anglia based on Hobsbawm and Rudé, 1970, pp152-170.

830 Hobsbawm and Rudé, 1970, p152.

831 All quotes from the *Norwich Mercury*, Saturday 27 November 1830, p2.

832 Hobsbawm and Rudé, 1970, pp154-155.

833 Hobsbawm and Rudé, 1970, p158.

834 Hobsbawm and Rudé, 1970, pp159-162.

835 Hobsbawm and Rudé, 1970, p161-p162. See also the Hampshire Chronicle, Monday 27 December, 1830, p 4 for report of Saville's capture and the Bucks Gazette, of Saturday 22 January, 1831, p3 for a report of the trial.

836 Material on Swing in Cambridgeshire and the North from Hobsbawm and Rudé, 1970, p165-p169.

837 See Hansard, House of Lords, 22 November 1830 vol 1 cc604-18.

838 Hobsbawm and Rudé, 1970, pp297-298.

839 Griffin, 2015, p275.

840 Quoted in Hobsbawm and Rudé, 1970, p298.

841 Hobsbawm and Rudé, 1970, p299.

842 See Griffin, 2015, Chapter 11 in particular.

843 Griffin, 2015, p231.

844 Griffin, 2015, p233.

845 Hobsbawm and Rudé, 1970, p101. For more on the trial see Griffin, 2015, pp233-235. The day after the trial, Griffin points out, five more machines were broken in east Kent.

846 Quoted by Griffin, 2015, p236.

847 Griffin, 2015, p245.

848 Hammond and Hammond, 1995a, pp291-292.

849 Hammond and Hammond, 1995a, p294.

850 Hammond and Hammond, 1995a, p295.

851 Quoted in Hammond and Hammond, 1995a, pp298-299.

852 Hobsbawm and Rudé, 1970, p275.

853 This and following quotes are from Loveless, 1837, pp6-7.

854 Marlow, 1971, p122.

855 See Ball, 2010.

856 From a poem written down by George Loveless when his sentence was passed, Loveless, 1837, p10.

857 Norman, 2008, p110.

858 Chase, 2012, p89.

859 Marlow, 1971, p42 and p45.

860 Information on early rural trade unionism, the GNCTU and Tolpuddle from Chase, 2012, pp134-136.

861 Information on the rules and initial meeting from Marlow, 1971, pp43-45.

862 Quoted in Norman, 2008, p46.

863 Marlow, 1971, pp47-48.

864 Quoted in Marlow, 1971, p61. The full cautionary statement is in Norman, 2008, pp47-49.

865 Norman, 2008, p36 and p38. Material on Frampton from Marlow, 1971, pp55-57.

866 Loveless, 1837, p7.

867 Loveless, 1837, pp7-8.

868 For these quotes see Loveless's account in Loveless, 1837, p8.

869 Marlow, 1971, pp78-79 has a good account of the trial as well as a detailed explanation of the "beautifully spun [legal] web" which was used to knit various laws together to prosecute the labourers.

870 Marlow, 1971, p67.

871 Marlow, 1971, p67.

872 The full text of the act is in Norman, 2008, pp53-54 who makes this point.

873 Loveless, 1837, p9.

874 Dorset County Chronicle, Thursday 20 March, 1834, p4.

875 Dorset County Chronicle, Thursday 20 March, 1834, p4.

876 Loveless, 1837, p16.

877 Loveless, Brine and others, 2005, pp15-16.

878 Marlow, 1971, pp107-109.

879 Marlow, 1971, pp110-111.

880 Marlow, 1971, pp112-113.

881 Marlow, 1971, p113.

882 Poor Man's Guardian, 11 July 1835

883 Quoted in Chase, 2012, p140.

884 Chase, 2012, p140.

885 Quoted in Marlow, 1971, p119.

886 Groves, 1949, p21.

887 Quoted in Norman, 2008, p111.

888 Marlow, 1971, pp126-130.

889 Norman, 2008, p112, and Marlow, 1971, p130.

890 Marlow, 1971, pp130-133 and Hansard for the House of Lords, HL Deb 28 April 1834 vol 23 cc95-103.

891 Norman, 2008, pp112-115.

892 Norman, 2008, pp116-118.

893 Figures and quotes from Hume in Norman, 2008, pp119-120.

894 Norman, 2008, pp121-123.

895 Marlow, 1971, pp198-200.

896 Loveless, 1837, pp20-21.

897 Marlow, 1971, pp208-209.

898 Marlow, 1971, pp210-211 and pp217-218.

899 Marlow, 1971, pp214-215.

900 Norman, 2008, p144.

901 Marlow, 1971, p235.

902 Marlow, 1971, pp227-230.

903 See Ball, 2010 for a discussion of this, particularly pp18-20.

904 A book-length study of the rising and its context is Reay, 2010, on which this brief account is based.

905 Reay, 2010, pp107-109.

906 Reay, 2010, p109.

907 Reay, 2010, pp110-113.

908 Reay, 2010, p130.

909 Reay, 2010, pp73-76.

910 Quoted in Reay, 2010, p77.

911 Archer, 2010, p15.

912 A verse of a newly written union song sung by men, women and children marching for the union in Leamington on 29 March 1872. Quoted in Groves, 1949, p50.

913 Arch, 1986, pp73-74.

914 Arch, 1986, pp74-75.

915 Alun Howkin's introduction to Arch, 1986, p xi.

916 Horn, 1971, pp24-25 and p29. In 1869, 10s was

worth about £5 in today's money.

917 Horn, 1971, pp28-35. Chapter one of Horn's book is an excellent summary of the condition of the rural working class in the Victorian era.

918 Groves, 1949, p32.

919 All these examples come from Groves, 1949, pp33-35.

920 Groves, 1949, p36.

921 Horn, 1971, p44.

922 Arch, 1986, p78.

923 Horn, 1971, p49.

924 Arch, 1986, p77, and Groves, 1949, p49 and p51.

925 Groves, 1949, pp49-50.

926 Groves, 1949, p53.

927 *Royal Leamington Spa Courier*, 6 April 1872, p7, and Baker, 1979, p23.

928 Groves, 1949, p53.

929 Groves, 1949, pp54-55.

930 *Royal Leamington Spa Courier*, 1 June 1872, pp6-7.

931 Quoted in Owen, 2001, pp40-41.

932 Owen, 2001, pp42.

933 Groves, 1948, p61.

934 Groves, 1948, p58.

935 Arch, 1986, p139.

936 Horn, 1971, p69.

937 Arch, 1986, pp139-143 and Groves, 1948, p61.

938 Groves, 1948, pp68-69.

939 Groves, 1948, p73.

940 Peacock, 1968, p6.

941 Peacock, 1968, pp8-9.

942 Groves, 1948, pp73-75.

943 Groves, 1948, p78 and Horn, 1971, pp106-107.

944 Groves, 1948, p78.

945 Charlesworth, 1983, p172.

946 Horn, 1971, p109-110. Groves, 1948, p81-83.

947 Groves, 1948, p83.

948 Groves, 1948, p101-104.

949 See examples in Peacock, 1968, p15.

950 Charlesworth, 1983, p173.

951 Groves, 1948, pp105-110.

952 Groves, 1948, pp113-114.

953 My account of the St Faith's strike is based on Groves, 1948, pp115-122.

954 Groves, 1948, p124 and pp127-128.

955 Sherry, 2014, p33.

956 Groves, 1948, pp139-140.

957 Groves, 1948, pp140-141, and Howkins, 2003, p24.

958 Groves, 1948, pp143-149.

959 Groves, 1948, pp149-151 and pp164-165.

960 Danziger, 1988, p73. A full account of the strike is in Groves, 1948, pp179-205.

961 Calder, 1992, pp418-430.

962 World Bank figures from 2016.

963 Howkins, 2003, p173.

964 Quoted in Howkins, 2003, p174.

965 Figures and quotes in this section from Page, 1976, pp6-8.

966 Howkins, 2003, pp175-176.

967 Lister, 2001, p94.

968 Howkins, 2003, pp228-232.

969 Howkins, 2003, pp226-227, and *Socialist Worker*, 21 September 2002.

970 Department for Environment, Food and Rural Affairs, 2017.

971 Quoted in Howkins, 2003, p233.

972 Monbiot, 2016.

973 Page, 1976, p18.

974 FAO, 2012, p18, and IFAD, 2016, p21 and p25.

975 Quoted in Empson, 2016, p86.

976 Quoted in Empson, 2016, p88.

977 Quoted in Empson, 2016, p89.

Index